SURRENDER

SURRENDER

40 SONGS, ONE STORY

BONO

 ALFRED A. KNOPF   NEW YORK   2022

THIS IS A BORZOI BOOK
PUBLISHED BY ALFRED A. KNOPF

www.aaknopf.com

Knopf, Borzoi Books, and the colophon are registered
trademarks of Penguin Random House LLC.

Pages 561–565 constitute an extension of the copyright page.

Library of Congress Control Number: 2022938826

ISBN 978-0-525-52104-4 (hardcover)
ISBN 978-0-525-52105-1 (ebook)

Drawings by Bono
Creative design by Bono with Gavin Friday
Jacket photograph © Anton Corbijn
Jacket design by Bono, Gavin Friday, and Shaughn McGrath
Author photograph © John Hewson

Manufactured in Canada
First Edition

For Ali

I hear the ancient footsteps like the motion of the sea
Sometimes I turn, there's someone there, at times it's only me.

—Bob Dylan, "Every Grain of Sand"

CONTENTS

CONTENTS

PART I

I can't change the world
but I can change the world in me.

—SFX Theatre, Dublin, December 1982

a bicuspid view of the world
starts way before

I am told I have
an eccentric heart . . . .

1

Lights of Home

I shouldn't be here 'cause I should be dead
I can see the lights in front of me
I believe my best days are ahead
I can see the lights in front of me.

I was born with an eccentric heart. In one of the chambers of my heart, where most people have three doors, I have two. Two swinging doors, which at Christmas 2016 were coming off their hinges. The aorta is your main artery, your lifeline, carrying the blood oxygenated by your lungs, and becoming your life. But we have discovered that my aorta has been stressed over time and developed a blister. A blister that's about to burst, which would put me in the next life faster than I can make an emergency call. Faster than I can say goodbye to this life.

So, here I am. Mount Sinai Hospital. New York City.

Looking down on myself from above with the arc lights reflecting on the stainless steel. I'm thinking the light is harder than the steel counter I'm lying on. My body feels separate from me. It is soft flesh and hard bone.

It's not a dream or vision, but it feels as if I'm being sawn in half by a magician. This eccentric heart has been frozen.

Some remodeling needs to take place apart from all this hot blood swirling around and making a mess, which blood tends to do when it's not keeping you alive.

Blood and air.

Blood and guts.

Blood and brains are what's required right now, if I'm to continue to sing my life and live it. My blood.

The brains and the hands of the magician who is standing over me and can turn a really bad day into a really good one with the right strategy and execution.

Nerves of steel and blades of steel.

Now this man is climbing up and onto my chest, wielding his blade with the combined forces of science and butchery. The forces required to break and enter someone's heart. The magic that is medicine.

I know it's not going to feel like a good day when I wake up after these eight hours of surgery, but I also know that waking up is better than the alternative.

Even if I can't breathe and feel as if I am suffocating. Even if I'm desperately drawing for air and can't find any.

Even if I'm hallucinating, 'cause I'm seeing visions now and it's all getting a little William Blake.

I'm so cold. I need to be beside you, I need your warmth, I need your loveliness. I'm dressed for winter. I have big boots on in bed, but I'm freezing to death.

I am dreaming.

I am in a scene from some movie where the life is draining out of the actor in the lead role. In the last moments of his life he is vexed and questioning his great love.

"Why are you going? Don't leave me!"

"I'm right here," his lover reminds him. "I haven't moved."

"What? It's not you leaving? Am I the one walking away? Why am I walking away? I don't want to leave you. Please, don't let me leave."

There are some dirty little secrets about success that I'm just waking up to. And from.

Success as an outworking of dysfunction, an excuse for obsessive-compulsive tendencies.

Success as a reward for really, really hard work, which may be obscuring some kind of neurosis.

Success should come with a health warning—for the workaholic and for those around them.

Success may be propelled by some unfair advantage or circumstance. If not privilege, then a gift, a talent, or some other form of inherited wealth.

But hard work also hides behind some of these doors.

I always thought mine was a gift for finding top-line melody not just in music but in politics, in commerce, and in the world of ideas in general.

Where others would hear harmony or counterpoint, I was better at finding the top line in the room, the hook, the clear thought. Probably because I had to sing it or sell it.

But now I see that my advantage was something more prosaic, more base. Mine was a genetic advantage, the gift of . . . air.

That's right.

Air.

"Your man has a lot of firepower in that war chest of his."

That's the man who sawed through my breastbone speaking to my wife and next of kin, Ali, after the operation.

"We needed extra-strong wire to sew him up. He's probably at about 130 percent of normal lung capacity for his age."

He doesn't use the word "freak," but Ali tells me she has started thinking of me as the Man from Atlantis, from that 1970s sci-fi series about an amphibian detective.

David Adams, the man I will owe my life to, the surgeon-magician, speaks with a southern twang, and in my heightened Blakean state I begin to confuse him with the crazed villain of *The Texas Chain Saw Massacre*. I overhear him asking Ali about tenors, who are not known to run around a stage hitting high notes.

"Aren't tenors supposed to stand with two legs apart, firmly rooted in the ground, before even considering a top C?"

"Yes," I say, without opening my mouth and before the drugs wear off. "A tenor has to turn his head into a sound box and his body into a bellows to make those glasses smash."

I, on the other hand, have been racing around arenas and sprinting through stadiums for thirty years singing "Pride (In the Name of Love)," the high A or B depending on the year.

In the 1980s the stylish English songster Robert Palmer stopped Adam Clayton to plead with him. "Will you ever get your singer to sing a few steps lower. He'll make it easier on himself, and all of us who have to listen."

Air is stamina.

Air is the confidence to take on big challenges or big opponents.

Air is not the will to conquer whatever Everest you will encounter in your life, but it is the ability to endure the climb.

Air is what you need on any north face.

Air is what gives a small kid on a playground the belief that he won't be bullied, or if he is, that the bully will have the air knocked out of him.

And here I am now without it, for the first time.

In a hospital emergency room, without air.

Without breath.

The names we give God.

All breath.

Jehovaaaah.

Allaaaah.

Yeshuaaaah.

Without air . . . without an air . . . without an aria.

I am terrified because for the first time ever, I reach for my faith and I can't find it.

Without air.

Without a prayer.

I am a tenor singing underwater. I can feel my lungs filling up. I am drowning.

I am hallucinating. I am seeing a vision of my father in a hospital bed and me sleeping beside him, on a mattress on the floor. Beaumont Hospital, Dublin, the summer of 2001. He is deep breathing, but it's getting shallower and shallower like the grave in his chest. He shouts my name, confusing me with my brother or the other way around.

"Paul. Norman. Paul."

"Da."

I jump up and call a nurse.

"Are you okay, Bob?" she whispers in his ear.

We are in a world of percussive, animated whispers, a world of sibilance, his tenor now become short tinny breaths, an *s* after every exhalation.

"Yesssss sssss sss."

His Parkinson's disease has stolen the sonority.

"I want to go home sssssss I want to get out of here sssss."

"Say it again, Da."

Like the nurse, I am leaning over him, my ear close to his mouth. Silence.

Followed by another silence.

Followed by "FUCK OFF!"

There is something perfectly imperfect about my da's exit from this world. I don't believe he was telling me or the very vigilant night nurse to fuck off. I'd like to believe he was addressing the monkey that had been on his back for a large part of his life.

He had told me in those final days that when accepting his cancers, he'd lost his faith, but he also told me that I should never lose mine. That it was the most interesting thing about me.

Emboldened, I read to him from a psalm of King David, Psalm 32.

David was in a fair bit of trouble himself. Da was not in the mood for a sermon and I saw his eyes roll, likely not to heaven.

> *While I kept silence, my body wasted away*
> *through my groaning all day long.*
> *For day and night your hand was heavy upon me;*
> *my strength was dried up as by the heat of summer.*
> *Therefore let all who are faithful offer prayer to you;*
> *at a time of distress, the rush of mighty waters shall not reach*
> *   them.*
> *You are a hiding-place for me; you preserve me from trouble;*
> *you surround me with glad cries of deliverance.*

Was this for him, or me?

The old man confessed his admiration for what seemed like me having "a two-way conversation with the man upstairs."

"Mine is all one-way, but knock it off, will you? I'm trying to get some peace here." Well, he didn't get it here, but I want to believe he found it there.

Where's there? Home.

I don't know if I know what that is.

I say goodbye. I take a deep breath and head off to look for it.

Spring 2015.

More cold white fluorescent light. Steel and glass.

Nausea.

This time it's no life-threatening affair. I'm staring into a mirror in the bathroom adjacent to a dressing room under an ice hockey arena in Vancouver, Canada. It's the first night of the Innocence + Experience Tour.

I was never vain when I was younger. I would avoid standing in front of mirrors. But here I am, in the white-tiled bathroom, staring at my own face to see if, on some second glance, it might become more attractive.

I can hear the rumble of a crowd through the walls, singing along to Gary Numan's "Cars": "Here in my car / I feel safest of all / I can lock all my doors / It's the only way to live / In cars."

I am in the future I dreamed of when I first heard this synthesizer song in the late 1970s. I can't believe that now, turned fifty-five, I've opted for the DIY bottle-blond peroxide of that period. The color of a chicken wing, as a Spanish reviewer will later suggest. The rumble from the arena only increases the curdling of excitement I feel. I walk back into the dressing room, itself a time capsule, and complain that it looks just like the one we had on the last tour. I'm told it's been the same one for twenty years. Green hessian, fairy lights, tobacco leather couch. After all this time, why is getting ready to walk out and meet 18,474 of your closest friends so nerve-racking? It's the opening night of a world tour, but as usual I'm not alone.

Larry has an angelic aura about him, the look of someone who's seen through to the other side. I think that perhaps he has, having buried his father just yesterday. Adam looks like the lead in an art-house movie. Unruffled. Edge is tense and intense, but just about able to cover it up.

As we do before every show, we pray.

Sometimes it can feel as if we're strangers, praying to find the intimacy of a band that could be useful to our audience this evening.

Useful? To music. To some higher purpose. In some strangely familiar way we are changed. We begin our prayers as comrades; we end them as friends finding a different image of ourselves, as well as the audience we're about to meet, who will change us again.

To be useful is a curious prayer. Unromantic. A little dull even, but it's at the heart of who we are and why we're still here as a band. Men who met as boys. Men who have broken the promise that's at the very heart of rock 'n' roll, which is that you can have the world but in return the world will have you. You can have your messiah complex, but you must die on a cross aged thirty-three, or everyone has the right to ask for their money back. We've turned them down. So far.

We are men who bear some scar tissue from our various struggles with the world but whose eyes are remarkably clear considering the vicissitudes and surreality of a life playing stadiums for thirty-five years.

Now, through the walls, I can hear Patti Smith singing "People Have the Power," the signal that we have five minutes and ten seconds before showtime, five minutes and ten seconds before we find out if we still have the thing that people have turned up for, which is not just our music or our friendship. What's on offer is our band as a chemistry set, a chemical reaction between our audience and us. That's what makes a good band great.

The roar of the crowd rises as we head down the corridor from the dressing room, a roar that turns this mouse into a lion. I have my fist in the air as I walk to the stage, as I get ready to step inside the song. I will try over the next pages to explain what that means. But after forty years, I know if I can stay inside the songs, they will sing me and this night will be not work but play.

Nearly twenty thousand people are singing the choral refrain of "The Miracle (Of Joey Ramone)," and as Edge, Larry, and Adam walk down to the front of the stage, I walk up alone to meet them from the opposite end of the arena. I walk through our audience, through this noise. In my mind I am seventeen, walking from my house on the Northside of Dublin, all the way down Cedarwood Road, on the way to rehearsals with these men all those years ago, when they were boys too.

I am leaving home to find home. And I am singing.

the miracle of Joey Ramone

Out of Control

Monday morning
Eighteen years of dawning
I said how long
Said how long.

I'm jumping around the living room of 10 Cedarwood Road to the sound of "Glad to See You Go" from the Ramones' *Leave Home.*

You gotta go go go go goodbye
Glad to see you go go go go goodbye

It is 1978, the day of my eighteenth birthday.

These songs are so simple, and yet they express a complexity that's way more relevant to my life than Dostoyevsky's *Crime and Punishment.* Which I've just finished. Which took me three and a half weeks to read. This album takes only twenty-nine minutes and fifty-seven seconds. Songs so simple that even I can play them on guitar. And I can't play guitar.

Songs so simple even I might be able to write one. This would be some kind of personal revolution, the reverberations of which might be felt all the way upstairs to the empty room of my older brother, Norman. Or, more important still, down the hallway to the kitchen, where the da is sitting.

My da, who wants to talk to me about getting a job. A job!

A job is a thing where you do something you don't really like for eight hours a day for five or six days a week in return for money to help you do the stuff on the weekend you want to do all the time.

I know I would like to avoid work. I know that if I could do what I love, then I would never have to work a day in my life. But there's a problem. Even in my pimpled teenage obnoxiousness I know that this is unlikely if I'm not great at something.

And I am not great at something. I am not great at anything.

Well, I'm a pretty good mimic. My friend Reggie Manuel says the reason I ran off with his girlfriend Zandra was all down to my Ian Paisley impression. I'm quite good at channeling the bellicose ranting of the Reverend Ian Paisley, leader of the unionists in the North.

"NOY SRRNDRRR." He would belch.

My Ian Paisley makes Zandra laugh so much that I tell myself she is vulnerable to my advances, but I also know she might dump me for Keith what's-his-face because it's not enough just to be funny. You have to be smart as well, and I am smart enough to know I'm not smart. Enough.

It wasn't so long ago that I was smart at school, but lately I can't concentrate on anything except girls and music. I'm smart enough to see a correlation.

I can paint quite well but not like my best friend, Guggi. I can write prose quite well but not as well as that gifted know-it-all Neil McCormick, who writes for the school magazine. I've played with the idea of being a journalist, fantasized about being a foreign correspondent, reporting from war zones. But to be a journalist, you have to do well at exams, and I'm having problems with exams. Problems with being in school to sit them.

And anyway, there's another war zone I'm involved in. In our street, at my house, in my head.

Why go all the way to Timbuktu as a war correspondent when there's so much good material under my bed? The fears and specters under my pillow are the reasons I sometimes don't want to get out of bed. I don't yet know that rock 'n' roll—punk rock in particular— will prove my liberation.

That it will end my occupation. Of my bed.

We have a brown leatherette couch in our living room at 10 Cedarwood Road. An orange-and-black sunburst carpet that runs flush to the walls and hugs our bare feet in the winter. We've just gotten central heating so that for the first time the cold does not chase us every morning from bedroom to bathroom.

We're rich.

So rich that my da drives a metallic-red Hillman Avenger. So rich that we had a color telly before our friends. A color telly is a big deal. In our house it makes real life look less real, and in my teenage years life for me, for Da, and for Norman regularly needs to look a little less real.

During the 1970s, color telly makes the green of the Old Trafford or Anfield or Highbury football grounds so much greener on *Match of the Day* than any green field out the back of our housing estate. The red shirts of George Best and Charlie George are ablaze. It doesn't do much for Malcolm Macdonald. What's the point of supporting Newcastle United in their monochrome kits when black-and-white is history?

My da says royalty should be history, too, but agrees with my mother that the queen looks great in color. Every year, my mother and father might laughingly argue about whether we Irish should interrupt our Christmas lunch to watch Her Majesty-ness give her Christmas Day speech on the telly at three o'clock. It's like the whole world has a weakness for the fanfare and parade, the royal pomp and circumstance. But war is black-and-white even when it's in full color. Parts of our country are at war with other parts of our country. Our next-door neighbor, Great Britain, has been a bully, and now we have grown some of our own. Blood is a crimson color on the news. More and more flags on our streets are branding public space with the divisive history of Ireland and England, but that doesn't stop us pausing to watch the Trooping of the Colour on the queen's birthday. It all comes alive on a color telly.

But even accounting for the U.K.'s punk rock, to a teenage boy in Dublin, England can never be as vivid as America. The "cowboys" introduce a whole other spectrum—John Wayne, Robert Redford, Paul Newman—and so do the "Indians," though they had no hand in their own drawing. The portrayal of the Apache, the Pawnee, the

Mohicans will influence the way punk looks. Then there's the urban lawmen like Clint Eastwood as Dirty Harry, Peter Falk as Columbo, or Telly Savalas in *Kojak*.

But fiction was nothing next to real American life. Nothing next to the dazzling Apollo space program, the most visionary of visions.

How mad these Americans are to think they could land a man on the moon, the kind of mad we Irish feel a stake in. And wasn't it one of our own royal family, John Fitzgerald Kennedy, who first thought up the idea of putting a man on the moon? That's what my da says.

A teenager in 1970s Dublin, I'm serious about turning the black-and-white world outside the ornament-cluttered windowsills of Cedarwood Road into the kind of color we have on that Murphy television. And if I want to see life differently, I want to hear it in a new way too. To move from the monotones of teenage hopelessness to the rounder, richer sounds of another objet d'art in our living room.

Our stereo.

We have a great stereo. It isn't just a record player to fill the house with the sound of my da's operas. It is also a Sony reel-to-reel tape recorder that is going to spin my life around. The Ramones, The Clash, and Patti Smith will reframe the world outside, but it had already started with The Who and Bob Dylan and a special obsession I developed with David Bowie, who, at first, I imagine as one half of a duo. Thinking *Hunky Dory* was the name of his other half, rather than the name of his fourth album.

MAY 10, 1978

A big day for an apprentice rock star of five feet seven and a half who swears he's five feet eight. That it's my eighteenth birthday is the least of it. We don't do birthdays well in our family. True, it's excellent to receive a £5 note from my da, but that isn't why today is special.

This is the day I will learn to do a Houdini-like great escape. Better than any Indian rope trick, I will make my black-and-white life disappear and then reappear in color. This is the day I'm going to write my first proper rock 'n' roll song and U2's first single. I have the miracle of Joey Ramone to thank for that. And his miraculous brothers. But without Edge, Adam, and Larry—my own miraculous brothers—no one would ever have heard it.

> *Monday morning*
> *Eighteen years of dawning*
> *I said how long.*
> *Said how long*
> *It was one dull morning*
> *I woke the world with bawling*
> *I was so sad*
> *They were so glad.*
> *I had the feeling it was out of control*
> *I was of the opinion it was out of control.*

I called the song "Out of Control"* because it dawned on me—and Fyodor Dostoyevsky might have had a hand in this—that we humans have little or no influence on the two most important moments of our life. Being born and dying. That felt like the right kind of fuck-you to the universe that a great punk rock song requires.

---

* The song was released on September 26, 1979, on an EP called *Three*, with two other songs—"Stories for Boys" and "Boy/Girl." The order of the songs was selected by listeners of Dave Fanning's RTÉ radio show, and Dave was the first DJ to play our first song. Dave has been the first person to play every new single of ours ever since.

3

Iris (Hold Me Close)

The star,
that gives us light
Has been gone a while
But it's not an illusion
The ache
In my heart
Is so much a part of who I am
Something in your eyes
Took a thousand years to get here
Something in your eyes
Took a thousand years, a thousand years.

Imagine a fifty-five-year-old man singing to his mother in front of twenty thousand people every night.

I mean what's up with that?

It's hard losing your mother at fourteen and all, but maybe he should be over it by now. Seriously.

As lead singer of the U2 group, I get a fair amount of harassment. Fair or unfair, it's part of the job description and most of the time I quite enjoy it. None of it compares with the kind of shit I accuse myself of, especially onstage when I can have all kinds of psychedelic, psychological stuff going on. There's a lot of static on that stage and in that crowd.

———

What's up with that?

That question above? An example of the more inane accusations I hear in my mind just before I step into the song "Iris." It's as if I have my own personal satan trolling at my shoulder, sowing doubt at every turn. The little divil sprays emotional graffiti all over the walls of my self-respect. But the little divil is me, so why would I put myself through this?

Someone has likened prayer to being on a rough sea in a small boat with no oars. All you have is a rope that, somewhere in the distance, is attached to the port. With that rope you can pull yourself closer to God.

Songs are my prayers.

BLACK CURLS AND CHURCH BELLES

I have very few memories of my mother, Iris. Neither does my brother, Norman. The simple explanation is that in our house, when she died, she was never spoken of again.

I fear it was worse than that. That we rarely thought of her again.

We were three Irish males, and we avoided the pain that we knew would come from thinking and speaking about her.

In 2014, on *Songs of Innocence,* I'd given myself a license to look back, to lift up stones under which I knew lay creepy-crawlies. What strands of memory I had left of my mother I'd attempted to weave into the song "Iris."

I would sing myself to her.

I would find her.

Three days before the album's release, I panicked. I'd gone off the idea of the song "Iris" going out into the ether of music releases, out into the world, this song by a fifty-four-year-old man wailing for his late mother. "Iris" felt, at the last minute, too everything: too soft, too broad, too exposed, too much for a band to have to suffer for a singer. This being initially a digital-only release to 500 million people (another story, we'll come to that), I tried to pull the song off the album. It wasn't as if a million CDs or vinyl albums would be consigned to a landfill. But digital too has deadlines, and I'd missed mine. Apple had loaded the album into its myriad virtual systems, and pulling the track would mean blowing up the world.

Or something equally bad.

I stared at the wall asking myself why this was still so raw, why Iris still hurt after all these years. How many years exactly? This is 2014, forty years later. And September—forty years to the month.

Really? What date exactly? I couldn't remember. I texted my brother. He couldn't remember. He called my uncle, but Uncle Jack couldn't remember either, though he remembered that "Gags" Rankin—my grandfather—was buried on September 9 because that's the last time he saw his sister Iris.

September 9 was the album release. Unbeknownst to anyone, *Songs of Innocence* was arriving in the world on the same date I last spoke to my mother. What are these serendipities about? Coincidence? I treasure the mystery of every cosmic rhyme and took this for some comfort that I was doing the right thing.

> *Free yourself to be yourself*
> *If only you could see yourself.*

That phrase became my mantra—"Free yourself to be yourself"—and the memories began to return.

Iris laughing. Her humor, black as her dark curls. Inappropriate laughing was her weakness. My father, Bob, from the inner city of Dublin, had taken her, and her sister Ruth, to the ballet, only to have her embarrass him with her muted howls of laughter at the protruding genitalia boxes worn by the male dancers under their leotards.

I remember at around seven or eight, I was a boy behaving badly.

Iris chasing me, waving a long cane that her friend had promised would discipline me. Me, frightened for my life as Iris chased me down the garden. But when I dared to look back, she was laughing her head off, no part of her believing in this medieval disciplining or the badness of the boy.

I remember being in the kitchen, watching Iris ironing my brother's school uniform, the faint buzz of my father's electric drill from upstairs, where our DIY da was hanging a shelf he'd made.

Suddenly the sound of his voice, screaming. An inhuman sound, an animal noise.

"Iris! Iris! Call an ambulance!"

Racing to the bottom of the stairs, we found him at the top, holding the power tool, having apparently drilled into his own crotch. The bit had slipped, and he was frozen stiff with fear that he might never be stiff again. "I've castrated myself!" he cried.

I was in a state of shock, too, at seeing my father, the giant of 10 Cedarwood Road, fallen like a tree. And I didn't know what that meant. Iris knew what it meant, and she was shocked, too, but that wasn't the look on her face. No, the look on her face was the look of a beautiful woman suppressing laughter, then the look of a beautiful woman failing to suppress laughter as it took hold of her. Peals of laughter like a bold girl in church whose efforts not to commit sacrilege just make for a louder explosion when it finally erupts.

She reached for the telephone, but she couldn't get it together to dial 999; she was bent double with laughter. Da made it through his flesh wound. Their marriage made it through the incident. The memory made it home.

Iris was a practical woman. Pretty DIY herself. She could change a plug on a kettle, and she could sew: boy, could she sew! She became a part-time dressmaker when my da refused to let her work as a cleaning lady at Aer Lingus, along with her best friends on Cedarwood Road.

There was a big showdown between them, the only proper row I remember. I was up in my room eavesdropping as my mother reared up at him with a "you don't rule me" tirade in her own defense. And, to be fair, he didn't. Pleading succeeded where command had failed, and she gave up the chance to work with her mates in Dublin Airport. Years later, returning home from tour, I would ache more than a little on meeting her great friends Onagh and Winnie at Arrivals. Iris had departed, but sometimes I could see her standing right there beside them.

SUNDAY MORNINGS AT THE TWO ST. CANICE'S

Hold me close, hold me close and don't let me go.
Hold me close like I'm someone that you might know
Hold me close the darkness just lets us see
Who we are
I've got your light inside of me.

Bob was a Catholic; Iris was a Protestant. Theirs was a marriage that had escaped the sectarianism of Ireland at the time. And because Bob believed that the mother should have the casting vote in the children's religious instruction, on Sunday mornings my brother and I were dropped with our mother at the Protestant St. Canice's Church in Finglas. Whereupon my da would receive Mass up the road in the Catholic church. Also called St. Canice's.

Confusing? Yes!

There was less than a mile between the two churches, but in 1960s Ireland a mile was a long way. The "Prods" at that time had the better tunes, and the Catholics had the better stage gear. Gavin Friday, my mate from the top of Cedarwood, used to say, "Roman Catholicism is the glam rock of religion" with its candles and psychedelic colors—cardinal blues, scarlets, and purples—its smoke bombs of incense, and the ring of the little bell. The Prods were better at the bigger bells, because, as Gavin said, "They could afford them!" For a fair amount of the population in Ireland, wealth and Protestantism went together. To have either was to have collaborated with the enemy—that is, Britain. This was the rather warped thinking in the 1960s and 1970s. In fact the Church of Ireland had supplied a lot of Ireland's most famous insurgents, and south of the border its congregation was mostly modest in every way. Very modest, very nice people. In fact, far from bigotry, niceness was the only thing you could complain about. Its garden fetes and bring-and-buy sales were much more a death-by-sticky-bun situation. The Church of Ireland could nice you to death!

My da was hugely respectful of this church community he'd married into, and so having worshipped on his own up the road, he would then return from his St. Canice's to wait outside our St. Canice's for his wife and children to come out and then drive us all home.

Iris and Bob had grown up in the inner city of Dublin around the thoroughfare of Oxmantown Road, an area known locally as Cowtown because every Wednesday it was the seat of the country-comes-to-the-city fair. It was next to Phoenix Park, which, the locals would tell you, was the largest city-center park in Europe, and where Bob and Iris loved to walk and watch the deer run free. Unusually for "a Dub," as inner-city residents were known, Bob played cricket in the park, and his mother, Granny Hewson, listened to the BBC for results of English Test matches.

Cricket was not a working-class game in Ireland. Add this to my da saving up to buy records of his favorite operas, taking his wife and her sister to the ballet—and then not letting Iris become a "Mrs. Mops," as he called it, even though her friends were—and you can sense there might have been just a tiny bit of the snob in Bob. His interests were not the norm on his street, that's for sure. Actually, the whole family might have been a little different. My da and his brother Leslie did not even speak with a strong Dublin accent. It was as if their telephone voice was the only one they used.

My da's family name, Hewson, is also unusual in that it is both a Protestant and a Catholic name. Visiting a posh pub during a U.K. tour, I once saw a charter for the beheading of Charles I, with one John Hewson among the seven signatories. A republican? Good. One of Cromwell's henchmen? Bad.

As a kid I could see that Hewsons tended to live in their heads while Rankins were more at home in their bodies. The Hewsons could overthink. My da, for example, would not go to visit his own brothers and sisters in case they might not want to see him. He would need to be invited. My mother—a Rankin—would tell him just to go on and drop in on them. Her family members were always dropping in on each other. What's the problem? We're family. Rankins are laughing all day long, and if the Hewsons can't quite do that, we do have a temper to keep us entertained. A big temper.

I might have a bit of that.

There's another difference. The Rankin family is susceptible to the brain aneurysm.

Of the five Rankin sisters, three died from an aneurysm. Including Iris.

JESUS, IRIS, AND JOSEPH!

My mother heard me sing publicly just once. I played the Pharaoh in Andrew Lloyd Webber's musical *Joseph and the Amazing Technicolor Dreamcoat*. It was really the part of an Elvis impersonator, so that's what I did. Dressed up as Elvis, I curled my lip and brought the house down. Iris laughed and laughed and laughed. She seemed surprised that I could sing, that I was musical, which is odd because I'd hinted at it often enough.

As a very small child, from when I stood only as high as the keyboard, I was transfixed by the piano. There was one in our church hall, and any time that I could spend with it on my own was time I held sacred. I would spend ages finding out what sound the keys could make or what happened if I pushed one of the pedals with my foot. I didn't know what reverb was; I couldn't believe how such a simple action could turn our church hall into a cathedral. I remember my hand finding a note and then searching for another note to rhyme with it. And another. I was born with melodies in my head, and I was looking for a way to hear them in the world.

Iris was not looking for those kinds of signs, so she didn't see them.

Iris was not a romantic; she was a pragmatic. A frugal woman who made her own clothes. When my grandmother decided to sell her piano, my hints about how well it would fit in our house could not have been any less subtle.

"Don't be silly, where would we put it?" No piano for our house. No room.

Iris had a second chance to sort this. When I was eleven, my parents sent me to St. Patrick's Cathedral Grammar School in the city center, a school famous for its boys' choir. At the interview

Mr. Horner, the principal, asked if I might have any interest in joining the choir. My heart stirred, but I had the nervousness of an eleven-year-old claiming a talent I hadn't really owned up to. Iris, sensing my embarrassment, answered for me.

"Not at all. Paul has no interest in singing."

For a child so evidently betrothed to music, my mother's behavior might seem a little odd, a little out of touch with her second son, but I don't think so. Iris was a problem solver, not a problem maker. Iris was just being practical.

FROM CATHEDRAL TO TEMPLE

Once we are born, we begin to forget
The very reason we came
But you I'm sure I've met
Long before the night the stars went out
We're meeting up again.

In September 1972, I was twelve and in my first year at Mount Temple. St. Patrick's Cathedral Grammar School had been unhappy for me and unhappy for them. The final straw was a Spanish teacher known as Biddy who I was convinced put lines through my homework without even looking at it. I was feeling bullied, but what began as a prank turned me into a bully myself. When the weather was good, Biddy would take her lunch from her clear plastic Tupperware box and sit on a park bench in the shadow of the magnificent St. Patrick's Cathedral, the largest in the country. Students from St. Patrick's were not allowed in the park at lunchtime, but I'd found a way to mount the railings and one day, with a couple of accomplices, successfully lobbed dog shit into her lunch box. It was revenge on her for shitting on our work. Some of it might have gone into her hair, and that was very bad. Unsurprisingly, by the end of that term Biddy wanted this little shit out of her hair, and it was suggested I might be happier somewhere else. Enter Mount Temple Comprehensive School.

Mount Temple was liberation.

A nondenominational, coeducational experiment, remarkable for its time in conservative Ireland. Instead of an A class, B class, and C class, the six first-year classes were D, U, B, L, I, and N. You were encouraged to be yourself, to be creative, to wear your own clothes. And there were girls. Also wearing their own clothes.

The challenge was the two bus rides it took to get there, the long journey into the city center from the northwest side and then out to the northeast. Unless you cycled, which is what my friend Reggie Manuel and I began to do. It was on one never-ending incline of a hill that we learned how to hold on to the milk van, and I'm not sure I've ever felt as free as I felt on those days cycling to school with Reggie. If the weather meant we couldn't cycle all the time, leaving us to the drudgery of the bus journey, compensation would come on Fridays by being in the city center after school with the chance to visit the record store Dolphin Discs on Talbot Street. The chance to stare at album covers like the Stooges' *Raw Power* or David Bowie's *Ziggy Stardust*.

THE MEN AND WOMEN WHO FELL TO EARTH

The only reason I wasn't standing in Dolphin Discs at 5:30 p.m. on May 17, 1974, is that a bus strike meant we'd had to cycle to school. We were already home when the streets around Dolphin Discs were blown to bits by a car bomb in Talbot Street, another went off in Parnell Street, and another in South Leinster Street, all within minutes, a coordinated attack by an Ulster loyalist extremist group who wanted the south to know what terrorism felt like. A fourth explosion struck in Monaghan, and the final death toll stood at thirty-three people, including a pregnant young mother, the entire O'Brien family, and a Frenchwoman whose family had survived the Holocaust.

I didn't dodge a bullet that day; I dodged carnage. Guggi's eleven-year-old brother, Andrew Rowen, aka Guck Pants Delaney, did not dodge it. He and his father, Robbie Rowen, were parked in Parnell Street when the blast hit. His father locked Andrew in the family van while he set about trying to rescue people from this destruction. Andrew watched in horror at the dismembered, purposeless bodies all around him. Years later I called him to ask if he would mind if I wrote about that day in a song called "Raised by Wolves." Hold on a sec, he said, and when he came back to the phone, he told me he was holding a piece of shrapnel from the original car bomb. He'd kept a little piece of the bomb for forty years, evidence of a trauma that had taken a little piece of him. His words. At fifteen he was in the newspapers for shooting an intruder who'd broken into the bicycle store he was minding. By twenty he was a heroin addict, sleeping rough on the streets of London. I wrote our song "Bad" about Andrew.

The Dalai Lama says you can only begin a real meditation on life with a meditation on death. Gothic stuff but something in it. Finiteness and infiniteness are the two poles of the human experience. Everything we do, think, feel, imagine, discuss is framed by the notion of whether our death is the end or the beginning of something else. It takes great faith to have no faith. Great strength of character to resist the ancient texts that suggest an afterlife.

At age fourteen, none of this was abstract.

DREAM SEQUENCE WHILE AWAKE

I'm fourteen on Monday, September 9, 1974. My father is carrying my mother in his arms through a crowd that splits open like a white snooker ball hitting a triangle of color. He's rushing to get her to the hospital. She has collapsed at the side of the grave as her own father is being lowered into the ground.

"Iris has fainted. Iris has fainted."

My aunts, my cousins. Their voices blow around like a breeze through leaves. "She'll be okay, she'll be okay. She's just fainted."

She she she . . . whispers in the wind . . . fe fe fe fainted . . . Irissss hasssss fainted. Before I, or anyone else, could think or blink, my father had Iris in the back of the Hillman Avenger, with my brother, Norman, at the wheel, twenty-one and driving the getaway car. But there was no getting away from tragedy that day. I stay with my cousins to say goodbye to my grandda, and then we all kind of shuffle back to my grandmother's house, 8 Cowper Street, where the tiny kitchen is a factory producing sandwiches, biscuits, and tea.

This two-up two-down with an outside bathroom seems to contain thousands of people, all of whom are miraculously being fed.

Only three nights ago, my grandda had danced and sung Michael Finnegan's reel, on his fiftieth wedding anniversary. He'd had such a high time that his children worried he'd wake in the night and not make it to the bathroom. They left a bucket beside the bed. My grandfather left this life kicking that bucket. That's right, he actually kicked the bucket, a massive heart attack on the night of his wedding anniversary.

Today the Rankin family of sisters, brothers, and cousins are all squeezed into this tiny redbrick house, and even though it's Grandda's funeral and even though Iris has fainted, we're kids, running around, laughing with the cousins. Until a door slams open. Ruth, my mother's younger sister and best friend, bursts through with her husband, Teddy, who is weeping.

"Iris is dying. Iris is dying," he says. *"She's had a stroke."*

Uncle Ted is starting to wail, but everybody wants to find out the story, crowding around them to unlock the news.

Iris is one of eight kids from number 8. She has four sisters—Ruth, Stella, Pat, Olive—and three brothers: Claude the oldest, Alex next, and Jack, who is married to Barbara, a couple who have become my other close family, the ones we share a holiday caravan with. Jack and Barbara are in a huddle with Ruth and Teddy. I look up to Barbara, who will step in for my mother in so many ways, and I see the weight of grief. It's as if gravity doubles up.

Barbara is struggling to stand. Ruth, the closest in age, and so much more, to my mother, immediately takes her elder sister's job and starts to get organized.

All this is taking place in the moment before someone realizes I'm here too, Iris's youngest. Maybe I don't need to be hearing this news, like this, just now. But I hear it. I'm fourteen and strangely calm. I tell my mother's sisters and brothers that everything is going to be okay. But everything isn't okay. And everything won't be okay.

Everything will be different.

Three days later Norman and I are brought into the hospital to say goodbye to my mother. She's alive but barely. The local clergyman, Sydney Laing, whose daughter I'm dating, is here. Ruth is outside the hospital room, wailing. And Barbara. And my father, whose eyes appear to have less life in them than my mother. Norman and I enter the emergency room at war with the universe, but Iris looks peaceful. It's hard to figure that a large part of her has already left. I am reminded that with faith the size of a mustard seed you can move a mountain. But this mountain is my mother's mortality, and it won't get out of the way. We hold her hand and say goodbye. There's a clicking sound, but we don't hear it. The sound of a switch. The machine that keeps Iris warm is turned off. Electricity. This mortal coil. Gone.

The stars are bright but do they know
The universe is beautiful but cold.

Sometimes, goes the old spiritual, I feel like a motherless child. What is it about the loss of a mother? Does something inside the child feel that the mother chose to leave?

Abandonment is probably the root of paranoia. John Lennon, Paul McCartney, Bob Geldof, John Lydon, so many rock 'n' roll singers lost their mothers at an early age. There must be something to this. A friend tells me of a parallel abandonment in hip-hop. Abandonment by the father drives that car.

SONG LINES: FROM IRIS TO ALI

Big drum sounds, big themes, big emotions. I've always loved the big music. Songs are my prayers. Songs are also where I live, and if you live in your songs, you want to make sure there's enough room. The size of the song is important. Your emotional life has to fit into it, and a lot of the emotions that I couldn't express as a young man living at 10 Cedarwood Road have since found expression in the songs of U2.

Those songs became my home.

In writing the song "Iris," I found myself meandering from singing about my mother to singing about Ali, understandable but unforgivable. A man should never make his lover his mother. It's a trick that a nurturing girl can fall for and a selfish boy can exploit, but it happened in that moment. I was singing for Iris, and then suddenly I wasn't.

You took me by the hand
I thought that I was leading you
But it was you made me your man
Machine
I dream
Where you are
Iris standing in the hall
She tells me I can do it all.

Kraftwerk's *The Man-Machine* was the first gift I bought Ali, who mostly seemed to listen to her father's record collection of crooners. I wasn't to know it, but Ali would become the one who would believe in me, now that my mother no longer could. I wasn't to know it, but years later when my father passed, Ali would explain to me that I somehow blamed him for the death of Iris and that the anger I had inside me, the anger that can still overtake me, was rooted right there.

Iris playing on the strand
She buries the boy beneath the sand,
Iris says that I will be the death of her
It was not me.

The rage that is rock 'n' roll.
All the rage that drives you off the page and onto the stage. Every night you sing yourself to it and through it.
I didn't kill her; you killed her, by ignoring her.
You won't ignore me!
Iris.
You're no longer singing the song; the song is singing you.
The journey away from self-consciousness is the most important journey for any performer to make; it is the hardest journey. But when you get it right, the stage becomes the place where you're fully at home, where in a strange way you're fully yourself.
Yeats got it.

O body swayed to music, O brightening glance,
How can we know the dancer from the dance?

5
GUGGI

10
Home of BONO
'a baritone who
thinks he is a tenor'
an actual tenor

CEDARWOOD
ROAD
and BOB HEWSON

140
MR FRIDAY2U

4

Cedarwood Road

I was running down the road
The fear was all I knew
I was looking for a soul that's real
Then I ran into you
And that cherry blossom tree
Was a gateway to the sun
And friendship once it's won
It's won . . . it's won.

My father was a tenor, a really, really good one. He could move people with his singing, and to move people with music, you first have to be moved by it.

I see my father standing in the living room of Cedarwood Road, standing in front of the stereo with two of my mother's knitting needles. He's the conductor. He'd conduct Beethoven, Mozart, and Elisabeth Schwarzkopf singing Richard Strauss's *Four Last Songs*.

Right now he's listening to *La Traviata*, eyes closed, lost in reverie.

He is taken by the music, no longer present. He is not precisely aware of the story of *La Traviata*, but he feels it. A father and son at odds, lovers cast away and returned. He senses the injustice of the human heart. His is broken by the music. He doesn't notice that I'm in the room looking at him. I won't know for many years what the opera was that was going on in his head, but music was clearly his only escape. He doesn't really notice much else.

There are only a few routes to making a grandstanding stadium singer out of a small child. You can tell them they're amazing, that the world needs to hear their voice, that they must not hide their "genius under a bushel." Or you can just plain ignore them. That might be more effective. The lack of interest of my father, the tenor, in his son's voice is not easy to explain, but it might have been crucial.

After my mother's departure, Cedarwood Road is becoming its own opera. I am locked in a house of three men used to shouting at the television now shouting at each other. We live in rage and melancholy; we live in mystery and melodrama.

The subject of the opera is the absence of a woman called Iris, and the music is swelling to stay the silence that envelops the house every time her name is mentioned. Which is never, because that's how these men are trying to deal with their grief. By pretending it is not there.

Just as Iris is not there.

Three men dealing with their grief by never talking about it. One of those men is just a boy who, as a result, even now has too few memories of his mother to dredge from the river of silence that sought to drown her out. A river of silence in which our hero himself might drown until his big brother throws him a line that will save his life.

Pulls him on a wooden raft that will take him to shore. The raft is a guitar, both lifeline and weapon.

My brother, Norman, has always been a fixer of the most practical kind, an engineer, a mechanic of the world around him who could pull things apart and put things back together. Anything. The engine of his motorcycle, a clock, a radio, a stereo. Norman loved technology and he loved music, and both came together in the large, chrome Sony reel-to-reel tape recorder that sat in the center of the table, taking pride of place in our "good room." Norman was entrepreneurial enough to figure out that a reel-to-reel machine meant he didn't have to keep buying music. If he borrowed an album from a friend for an hour, it was his forever. His vast library of songs and albums occupied most of my interior life in the early 1970s. From The Beatles to Bowie via the Rolling Stones, The Who, and even the folkies Bob Dylan, Leonard Cohen, and Neil Young.

Because Norman, seven years older than me, was already a workingman when I was in Mount Temple, the reel-to-reel was my only company when I got home from school. Some late afternoons I'd be so hungry but would forget who I was and where I was. I'd stand in front of the stereo, just like my father, and let the house burn down while I listened to the opera. *Tommy* by The Who. A rock opera. Charcoal smoke would fill the kitchen and seep into the living room.

Norman taught me to play guitar. He taught me the C chord, the G chord, and, much more difficult, the F chord, where you had to hold down two strings with one finger.

Especially difficult when the strings are quite a way from the fret board, as they were on his rather cheap guitar. But with his guidance I learned to play "If I Had a Hammer" and "Blowin' in the Wind." He had a Beatles songbook that took me further. It wasn't just chords and sheet music; it was full of surreal paintings of their songs. While my friend Guggi tried to copy the images, I worked out how to play "I Want to Hold Your Hand," "Dear Prudence," or "Here Comes the Sun" on my brother's guitar.

Norman and I fought a lot. He had a bad temper, but he was a clever boy who, like his da, should have gone to university. He'd won a scholarship to a very well-regarded institution called simply the High School, a renowned Protestant secondary school that leaned in the direction of maths and physics but was famous for having been the alma mater of William Butler Yeats. But Norman never felt very comfortable there with his secondhand uniform, secondhand books, and the secondhand religion of his Catholic father. He felt inferior to the Protestant boys from the Southside.

Norman was upbeat by nature, except when the melancholy had him. Then it really had him. He was close to Iris, and I would overhear him talking to her about girls he liked and how he found them hard to approach. I remember Iris helping him with his acne. Like Norman, Iris was a mechanic too, a mechanic of the heart.

MY SECRET NERDY SELF

I don't remember exactly when I learned to play chess, but it was likely summertime in the seaside town of Rush, just outside Dublin on the north coast. Grandda Rankin—my mum's da—had an old railway carriage that he'd turned into a summer chalet. There was nothing much to do at "the hut." There were card games like patience and 22, but even as a kid I wasn't much interested in luck as a subject. I was interested in my da, and if he wasn't golfing or reading or hanging out with his brothers-in-law, I would try to catch his attention. I craved his affection. I remember walking the pier and the warmth of his hand on my neck.

When I was around eight or nine years old, he taught me to play chess, and I quickly took to its permutations and combinations, beginning to form my own openings before studying the tried and tested ones.

At first I thought he was letting me win, but eventually I noticed he wasn't. This was how to take his attention off whatever he was thinking about and put it on *me*. To best him, to beat him! Bob didn't like losing, and maybe that's where I learned that I didn't either. As I played, I came to learn one of the most important lessons in my life, that chess was not a game of luck but a game of strategy and that good strategy usually trumps luck. Even bad luck.

Long before my teenage life would be crushed and uplifted by the two great forces of girls and music, I developed a secret life with local chess players. Niall Byrne, from two doors up, Joseph Marks from Cedarwood Park, two brilliant boys. And fun too. As we got better, it became harder to find good games, so we started playing in adult chess tournaments. It doesn't take a psychological genius to figure out why adult slaying was a thrill beyond any other. I loved going up against grown-ups who would start out dismissively reading their newspapers—so beneath them to be playing children. Lightning chess was a favorite. To be sitting there at age ten, annoying the face off people five times your age, chasing them around a chessboard. That was a whole other order of fun.

It was dawning on me that while I could do stuff quite easily that a lot of people found hard, I found difficult a lot of stuff that others found easy. I'm not sure if it's dyslexia, because I'd had no problems reading, but while I was doing okay at school, I was starting to get anxious that I wouldn't excel. My quality of work had improved when I'd first arrived at Mount Temple, and I'd done better in class than at St. Patrick's, but when Iris died, I lost all concentration.

Teachers lamented my scrawly handwriting when my father's letters to them about me were such beautiful calligraphy. They asked why I hadn't noticed leaving complete sections out of essays or why I could do higher maths but not lower. I wasn't able to explain myself.

While I loved poetry and history, I didn't feel as clever as my friends. I started to feel stupid and, because of that, became angry. I was afraid deep down that I was average. I didn't realize that my whole life would be pitted against the concept that anyone is average. "No man need be a mediocrity if he accepts himself as God made him" is how the poet Patrick Kavanagh put it.

I was losing my self-confidence in all kinds of ways. I stopped playing chess, not because I wasn't loving it, but because I began to think of it as "uncool" and I had no mother to tell me that nothing cool was "cool."

Away from the chessboard Bob and I were competing in conversation, and if I wasn't giving him a lot of lip, I gave him enough for occasional escalation. We'd fought a lot before Iris died, but we fought more after. Much more. Our arguments were mostly verbal, and only occasionally would he speak of restraining himself lest he have to clatter me. In truth, from when I was fourteen, he knew that wouldn't work out well for himself. Things would go off unpredictably. Norman winding it up. He'd come home from work and I'd be in the house watching the telly, not doing my homework, not having prepared the tea. He would give me some lip. I would return it. Maybe Norman or I would end up on the ground. Bob half whacked me a few times, but I never responded, although I held him a couple of times.

Sleepwalking down the road
I'm not waking from these dreams
Alive or dead they're in my head
It was a warzone in my teens
I'm still standing on that street

Still need an enemy
The worst ones I can't see
You can . . . you can.

But there's something between the father and the son. A thickness of atmosphere, some kind of wall of air that, if punctured from the son to the father by way of a blow, will mean things are never the same again.

Norman was angry.

Bob was angry.

I was angry.

Part of my rage was knowing I had something but not being able to uncover it. Knowing I was clever but not being able to be clever in school.

But there was rage about my mother too. I'd had faith she'd make it through and she didn't. I told her sister she was going to make it. I comforted my aunts, saying that we were all going to make it through.

But prayers aren't always answered in the way you want. I didn't know that then.

That's a part of my rage and maybe even some wild, irrational blame that he, the head of the house, was responsible for the destruction of it.

He must be to blame if we're all in this trouble.

THE OPERA THAT WAS BOB

Although Bob Hewson was himself betrothed to music, in tune with his wife he also did not suggest we get a piano. Nor ever ask me about how my music was coming on. He loved to talk about the opera, just not to his sons. He read Shakespeare; he painted and acted. For a working-class Dub, this was not unheard of but was unusual. He had rarefied taste.

But music was his great passion. For years after Iris died, he would reduce a room of relations to a puddle by breaking into Kris Kristofferson's "For the Good Times." I still wonder if he was singing it from my mother's point of view: "I'll get along, you'll find another," etc. Quite the manipulator, he could crack open a heart like it was a boiled egg with some high falsetto singing. He really was a fine tenor and once told me that I was "a baritone who thinks he's a tenor." One of the great put-downs and pretty accurate.

I am a baritone who thinks he's a tenor.

When I think of opera and my da, it's not just watching him get lost in *La Traviata* or *Tosca*, or, later, seeing him onstage with the Coolock Musical Society, his face caked with orange makeup, singing everything from *The Mikado* to *H.M.S. Pinafore*. When I think of opera and my da, I think of opera in the tortured sense because, though Bob Hewson might have sung light opera, he was heavier than that. And "operatic" is also the operative word in describing our relationship. I was an angry teenager; he was an angry grown-up, an Irish male who didn't know what to do with a young teenage boy. A creature of his time, he was not that interested in his kids and now he was the only parent, and he didn't like it. I was interested in his interest, but I, too, had the seeds of a performer, and above all else performers don't like to be ignored.

> *If the door is open it isn't theft*
> *You cannot return to where you've never left*
> *Blossoms falling from a tree, they cover you and cover me*
> *Symbols clashing, bibles smashing*
> *You paint the world you need to see*
> *Sometimes fear is the only place we can call home*
> *Cedarwood Road.*

You can see the through line of this melodrama. Son blames father for the loss of his mother and the ending of his home life. The young buck takes on the old buck.

Patricide. The stuff of the great operas. U2's music was never really rock 'n' roll. Under its contemporary skin it's opera—a big music, big emotions unlocked in the pop music of the day.

A tenor out front who won't accept he's a baritone. A small man singing giant songs.

Wailing, keening, trying to explain the unexplainable. Trying to release himself and anyone who will listen from the prison of a human experience that cannot explain grief.

Maybe Bob didn't take me too seriously as a teenager because he could see I was doing a great job of that myself. But I can still hear his voice, in my head, especially when I sing. I thought he was standing in my way, but perhaps he just wanted solid ground for his son, and there wasn't much of that in Dublin in the 1970s. Bob thought that to dream was to be disappointed, and he didn't want that for me.

I got to thank him for his patience.

I never got to apologize for being such a prick—until he was gone.

After Iris died, 10 Cedarwood Road stopped being a home. It was just a house. Most days I'd return to it from Mount Temple holding a tin of meat, a tin of beans, and a packet of Cadbury's Smash. Cadbury's Smash was astronaut food, but eating it did not make me feel like David Bowie's Starman or Elton's Rocket Man. In fact eating it was not a lot like eating at all. But at least it was easy. You just put boiling water on these little dry pellets, and they shape-shifted into mashed potato. I'd add them to the same pot in which I'd just cooked the tinned beans. And the tinned meat. And I ate my dinner out of the pot sitting in front of the color TV, even though this was a particularly black-and-white thing to do.

I don't enjoy cooking or ordering food, which may go back to having to cook my own meals as a teenager. That was when food was just fuel. We used to buy a cheap fizzy drink called Cadet Orange because it had enough sugar to keep you going but was so foul you would want nothing else down your throat for hours. We drank it after I'd spent my food money on something more important—Alice Cooper's 45 "Hello Hooray," for example.

Sometimes such a musical purchase—Santana's *Abraxas* or Black Sabbath's *Paranoid*—required I invest the grocery money for the whole family. On those occasions, I confess, I'd sometimes have to borrow the entire grocery list . . . and fail to give any of it back. It was easy . . . apart from a whole loaf of sliced bread which was difficult to hide up your jumper. Being honest about my dishonesty, I didn't feel good about it. At age fifteen, I put away a life of crime and punishment, and turned back to commerce and selling calendars.

TAKEOFFS AND TAKEAWAYS

Fate and fortune arrived in 1975 when Norman got a job in Dublin Airport. Airports in the 1970s were even more glamorous than color television, especially if you were a pilot.

Norman had applied to be a pilot, but his asthma disqualified him from their trainee program, and instead he got work in Cara, the computing department of Aer Lingus, the national airline. Computers, Norman told himself, were even more glamorous than airports, and he committed—just as soon as he'd made some money—to learn to fly small airplanes.

Watching jets take off and land is a weird and wonderful meditation. For people like Norman it can become an all-consuming passion, and thousands of Irish plane twitchers would turn up at Dublin Airport each weekend to see flying machines defy gravity, taking off for somewhere else, somewhere different. Every flight was a subconscious reminder that there was a way out of Ireland if it was needed. In the 1950s and '60s, more than half a million Irish people bought themselves one-way tickets out of the country.

The good fortune for Da, Norman, and me at 10 Cedarwood Road, just two miles from the end of Runway 2, was that Norman managed to talk his bosses in Cara into allowing him to bring home the surplus airline food prepared for Aer Lingus passengers. The meals were sometimes still warm when he carried them in their tin boxes into our kitchen, to be heated in the oven for twenty-three minutes at 185 degrees Celsius.

This was highly exotic fare: gammon steak and pineapple, an Italian dish called lasagna, or one where rice was no longer a milk pudding but a savory experience with peas. I told Norman that this was the worst dessert I'd ever had.

"It's not dessert, and by the way half the world eats rice every day."

Norman knew stuff other people didn't. Imagine eating rice pudding as your main meal every day. If my father and I were proud that Norman had removed the need for us to buy groceries or even to have to cook, after six months the aftertaste of tin was all we could remember. Secretly, at night, I took to eating cornflakes with cold milk instead of the airline food.

I thought salvation had arrived in the form of another culinary miracle, this time at Mount Temple, when the end of the lunch-box era was announced and the age of school dinners dawned. Imagine a fanfare of trumpets and cheering at assembly, that's how excited we all were. But I was punching the air only briefly. The school dinners, the headmaster, Mr. Medlycott, explained, would not be cooked in the school canteen. It wasn't big enough. Instead, they would be arriving by van in tin boxes . . . from Dublin fucking airport! They would be heated, he announced proudly, at 185 degrees for twenty-three minutes in new ovens the school board had paid for.

I'd never been on an airplane, but already my romance with flying was over. Airplane food for lunch and airplane food for tea was more than any apprentice rock star could handle. In time, the apprentice with his band would take to the skies, and on those early Aer Lingus flights I would look out of the window and try to see Cedarwood Road. As I finally left this small town and small island and rose above these flat fields, this dull suburbia, my mind filled with memories of the phone box on the street, teenagers with broken bottles and hearts, sweet and sour neighbors, and the vibrant branches of the cherry blossom tree between our house at number 10 and the Rowens' at number 5. At which point the air hostess would arrive and place one of those little tin trays right in front of me.

MR FADAT 2 U + the Gnan

GAVIN & Guggi
I was coming to understand that you have
the people you need right there beside you
if you can see them. Guggi and I had so much
in finding each other but we were missing
something. Someone —

Stories for Boys

There's a picture book
With coloured photographs
Where there is no shame
There is no laugh
Sometimes I find it thrilling
That I can't have what
I don't know
Hello hello

Was I eleven or twelve when I first read *Lord of the Flies*? William Golding's story is about a group of British schoolboys, around the same age and a little younger, who have crash-landed on a Pacific island while being evacuated during a world war. It's a story about how fear of one another—or fear of "the other" in a metaphysical sense—can shape our imagination and twist our thinking. It's a story about the end of innocence that still shapes my thinking and writing today. And a story that will sketch out the first U2 album, *Boy*, including its cover and final track, "Shadows and Tall Trees," which borrows its title from chapter 7 of the book:

Who is it now? Who calls me inside?
Are the leaves on the trees a cover or disguise?

I walk the street rain tragicomedy
I'll walk home again to the street melody.

Walking down Cedarwood Road one evening, I watched the streetlights shrink and enlarge my shadow and noticed how the telephone poles made stark silhouettes like shriveled conifers. People talking behind the door of the cream-and-green phone box seemed to signal that away from these inexpensively built and modestly mortgaged housing estates of the 1950s and 1960s there was another world to explore. There weren't many trees on our road; the one I remember was the cherry blossom, which miraculously grew out of the stony gray concrete of number 5, a crescendo of flesh tones, pink and pretty. Feminine. In the early summer a kind of luxury fell from its branches, scenting the more modest lives of the Rowen family, who lived there. The tree seemed both sexual and spiritual, and while it made no sense, it also made every sense dance a little. Any suburbanite walking past was reminded that somewhere out there was the possibility of a life of intense color.

APOCALYPSE NOW WITH THE ROWENS

I've been best friends with Derek Rowen, or Guggi, since I was three years old and he was four, this despite his claim that he befriended me only because we had a swing in our back garden.

Guggi not only gave me the name Bono; he gave everyone in his family new and surreal names. Like Clive Whistling Fellow, his older brother. Like Man of Strength and Arran, his younger brother. Guck Pants Delaney, younger still. Glennich Carmichael, his first sister.

Little Biddy One-Way Street, his second sister, then Hawkeye and finally Radar, his youngest brother, who appeared on the cover of two of U2's early albums, *Boy* and *War*. There was one other sister who was born just before he left home, so he called her by her actual name, Miriam.

The name Bono is not the only name Guggi put on me over the years.

I had many, each more ridiculous than the last. The names we gave each other were not merely to make each other laugh but also to illuminate something of who we were, beyond those names given to us by our families at birth, before our personalities were known. The names were supposed to describe the shape of your spirit as well as your physical characteristics. Bono was short for Bono Vox of O'Connell Street, but the boy Guggi was no Latin scholar. "Strong Voice" was an accidental translation. Bonavox was a hearing aid shop in Dublin. He just loved the noise the name made in his mouth. Gradually, Bono Vox of O'Connell Street got shortened to Bonmarie and then to Bono. Previously I had been Steinvich von Heischen, and I was grateful when that phase passed. I called the boy from number 5 Guggi because that's what his head looked like to me, if you tried to represent it in sound. A sound painting. Say "Guggi" and look at him and you'll see what I'm talking about. Perhaps.

The Rowens—three sisters and seven brothers—lived five doors down from us, although you could barely see their house for all the secondhand cars parked around it. Robbie, Guggi's father, was a fiery religious man who was ready if the end of the world arrived suddenly. Mr. Rowen spent most Fridays reading the small ads in the *Evening Herald* in search of stuff that might be needed for the coming apocalypse. Stuff like five hundred tires. Or a 1957 Oldsmobile. Or a garden of chickens and turkeys. Live ones, that is, not frozen ones, to be eaten or sold.

I would sometimes cycle to Mount Temple with Trevor Rowen— the Man of Strength and Arran, later shortened to Strongman. He was an asthmatic whose wheezes and adenoidal voice projections made all the girls drop their guard for him. A genuinely sweet soul who, to protect himself, was capable of some savage humor and malevolent fun. Tidy and organized, he would prepare for the school journey by staring into the hall mirror for a few minutes to check his look was just right, his jeans tucked into socks and ash locks brushed into a quiff. He would later play bass in the Virgin Prunes like a caveman kept from his cave.

Andrew Rowen would end up in three U2 songs, "Running to Stand Still," as well as "Bad" and "Raised by Wolves." Andy, who'd received his name Guck Pants Delaney at age two after a nappy accident, was known for a near-photographic memory. He probably had the highest IQ of any kid on our street, and sometimes it seemed he had memorized the *Encyclopaedia Britannica*. He could remember turning two. He could remember a lot of things he would have liked to have forgotten. His party piece was fielding obscure questions on any subject.

Doing my homework one day, in the little box room in Cedarwood Road, I looked out the window as Guck Pants went by on a unicycle. Playing the trumpet.

Along with his apocalyptic mindset, Robbie Rowen had a wonderful sense of adventure and often took me, with all of his children, to places I'd never have otherwise gone. He took us exploring country lanes at the back of Dublin Airport to pick blackberries in August. Or to the "hole in the wall" beach to sail on inflatable rafts. He taught me to ride motorcycles, putting me on my first moped at eight and a Honda 50 at ten. And he taught me how to sell things.

I've often said that I come from a long line of traveling salespeople, people on my mother's side, and I still consider what I do sales. I sell ideas, I sell songs, and occasionally I sell merchandise. The merchandise began with Robbie Rowen when, in February 1972, he bought a job lot of unsold calendars. A thousand 1972 calendars, going cheap because, well, we were already two months into the year.

Guggi and I went door-to-door on our local roads, trying to sell these calendars with their "professional photographs." Asked if we were not a bit early to be selling next year's calendar, we'd explain that no, we were selling this year's calendar.

"But, Mrs. Byrne, you don't really need the first couple of months, do you?"

THE GOSPEL ACCORDING TO GUGGI

Guggi taught me two things that would change the direction of my life.

1. It was his idea that we split everything fifty-fifty. If he had fifty pence, I had twenty-five pence. In the same way if we were hanging with a larger crew, we shared everything with everyone. It was the way he saw the world.
2. Guggi introduced me to the idea that God might be interested in the details of each of our lives, a concept that was going to get me through my boyhood. And my manhood. (The idea that there is a God, I now recognize, is preposterous for many people. Still more that such omnipotence, if it existed, might be interested in a teenage boy's growing pains.)

When Guggi tells me about Robbie's mood swings and the anxiety involved in ducking out of their way, it seems remarkable that his own spiritual life survived. For all the talk of heaven, he felt like he was in hell at times. His mother, Winnie, was the guardian angel.

"ARE YOU SAVED YET?"

On occasional Sundays, Guggi took me to Merrion Hall, a Holy Roller church meeting for the very evangelical. The Rowens went to church three times on the Sabbath, which I could never figure out, and in the evening they went to a place called Boys Department in the YMCA.

"Are you saved yet?"

My mother was laughing when I came home that first night. She was familiar with the Boys Department kind of evangelizing. But listening to the speakers at these meetings, I was further attracted to the God of the scriptures that they read from. I wasn't sure I'd ever encountered such a presence in our lovely little Church of Ireland in St. Canice's. I had met and briefly dated the clergyman's lovely daughter, so maybe I was distracted. I did have a sense of the divine, but it was inchoate and formless, so when I started to uncover clues about the nature of this presence, I was fascinated. The Bible held me rapt. The words stepped off the page and followed me home. I found more than poetry in that Gothic King James script.

Soon I started to enjoy a modern translation, the Good News Bible, which I discovered when I accompanied Guggi on a YMCA

Christian summer camp in Criccieth, on the Llyn Peninsula in North Wales. I'd never been away from my family. I'd never been out of Ireland. I'd never met such religious devotion. Even the football and hockey teams had biblical names; you could be playing for the Ephesians or the Galatians. It was a little mad but also moving and persuasive. I was taken in by the camaraderie and touched by the preaching.

I'd always be first up when there was an altar call, the "come to Jesus" moment. I still am. If I was in a café right now and someone said, "Stand up if you're ready to give your life to Jesus," I'd be the first to my feet. I took Jesus with me everywhere and I still do. I've never left Jesus out of the most banal or profane actions of my life.

Had I been familiar with that quotation attributed to Saint Augustine when addressing the Lord—"Give me chastity and continence, but not yet"—I'd have understood it. On these trips abroad, Guggi and I shared more than an interest in the scriptures. We were girl mad and had made ourselves available for French-kissing experimentations by the girlfriends of older boys. Nothing to complain about, but we needed to find our own girlfriends. In Criccieth my eyes fell on the very not mendacious Mandy, without doubt the most beautiful girl in all of Wales. It was as if she'd been swept up on the beach, dark and gorgeous in a black bikini. I was thirteen, she was fourteen. I so wanted to be sixteen and have her never let me go. Which she did quite easily now I think of it.

GANGS OF NORTH DUBLIN

I'm not sure a professional psychologist would agree, but something in me understands that until we deal with our most traumatic traumas, there's a part of us that stays at the age at which we encountered them. For a long time that has kept me at age fourteen, when I hit puberty and Iris died.

There's part of me that's still the boy with the baked bean face. I've seen photographs of my freckled face before that time, and it was kind of open and round. A bold face, but clear. At fourteen the baked bean started to grow a nose; I remember spotting the angle starting to arrive on the circumference of the bean. Luckily enough, another angle arrived to balance it; that was my chin. I got some spots but not that many. My face changed, but part of my worldview froze. The pimples started to grow on the inside.

Guggi and I became best friends for a host of reasons, but our relationship with our fathers must be high up on the list. Sons taking on fathers, what's new? We expressed our angst through our love of fighting, martial arts, boxing, wrestling. We beat the shite out of each other on a regular basis. Isn't it true that we turn the world into the shape of our pain? Guggi and I didn't know we were fighting our fathers, but we found enough stand-ins; in fact there was a queue. So we scrapped our way through teenage years.

You could say our friendship was sealed because at home we felt we were in exile. In time art became our passport. Music.

We wrote stupid songs and painted and drew each other. The shading and detail that Guggi could deliver with a cheap blue Biro was confounding to anyone who observed it, not least to my da, who loved to paint with watercolors, especially over black-and-white photographs.

We faced our fears. Our fears threw us in the direction of fearlessness, hyperbole. We wanted to start up our own country or at the very least a city or a town. Or a village, an alternative community that we would call Lypton Village. We had our own language, our own surreal sense of humor. We were dadaists before we knew about such art movements.

Tired of fighting with our fists, Guggi and I took up the fight with our fingers, me on the fret board of Norman's guitar, him painting and drawing, both of us pointing fingers at the stupidity of the world of our enemies. Our only weakness a sneer of superiority. We laughed a little too hard.

But I was coming to understand that you have the people you need right there beside you if you can see them. Guggi and I had so much in finding each other, but we were missing something. Someone.

In my imagination
There is just static and flow
No yes or no
Just stories for boys.

Enter Fionán Hanvey from 140 Cedarwood Road, soon to be renamed Gavin Friday. Mr. Friday to you. A man who would show
Guggi and me what an artistic life looked like and the cost of living
it out loud.

Gavin's ma, Mrs. Hanvey, let her sensitive son take us into the
"good room" of 140 on Monday nights, where we would look at the
art of Picasso as well as listen to the art of David Bowie and T. Rex.
In 1975, the year before punk rock, before the shorn roar of The Jam
and the Sex Pistols, we would draw or sketch or listen to our musical fascinations. Gavin was as pretty a curly-headed boy as T. Rex's
Marc Bolan, a beautiful face with a perfectly balanced forehead and
jawline, well-drawn lips, and, in his own words, "a perfect nose."

I first met Fionán on Cedarwood Road, with screw-down hairdo
and Day-Glo paint on his jeans spelling out "ENO." David Bowie
and Marc Bolan seemed on his mind constantly. He was cooler than
us. Guggi had become friendly with him because they were both
dodging the judgment of their fathers, but we never really got to
know him until a teenage party at my house where he and his mates
Frank Mangan and Damian Kelly were so messy we had to throw
them all out.

Earlier, flirting with Ali and her best friend, Jackie Owen, these
boys had discovered that comprehensive girls were comprehen-
sively quicker and smarter on a lot of stuff. Plus these girls were
"Prods." Gavin, who'd never really rubbed up against Protestants,
was a little intimidated. But the Bolan impersonator had made his
mark and, from that day, would always be informing me of where I
was in the world of music, eventually to roam the U2 planet himself,
as a veritable *Tyrannosaurus rex*.

An apprentice rock star for sure with only one thing holding him back, which was the same thing propelling him forward. He couldn't play an instrument, and the sound of his voice was mostly a wail. No wonder the voice and persona of Johnny Rotten would be so pivotal for so many of us. At full tilt the Pistols made music for marching armies to charge to as they mounted the battlements of any enemy.

That common alarm with our fathers, that was the other reason why Guggi and I, at sixteen, were going to be friends with Gavin Friday for life.

Fathers who at some point had *all* answered to the name Bob.

Pascal Robert, Gav's da, was one of the biggest obstacles in his son's path to freedom of expression. With his slicked-back teddy boy hair and handsome face marbled with fine lines of pink and red from a few too many last drinks in the Ballymun House, he was quite the character to have standing in your way.

"Hello, Mr. Hanvey," we'd say as he crossed the road purposefully to avoid his son and his friends in their Day-Glo battle dress.

"Call me Pascal," he'd shoot back. "Mister is the name for a fool."

"Yes, Mr. Hanvey."

Truth is Gavin had other enemies: his effeminate looks, even graffitied for the sake of punk, were an affront to the laddish boot-boyism of the time.

"I will stab your face" comes to mind as one of the great rejoinders I overheard from someone offended by Gavin's good looks. "Handbag Hanvey" had not yet declared himself gay, but the hail of blows and abuse revealed more about the people in his way and their own sexual psycho nightmares than Gavin's. Maybe there was something defiant in Gav that was the excuse for provocation; there was a pride about this boy who had survived several attempted robberies on his innocence. "Darkness gathers around the light."

Gavin would be a vital player in the future creative life of U2, both in the emergence of our records and in executing our live shows.

Rock 'n' roll is the sound of revenge, all right.

Looking back, I can see it up and down Cedarwood Road.

In number 1 lived Anthony Murphy, renamed Pod, a gentle tough guy who could always stand his ground and would soon sit behind the war drums that Gavin and Guggi would require when their band arrived, along with Reggie Manuel, from nearby Ballymun Avenue, who would become their manager.

Two musical groups would be born from this community: the Virgin Prunes—with Guggi and his brother Strongman, with Gavin, and with Edge's older brother, Dik—and U2.

Two musical groups who were a reverse image of each other. If they raised hell, we were digging for heaven.

These were the families we chose to be in, not the ones we were born in. It's almost a cliché, but if Guggi and I had not found this other life, I wonder where running from our families would have led us. A very different kind of dance.

⊕DIARY

NOV 1976 a big week for me at
the ROCK NROLL HIGH SCHOOL
that was Mount Temple Comprehensive

Song for Someone

You got a face not spoiled by beauty
I have some scars from where I've been
You've got eyes that can see right through me
You're not afraid of anything they've seen.

In the grounds of the former Mountjoy and Marine boarding school, with its redbrick buildings and clock tower made famous by Christopher Nolan in *Under the Eye of the Clock,* sits our school. Mount Temple Comprehensive, one of Ireland's first nondenominational coeducational high schools.

A science block, a maths block, and a small outbuilding for home economics, but the main Mount Temple is a single-story cinder-block building of three corridors—one green, one yellow, one purple—cross-sectioned in the middle by a wider corridor known as the Mall. On the Mall is where I first see Adam Clayton, where I first spy Larry Mullen with his beautiful girlfriend, Ann Acheson, where I first come face-to-face with David Evans, whom no one has yet named the Edge.

September 1973. I am becoming aware that the life of a romantic can sometimes be confusing for the heart. I have evidence, I am reading Shakespeare's sonnets. I know one thing for a fact: despite all the hormoaning and teenage angst, girls are more interesting than boys, mentally, physically, spiritually. I am wowed as I enter my second year at Mount Temple and determined the wowing would turn into wooing. It's the first week back from school holidays when I notice two pretty first years heading to their class and throw myself in their way.

"Do you know the way to the science lab?"

"No, we're first years. We've just got here. Aren't you a second year?"

"I'm lost," I reply. "I'll probably always be lost."

The girls laugh the way that girls laugh at stupid boys who say stupid things, and they walk off. I don't let myself notice the lack of interest and instead ponder whether the blond one and I had some chemistry. Maybe not. Her friend? Definitely not. Her friend with dark curls, an orange sweater that must have been knit by her mother, a tartan skirt, and Wellington boots. Who dresses like that?

She is not demure but seems to demand that no one notice her, including me. This is the first time I've set eyes on Alison Stewart, but I do not know she already has eyes for me, that her friend Sharon has been winding her up for a year, telling her that she and I were born to be together.

I have no hint of that on this first encounter, but something has me enchanted. Her brown eyes brought me somewhere else, her skin tone suggesting farther-flung places than the normal Spanish explanation for the "dark Irish." She looks brainy too. I know I fancy bookish girls. Girls who look as if they do their homework, who might develop a fine sheen of perspiration in the overheated library. Girls who look as if they might do *my* homework.

It took a few terms, but eventually I asked Alison—Ali, she prefers—to our youth club in St. Canice's parish. We called our Friday nights the Web, which is what it was, an equal-opportunity trap because the girls were just as interested in the passing prey as the boys. The Web because we disguised it being a church hall by hanging large nets and lighting it with a single red bulb. I suggested the catchphrase "Get your fly caught in the web." (I know.)

Another Friday night, not long after, under a concrete awning on the school playground, when I first kissed Alison Stewart. Pure joy. If slightly desperate. Kissing was not on the school curriculum, but I figured it was something you could get better at if you found the right accomplice. Alison seemed to suggest there might be room for improvement.

It had been only months since Iris had died, and I had no inkling that her departure would leave me in the hands of another spirit guide, a perfect soul to make my own imperfections my strength. The atom having been split, the force was being released, but in that moment next to the bicycle shed West Finglas looked not one tiny bit moved or changed. Neither did Alison Stewart.

We didn't go out.

I told myself I was still getting over the rector's daughter. And, anyway, I was actually going out with Cheryl.

And I fancied Wendy and Pamela. And Susan.

Bottom line? My mother's death, an event I was in denial about. My heart had broken down, and after these months of grief it was starting to go to sleep. I didn't want somebody waking it up.

In the next couple of years Ali and I shared a few intimate moments, but epiphany did not arrive until I was sixteen, in fifth year. My friend Reggie Manuel, who believed in Ali and me, was giving me a lift home on the back of his Yamaha 100, when I saw a kind of vision of Alison Stewart crossing the school square. Maybe it was the exhaust fumes of the two-stroke petrol engine refracting the image, but she appeared to float, turning to water in my mind, the coolest, clearest, stillest water. The heat haze made a mirage of her, and in that moment I was in the desert, a parched, wayward soldier like those I'd seen in some art movie about the French Foreign Legion. As if on horseback, I rode out of the gates of Mount Temple holding on tight to Reggie's good judgment. It was a different song in my head that day, probably "School's Out" by Alice Cooper, but please substitute The Undertones' "Teenage Kicks" if you need a soundtrack for this moment. I knew I had to ask the future out on a date.

An adult date.

In those few years since we'd met, I'd never forgotten our first desperate kiss, but as my schoolwork had tumbled and my personality soured, something inside me said I wasn't good enough for Alison Stewart. The only thing keeping me keeping on, as Bob Dylan sang to me in "Tangled Up in Blue," were the songs I was starting to hear in my head and the encouragement of friends like Reggie Manuel the Cocker Spaniel.

It was Reggie again who talked me into turning up at Larry Mullen's house, one afternoon after Larry had pinned up a notice in school.

Reggie who drove me to Larry's house on Rosemount Avenue on the back of that Yamaha for a meeting that would define the course of the rest of my life.

ON THE DRUMS

"Drummer seeks musicians to form band."

How casually our destiny arrives. Quite a few wannabes had responded to Larry's invitation on the school notice board, and now, classes out for the day, we were all packed in the oven that was Larry's kitchen.

How did we fit all the drums, the amps, and the apprentice rock stars into such a small room that first time we got together? Guitar and bass might have been squealing for attention with their amplifiers and distortion pedals making loud arguments for being there, but it was the drums that filled both physical and musical space.

On that first Wednesday after school it felt as if no one was in tune but Larry, who appeared quite at home around all this metallic chaos.

Well, he *was* at home. It was his kitchen. Everything I still love about Larry's playing was present then—the primal power of the tom-toms, the boot in the stomach of the kick drum, the snap and slap of the snare drum as it bounced off windows and walls. It was a beautiful violence modulated by the shining gold and silver armor of the cymbals, oddly orchestral, filling out frequencies. This indoor thunder, I thought, will bring the whole house down.

Soon I noticed another noise, an exterior one, the somewhat high-pitched sound of girls giggling and shouting outside the window. Larry already had a fan club, and over the next hour he would offer us a lesson in the mystique of the rock star. He turned the garden hose on them.

Adam Clayton was there on bass. I couldn't quite make out what he was playing, but he really looked the part. David Evans, despite the clangorous din around him, had the coolest aura of anybody. He didn't have to be in tune with anyone else, because he was in tune with himself. In the room briefly was Neil McCormick's brother, Ivan, Larry's friend Peter Martin, who owned a pristine white Telecaster replica that looked as if it had just come from the shop window (he was happy enough to lend it to me, but was probably not so happy about my fingers bleeding all over it), and David Evans's older brother, Dik, a well-known brainbox. Dik and Dave were so clever that they built an electric guitar from scratch. So clever that they used to try to blow each other up with chemistry experiments and, according to their next-door neighbor Shane Fogerty, did blow up the Evans garden shed one day. They had a reputation as weirdos— pleasant weirdos, but weirdos nonetheless.

ON THE GUITAR

My first memory of David Evans is a geometrical one. The angular face on this boy who was leaning up against the wall of the Mall at Mount Temple, plucking a complicated guitar line from a progressive rock group called Yes. He didn't look Irish, he didn't look Welsh—although Wales is where he came from—he looked like a Native American. Or at least my idea of what a Native American looked like. His hair was brushed forward, and he was beginning, I guess you'd say, to get cool.

In 1976 he was fifteen, a year younger than me. He was in class with Ali, and it was said they were the best in their year. It was also said that he had a crush on her, that they might have gone for walks and things like that. My party piece with Ali—whom at that time I was not, technically, going out with—had been teaching her how to play George Harrison's "Something." On guitar. When I couldn't actually play guitar. Now I had come up against a real guitar player. David Evans could play anything he wanted. Which might be shorthand for he could have anything he wanted.

This very intricate guitar part he was picking out right now on the school corridor was from a Yes album called *Close to the Edge*— I know—and it involved harmonics, those bell-like notes he would later make famous. To this day we debate for hours why I think progressive rock was a bad thing. Edge always comes round to my viewpoint and then completely ignores what we've just agreed on. Progressive rock remains one of the few things that divide us.

On a family trip to the United States in 1977, Edge would buy his first guitar from a shop on West Forty-Eighth Street in Manhattan. It was a Gibson Explorer, the same shape as his head, with a big chin and a cone brain. Somewhere around here he received his official name of the Edge, although officially it had more to do with the sound of his brain than the shape of it. When Edge played the guitar, he went into a kind of trance. He didn't really know what he was doing, he didn't know the name of the chords he was playing, and sometimes that's still true.

Edge has enough musical theory to guess, but in truth he is feeling his way through the musical scale, looking for notes, for a particular order of notes that other people haven't used. Looking for the space between them, the gaps in between notes. Looking to pare down everything to the most minimal expression.

Edge is a minimalist by nature. I am not. I am a maximalist.

Edge has a poker face. I do not.

You could be sitting opposite Edge and never know that he had four aces and a two of clubs. Or nothing at all. One of the great bluffers.

There's stuff you can learn from people who don't tell you anything.

Like how not to react when there is a crisis. Like how to stay still and maybe even unearth levity from the seriousness of a situation.

Edge is the silence inside every noise. He's the light inside the paint.

ON THE BASS

Adam Clayton was a true believer in rock 'n' roll. Music is all he ever wanted to do. He had the style, the attitude, the ambition. The only problem was that he couldn't play. This was no automatic disqualification . . . at the time I couldn't really sing. But Adam had a kind of musical dyslexia where he could play the most sophisticated parts or the most simple but not so much in between. This unusual combination meant the normal discussion between bass, drums, and guitar could be a little random and stressful in a rehearsal situation. The Edge, the most musically gifted of any of us, covered the cracks. He desperately wanted his childhood friend to be his teenage bandmate.

Edge had witnessed Adam, age eight, being banished from family and friends to what Brian and Jo, his parents, described as "the best boarding schools." The Claytons, Malahide neighbors of the Evans family, imagined the best kind of life for Adam, the kind of life they would have been familiar with from "the colonies" and the British upper class that Brian knew as a pilot in the air force.

They'd learned about some of the finer things in life from living in air force bases in Yemen and Kenya and were going to make sure their three children—Adam, Sindy, and Sebastian—would not have the kinds of humble beginnings they'd had. Unfortunately, this created a kind of cultural trauma for Adam where he felt he didn't properly fit in anywhere. Worse, he felt spat out of the system as a result of not conforming to it. The injuries were not obvious at first. In fact the armor he wore that first day as he swaggered into Mount Temple Comprehensive was so convincing and cool that his old friend from Malahide David Evans didn't recognize him.

He must have been shitting his pants to walk through the yard in what some would have mistaken for fancy dress—wild curly blond Afro, afghan coat made from sheep that looked as though they were still alive, and a Pakistan '76 T-shirt to keep it real. There was a clinking sound of dull bells from steel bracelets ringing around his wrists. What a sight and what an opening line to impress the tough guys from very different circumstances on the Northside of Dublin.

"Where might I find the smoking room?" he asked, in perfect Queen's English.

For the lads and lassies that smoked behind the bicycle shed it was a clear signal . . . this boy knows nothing and everything. They fell in love with him. Adam dodged difficult students and teachers with the same strategy. Perfect manners. He would read English novels in French class and drink coffee during maths from a flask he kept in his satchel.

"Unteachable" was one teacher's reaction. "Too smart for the school curriculum" was another, and likely truer, analysis. Adam was going to be serious about art and life but certainly not school. School was for fun. Rare is a man so at home in his own body, equally celebrating or mocking all bodily functions, and particularly delighted with his own penis.

Invited or not, you were never surprised to find him giving it some air. Talking to him with your girlfriend, it would dawn on you mid-conversation that Adam was nonchalantly relieving himself on the grass. If his legendary naked run through the corridors of Mount Temple was partly designed—successfully—to get him expelled, it was also about the sheer joy.

Adam might have been the most fun at school, but he was the first person to be serious about our band. It wouldn't be long before he'd talked someone into printing up cards bearing the legend "Manager of U2." His posh accent and air of casual confidence got him off the hook for all kinds of unusual behavior in 1970s Dublin.

When he didn't have the cash for his fare, he would offer the bus conductor a "check"—meaning his name and address on a blank piece of paper. Often he was thrown off anyway, but some drivers were so impressed by his creamy tones they let him take his free ride.

A natural entrepreneur, Adam organized our earliest shows and signed up Steve Averill, the singer of the infamous Irish punk band The Radiators from Space, to be our mentor and come up with a better name for our band than The Hype. Steve was a neighbor of Adam's and Edge's in Malahide and, despite the punk rock attitude, the nicest man on the Northside. He would become critical in art directing the visual language we developed over several decades, but he started the job just by being big brotherly to Adam and finding us our name.

U2.

There it is, a letter and a number, perfect to print large on a poster or a T-shirt. If I think about it as a spy plane, as in the U-2, I like it. But if I think about it as a bad pun, as in "you too," I really don't. I don't think I voted for it, but I certainly didn't stop it. I'm one in four, and a real rock 'n' roll band is not run by the singer. Led maybe, but not run. I definitely stopped The Flying Tigers, which was Steve's second suggestion.

Such was Adam's confidence that it took us a few months to discover his musical bluffing, that he was not playing the right notes in the right order or in any particular key. It didn't seem to matter. In 1976, with rock about to get turbocharged by punk, Adam was the spirit of rock 'n' roll, a kind of posh Sid Vicious. If Larry gave life to the band, it was Adam who believed this band could give us a life.

In our earliest rehearsals, Dik was in the band, and it would not be unusual for me to call out a song, say, the Rolling Stones' "Satisfaction," and find that Dik was playing "Brown Sugar." This was not because he didn't have a highly tuned musical ear—he really did—but because Dik lived in a kind of impenetrable bubble where the thing that was going on in his head was not always the thing that was going on in the room. At this time, Dik would argue, in a parallel universe "Brown Sugar" *was* the correct choice.

"Is Dik really in the band?"

Larry wasn't sure what to make of Dik.

"I mean Dik is a nice guy and everything, but is Dik really in the band?"

Eventually, it became clear that Dik was going to university and wouldn't be able to rehearse with us, so the question was answered without Edge having to explain to his brother that Larry wasn't sure Dik should be in the band. Shortly after Dik left, Larry sidled up and asked, "Is Edge really in the band?"

Edge really was in the band, and in the coming weeks it became clear that Larry, Adam, and I were also in the band. The four of us. Slightly to our disbelief and with thanks to the experiment that was a progressive educational establishment, we began to rehearse in the school music room on Saturdays. Thanks also to some allies on the teaching staff, music teachers like Mr. McKenzie and Mr. Bradshaw, our history teacher Donald Moxham, and our sometime housemaster and sometime English teacher Jack Heaslip.

It was in the music room that I discovered that the songs I couldn't play on my brother's acoustic guitar sounded a lot better when I couldn't play them with Dave, Adam, and Larry.

Not just the songs of The Beatles or The Beach Boys or Bob Dylan. Our own songs. It was in the music room that I discovered songwriting by collective. As unlikely as it was to dare to think we might be able to write songs, I really did have melodies in my head since I could remember. And maybe because Adam, for years, had been jotting down ideas for lyrics, no one laughed when I suggested we try to work on some of our own ideas. And when we did, they sounded simpler and more convincing than the cover versions we'd been playing. Covers we weren't very good at playing. It is not an exaggeration to say U2 began to write our own songs because we couldn't play other people's.

Baby steps for a baby band.

It was almost as messy, but for me this was like being born. Punk rock slapped me on my naked arse and I just started wailing. Almost in tune.

It was also in the music room that we had our first audition, a year and a half after that first meeting in Larry's kitchen. It was for a television producer by the name of Bil Keating and it came after Steve Averill had explained to us that if we could make an impression on this man, we might get ourselves on television.

Television?

A new arts program for children called *Young Line.* It sounded pretty un–punk rock but still . . .

Television!

It felt as if this could be our big break as we waited for the arrival of the TV producer one day in the spring of 1978. This could lead to national exposure, to world domination.

Unfortunately, when the talent scout arrived at the door, we were in the middle of a big fight about what to play.

How to start and how to end it.

"Ssshhh, let him in . . . what are we going to do?"

"Open the door . . . open the fucking door."

"I hear you've written your own songs," said the TV producer.

"Yes," I replied, panicking until suddenly inspired with a very dishonest idea that might just work. I stared into the honest eyes of Dave Evans, and somehow he knew what I knew we had to do.

"Yes indeed," I continued. "This is one of ours. It's called 'Glad to See You Go.'"

Edge then gave the look that he gives to this very day when communicating onstage with Larry and Adam. It's almost not a look at all, more a kind of psychic direction they seem to understand, and immediately they turned on a sixpence, smashing into the not-very-but-quite-famous Ramones tune "Glad to See You Go."

We nailed it.

We nailed the VIP to the classroom wall, who couldn't believe these kids could deliver such melodic brutality. We won the spot on *Young Line,* and when it came to the show, we naturally switched out "Glad to See You Go" for one of our own songs, "Street Mission."

No one noticed.

Another miracle attributable to Joey Ramone.

LIGHTNING STRIKES TWICE

I still pinch myself that that week in 1976, the week I'd joined the band that was to become U2, was also the week that I formally asked Alison Stewart to go out with me.

Nothing would ever be the same. The sky didn't split, the rain didn't stop, and we were not looking down from a hill over the city. Actually, we were standing at the bus stop on the Howth Road, waiting for the 31a. It was 4:30 p.m. on a Thursday when we had our second kiss.

Though the day outside wasn't looking that interested, inside my freckled head music was forming out of the noise, a top-line melody emerging from the din. In my confusion I had found clarity, this young woman who was clear as a wellspring. In my vision she was walking through water again. She became water.

I dived in.

> You let me into a conversation
> A conversation only we could make
> You break and enter my imagination

Whatever's in there
It's yours to take

Wednesday was a half day at Mount Temple, a free afternoon like a stolen piece of the weekend in the middle of the week. I'd always been awake, sexually speaking, but around Ali I was wide awake, eyes pinned, senses on overload. Her presence was disturbing as well as comforting. While I really wanted to be on my own with her, I was determined not to foist myself on this perfect person because I'd developed a bit of a reputation as a man about youth club. But on this afternoon I talked Ali into visiting 10 Cedarwood Road, offering a tour of my minimalist box room with its single naked light and its minimalist single bed. It was not a plot to get her into my bed—not consciously—but that's what happened. What joy. We never discussed the sex that we were not going to have; we just started romancing each other in sweet, then humorous, then serious ways.

At which point the sound of a front door opening. Our front door.

Enter my da, home unexpectedly early. Ali staring at me in an undressed state of shock. She'd never met the man.

"What are we going to do?" We gasped.

Panic, I thought.

"Get under the bed," I blurted.

"What!"

Her look said I had to be kidding. My look said I wasn't. If she didn't know Bob Hewson, I knew him quite well.

"I can't fit under there."

"You can. You must."

She did.

Just as Da reached the top of the stairs and entered my room.

"What in the name of God are you doing in bed at this time of day?"

"I'm sick," I lied, although I was now actually feeling a little nauseated, as if I were at a crime scene, as if I were the crime.

"Eh . . . eh," I stage-whispered. "A sore throat."

Of all days to have my father, Master of the big Panto and little Opera, show me affection, he would choose this day. Choose this day to sit down on my bed and ask me all kinds of concerned questions about my well-being. Alison Stewart, meanwhile, suffocating under the weight of two Hewsons, inches above her.

This is a situation, dare I say it, condition, she will not shake off easily.

the gibson
explorer

IRIS   PAUL

the yellow
house

7

I Will Follow

A boy tries hard to be a man
His mother lets go of his hand
The gift of grief
Will bring a voice to life.

"The elephant in the room" is a phrase I enjoy, having at different times been either elephant or room. We can lose ourselves in situations or conversations and miss the obvious. We're looking for someone to save us or a solution to a problem, and they're right in front of us hiding in plain sight.

Hanging in our house is a wall-sized piece of art by the filmmaker Wim Wenders. *The Road to Emmaus* is a recent photograph of that road, just outside Jerusalem, where close friends of Jesus are said to have walked with him, without knowing it. A couple of days after his crucifixion. There's a rumor he's alive and no one can find the body.

His friends are confused, grief-stricken, terrified, and oblivious to the identity of this stranger until the moment when he says goodbye. Now they wake up to the possibility that the very heart of their faith has been beating loudly at their side. If only they'd had eyes to see.

I have taken flights where the person seated next to me, the person I was dodging having a conversation with, turned out to hold a valuable piece of the puzzle of my life that I would be lost without. When you're open, a hitchhiker—a "randomer," as my daughter Eve calls them—can become an angel. When you're least expecting one. And not just people. Places, too, can spark a rare connection that is initially hidden.

OUR YELLOW PERIOD, COTTAGE AND CHEESE

U2's third proper rehearsal room—after the music room at Mount Temple, and Edge's seven-foot-by-nine-foot garden shed—was a small cottage backing onto a graveyard in north County Dublin. The graveyard my mother was buried in. In the Yellow House, as we called it, we had an electric heater on which Larry would toast his and Edge's cheese sandwiches.

Myself and Adam brought nothing with us and would, literally, eat their lunch. The two of us were united in our love of stolen food. He also liked leftovers. At school lunch Adam, "the posh boy," would stand beside the slops bowl and fork out of the food bin an odd potato that looked unused or three-quarters of a sausage floating like a body in a cold sea of beans. I would see Adam all through our touring life eating the leftovers from trays put outside hotel rooms, half a cheeseburger here, a slice of cold pizza there. Larry's diet was more discerning and less public, a generally more discreet diner. More discreet all round. Larry was a good-looking teen who didn't like to be stared at by girls or guys.

Now, you might ask, why would a man like that want to be a pop star?

Why would a shy fella put a sign on the school notice board inviting musicians to jam in his kitchen? I cannot fully answer that question, but I'm very glad that he did. Long before his idea paid for all our lunches, I credit his generosity for sharing his own.

Edge, on the other hand, would forget to eat. Still does. I often wondered if that had something to do with the fact that every day for seven years his mother, Gwenda, had packed him cheese sandwiches.

Every single day he ate those cheese sandwiches. Not always enthusiastically, but he ate half and I ate the other half. It wasn't that his mother didn't have the means for a more varied lunch box, just that she'd forgotten what she gave him the day before.

Like her son's, Gwenda's mind was often elsewhere.

Discomfort Food

Chip Sandwiches

Fried Anything (Best of all the Batterburger. Buy the burger and you get battered.)

Cornflakes (Breakfast, Lunch, Dinner)

Smoked Cod (For an Irish teenager about to eat fish, it's important that the fish not look or taste like fish.)

On this day in the Yellow House I'm eating a toasted cheese sandwich from Edge and a toasted ham from Larry. It's a wonder they're even speaking to me, let alone opening their Tupperware for me. Today, not for the first time, I have been screaming and roaring at my bandmates for reasons that, I can admit now, don't stand the test of time. It's the usual old shite. They've been playing too fast or too slow or just not being on the street below as I'm about to jump off a high building.

This melodrama is not very important and it feels like the most important thing in the world. Forget Ireland bursting into paramilitary flames or the promise of a nuclear winter that we all live with in the late 1970s. No, the most pressing issue facing humanity on this day in the winter of 1978 is that this band is not being good enough musicians.

You could understand this argument if (a) they were not good musicians or (b) I was a better one.

Which I most definitely was not, but still my shouting head is spouting unforgivable invective for which now, all these years later, I ask their forgiveness. This was not a one-off. This was a way of life at our rehearsals. With hindsight maybe I can psychoanalyze the situation and see it as a way of *avoiding* life, hurting to avoid the hurt. Maybe.

Or, perhaps just a very bad attitude.

One thing is sure: as a musician my grasp is a lot further than my reach. I can hear the music in my head, but I'm not able to play it. I'm like someone who can't paint, who can't even sketch, trying to use the hands of other artists. A lot of my rage is my inability to express myself, which is true of a lot of people. I've had only a few guitar lessons and so am very dependent on these three comrades. I'm having to subsume my ego because without their ability to express themselves I have nothing.

Less than nothing.

A void, a black hole.

Today the only thing that's on offer is a swollen ego.

I am trying to explain how fresh and exciting the new Public Image Ltd. song "Public Image" is, how its nihilism is the final nail in the coffin of all the blues-based rock we had grown up with. It sounds, I enthuse, like an electric drill into your brain, or an electric knife through the carcass of the past, or a forklift to remove any obstacle in your way. (You get the idea.) It's so incisive. No fat, no beard on the guitar sound. It's beyond punk; it's post-punk. ("Post-punk," yes, that's what they would call it. That's what they would call us.)

A great song, I explain to everyone—as if I've written the manifesto—can be written on two strings over two chords. That's how post-punk John Lydon is. We've gone from three chords to two. This is maximum minimalism!

I'm trying to get Edge to play the sound of an electric drill through the spinal cortex, but he doesn't know what I mean. (In retrospect I see that this was like a graffiti artist telling a great landscape painter to use a spray can.) Edge is losing patience, and I'm becoming even more frustrated. So frustrated that, from around his neck, I seize his Gibson Explorer, that triangular science fiction electric that he bought with all his savings in New York. I wrap it round my neck instead and start making a wild and dangerous squeal of a sound.

"Go on," says Edge. "Keep it coming. You're nearly there."

"You like it?" I ask, surprised.

"I'm not sure I like it, but it does sound like a dentist's drill. Let me see if I can take it somewhere."

In this ego-filled and ego-less moment a song that will be called "I Will Follow" is forming. Edge and Adam figure a complexity to the ringing drones that makes for an appealing harmonic, and when Edge goes to the lower drone (a ringing E and D string, fretting on the second and third strings to make the chords E over D followed by D added ninth—if you're interested) after Larry goes all Joy Division with another Teutonic drum fill, I come up with the chorus chant and lyric:

> If you walk away, walk away
> I walk away, walk away
> I will follow.

The repetition and percussion of "walk away, walk away" is a mantra, is like Jimi Hendrix's wah-wah pedal, a rhythm hook that catches you under your skin.

We knew we had something.

"What's it about?" we asked each other.

"The song is a suicide note," I intoned. "It's about some kid who wants to find his mother, and even if she's in the grave, he'll follow her there."

Pregnant pause.

What no one in that rehearsal room, including me, had thought about was Iris Hewson resting under the ground not a hundred yards from where we were playing. In all the time we rehearsed there, I never thought about it or even once visited her grave. My mother was dead. Literally, but also emotionally, to me.

So I thought.

Self-denial is a remarkable psychological trick, sometimes necessary, I guess. The truth is that the enduring appeal of that song is truly not as nihilistic as a suicide note. In its sound or its state of mind it's a song about a mother's love. A song about unconditional love. Agape love. Eternal love. More usually described as a mother's than a father's.

A lot of people know Jesus's story of the prodigal son, a young man who squanders his father's inheritance on fun and frolics and after a while falls on hard times and has to head home humiliated, with not even a hat to hold in hand. What few readers pick up is the description of the good father, who is not at home waiting for the return of the prodigal but instead is out in the farthest field looking and longing for him. More likely the mother.

If you walk away, I will follow.

STUPID, PIGHEADED LOVE

There's something both clever and stupid about love. Sometimes love doesn't only cover the cracks; it doesn't even notice them. Slowly but surely Ali and I had been falling in love, and as we were investigating love in all its manifestations, we were getting close to a group of Christian radicals called Shalom. We were experiencing an effect that we still understand to be true today: that the closer we felt to our Maker, the closer we were to each other.

The Shalom group were practicing a kind of naïve first-century Christian life that anticipated few possessions but plenty of miracles. Their members might not know where their next meal was coming from, but they knew their way around the Bible. It was a rigorous and demanding life that attracted some eccentric characters.

My feeling was always that the more eccentric the better. Already being part of the Lypton Village crowd, which also specialized in eccentrics and freaks and firebrands, we found it normal to begin hanging out with the street preacher Dennis Sheedy. We met him outside McDonald's, where, believe it or not, the punk scene in Dublin sometimes hung out. McDonald's on Grafton Street, which still had some kind of fifties Americana about it in those days. Dennis would point out that the French fries weren't made from potatoes but potato powder.

"Then why do you spot the occasional piece of potato skin?" I queried.

"They spray them on for effect" was the truth teller's riposte. "Don't get me started on the gherkins."

Dennis was a kind of latter-day Jeremiah, the Old Testament prophet, but instead of going for the people of Israel, Dennis was going for the people of Dublin, preaching the gospel on city center thoroughfares like Henry Street. Granted he could be a bit of a forest fire; still we had a lot of affection for him. We still had it twenty years later when Dennis arrived at Mr. Pussy's Café de Luxe in fishnets, high heels, and bright pink lipstick. Still preaching but with a little less thunder. Love is the higher law.

OUR FIRST OFFICE . . . THE RAIN

Blind faith will not get you there, but it will get you started.

It took us from rehearsals in the Yellow House to actual gigs with actual people paying to see us. Shows that were erratic, sometimes surreal, but occasionally transcendent. McGonagles was the preeminent Dublin punk venue of the day, complete with all the accoutrements of a 1940s ballroom dragged reluctantly into the 1970s—the sticky-carpet wine bar, the fake plastic trees at side of stage. Later I discovered that my father and mother, Bob and Iris, used to dance there when it was called the Crystal Ballroom. We were given a Monday slot, the night the music business went out on the town, and if it was never going to be full, there was a clientele of sorts, an audience to poach from their drinking. If we could be good. Or even great.

We always had excitement in the mosh pit at the front of the stage; we'd made sure by asking our friends along, persuading them to impersonate an excited crowd. Or maybe they weren't impersonating. Walking onstage, I could hear Ali, Ann, and Aislinn, our girlfriends, screaming as if we were The Beatles, while Gavin, Guggi, and the Lypton Villagers kept their cool. Until finally they exploded in punk rock spasms. The editor of the local music paper *Hot Press*, Niall Stokes, was often there along with Mairin, his wife, and Bill Graham, the paper's star writer.

It was Bill who had introduced us to Paul McGuinness, a fellow student at Trinity College. Bill seemed to believe in U2 as much as we did, and visiting his brain was like the tutorials I'd never get by choosing not to go to college myself, a decision I hadn't yet told my da about. After Steve Averill, Bill rapidly became our second spirit guide and, by connecting us to Paul, introduced us to our third, who became our fourth, fifth, and sixth. There would be no part of our life Paul would not help shape, becoming the most critical of allies, even if it did not always feel that way.

One night after a show I am standing with this man who will deliver the baby band that is U2 to adolescence and near adulthood. We are standing in our first office, the Rain. Our office is anywhere we happen to be meeting our manager, and tonight our office is outside McGonagles. In the rain. It's early in our relationship, and we're still sizing each other up. He hasn't delivered us a recording contract with a U.K. record label that will fund us as we set out to superstardom.

We are working on an understanding that he will provide us with this manna from heaven, but as the broken neon of the club fizzes and splutters around us, it's a "not yet" situation that I'm picking up from his body language. We are in talks about talks. Talks that are turning into a white-hot argument. I am finding it difficult to swallow the information that not only is the record contract not imminent but neither is the arrival of the much-discussed van that might at least transport us to the place where we might afford to eat outside our own homes, maybe even sleep outside the patronage of our parents. I have no doubt that a van is the most essential piece of equipment for any up-and-coming punk band. As important as guitar, bass, and drums, I tell him. As if he doesn't already know.

ME: "In Ireland it's how a band gets from one gig to another and gets to make a profit, because without one, our shows barely pay for the van hire."

PAUL: "Tell me something you know something about."

ME (earnestly losing the plot): "Paul, can't you see the transformative power of such a vehicle? If you were a real manager, you'd be getting us a van."

PAUL: "We don't have the money for a van, Bono. It's too soon."

ME (not making sense): "You've got the posh accent, but you
   don't seem to have the cash that goes with it."
PAUL: "That's a mad sentence! Bono, you need some patience
   and perspective."
ME: "Tell that to my da."
PAUL: "I'm happy to. I've already spoken to Adam and Edge's
   families."
ME: "Let's put it this way. If you aren't getting us the van, we—
   the four of us in the band—are going to have to get it. Which
   means we need a record deal, which means you need to go to
   London and get this sorted."
PAUL: "Bono, you can only go to London for the first time once,
   and the band is not ready to go to London yet. The band is
   not where it needs to be."
ME: "Well, if *you're* not going to get us a record deal, who is?"
PAUL: "Good question."
ME: "It's starting to sound like you're not committed to us, not
   enough; otherwise you'd find us a van."
PAUL: "How can I not be committed enough when I've been
   standing in the rain with you like this for nearly forty-five
   minutes?"
ME: "That is a point."

Paul was the only man I needed to be standing in the rain with at
that moment. At the right time a stranger or a friend or even the
physical landscape we need will find us. But not always do we discover their role.

THE CLEANEST CON ON THE PLANET

Flash forward a few years, after I'd left the home I'd grown up in at
10 Cedarwood Road. My father kept getting broken into. I tried to
talk the old man into moving, but he wasn't budging, so one day
I told him a white lie, that I'd bought a modest apartment in the
beautiful seaside town of Howth, overlooking a small beach. He'd

be doing me a favor if he could caretake it while renting out Cedarwood Road, adding an extra few bob to his pension. He stayed there until he died. He loved the place, and it seemed to love him back.

A few months after he moved in, my auntie Ruth called in to see his new surroundings and broke the news that she and her sister Iris—my mother, his wife—swam on that beach all through their teenage years.

Iris wouldn't notice the long train journey out to Howth, she said. It meant so much to bathe there and lie in the sun, on the odd occasion when it would lie with her.

Flash forward another couple of decades, and Paul is driving me to the Ferryman pub on the docks in Dublin. The Ferryman hasn't changed much, but the chrome-rimmed wheels of Paul's black Jaguar XJ8 are just a little bit more upmarket. I'm meeting Jon Pareles, music critic of *The New York Times,* who raises questions that I cannot answer by going around or even over. Origin stories. About me.

"How did you get along with your father when you were growing up?"

At which point two hard men enter the pub. I know they are hard because I feel the hairs on the back of my neck go up and I have no hairs on the back of my neck. In their thirties but looking forties, one of them with a stuck-on grin, one with badly stained tobacco teeth, and they begin to play pool, but I clock them clocking me and after a while they come up.

"Aw right, Mal? Everything okily dokily? You know what I meal?"

If you're ever stuck in a tough part of our town, it could be helpful to try swapping out your *n*'s for *l*'s. Dublin is much richer for a whole host of dialects.

Him: "Youse from Cedarwood, aren't youse? I remember youse. Youse lived right opposite the turn for Cedarwood Grove. Number 10, wasn't it?"

"Yeah," I said, secretly pleased that my choice of venue with *The New York Times* had led to an authentic encounter with some of the characters I would have had to negotiate as a teenager.

"You've got some memory," I threw back. "I'm not sure we've met. This is Jon. Your names are?"

He cut me off.

"No, we've never met and you wouldn't have wanted to have met me."

I don't blink.

Pareles blinks a few times in a row.

"Agh, nothing, I'm only messing with ya. Youse all right, youse have done good. We're all proud of you."

"Thanks, man," I said, forgetting to swap the *n* out for an *l*.

"Do you remember youse used to get a lot of break-ins? Back in the early '80s?"

"Yes," I answered, looking at Jon, his face suddenly a little paler. "What of it?"

"It was just a few bob, tellies, a stereo, and I remember once a kettle. Oh yeah and a jeetar. Was it your jeetar?"

"No, it was my brother's."

"The leather jacket. Was that your brother's?"

"No, that was mine."

"Some reel-to-reel tapes, never listened, were they your songs?"

"No."

My blood was starting to boil. I was doing the maths on the various outcomes of this conversation if the situation melted down, if I melted down.

Then out of the blue a poetic thing emerged, something I've never understood but never forgotten.

"You know, we never made a mess?" he asked, looking at me with dignity as well as defiance in his eyes.

"You know, we never smashed up your da's place, and on a point of fact on one occasion we made a cup o' tea and we fuckin' cleaned up. Washed and dried the fuckin' cups."

I am now a little all over the place myself because the man with the tobacco teeth was not lying, it was an episode that was much discussed in our family, so here we are with the cleanest con on the planet.

"But we robbed the fuckin' kettle . . . hahahaha!" A big laugh out of him.

ME: "What was that about?"

HIM: "Listen, we were banging up a bit o' gear. You get stuck,

you know. We knew your da wasn't stuck. He had you. Am
I right? Did you get that? We never made a mess; we didn't
want to be robbers. We were just junkies who needed a bag.
That simple."

ME: "What are you doing now?"

HIM: "Just got out."

ME: "What were you doing?"

HIM: "Some heavy bird."

"Jail time," I said, translating for *The New York Times*. "What for?"
"A bit of the armed robbery, you know yourself."
"Eh, no," I didn't say. I actually nodded, as if to an accomplice.
I looked at Jon, who was looking at his Aiwa recorder, no longer a
critic, but a reporter of a crime, albeit one twenty years old.

If you're where you should be, you'll meet whom you need to meet.

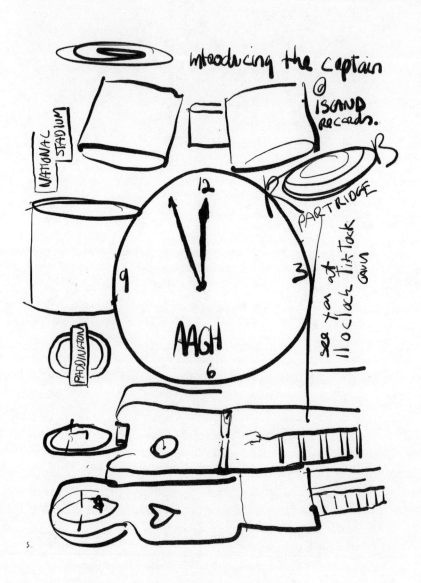

Introducing the captain @ ISLAND records.

NATIONAL STADIUM

PARTRIDGE

see ya at 11 oclock TikTock onn

AAGH

12

9

3

6

8

11 O'Clock Tick Tock

It's cold outside
It gets so hot in here.
The boys and girls collide
To the music in my ear.
I hear the children crying
And I see it's time to go.
I hear the children crying
Take me home.

The train lays down a rhythm track. It keeps its own time, slowing and speeding until the Welsh-accented towns and valleys give way to the cheers and jeers of the English countryside, which eventually engorges us, and we descend into the underworld of London. Here in the tiled tunnels, the drumbeat crescendoes in volume until we are spat out onto a station platform in Paddington, London W2.

This is it.

The belly of the beast.

Orpheus in the underworld with a cassette player instead of a lyre.

Orpheus and his lover, Eurydice, but it isn't the beguiling Eurydice who will need saving; it's Orpheus himself. She's here to save his life because she knows if he doesn't become who he is here, he will never have one. This is the story of how Eurydice saved Orpheus from his own hell.

The story of how Alison Stewart saved me. From myself.

Ali had faith. She believed in me, and she was sure the God she prayed to could breach the distance between what we had and what we didn't have, in the way of talent and tolls. Our faith was our ferry for sure, and faith is a remarkable thing, not least because it can cover up a lot of stupidity. For instance, the way these two Irish teenagers didn't have a place booked to stay on this first trip to London. We slept that night in Paddington Station. (With Guggi, I'd already learned to sleep in phone boxes where, standing up, we became a bed for each other.) This was less Dante and Beatrice and more Jonah and the Whale, but our hearts were like trains as, next morning, we climbed the steps to the daylit overground, to stare up close at a world we had only ever seen on the news or glimpsed in fiction.

THE SACRAMENT OF FRIENDSHIP

On all the journeys I've taken, I've sought a guide. Even with the compass of faith I'm looking for the right company for the ride. For some spirit guide physicalized in a person. The sacrament of friendship.

I'd first learned about friendship with Guggi and saw how it opened up my life to new possibilities and adventures. I discovered early that I was collaborative by nature. I began to understand that the world is not so scary if, around every significant corner, somebody is waiting to walk with you on the next part of the journey.

Slowly but surely, after Iris's death, Ali had become my companion. We weren't always sure who was leading whom, but we felt that the Spirit was with us and would lead us if we were open to the possibility.

If Reggie Manuel had got me to that first rehearsal with the band, now it was Ali taking me to London, where I would surely find a record deal for the band so we could get our music out there and, maybe even more important, a record deal that would pay for the elusive van, which would, in turn, fund us as we set out on the path to superstardom. Or at the very least stop the old man from sending me to college or, worse, making me get "a real job."

We'd seen photographic evidence of what was happening with the punk scene on the King's Road, but nothing could prepare us for this Day-Glo mix of beauty and badness, the rags of rage, the stylish violence of Vivienne Westwood and Malcolm McLaren's boutique called Sex. Bondage seemed to be a theme, but even through the parody I couldn't help wondering if there was some other subtext in all this submission and domination. Parts of British punk

The Ten Commandments of Punk

Thou shalt know everything by the time thou art seventeen, with a great and sure certainty.

Thou shalt proclaim the year zero and not honor the past because the new alone shall count.

Thou shalt wear a garb of torn leather jacket and trousers, with accessories bearing a hint of S&M, with thy feet shod by Doc Martens.

Thy T-shirt, like thy lyrics, will bear a slogan to offend.

Thou shalt be bored, angry, pretty vacant, or at least faintly pissed off.

Thou shalt have no more heroes, nor accept anyone in authority.

Thou shalt bear an adjective for a surname like Rotten or Vicious.

Thou shalt connect with thy audience so that they may invade thy stage or receive thy spit in their eye. Let them mosh.

Thou shalt speak the truth in a fake cockney accent, even if thou art Irish or went to a minor English public school.

Thou shalt not grow old lest thy come to realize the biggest authority thy will need to defeat is thine own self.

rock were very . . . British. The "new boys" club could face a flogging in the music press that might go way past criticism. A kind of
spanking. For a working-class revolt, viewed through the eyes of
an Irish teenager, this looked a little too much like the humiliation
we'd heard about in British boarding schools. It was really exciting
though. Some magnetic writers emerged, and those weekly put-
downs made for a great read. If the cruelty was sometimes off, it
was mostly coming from a place of passion. There were rules on
what you could listen to or how you could dress, a certain funda-
mentalism that felt not so dissimilar to what I was struggling to
negotiate at home.

At times British punk was an art school experiment that had escaped
from the lab to run down suburban streets with the proletariat. Punk
in London stenciled "NO FUTURE" on walls and T-shirts because
it rang true for a generation of people who sensed their country was
on the verge of crisis.

No future? In our Dublin it felt as if there were no present, let
alone past or future. In our band we felt estranged from any traditions we could have held on to. Growing up in Ireland it felt as if the
future was always somewhere else.

Over the border and across the water, cities, towns, and indus-
tries that had once made Britain great were bullied into believing
their new industrial problems were due to union militancy and not
the emergence of globalization, a project that would benefit much
of the world but also demand a toll of reciprocity from its creators.
The world was changing, old-world jobs in steel, coal, and steam
now being delivered more cheaply, often by the very countries
the British had colonized. Soon independent India and Bangladesh
would demand their share of the free market while providing much
cheaper labor.

So many of us born in the 1960s were looking for personal independence, a restart to a clock that no longer recognized our face.
We were looking to music for some kind of liberation. Or revolution. We felt claustrophobic. I related to the straitjacket worn by
the singer of the Sex Pistols. His name was Johnny Rotten and his
bandmates were refusing to be in "showbizness" in a very, er, showy

way, swearing at the media as well as on the media. Their music was year zero, the big bang of punk, not so much outrage as just rage. It was the sound so many of us heard inside our heads. For our generation "Pretty Vacant" was a thrilling "fuck off" to anything that had come before. Teenage terror.

It replaced the glam rock that had come before, and that era's more obvious femininity, with a kind of manic machismo dumping the traditional binaries. Bowie as a bootboy spray-painting T-shirts as well as walls. The Pistols single "God Save the Queen" was released in the year of Queen Elizabeth's Silver Jubilee, and they were banned from the BBC.

Johnny Rotten wrote the lines "We mean it, man!" and sang them with a leer: "No future for me."

Ideas for songs became more important than the ability to execute those ideas. Having something to say mattered more than how you said it. The picture didn't have to be pretty for a boy or a girl. Think *American Idol* and imagine its opposite. That was punk rock. U2 wouldn't have made the grade on those showbiz terms either. When we saw The Clash play in Trinity College Dublin in 1977, it was like an invitation to step up out of the audience and onto the stage.

The Clash sang about how they wanted to join in the race riots they witnessed in Notting Hill in 1976: "White riot, a riot of my own . . ." We wanted a riot, too, but our rebellion was directed somewhere much more nebulous than, say, "the establishment." We were rebelling against ourselves and, okay, maybe the generation of bands who'd gone before.

Maybe this was the last time a generational war was waged with music. Out with the flares and long hair of my brother's musical heroes. Even The Beatles had worn beards. (They'd have to go.) The Rolling Stones just about got away with it, but The Who would have to shave. Even though they were good at bad behavior, Led Zeppelin were also to be banned, mainly because they were too popular with your older brother or sister.

Walking down the King's Road in Chelsea with Ali, we stopped at a large sign: "World's End." The site of the original World's End public house. And no better place for a drink at this moment of endings and beginnings. All music from before this day shall not be allowed. Stars are now the enemy. "No more heroes anymore," as The Stranglers put it.

It was exciting to be in this city that felt like the capital of the world as the world was irrevocably changing.

I was not afraid.

What was there to fear except failure, and that was mine anyway. I was afraid.

Afraid I couldn't quite belong here.

Ali was more punk than me. Ali could never be anything other than herself, which was very annoying because she wasn't really looking to be liberated from anything. Except her earnest boyfriend. It was I, not she, who was intimidated by the style fascists. Taking a morning to explore Piccadilly, she was not in the least bit beholden to the punk rock circus. She was in her own category. But we did need an actual bed to sleep in that night, and while we had only £37 between us, we also had a big red London busload of faith. It would all become clear.

Wouldn't it?

We had put the trip into the hands of prayer and expected the divine travel agent to sort our mess out. Everything we need is right under our feet, we told ourselves. We just needed to hear some hint in this honking metropolis. We'd heard you could find bed and breakfast on the Edgware Road, and our walk took us past cockney and plummy shouts and suggestions, through Jamaican and Indian accents, until we reached a nondescript Victorian building called Stewart House. Clearly a sign.

"Your da will be pleased."

In our heads we were first-century Christians feeling kind of radical (but maybe just annoying) as we wide-eyed stared at the Camden Lock Mohawk tribes on Sunday morning, a big bold *A* splashed on the back of their black leather jackets.

ALI: "What does *A* stand for? Is it Adam and the Ants?"

Ali had never heard their music but loved their name.

ME: "No, it's for 'anarchist.'"
ALI: "This is about fashion, right? They're not really anarchists?"

"I dunno, I'd say some are serious," I said, walking with a little more machismo, releasing her hand from mine as I explained that "anarchist" means "not being beholden to any rules."

ALI: "To any rules or just to anyone else's?"
ME: "Listen, these are our kind of people. I'm pretty sure Johnny Rotten is one."
ALI: "Didn't he also describe himself as an Antichrist?"
ME: "He was joking. It's an Irish thing. My mother used to call me a little Antichrist."
ALI: "She wasn't joking . . ."

Finishing our bacon and eggs, we agreed with each other that Jesus was a kind of anarchist and the Holy Spirit "like a wind," as the Bible had put it. "No one knows where it comes from or where it's going."

I muse on how this must have been on Bob Dylan's mind when he wrote, "The answer, my friend, is blowin' in the wind." Surely this was what Van Morrison was on about when he sang about sailing into the mystic?

Ali tolerated this furtive thinking and listened when I explained that Van Morrison and Bob Dylan were the first singers to encourage me to believe in what you can't see. We both got the idea that what you can't see matters and that it matters to some people more than matter. (Or something like that.)

We were in London only because Paul had said we weren't ready for him to bring our music here, and we decided we'd do it ourselves. So, now that the Holy Spirit had found me and Ali our lodgings, all I had to do was to generate some critical acclaim. And get signed. And find a cool producer. And I had seven days.

I headed to the West End and the first-floor offices of *Record Mirror* near Shaftesbury Avenue. I bluffed that I had an appointment.

ME: "I've come to meet Chris Westwood."
RECEPTIONIST: "Oh yeah, hold on a second."

I couldn't quite believe it when Chris Westwood, one of the writers whose stories we read every week, came out to reception. This was more straightforward than I'd anticipated.

ME: "Chris, I loved your 'In Search of the Cure' piece. This is our demo tape; we're called U2."
CHRIS: "Oh, great, thanks very much."
ME: "I'll be back in an hour then."
CHRIS, looking confused: "An hour?"
ME: "Yeah, we're from Dublin and only here for a few days so I just need to know what you think. If that's okay?"
CHRIS, uncertainly: "Er . . . sure."

I pulled off the same stunt with Dave McCullough, a well-known writer at *Sounds,* a more punk indie weekly. We'd been introduced to Dave through Philip Chevron, Steve Averill's foil in The Radiators from Space, who'd recorded *Ghostown,* one of the best-ever Irish albums.

My luck ran out at the *NME,* which was a shame because there were a few writers there who I so enjoyed reading. Paul Morley's cover story on Joy Division, with Anton Corbijn's stark black-and-white photography, had introduced me not only to Anton's work but to a whole new world centered around Manchester's Factory Records and the genius of the singer Ian Curtis. But two out of four music weeklies wasn't bad, and both writers liked what they heard and wanted to meet up.

The demo was the best of two studio recordings we'd made. One had versions of "Shadows and Tall Trees," "The Fool," and "Stories for Boys" from Keystone Studios with Barry Devlin, and the other "Alone in the Light," "Another Time, Another Place," and "Life on a Distant Planet" recorded at Eamonn Andrews Studios. I'd packed fourteen cassettes for the trip, planning to get them into the hands of all the A&R people at London's record companies I could—in particular, Nick Mobbs at Automatic Records. He'd signed the Sex Pistols. The actual Sex Pistols. He might as well have signed Queen. I mean he might as well have signed *the* queen.

And he liked our demo. Wow. This was easy.

I was a door-to-door salesman again, a hustler whose merchandise was the hopes and dreams of a band who on one level we knew had almost nothing in terms of prowess but on another level we hoped might have "everything" in terms of promise. One of my best mates, Simon Carmody, singer in Dublin punk band The Golden Horde, had a phrase to describe more evolved talent than ours—acts that might play better or just look better, hipster acts who seemed to have everything. "They have everything but 'it,'" he'd say.

"It," he explained, was the thing, the chemistry, the magic, the indeterminate determinedness.

In our own heads we had nothing but "it."

When I listened to the all-important late-night shows on BBC Radio 1, so often a band felt like concept over communication. But a session on the legendary show of John Peel could make or break a band. We'd sent him a demo, but he'd passed on us. The man whose taste had broken The Undertones and Stiff Little Fingers would not go south of the Irish border for U2.

Edge has always had the best take on people who don't like U2. "They're just not trying hard enough," he deadpans.

That rang loudly in my ear as I stepped inside a red phone box to call John Peel at home, a recollection that troubles me because I must have hustled the number from one of the music journos. They shouldn't have given it to me and I shouldn't have rung it, but I wanted to see if I could get John to try harder with U2. I was the David to this Goliath of the radio waves, who'd championed everyone from Pink Floyd to Roxy Music and David Bowie. I got through, but the indie champion was less than pleased.

"What's going on? Who is this?"

"Listen, I'm from a band called U2 and I wanted . . ."

"What are you doing calling this number?"

"I'm sorry. I can't talk for long. I only have a few coins."

I didn't need all my coins. I heard a woman's voice. Someone put the receiver down. Evidently I was not on his wife's playlist either.

A day or two later I headed to the BBC to try to collar John on the way into his evening show. Security wouldn't let me past but promised to give John our demo. History does not record whether it reached him and if he played our songs, only that he never came to an appreciation of U2. I'm sure it had nothing to do with the stalking, just that he wasn't trying hard enough.

THE MANAGEMENT CONTRACT

The Battle for Britain had begun, but I had more medals than wounds, and returning to Dublin after that first week away in London was a good feeling. Ali felt we'd been through something significant together and that we were becoming comrades as well as companions.

We knew something had shifted and not just between us. There was excitement about the band in "the inkies," as the music papers were known. Punk rock had been a bumper crop for them, each inkie vying to be "the bible" of this new underground scene that was now going overground. *Melody Maker, Sounds,* and *Record Mirror* all printed stories about us based on the demo tapes I'd delivered in London. *Record Mirror* was particularly enthusiastic, and by the time we eventually got to London as a band, they'd put us on the cover. *Record Mirror* wasn't as cool as *Melody Maker* or *NME*, but to be attracting this kind of attention as an unsigned band when we were still eighteen and nineteen created a bit of a stir in Dublin.

Dublin always had one eye on London.

"See?" I said to Paul McGuinness. "Do you still think we're not ready for a record contract?"

"Well, you don't even have a management contract," he said. "And if you want me to do any more work on this, I suggest you put that right."

We weren't sure how to take this aggressive-defensive reaction, coming from a man who hadn't judged our demos seriously enough to take them to London himself. So one Saturday afternoon in October 1978 the four of us went to "have a talk" with Paul McGuinness in his apartment on Waterloo Road.

A wide tree-lined avenue in an area famous for its postal address—Dublin 4—Waterloo Road is a kind of suburb for the intelligentsia, every other address boasting a writer or editor, an advertising or TV exec, a news commentator or news maker. Dublin 4 was home to the national television and radio station RTÉ, the station's 110-meter mast surveilling the whole neighborhood. Paul lived with his wife, Kathy Gilfillan, in an apartment in a large, high-ceilinged Georgian town house, handsome granite stairs leading up to a big blue oak door.

This is a man who knows how to live, I thought to myself. I bet he'll have something we could eat in his fridge. We were all a bit hungry, and I had been delegated the task of requesting whether we might make ourselves a sandwich or two.

"Sure, take whatever you want."

I looked around the kitchen as if it were my first time in one. There were all kinds of sights and smells that I couldn't quite put a name to. This Kathy must be a chef or something. It was with some disappointment, on opening their fridge, that I could find only an impenetrable lump of rock-hard cheese, which proved impossible to cut. Had these people no idea that in 1978 it was now very easy to get cheese in slices or even soft, in tinfoil triangles? When I offered this advice to the man who would be our manager, he looked at me in disbelief, as if I were a Neanderthal.

"I think you might have invented something brand-new right there, Bono," he said, guffawing. "A Parmesan cheese sandwich. That's one for the books."

While I pretended to get the joke, he pulled out a management contract, explaining that if we wanted him to get serious we'd have to do the same. If we wanted him traveling to London to capitalize on this media interest and get the band a record deal, we needed first to sign a deal with him.

We were stunned. This wasn't very punk rock. In fact it felt kind of corporate, and we said so.

"Well, a band is a corporation," he responded in his confident, grown-up baritone. "Just a very small one. If you want it to get bigger. You'd do well to get a lawyer."

Actually, I said, we thought of ourselves as "a cooperation." Paul liked that, and as we were to discover, he had no patience for musicians who were in denial that they had to be organized for their art. That was all a bit too hippie for Paul McGuinness.

He didn't like hippies.

In the religion that was punk rock, hippies were apostates. Punks good; hippies bad.

Paul was speaking our adopted language. Another clue he was the right man for the job. Adam's and Edge's parents had met Paul and been impressed with this middle-class college-educated twenty-something who brought them the gift of a honeycomb. Or was it a pineapple? Either makes me laugh as I'm writing.

But there were a lot of questions to be answered before we could sign a legally binding agreement in which he wanted 25 percent of the gross earnings.

What? Yes. You read that right. Twenty-five percent.

We were beginning to understand the word "negotiation." Not that we acceded to Paul's first line of demands—we didn't—but this was the moment when the penny dropped that this is how the pennies drop. We felt we were over a barrel and took his advice to get legal advice.

A few weeks later, armed with the wisdom of our legal counsel, we arrived back at Paul's apartment to "negotiate." To Paul's evident and mounting annoyance we slowly pored over the elements in the contract that we didn't agree with.

At a dramatic moment Paul exited the room and Kathy entered, plainly not that happy to see us. Kathy was Paul's secret weapon. A northern Protestant, she had met Paul when they were studying at Trinity College. They enjoyed being as smart as each other; it was a one-plus-one-makes-three situation. Playful when they were sure of you, neither felt the need to resolve any tension that might enter the room. Paul rarely made small talk. Kathy had this way of looking through you as if you weren't there. I later found out she couldn't see you with her contacts out. She was sexy in a way I hadn't met before, if you find a woman who can skewer you intellectually sexy. Which I do. From the very beginning it was clear Kathy was our manager's manager. For all his single-mindedness her opinion mattered more than anyone else's to him.

"It's outrageous that you won't sign this deal," she said. "Paul works in the film business, and that's where he should be staying. This is a madcap idea anyway, and now you're saying you don't trust him?"

"Isn't trust both ways?" inquired Larry.

"You're giving up nothing," she shot back. "Paul will be giving up everything."

It was hard to get past that.

Feeling the power of the power couple and starting to lose our confidence in this negotiation thing, it was time for some drama of our own. A dramatic exit, explaining to our host that we needed time to think and then retreating to our war room in a hamburger joint called Captain Americas on Grafton Street. We couldn't afford the milkshakes, but at least they wouldn't throw us out.

After a heated discussion, we came to a conclusion: we would fire Paul—from the agreement we hadn't signed—and hire Billy McGrath, who managed a group we admired called the Atrix.

"I'm sorry but I couldn't help overhear you."

The speaker, a pale-faced man in his late twenties, had been sitting at the next table while we were talking.

"I know the person you're talking about, Paul McGuinness," he continued. "You're about to make the biggest mistake of your life if you get rid of him."

He told us he managed local show bands, which is how he knew Paul, who represented a folk rock band called Spud. His name was Louis Walsh, later to become the manager of Boyzone and Westlife, among Ireland's most successful pop acts, and then famous in his own right as a judge on the talent show *The X Factor*.

We didn't fire Paul McGuinness or he us. In the end both parties "negotiated" a compromise where Paul would be paid 20 percent of the net after expenses. In other words, the same as each one of us.

Sometimes you don't know when you've made a decision that will alter the course of your life. This time we knew.

We knew that with Paul on board we were on a different kind of ride.

That he and Kathy had been so blunt and kind of anxious was a clue into how serious they were taking this decision. For the next thirty-five years the four of us became a cooperative with Paul.

Exciting. Beyond exciting.

We now had a manager fully committed and ready to represent us with "music executives" from London who were starting to "show interest" and talk about "discovering" us and "signing the deal."

THE MUSIC PUBLISHER

Bryan Morrison was a music publisher, another industry executive with public school pretensions and an attitude to go with it. He was, we were told, a big deal, representing the likes of Pink Floyd and the Pretty Things. When he flew to Dublin to watch us rehearse in the Yellow House, we were determined to show him the best of Ireland.

We took him to the local pub for lunch, as you do. We didn't love this pub, but it would no doubt serve up some authenticity along with the semi-frozen burgers. It did not disappoint on either front. A faint look of disgust crept across Bryan's face as he peeled back the bread on his bap to reveal the pale and pink flesh within, set off with a light garnish of green mold. He was soon distracted, the smaller gents' bar proving unusually noisy for a weekday afternoon. Actually, through the walls in the larger public bar, it was not just noisy; it was kind of riotous.

"Brits, out! Brits, out!"

Ah. The familiar chant, accompanied by a cappella renditions of some favorite rebel songs. All pretty intense and our nervous-looking guest evidently wondering if he was the Brit who should be getting out. We tried to tiptoe around it, but in the end we had to explain that this was likely a meeting of a local branch of some republican organization who, judging by their choice of songs, were not "nonviolent" . . . Let's put it that way.

Bryan, now decidedly paler, looked as if we'd walked him into a trap and promised us an advance of £3,000 for our publishing, with a further £3,000 after we signed a record deal.

It wasn't a lot, but it was a lot . . . if you know what I mean. He'd heard our demos and figured if we could write songs at this level as eighteen- and nineteen-year-olds, we were a good investment. We'd heard of bands signing publishing deals for £30,000 or even £50,000, but £6,000 would hire us a van and the equipment we needed to get to London and play some shows. And in London we'd surely get the record deal.

It was all coming together until, out of the blue, days before we were due to leave, Morrison halved the deal. He was calculating we'd have to swallow the new terms because Paul had already booked the venues and made all the arrangements. He was wrong.

It wouldn't be the last time in business a face would change from angel to devil, and it wouldn't be the last time we would not let money push us around. But how would we fund the trip? After much wailing and gnashing of teeth, we went, cap in hand, to our families, who, between them, came up with £1,500. Screw Morrison, we thought, but now, in hock to our families, we really had to bring home that record deal.

Fifteen hundred pounds would get us to London, to the city where we would surely secure the holy grail that was a record contract. We now had friends in the music press, and there was enough interest to even have our manager interested. We just needed to be at our best, which would mean at least being rehearsed.

This was why, on the way to those rehearsals, when Edge was thrown through the windscreen of the car that Adam was driving, Edge did not go straight to a hospital.

Fate arrived in the shape of a large white van on the other side of a small humpback bridge. This was not the white touring van that would take our band toward its destiny but one that would drive right over our destiny. A van that Adam saw too late and could not squeeze by.

Being Edge, he'd had the presence of mind to put up his hand to protect his head as it sailed through the glass. His whole body doesn't go all the way out but as he bounces back into the car, the back of his head catches the frame of the screen.

A bloodied head and a lacerated hand, which took the main impact. Was he in shock? He says he can't remember, but either way he picks up his guitar, walks about a mile to the nearest bus stop, meets Larry and I for our last band practice before that night, reunited with Adam, and we all take the B&I ferry to the other side of the Styx that was the Irish Sea.

Later, a doctor straps Edge up, but on our ferry crossing to Liverpool he is in agony, alternately putting his hand in ice or holding it high above his head. The holiday trippers don't seem to be throwing up in the choppy sea, but the four of us are sick to the stomach. On tour with borrowed money and on borrowed time and now our only real hope—Edge's hand-to-eye coordination—is at serious risk. In Liverpool and heading straight to the hospital for treatment, Edge will not allow the doctor to bind his fingers or his thumb.

"We've got these shows to play . . ."

We played the Moonlight in West Hampstead the next night, the 100 Club a couple of days later, and then the Hope and Anchor. One night we were billed as V2, which at the time we felt was a lot more punk rock than U2.

We stayed in a small flat in Collingham Gardens, in London's Kensington. It was a squash, but so were the venues. Some of them held crowds of only a hundred, and we couldn't half fill them. Or even a quarter. At the same time the music seemed offended by this, it seemed to be demanding a bigger audience. These tiny audiences made us self-conscious. Edge's injuries healed over the next couple of weeks, but our performances were still erratic—from pretty good to not pretty and not good and, some nights, not bad to quite mad. Or both.

I'd developed this move where I walked into the crowd—this really quite small crowd—to request the loan of a cigarette and lighter from an unsuspecting punter, sometimes looking the other way or sitting up at the bar. I would cock the lighter, as a cowboy might cock a pistol, shooting sparks into the darkness of the venue as our lighting tech John Kennedy turned the lights on and off, creating a dazzling strobe effect. As long as the lights were turned off, and on, in exact sync with my own cowboy moves. Which they generally were not. Such calculated spontaneity was our stage show at the time. Until it wasn't. We've done a little more work on lighting and performance in the years since.

We didn't get the record deal. Every single label passed on us.

One night a talent scout would see our potential and the next night bring their boss and find themselves embarrassed at a lukewarm show. At CBS Records a young Chas de Whalley lost his job trying to sign us. His boss, Muff Winwood, brother of the singer Steve and known by us from that day forward as Duff Windbag, said he'd consider signing us if we let go of Larry. Sorry, Windbag, no deal.

Another pass came from Nigel Grainge at Ensign Records, whose brother Lucian tagged along for a show. After his pal Chas got the heave-ho, Lucian felt bad and always kept an eye out for us. Back then he was our age and just as desperate. These days, still as desperate, Sir Lucian heads Universal Music, controlling one-third of the world's recordings. I guess he is officially our boss, although we like to see it the other way around. Paul regularly reminds him that he got in for free at the Moonlight Club in North London in the summer of 1980. Lucian regularly reminds Paul that he's been picking up the tab ever since.

Of these dozen or so gigs, reviewers seemed to catch us on the better nights, and we ended up with some good notices even in the hallowed inkies. On our return to Dublin the headlines were confusing. Some seemed to suggest U2 was "the next big thing," that we had "made it in London."

It felt nothing like that, and as I look back now, I see that the kind of brokenness that was our band on that first injurious tour of the U.K. has always been part of our appeal. There is something about our band that can never be too cocky or cool. Our best work is never too far from our worst, and when we get too professional or too hip, our audience seems to shrink. It's as if we need to be up against the odds.

As the seventies played out and the eighties arrived, I stayed over with Ali's family for New Year's Eve. It wasn't that great a celebration. We'd just played the Arcadia Ballroom in the rolling city of Cork, home to Joe O'Herlihy and Sam O'Sullivan, both of whom will travel with us on the road for the rest of our lives. It was a night filled with magic but not so much that it could make us forget that there was no sign of a record deal or a van of any kind. No legitimate suggestion we could give our lives to a career in music. We watched the highlights of the year on telly: John Paul II had come to Ireland and John Hume became leader of the SDLP, none of us guessing at the giant he would become. For U2 the year seemed to have fewer highlights and more question marks. The main question being whether we had another year in us.

I was feeling pretty low about it all. So many things seemed to be going wrong.

Waking up on the first day of the new year on the inflatable bed in my future in-laws' front room, I feel the cold. It's really cold; we're about to have the coldest day of the century in Ireland. But the room warms up when Ali walks in. She's wearing a Day-Glo orange fake-fur dressing grown that her mother has made for her, and she is so achingly beautiful that it is all I can do to try and stop thinking about what might be hiding inside that dressing gown.

"Are you depress-*ed*?" she asks, with comic emphasis firmly on the final syllable.

Depress-*ed*.

Yes, I figured, there was a kind of depress-*ed* on me. What am I going to do?

I'm harboring some growing doubts about our prospects as a going musical concern.

Terry, Ali's da, doesn't mind too much, but my da is more worried. The real worry is inside me, the fear that this will be another report card marked "fail."

Adam is talking about going back to London. He'd worked in a fish market and had a relative there who's offered him a real job. There's talk of Edge going to Kevin Street technical college. Maybe Larry would go back to his old job as a courier.

The numbers didn't add up. We couldn't seem to earn enough to pay for a life as musicians.

It was a shitty feeling.

It was what failure feels like.

Fail. Fail again. Fail better, says Samuel Beckett. Well, I had two out of three.

Failure is the feeling you get watching a van that you know you should be in driving off without you. Or worse, over you.

Failure is the feeling you get watching the crowd move out of the way of the record company people as they leave the room halfway through your set in the Baggot Inn. It's a small crowd and everyone knows who everyone else is and everyone knows your dreams are in the room.

Until they aren't.

Lying there on the inflatable bed in Ali's front room, I seem to get stuck on that Baggot Inn show, and in particular returning home afterward. The farcical kicking I offered my Arsenal bag as I chased it down Grafton Street on the way to catch the last bus back to Cedarwood Road. There was nothing in the bag but soggy wet clothes and the stink of black leatherette jeans, pooling the sweat. I see the laughing head of Pod from No. 1, the first drummer of the Prunes. Pod could see the funny side of this tantrum. He could usually find some mirth in the moment.

Failure is a recurring nightmare where I'm back working in a petrol station in the middle of the oil crisis, Norman suggesting I consider a career as a "fuel injection technician." My auntie Ruth had got me the job that past summer, at the Esso station on the airport road, and it had seemed perfect. I could write lyrics in the long gaps waiting for the cars to come in. But then came the oil crisis and long queues of cars lining up and no chance to write lyrics.

But maybe worse than all this?

Failure is when you give your enemies the confirmation they were right all along to have you on their shit list.

If failure was around us, it still couldn't quite have us. Somehow we kept the faith. Or maybe the faith kept us. Faith was propelling us all through this. In a look we shared, or in taking time out or a more intentional moment together, Edge, Larry, and I believed our prayers would turn things around. Our punk prayers. Adam wasn't reading from the same hymn sheet, but he still believed music could save us.

There was a kind of comedic aspect to this willful determination to stay in the game, like that scene in *Monty Python and the Holy Grail* when the Black Knight is losing his limbs to the sword of King Arthur.

An arm, another arm, a leg . . . but still the knight won't submit. Arthur: "Look, you stupid bastard, you've got no arms left."

The Black Knight: It's "just a flesh wound!"

It's hard to explain now because, of course, nothing is inevitable. It's easy to fall into a narrative that suggests destiny had you in its hand, but there was no such narrative. But if you have staying power, and we did, there's always a chance a new thought might arrive, and a few weeks into the new decade that thought did arrive.

A canny thought. Also a cynical, ballsy, and mischievous thought.

THE AGENT

A thought that came from Dave Kavanagh, the entertainments officer of University College Dublin. Dave had booked most of the English punk bands when they played Ireland and was now booking U2. One of the smartest and funniest people in the business, I still remember some of his favorite lines, all delivered in a lightly broiled Dublin accent. Often directed to Paul or to me.

"Once a man has acknowledged his own greatness," he'd say, "it is imperative that it is acknowledged by all others at all times . . . otherwise it is extremely hurtful."

Somebody you didn't want to meet? This was a "two-bullet situation." If you shot them and missed, "always keep a second bullet handy to shoot yourself."

When entering a location where the sense of our own good fortune is all around? "I see the suffering continues."

Known for being quite the gambler, Dave would tell me that "worried money never wins," and, when he lost, that "racing was the real winner here today."

It was this great gambler who was the perfect person to suggest one of the great bluffs in the story of our band. What if we ran with the hype generated by the inkies, and winning the *Hot Press* reader's poll, by announcing a homecoming show as a victory lap for a race we hadn't won? What if we surfed the wave of local goodwill and had it bring us to shore in a venue that would normally be off-limits for a local act? The National Stadium, for example!

What if we played the National Stadium?

The actual National Stadium.

The venue was in fact a boxing arena on the South Circular Road with a capacity of 1,200.

We might be good for 200. Maybe 250.

On the night of February 26, 1980, the entry price to the great hall was that you were breathing, even just a little. It soon became apparent that this was a free tickets a-go-go, and the venue filled up with all kinds of people. People with a vague interest in us, people with no interest in us, people who had never heard of us, people of no fixed abode who were looking to keep warm, and people whose only interest was to see us fail. All of which meant that the place was about half full when we hit the stage for our triumphant return. And if it was a pretty good show by our own erratic standards, for one man at least the gig was exceptional. That was the A&R man.

THE A&R MAN

There was a rumor that Nicholas James William Stewart was a community relations officer for the British army in Derry and had seen The Undertones play. How this tall toff Harrovian could meld in among the Irish even in his civvies would be a mystery to anthropologists everywhere. He loved his music much more than parade ground dressing up, and he'd left the army to work as a talent spotter for Island Records. Island Records, home of Bob Marley, home of the great Lee "Scratch" Perry, home of the glam rock heroes Roxy Music.

The Captain, as we would come to call him, had flown to Dublin after hearing his colleague Rob Partridge enthuse about this band, named after a spy plane, that by stealth had broken big enough locally to play the National Stadium.

Stadiums were common enough for superstar acts, but what was an unknown teenage band doing in such a venue?

On his arrival, illusions of football or rugby stadiums gave way to the sight of a rather more modest boxing ring. We had done what we've always done well. We'd bluffed. If you build it, they will come. And they did. Sort of. Three hundred and seventy-six of them plus 157 who never paid a penny. We took to the ring—sorry, the stage—in one of the most important rounds of our life.

As I looked out on this, the biggest crowd we'd ever played to, I saw so many faces I did and didn't recognize. Whatever reasons people turned up, as fans or as friends, out of curiosity or to witness calamity, within a few songs they were willing us to win the night.

Edge's wrist was repaired, our confidence restored, and the songs were played in and after so many not-that-great shows. Tonight I had the definite feeling that even if our music didn't yet fit the size of the room, it could fit the size of the occasion.

In that ring in that stadium, we didn't hear the bell; we didn't even notice the referee or the judges. But the only judge that mattered noticed us.

"Island Records is ready to sign you," said Captain Nick Stewart. "No doubt about it. Don't need to check this by my boss. Let's work out the deal right now. Island Records are in."

I felt dizzy. We were all disoriented.

"Are you sure?" inquired Paul. "The last A&R man who tried to sign us was fired by his boss."

"I have both instinct and instructions," said the Captain.

I looked at Edge, who looked at Adam, who looked at Larry, who looked at me. We looked like we'd gone sixteen rounds with Joe Frazier. But, funny thing, that deep tiredness that follows failure, now it began to seep out of us. Smiles replacing smirks, "So, what did you think?" replacing "So what?"

It wasn't eleven o'clock; it was five past midnight. No one raised an arm like a victorious fighter or hung a brassy belt over the cuts and bruises . . . and yet it felt as if we'd won gold.

Paul nodded, a "this is for real" nod, but I don't think we fully believed it until a month later when we found ourselves in the ladies' toilets at the Lyceum Theatre in London. We signed a worldwide recording contract with Island Records and became professional musicians . . . in the ladies' toilet of one of the oldest theaters in London's West End.

"The gents' is full, the ladies' better lit," explained our manager, now being paid to make this kind of lateral proposal.

———

In the early nineteenth century, the Lyceum had been the original London opera house hosting many an Orpheus to descend nightly into the hell of no applause. Now it was hosting melodrama of a different kind. Not just the raincoat-wearing post-punk music of the bands onstage this March night, but some kind of upstart Irish opera, beginning to find its voice. As far as I was concerned the faded gilt glory of this place was La Scala, the actual home of opera, the ones that my father would conduct his way through with my mother's knitting needles. La Scala—"staircase"—this was our way up and out.

I couldn't help thinking of Ali, not least because it's her birthday. This Orpheus in this underworld was about to swap his cassette player for a mixing desk in a recording studio. In the myth Eurydice perishes when Orpheus stops to look back at her, and that's where Ali and I would part company with the rules of this underworld. I have no doubt that it is I who will disappear, if I ever fail to look for her.

> and it was not from any dullness, not
> from fear, that they were so quiet in themselves,
>
> but from just listening. Bellow, roar, shriek
> seemed small inside their hearts. And where there had been
> at most a makeshift hut to receive the music,
>
> a shelter nailed up out of their darkest longing,
> with an entryway that shuddered in the wind—
> you built a temple deep inside their hearing.
>
> —Rainer Maria Rilke, *Sonnets to Orpheus*

We signed on the dotted line, but the check was apparently in the post. So like most other nights, I'd need to borrow some cash to get home. I blagged it off the Old Harrovian.

we can debate whether information
or matter is at the heart of the
physical universe, but there is no argument
that the essential building block of
the rock n roll solar system is
the Van

9

Invisible

I've finally found my real name
I won't be me when you see me again.

Managers and rock bands do not have a great history. The record business is littered with unscrupulous managers and unmanageable artists. The manager can be the person who sends you on your way into the promised land of rock 'n' roll or the one who bars your way. For the four of us, our record contract was now a passport into this strange new land, but we still felt like illegal aliens. Without Paul McGuinness we might not be here for long.

One thing had changed immediately which was sure to impress my dad, if not Ali. I was now being paid to have these waking dreams. A lump sum that came out around thirty pounds a week each, although Paul was quick to remind us that was thirty Irish punts, not English pounds.

"And what are you being paid, Paul?"

"You don't pay a doctor what you think you can afford to give him," he replied. "In the film business I might charge one hundred pounds a day. Am I giving up my job to work for thirty pounds a week? I don't think so. I will borrow the difference."

"But I thought we were all in this together?" I parried, knowing Paul could not live on thirty quid a week. Ever.

"I am now the professional and you are my clients. Your thirty pounds a week is modest but meaningful. Not only do you need me; there are other professionals who will also be essential. An accountant, a new lawyer, and, if you're to move on from demos to actual recordings, a producer. All of these people you'll have to pay properly. And they will all want to be paid more than you have. That's why you need me."

THE PRODUCER

Record producers are more like film directors than film producers. They don't write the script, but they have to get the best performances they can out of the cast and they have to frame it just right. The band of the moment was Joy Division from Manchester, and the production genius who'd made their debut, *Unknown Pleasures,* was Martin Hannett. There was no chance of his taking on an unknown band from Dublin. But that's what he agreed to do, and lo and behold the sacred talent of Martin Hannett came to steward our first release on Island Records.

"11 O'Clock Tick Tock" was our attempt at Weimar cabaret. Gavin Friday had got me listening to the music of Kurt Weill and studying the lyrics of Bertolt Brecht, and it was starting to show.

Imagine me singing the "la da da da" in a German accent, and you'll get the picture. The lyric was a portrait of a gig we'd played with The Cramps at London's Electric Ballroom, a night when I was mesmerized by the studied lostness, the gothic hair, the sepulchral white faces of the audience. The Cramps were clever, spooky, and cool, but just a little too coldly apocalyptic for me.

> *A painted face*
> *And I know we haven't long*
> *We thought that we had the answers,*
> *It was the questions we had wrong.*
>
> —"11 O'Clock Tick Tock"

Millenarianism. A song for the end of the world. Martin created a remarkable soundscape, ending with a very long guitar solo that was completely against the rules of punk rock. But despite good reviews, the record company was against his producing the album.

If Martin was highly experimental in the studio, he was also experimenting with highs outside the studio, and his experiments were taking him into some dark corners. We didn't care about that, we cared about him, both humorous and luminous, but the record company was not budging.

Enter a second producer, flown to Ireland to see us play in Galway.

When Steve Lillywhite walked into the dressing room at the Seapoint Ballroom, he looked as if he could have been in our audience. Only a few years older than us and certainly as fresh-faced, he had that kind of English can-do Scout leader attitude that you'd find on children's television.

"He looks like that fella on *Blue Peter*," said Adam.

"Acts like him too," added Edge. "Except no children's TV presenter has produced *The Scream*."

The Scream, the debut album by Siouxsie and the Banshees. With its otherworldly and Ramones-like simplicity, it resonated with us because it felt as if it were made by nonmusician musicians. Although his hair was dyed peroxide blond and he wore a leather jacket, there was nothing punk about Steve Lillywhite. He was completely transparent. In all the best ways. You could see right through him. There was a kind of worldliness in punk rock, an "I'm so bored with the U.S.A." kind of jadedness that would never become Steve. He had a joy about him, a sense of innocence. From a distance, you might think he was cool, but up close you knew he wasn't . . . and we were so relieved.

THE RECORDING STUDIO

Previously, Steve had always been the kid in the recording studio, but with us he was like one of us. He had no idea that it was his naïveté that made him great. That it was his lack of worldliness that made him powerful in this world. Steve was a kind of synonym for us.

He came to us after producing the Psychedelic Furs and straight from sessions with Peter Gabriel on his third solo album. Steve was determined that we wouldn't sound like any other band. The album would be called *Boy,* and we—and he—stayed like children. We were pretty tight from all the touring, and the sessions with Steve turned into a kind of playpen, the five of us on a sugar rush of excitement for the music.

We were working in Windmill Lane in Dublin's docklands, a sort of science fiction wonderland. With its state-of-the-art video editing suites and film production facilities right up the stairs, it was unlike any building in the country of Ireland. This was dirty old Dublin, a city shape-shifting right in front of us, a new Ireland beginning, in the early 1980s, to crawl out from under its past, to shake off its own inferiority complex.

Why couldn't we make homegrown music that was way ahead of the rest of the world?

Recording "I Will Follow," we used bicycle wheels as percussion, turning the bike upside down in the hall of Windmill Lane and using forks and knives in the spokes for rhythmic effect. In a break in the track we threw milk bottles up in the air and let them bounce down the tiled hallway, their off-key musical contributions a novel addition. Adam and Steve forged a particularly close friendship, staying up late after the rest of us had left the studio, spending the night innovating on bass lines. "Let's try it" became our mantra, and even all this time later *Boy* sounds singular and distinctive.

FINDING MY VOICE . . . BUT MOSTLY OTHER PEOPLE'S

Singers are often good mimics. Stand next to someone long enough and I can walk off with their voice or at least their accent.

Listening to Siouxsie Sioux on repeat, I copped her taut "banshee" singing style, and while I couldn't quite pull off her Kabuki iciness, she's certainly one reason the boy from Cedarwood Road doesn't sound like what you'd expect in a boy from Cedarwood Road. It's more girl from Bromley, South London. Or boy from Bromley, the other famous resident of that neighborhood being David Bowie, an influence I've never wanted to shake off. But despite my mannered singing, Steve got some good performances out of me.

"Sing the lyrics," he'd say to me. "Not the person you want to be. Sing the person you are."

Truth be told, the lyrics were not quite ready to be recorded. They were unfinished thoughts or sketches. I hoped what I was sketching was more interesting than most first-time lyricists but also that this subject matter deserved more original rhymes, more complete thoughts. That said, there was a clarity of purpose in this portrait of the artist as a naïve young man determined to stay that way. A paean to an innocence that wasn't being easily let go, a rejection of worldliness and world-weariness at a time when the deflowering of innocence was a central story in rock 'n' roll. That very defiance has me able to listen to those songs still, though I now see the darker shades suggested below the covers of that innocence.

"In the shadow, boy meets man."

I would later find myself repeatedly explaining to critics and fans that the image of adolescence suggested in the song "Twilight" didn't mean that as a boy I actually met an older man in the shadows, even though I do remember being accosted by a stranger when I worked the petrol pumps on the road out to the airport.

Nor was "Stories for Boys" about masturbation. (But then again, now that I think about it . . .)

I see now that "A Day Without Me" as well as "I Will Follow" carry an unconscious reference to suicide. Suicide offers quick authority over a life that feels it has lost all agency.

The sorts of kids who write songs or poetry or paint pictures are the sorts of kids who feel too much at times. The sorts of kids whose feelings can overpower them. In writing this now, I am brought back to the green briar and leafy trees at the edge of the school grounds in Mount Temple. I am brought back to a fretting teenager standing by the train tracks and imagining the comfort they might offer if I lay across them and gave up on hope and love.

But I had faith.

Somewhere in there, I had faith in the next step. One step, then another. The next steps on the journey home.

That first album, *Boy*, would be at odds with the history of rock 'n' roll, where escaping innocence, if not defacing it, is the rite of passage you score with your music. In *Boy* we were writing an ode to an innocence we were determined to hold on to. Some part of us wanted to be men of the world, but a greater part knew we were so much more powerful as boys who didn't know too much about "the world." For all my curiosity I wanted to write about what was going on beneath the surface of the skin because mine felt porous, oversensitive to everything around me. I didn't need any extra stimulation. It was as if I couldn't brush past someone without feeling them intensely. I wanted to write about the human spirit because I was trying to better understand my own. I wanted to sing about it because I could sing myself to somewhere I wanted to be.

That cover image of *Boy*, the photograph of a boy's face taken out of the chemical tray before the image had fully developed, was a boy hardly in the world. A boy from Cedarwood Road staring in wonder at what's going on around him. It was in the Photographic Society in Mount Temple that I first watched with wonder how photographs are developed by dipping, into chemicals, photographic paper with an image burned into it. I loved the image before it was fully formed, when it was in neither one world nor the other, just coming out on the paper. That's what I wanted for our album cover, the face of a boy coming into focus.

The album made a serious impression, and in country after country the boy was received into the open arms of a world that wasn't expecting this beautiful, guileless child.

The boy was off and running, and finally he now had a van.

THE VAN

We can debate whether information or matter is at the heart of the physical universe, but there is no argument that the essential building block of the rock 'n' roll solar system is the van. You get nowhere without a van; it's not just a mode of transport that separates the real from the phony. The van is a time machine, the perfect size for the fledgling rock 'n' roll community: some musicians, a tour manager, a roadie or two, sometimes a manager. Later it may grow wings and become a private plane, but it will always feel roughly the same size as the van.

I am now ready to accept that the reason Paul McGuinness had taken such a long time purchasing our own van was that Paul did not want to drive one. Driving a van was not why Paul wanted to manage a rock band. For Paul even sitting in a van seemed a stretch too far, and far too far from a stretch limo.

The whole point of getting the record deal was that we could now afford not only somebody to mix our sound but also someone to drive us. In September 1980, U2 got a white van and a tour manager, Tim Nicholson, to drive it. A VW with plastic beads and fake sheepskin, it was going to take us out of Dublin and around Ireland, up and down the M1 in England, and all over Europe. We were Hannibal with a Volkswagen elephant to take us across the Alps.

Van Playlist, First U.K. Tour (on Cassette)

The Associates, *The Affectionate Punch*

The Clash, *London Calling*

Peter Gabriel, *Peter Gabriel*

The Pretenders, *Pretenders*

The Teardrop Explodes, *Kilimanjaro*

Joy Division, *Unknown Pleasures*

Skids, *Days in Europa*

Pauline Murray and the Invisible Girls, *Untitled*

David Bowie, *Scary Monsters (and Super Creeps)*

Echo and the Bunnymen, *Crocodiles*

Giorgio Moroder, soundtrack, *Midnight Express*

Blondie, *Parallel Lines*

THE FERRY

I love the happy sadness of disembarking from the van after driving onto the B&I ferry, leaving behind the sounds and smells and the squealing seagulls of Ireland. The seagulls follow the boat for miles and miles until the moment comes where they call off their harassment and get bored of their amped-up screech.

The country has let you go; it is the moment you are untethered. You are free. I would stare at the frothy wake left by this giant van-eating vessel and let it be just that—a wake for the old me. I felt brand-new. True, on board there might be retching and vomit, spilled drinks, and fitful sitting-up sleep, but you're headed "somewhere else," and eventually you see the promise of another land. And its seagulls. You climb back into the sealed universe of the van and resume your sitting-up sleeping, now also sitting-up eating and talking and listening to music. But no longer sitting up . . . and throwing up.

As we listen, the white elephant drives us all over Europe, first to London and four shows in Soho in September 1980. Enter another inanimate member of the dramatis personae.

THE FLAT

Paul didn't like sleeping in vans, but he made up for it with a great eye for posh accommodation even when we couldn't afford it. In 1980 he struck a deal on some rooms in Orme Square off the Bayswater Road, opposite an entrance to Hyde Park, a base from which we could shape our first proper U.K. tour, the Boy Tour.

In order to pay for such fine digs, we did not stay in the regular hotels that a band stays in when they're playing cities like Liverpool and Brighton and even Manchester. After our shows, still damp in our stage gear, we saved the cash and drove back to London. Back to the bright lights and cynicism of the capital. Of course London was Babylon. London was Egypt. And London was *great*. London was the centrifuge of all the music we cared about. Not least because of another member of the cast in this great play we find ourselves in . . .

"There's an 'A' bomb in Wardour Street" was a blast we heard on the radio in 1978 from another favorite band, The Jam, who unknowingly directed us to playing, two years later, a Monday-night residency in the Marquee Club in Wardour Street. In London we played everywhere, but the big bang for us was the Marquee Club. The first Monday we were half full. The second completely rammed. The third there were queues around the block.

The fourth? Mayhem.

"U2 could happen to anyone" was how we'd put it on our DIY posters and little round badges, and now it felt as if this childlike boast were becoming real.

One morning we arrived at the venue to find the metallic knockout singer and bass player Lemmy, the Ace of Spades in the flush run that was the group Motörhead, helping our crew unload and set up our gear. He'd asked to be locked in through the night before to play *Space Invaders,* but he told us that the roadie work was a good way to get him down from the adrenaline of all those aliens he had to shoot up on-screen. An early punk prototype and rock 'n' roll savior, Lemmy would come to see us a lot in those days, even though we didn't have much to offer him.

A venue attains its own legendary status, and playing these early shows felt like being up against all the great bands who had played here, whom we knew we'd never touch.

Famously, The Who had made the Marquee Club their own with their maximum rhythm and blues, and no band had their joy and despair and defiance. Some punk bands got the rage, got the guttural churning, got the death rattle, but not the grandeur. We wanted to bring some of that grandeur to punk rock, and there are moments where we come close in songs like "Twilight" and later "Gloria." For the grandeur you need another member of the dramatis personae . . .

THE FANS

Our fans were often the same age as us, and we would prove to ourselves and them that we were the real punks. We were zealots of a kind with a determination not to surrender our values to the big cities, but rather bring them our true punk values like respect for the people who were paying to see us. We'd make it our business to stop and talk, to sign autographs. We wanted to fuse with our audience in the way no punk band had been able to. And as the singer, I had to create that fusion, to make a chemistry set of the crowd, by rubbishing the very idea they were a crowd. This was not just a nucleus of unstable atoms banging into each other; this was a gathering of sentient beings who for those few hours every night played the most important role in the drama, transporting the band and therefore themselves to some place neither had been before. Finding some moment that none of us had occupied before, or would ever again.

Think about that.

It was as if we were looking for a door to somewhere else, a world that didn't exist, a night outside ourselves. But escaping self-consciousness is not easy when the singer himself is so self-conscious that he finds he has to climb inside the music rather than just perform it. It will require some kind of trick for band and audience to disappear into each other, some pseudo-religious ritual that becomes truly religious. A communion of band and fan both in pursuit of some kind of elevation, a night outside ourselves.

This all takes place on . . .

THE STAGE

In the dark the first glimpse is all important. The shadows of the crew crossing the stage, checking the lines. "The wee red lights on the amplifiers," as Jim Kerr from Simple Minds would point out, "they're kind of landing lights on a runway; the spaceship you're flying this night will return but not right away."

Trajectory is everything in this moon shot. We have two songs,

"11 O'Clock Tick Tock" and "I Will Follow," that can provide the necessary liftoff.

But ten, nine, eight, seven has nothing on a punk rock singer yelling ONE, TWO, THREE, FOUR.

Will these assembled people just stand, listen, and observe, or will they, too, get airborne? That's the excitement the punk band lives for, the vertical lift of the audience as they defy gravity and jump up out of their skins. It has to happen on the first note, or it's not going to happen at all.

Hydrogen and oxygen at the right temperature. Boom. The release of the binding energy.

People shouting your name, you forgetting yours. Forgetting where you come from.

You belong only to the here and now. This is no Oceanus of faceless faces; you are trying to make eye contact with everyone. But you can't . . . until you can. If you get it right, you've not just eyeballed everybody in the front row; you've eyeballed everybody in the venue. And there's no one who doesn't think you might follow them home, that you might pick their pocket or preach them your gospel or make out with them. Or their sister. Contact has been made, real and imagined. And we're discovering another player in this epic drama . . .

THE NIGHT

Sometimes the night inspires unplanned communication between band and audience. Now you do end up on top of them or they on top of you. You resent the stage so much you jump from it and dive into the arms of anyone who'll catch you. They hold you up, scratching, biting, and kissing—they don't seem to mind—until now, with the last song, you find yourself leaving the stage behind, now elbowing your way through the crowd and heading out the back door of the venue. You find yourself walking home through a warren of Soho streets with names like Carnaby, Greek, and Dean, eventually arriving back at this most peculiarly upmarket address in Orme Square.

London is too easily described as Babylon, and we innocents

abroad are just discovering sex, still inquiring about the power and corruption that so easily exploits it. I was curious to know what was going on behind these shop windows of desire, to understand what was being bought or sold down those alleyways, but while this path was full of interesting people, it was also littered with songwriting clichés, ground too well trodden. From the delightful discovery of sex in the backseat of a Cadillac or the front seat of a Corvette— depending on whether you're listening to Chuck Berry or Prince— this was dramatic subject matter but not exactly fresh paint. The great Philip Lynott had pulled it off with "Solo in Soho." A few years later so too did Shane MacGowan and The Pogues with "A Rainy Night in Soho"—has a better song ever been written about the City of London? Even if we'd wanted to, we wouldn't have known how to paint those pictures; the point is you've got to sing your life. "Sex & Drugs & Rock & Roll" was an Ian Dury song we all loved, but truth be told we didn't know what it was about.

I hadn't done drugs since sniffing Lady Esquire shoe polish when I was fifteen. I didn't need to. I felt the pinch of wonder. I felt everything sharply, the people we met, the sensation of being in a body, of eating or drinking. I knew there was darkness in the world, but I was sure it would not overpower us; rather, we would let ourselves be overpowered by the beauty of our discoveries as we traveled through this world. Railway stations and underground trains, the commons, a magnificent oak in a park, the redbrick Victorian buildings of England and Wales, the Georgian splendor of Edinburgh, of Glasgow with its occasional black eye.

And the beautiful searching eyes of our audience. Every night, the show. The ragged and sometimes glorious show, after which we return to . . .

THE DRESSING ROOM

After the conquest, the inquest. It was often me asking the hard questions, distracting the band from my own inadequacies because in truth they were becoming a firestorm of talent, so tight and innovative a power trio. I was a lightning rod for sure. I had the front to be front man, but if you saw round the back, I wasn't as on it as I should have been. Not in terms of craft. As a performer I was spasmodic, an electric eel in black plastic pants, more shouting at God and less singing to the heavens. I should have been kinder on the band members, who were invariably good and often great, but occasionally all three would round on me.

Why was I being such a dick risking the show and myself climbing up onto the balcony?

Why was I having a go at the bouncers?

Or making a show out of myself scrambling up some unsecured speaker stack?

Making a show out of yourself? Isn't that the whole point of being in a rock 'n' roll band?

We were hard on each other. What went wrong during a show was a longer list than what went right, but still, after the postmortem, we'd always head out to meet the fans, then head for the van and the road home. Laughing at each other, listening to some new band on cassette, or—the bad show—letting silence play on the stereo and thinking about how we could be better at being in a band.

We were still prayerful, and still to work out how to be "in this world if not of it." How to be in the van but not run over by it.

You'd have to feel sorry for Adam, back at the flat or the hotel. All a man wants to do is live the dream of four strings, but there's his three bandmates huddled together in their rooms, agonizing over whether this dream is a vision we share. Three apprentice zealots, locked away in prayer and meditation rather than banging out a mix tape. One night in a hotel, a woman, arriving to service one of our rooms, found the three of us praying and joined in with us. We met all kinds of unexpected strangers who encouraged us to find the answer to a simple prayer: In a broken world how could this band play any role? Strangers or angels, we seemed to meet the right person at the right time, new players clearing their throats and preparing their lines like . . .

THE TOUR MANAGER

It's 1983 and we're driving back from a gig at the Bristol Beacon, formerly known as Colston Hall. The first time we played Bristol in

1980, it was to a few dozen people in Trinity Hall, but tonight was important because Bristol has a real music scene from Pigbag to The Pop Group and eventually one of the most important bands in the history of music, Massive Attack.

Edge is up front in the passenger seat pretending to be asleep. Adam, stoned, is looking out the window. Larry is asleep and I'm nearly there. Our new tour manager lives in Bristol, but he's driving us back to London and talking up a storm on his favorite subject.

Bees.

The secret life of bees.

Bees mean a lot to Dennis Sheehan; he's a beekeeper himself, which is why Edge is no longer pretending to be asleep but is now pretending to be awake. But since Dennis joined us six months ago, he has already explained to each one of us separately and collectively that "the wingspan of a bee relative to the body mass makes no sense and physics cannot explain how they can fly." Which is why Edge is now actually asleep. Before I let Dennis's honeyed tones put me out, I marvel not at the miracle of aviation that are bees but at the miracle of Edge being able to sleep with his eyes open and his remarkable ability to nod and grunt in all the right places.

In 1982, Dennis Sheehan, a few years older than us, became our tour manager. Born in Wolverhampton, England, raised in Ireland, he has already worked with Iggy Pop and Patti Smith, been personal assistant to Robert Plant, and come of age with Led Zeppelin. We have no idea that he is going to be with our band for the rest of his life. Dennis had a moral center based on the Catholicism of his youth, and he would become one of our guides as we drove out into this new world. At his funeral in 2015, after a collection of moving eulogies capturing his kindness and strength of character, Robert Plant whispered in my ear, "And let's not forget—in his day, one of the great hammer men!"

Paul McGuinness may have got us entry into the promised land, but he was no man to deal with customs and excise. Dennis was that man. He had a strategy that Paul and sometimes even the band found stressful. He wore a jumper; that's right, a woolen pullover. Sometimes even a Dennis the Menace jumper, which was just not very post-punk. Or funny. But surprisingly effective if you were a frosty-faced gatekeeper at passport control.

Border guards and rock bands do not have a great history, what with all that rooting through your personal stuff, drug busts, rectal examinations. Rock stars know a natural predator when we see one. Unless it has a recording contract and a wet pen, the lamb will instantly lie down with the lion.

We're in Berlin in 1981, being pulled into a little room by customs officers who believe drug smugglers like to dress up as rock bands. Our work is borders, crossing them. Borders are a big attraction for me, leaving one country on the way to another, leaving one thought on the way to another, leaving our teens for our twenties, leaving East for West Germany.

The liminal is the place to be. The bleeding edge.

The demilitarized zones of the psyche, the gray ones of the heart. No-man's-land is yes-man's-land.

Albums are travelogues. Geographically, philosophically, sexually.

An artist searches for territory yet to be discovered and, better still, places on the way to somewhere else.

The poet loves a crossroads.

Berlin. Sarajevo. Istanbul. To live in Europe is a daily grace, this Babel of different tongues all wishing to speak a common language. Coherence. Even the mad Eurobabble of Brussels is a sanity of sorts, if you count the cost of all the lives lost to borders. Europe became a fascination. I had grown up a European without knowing much about Europe, but over the coming years I embark on my own grand tour.

Europe. The miracle landgrab that is Amsterdam or Venice.

Europe. To wake up in Madrid across the road from Picasso's *Guernica* hanging right there in the Museo Reina Sofía, a few minutes' walk from Velázquez's *The Triumph of Bacchus* in the Prado.

Europe. To play music on the same field as Real Madrid or where Barcelona plays their percussive soccer.

Europe. To roll down the Spanish Steps of Rome and discover the room where Keats lived and died, to feel the chill humiliation of a poet's begging letters.

For you, a suburban boy from Dublin, to be able to walk back to your hotel past Fouquet's in Paris and know that's where James Joyce ate his dinner most evenings. Even to be turned away for not being appropriately attired felt vaguely poetic. And deserved some kind of poetic response. I bought a fish at the market and dressed it in a brand-new Comme des Garçons suit that I couldn't afford and insisted on delivering it to the maître d' as a gift. ("From James Joyce.")

Festivals in Europe would teach us how to communicate on a grander scale. We often shared the bill with the Scottish group Simple Minds. Proximity to the band's ecstatic music changed us while Jim Kerr's lyrics changed the way we saw the great European cities we were touring together. REM's Michael Stipe's lyrics changed the way we saw America. He also had one of the great voices of any geography. At a festival in Milton Keynes in the U.K. he tells us he's so proud to have his voice compared to Dolly Parton's. At his side, Peter Buck, the giant shadow puppet on guitar, so believes in rock 'n' roll it cannot but return his love. Mike Mills on bass and backing vocals mashes the '60s and '70s into the '80s. Bill Berry, the drummer, who will leave them down the line after a health scare. But this was a band that made the whole world want to visit Athens, Georgia, not just me.

I would have paid to visit such places, but we were being paid. Discovery and exploration should be ends in themselves, but as we took to the road, the itinerary of our band had venues attached and a growing audience to greet us. Even when the halls were empty, this was a great adventure; even when there was nothing heroic about this "heroes' journey," it felt mythic. Some epic drama of scene and stage set, of cast and costume change and character . . .

THE MANAGER

It was in the van that we got to better understand Paul McGuinness.

Manager? Mentor may be closer to it. Dementor at times. We would learn more about the music business from this man than from anyone else, and that's because he was always learning himself, swallowing sections of the business whole: U.S. radio, French

airplay, the effect of federal politics in Germany on regional popularity, the too comfortable relationship between agent and local
promoter. This man more than anyone in the band wanted to make
us the most successful group in the history of music, and if you're
counting financial success as a measure—which he was, even if we
weren't—he would tell you he pulled it off. He understood that a
band needed to do business as well as it does music or else the business would undo the music. The company he founded, Principle
Management, was going to do things right, and Paul McGuinness
would put manners on an industry not known for having any. He
would be our guide through terrain that had chewed up tougher
and cleverer people than us.

A guide that did not travel economy.

Paul was not a snob, but he could out-snob anyone. He had a
great fondness for people but believed deep in his soul they needed
him much more than he needed them. Money couldn't pay him as
a manager; respect was the toll. Rumor was that money couldn't
pay him as a waiter either. While a student waiter in a restaurant, a
patron had left an inconsequential tip, and Paul had run down the
street after the diner, returning his loose change with the words
"You obviously need this more than me."

Entitlement? Arrogance? I think it was faith in himself and, later,
in us. Not faith in any divine hand, but faith in the project.

A "per diem" sounds like a Latin novena, and it *was* a kind of
"indulgence," this daily allowance a record company paid a touring
band so they could stop at motorway services and eat a proper meal.
For Paul, Dennis, and the four of us, it was often fish and chips and
a few cans as we saved up our per diems to buy some posh bottles of
claret to savor in our posh digs at the end of the week and quiet the
angry god that was our manager.

Paul would be irritated that our rags-to-rags story wasn't running
to his plan. He'd be annoyed that the English music media didn't
understand U2 because, he claimed, the English don't understand
emotion: "Your emotional temperature is too high; they want you
to be cooler."

"They get fashion but not opera," said the man whose father
was a bomber in the RAF, a man who grew up as a teenage mod
in Bournemouth. Paul would mark each milestone in our success

by calling for a lunch "somewhere interesting," somewhere where the star in the room would be the chef. Even early in the 1980s we began to observe that the stops on our European tours appeared to be booked around the location of Michelin-rated restaurants. Query why we were playing only one night in Marseille but, say, three nights in Lyon, and Paul wouldn't even answer the question.

"By the way, have you met my friend Paul Bocuse, the greatest chef in France, if not the world?"

Paul staring at us as if we were the swine he was buying pearls for. "If only," the look on his face says, "I hadn't left the film business."

While we happily acquiesced to business lunches—record company, agent, local promoter—Paul would never talk business at such tables. It was beneath his urbanity. He would talk history, politics, the latest biography, the movie business, music industry gossip, and all the way back to what had been ordered for the table.

The business of U2 was rarely on the table, even though the four of us were around it.

The military never left Paul. He was the right man at the right time, our own Winston Churchill, with a strategy to take the band to Britain, Europe, America, and the world. He referred to an album release as a "campaign" in which a war room and cabinet were necessary. But he would only go to battle after a bottle of Taittinger, a 1947 Barolo, and, sometimes, a Sauternes. Only after the posh meal would Paul McGuinness ride the sugar rush to the theater of war that was the music business, marshaling all the troops under his command. An extra Armagnac and he'd soon be contemplating other invasions—the next table maybe, or a radio station that wasn't playing our song. While we were under the table, sleeping off the lunch, Paul was up from the table, his abbot-like face breaking into laughter at another grand plan, spending the afternoon moving the pieces round the chessboard in a way no one had done since Brian Epstein or Kit Lambert or the rest of that rare breed of great rock 'n' roll managers with public school accents.

I loved Paul in those moments at the table, brilliantly illustrating the worth of our band by not ever talking about us. I loved his baritone, his sonority, his command of the English language.

To sit with him was to receive a master class in the art of conversation. Not to mention good ordering. A rarefied appetite and a capacious mind. An impressive, even scary man who looked as if he belonged astride a great horse. A man not born with a silver spoon in his mouth but absolutely sure he would be feeding us with one.

And a man with a temper. A legendary temper. Nowhere better captured than in an episode on the Boulevard Périphérique in Paris in 1981, when Paul attempted to set fire to his own car. His blue Lancia having broken down after running out of oil, Paul had had enough of Larry's knee in the back of his driver's seat, and we had to physically restrain him as he removed the fuel cap and attempted to throw his lit cigarette lighter down the shoot. Larry might have laughed a little too hard.

Paul could also be very emotional, and at some shows the tears would be rolling down his face, but as a rule, in those early days, he was a man built for combat. Our Churchill didn't smoke many cigars, but if you got in his or his band's way, it's fair to say he would roll you, smoke you, and dump you in an ashtray.

It was Roosevelt who claimed, "The only thing we have to fear is fear itself," but it was Churchill who lived the line. The genius of his leadership was not just his fearlessness but his faith in his fellow countrymen, faith in himself, and, when it came to World War II, faith in America. Our Churchill too. As much as he loved the U.K. and delighted in our European explorations, Paul had figured out that the United States would likely be our promised land. Our exodus would be westward.

Before we had a formal release planned, Paul had sent imported copies of our debut album, *Boy*, to alternative college radio stations across the United States, having the effect of hurrying Island Records along and upping us as a priority. It also meant that when we decided to do a tiny exploration tour of the East Coast of the United States, there was a tiny group of explorers to greet us. The Irish invasion was more of a commando raid than the famed British invasions of The Beatles or the Stones, but everyone involved sensed this might be some kind of appointment with destiny. For a student of rock 'n' roll, or whatever you want to call it—post-punk or post-post-punk—this music was and is an American format. We might have denied ourselves certain chord sequences made famous by American rock 'n' rollers like Chuck Berry and bluesmen like Robert Johnson, but in the end that's where groups like The Who and the Rolling Stones all got their inspiration. The Beatles were a little different, but even they worshipped Elvis as the fountainhead. It would be our biggest leap of faith yet, a leap across an ocean.

BORN (AGAIN) IN THE U.S.A.

On a cold and wet December day in 1980, my first impression of John Fitzgerald Kennedy Airport is the decibel level: human voices drowning out the sound of aircraft landing, as if everyone spoke through loud-hailers. The baggage hall is a fairground of accents and skin tones and high-volume babble. But people seem to be screaming at each other in a good-natured way. Only at Customs do the voices appear cross and detached.

"Stand back, sir!"

"Do not cross the line!"

"Passengers from Ireland, please have your yellow forms ready . . ."

Larry is laughing at the idea of Ireland being told we have a "special relationship" with America.

"They tell everyone that," says Adam. "The British for sure, and they have a Columbus Day for the Spanish."

"Should I tell them St. Patrick was Welsh?" wonders Edge.

It's funnier still when we discover that Paul has organized a black stretch limousine to pick us up. Only in America would they make a car this long. In our heads we've already moved from watching movies to being in one. Paul asks the driver if he can find WNEW on the dial, thinking there's the smallest chance our single "I Will Follow" might be on rotation. Instead, like frozen breath on a windscreen as our route reveals the majesty of the Manhattan skyline, we hear the mantra "All or Nothing At All," Billie Holiday's ode to running away.

We're staying at the Gramercy Park Hotel on Lexington Avenue, a fairly run-down establishment not far from Hell's Kitchen and just up the street from a park of the same name. Walking from the limo to the street corner opposite the snow-covered park, I've never felt more at home in my fake-fur coat until a funny-looking man stops on his bicycle and asks my name. I can't speak. I'm so terrified that I can only utter a small tinny sound.

"Bono," I bleat. "Bono from U2."

The next night, our first show in New York in a place called the Ritz, Paul tells us there will be some important people here to see us. It doesn't look that way to me from the stage; it doesn't look like there's anyone here to see us on this Saturday night. It looks like everyone is here to see each other. I'm nervous, overcompensating for the feeling of being the background noise to someone else's good time. Up on the balcony, which wraps itself around the club, I can see people engrossed in each other, committing the crime of sitting at tables in a rock show. This is a hanging offense for a hangman like me, and so I decide to embarrass these people before they embarrass us and leave. My anxious invective is not quite the punk protest I was hoping for. Not even that imaginative.

"Stand up," I yell toward them. "Stand up . . . yeah, you old guys in your suits . . . stand up. If you're able."

Awkwardly, it transpired, there were some important people there to see us that night. People from the record companies and radio stations who'd heard some good things about us and bothered their arses to show up and welcome the U2 group to their city. They were the ones sitting at tables on the balcony. Oops.

"Well done, Bono! Well done . . ."

Backstage, Paul has steam coming out of his I-can-hear-everything ears. "You've just insulted the only people who actually came to see you tonight. Well done—good for you!"

Three nights later we walked offstage up the road in Buffalo, New York, to the news that John Lennon had been gunned down in New York City. I felt as if we had lost a navigational system, that we were now lost in America. For all his fragility and cocksure defiance, John Lennon was as close to a musical conscience as we had. Hearing him sing, "Oh my love, for the first time in my life / My eyes are wide open," I knew I'd heard a hymn to the universe.

When the North Star of your own faith is becoming obscured, when you feel as if you're in stormy seas and low visibility, who are the lighthouses? John was a light to us.

The previous year, 1979, I'd started writing him a letter to ask if he'd produce *Boy*. We'd written a song called "The Dream Is Over" sparked by his throwaway explanation of the demise of the Fab Four. Now, as our dream was beginning, The Beatles' dream was over. In the years to follow, I would try to honor his wild peacenik imaginings with some of my own. Without sensing him in my ear, I can't believe I would regularly have torn an Irish tricolor into three pieces, holding only the white center, to protest the sectarian violence in our island of Ireland. I wouldn't have been climbing to the top of the rigging of a festival stage holding a white flag if I hadn't been thinking of John's "foolish" acts for peace.

I still interrupt the juvenilia of our teenage song "The Electric Co." with a chant from "Instant Karma!": "Well we all shine on / Like the moon and the stars and the sun."

Our first bite of the apple is sour and sweet at the same time, but Paul knows that to really understand America and have America understand us, we'd have to get beyond the coasts. His strategy was to not play the college circuit, even if it held our biggest audience. Colleges, he said, weren't real; the audiences are only visiting the locale. He wanted us to win over real urban venues, however small, because these audiences are the heart of a city and would stay with us in the future. Which is why the following spring, just a few months later, we're back in the U.S.A. for a sixty-date tour. Which is when a new character arrives onstage . . .

THE TOUR BUS

When we set out on that first proper tour of the United States in March 1981, our white van had morphed into a giant blue bus that would take us through what Paul called "the land of our opportunity." Sitting up front with Billy the driver felt more cinematic and less novelistic than driving through Europe. Now the windshield was wide-screen, and each of us took turns up there, marveling at the sheer size of America through the window.

The freeways and our time on them were longer; the cities were taller and, outside the East Coast, harder to reach. But the coach slept eight in coffin-like rectangular pods, curtained for privacy, and stacked one on top of the other in the middle of the bus. The quiet room was down the back along with a bigger shared space including tables, while a makeshift kitchen sat up front.

You couldn't not be reading Jack Kerouac's *On the Road* or Sam Shepard's *Motel Chronicles* or not notice, as you looked up, arriving in another town, how American place-names are also titles. Even the cheapest hotel room becomes a palace when you can look out over the richness of the Mississippi delta.

New Orleans, an overripe fruit just turning, the noble rot, the grand oaks, the dribbling humidity.

Arizona, what parched land to build on, what unreasonable sun to build under.

Marvelous, meaning utterly a marvel. American endeavor building towers of steel and glass out of melted sand.

Texas, a flat continent of freeways and fields, cities poking their heads out of black sticky ground. Black gold and white privilege standing over it, still struggling to be free from race and Civil War politics. The Bible Belt and its unchristian undertow leaving welts on the bare bottoms of unbelievers.

The forked lightning of Dallas and Houston, the dust storms and intellectual static of Fort Worth, the bohemia of Austin.

Nashville, the buckle of the Bible Belt where songs of praise live in the office next door to songs of redneck braggadocio, so Irish it feels too familiar.

And the liberal coasts, the undulations of San Francisco, the Tenderloin, City Lights bookstore, and back east to the Boston Celtics and the Ivy League, to Washington, Philadelphia, New York, where we started out.

It was a year after the October 1980 release of our debut album when I realized how right Paul's strategy had been. Edge and I were stopped at some lights in Los Angeles and noticed "I Will Follow" being played on a radio station in a car to our right. And also being played on another station, in a car to our left. Beautifully out of sync.

The boy was sprinting. We had to run to keep up. The shows came and came and came. Ireland, the U.K., Europe, the United States. Back home in Dublin, the press was cheering us on at the signs we were going to "make it in America."

> You don't see me but you will
> I am not invisible

But there was no ticker-tape parade when we got back, only "the ol' man," as Norman and I sometimes called him. And he was determined to conceal his pride at our success, a pride I'm fairly sure was just under the surface. Still, there was something reassuring, something right, about the abuse.

"This is not a Holiday Inn, by the way. The same rules apply. Don't you be getting a big head."

"But my brain needs one to make up for my small penis," I shouted back.

"Oh, you're very funny" was his not-so-funny return, followed by a weary sigh.

I'd graduated to Norman's bedroom and I lay on the bed, staring at the poster I'd just put up of Peter Saville's design for the debut LP by Orchestral Manoeuvres in the Dark.

"What am I gonna do about Alison Stewart?" Ali.

Three letters filled my mind.

I'd missed her out on the road, and it was good to discover that she'd also missed me. That our relationship had not been jeopardized by our time apart as the band reached for success. She was excited for me, if a little wary of what baggage success might bring with it. Self-consciousness. Success has prying eyes. You can pull the curtains on yourself or have them pulled by those closest to you.

Success can encourage friends and family to become a little too cynical or too respectful of its nosy gaze.

Are they still the same boys who left Dublin to go find a record deal? Ali's angle was, why would anyone want to stay the same?

She was happy because she knew music was my freedom. Freedom from having to get a real job or freedom from having to prove myself. Freedom to explore the wider world and my place in it.

Or was that "our" place in it? I found myself thinking in the third person, I was moving from I to We.

> There is no them
> There's only us.

Sitting outside 10 Cedarwood Road in my white Fiat 127, I recounted how the record company had hired a limousine to take us to a signing in a cool L.A. record store. We were so embarrassed we'd parked the limo around the corner and walked the last hundred yards.

"Did you get mobbed?" she teased me.

No, I explained, without the limo no one recognized us, and so we had to walk up to all these cool-looking people and explain that these uncool people had the signatures they were looking for. The impish little motor seemed to shake with our laughter.

"So your ego can still fit into this limousine?"

Ali was staring at me in that white coat and clipboard way I've become familiar with over the years. A way of looking at me as if she's an X-ray machine searching for fractures of the exterior or interior kind.

She looked in and around and through me and smiled. She reads me. She knows me. She's always known me.

If Ali was proud of what we'd achieved with *Boy*, so was our whole community of friends and families.

Except for one small corner of it.

Christians and those who play the devil's music do not have a great history. Shalom, the house church community that meant so much to Larry, Edge, and me, was worried we were falling away from our faith.

I explained to our pastor, Chris Rowe, and his wife, Lillian, that things were better now, that our little church group would not need to worry about funds in the future. We would be able to provide.

"It's the Lord who provides," he reminded me. It was a warning shot. There was more to come.

10

October

October and the trees are stripped bare
Of all they wear.
What do I care?

October and kingdoms rise
And kingdoms fall
But you go on
And on.

I have, as the reader is discovering, some anger management issues. I would not stand up to myself in certain circumstances. The only person who has ever stopped me in full, foul flight was this Zen Presbyterian we call Edge. At a show on the Boy Tour in New Haven, Connecticut, I had completely lost it to the point where I actually lifted up Larry's drum kit and threw it into the crowd. Adam and Larry sought cover, but Edge held his ground, and as I ran toward them, he caught me with one on the side of the head. That slowed me right down. Never pick a fight with someone who earns their living from hand-to-eye coordination at that level! And then the shame of it all descended as the good people of New Haven looked aghast at these Irish people getting all Irish on themselves.

No sooner had Edge hit me than he was apologizing. Of course.

This is the mark of the man. He's always been like that. He couldn't bear a grudge.

He couldn't even remember the grudge he was supposed to bear. Only three, perhaps four, times have I seen Edge in meltdown. The first time was in 1979, during another car crash rehearsal, people playing in different tempos and keys, me screaming at the band as if all three of them were the culprits. Edge, doubtless aware he was the only one making musical sense, picked up his guitar to throw it in my direction, stepped forward, seemed to wrestle with it in midair, and then stopped himself. He put it carefully back down on its stand, stormed out of the room, slammed the door, and, before the sound of the slam had reached our ears, reopened the door and walked back in to apologize. That was his rage. He wrestled with it because it was his guitar and he didn't want to break the guitar. He plays the same guitar now.

We recorded our earliest musical ideas on a cassette player, and when we played it backward, it made a squeaky, babbly sound. For me that was always the sound of Edge's brain. For all his tranquility there's something screaming in there. But he's such a strong will he's squeezed the scream into silence.

When I'd first started listening to *Marquee Moon* by the group Television, I recognized in Tom Verlaine's and Richard Lloyd's playing something of Edge's stoic quality and his desire as a guitar player to tell stories. In punk rock, guitar solos were banned as self-indulgent. One might be permitted as long as it was short, to the point, and very melodic, but if it was going to be longer, it had to tell a melodic story. Some of the best solos were on *Marquee Moon*, and my hunch was that as well as stepping away from the blues, we should go a little sci-fi. The blues were notes that people were too familiar with, notes it had become difficult to surprise people with. When Lemmy was in Hawkwind, there was something of the sci-fi in a futuristic song of theirs called "Silver Machine." And the same in an echo machine on Pink Floyd's *Animals*.

Edge rented a Roland tape echo to try out in rehearsals, where we came up with the hook for "A Day Without Me." Soon after, in Dublin music shop McCullough Pigott, he found an echo pedal by Electro-Harmonix called a Memory Man, which took root by his foot, the size of a box of chocolates, stainless steel, with knobs. It was not digital. It was analog. You didn't punch in numbers; you had to figure out what tempo you wanted to play at. You'd hit one strike and hear the chet-chet-chet and the echo-echo-echo would follow. Edge's foot was on that Memory Man and its replacements right until the year 2000. The echo and reverb of the Memory Man turned even the smallest punk club into a cathedral. An ecstatic church music.

HYMNS AND ARIAS

For a man who spends so much time in the future, Edge always carried some deep past in his soul, likely an obscure village in Methodist Wales. Edge's father, Garvin, was a mechanical engineer, a churchgoing one. Edge's mother was a schoolteacher, a churchgoing one. Science and faith were not antagonists in their house. His parents were hymn singers, and in Wales hymn singing is stadium rock.

> Guide me, O thou great Jehovah,
> Pilgrim through this barren land;
> I am weak, but thou art mighty;
> Hold me with thy powerful hand;
> Bread of heaven, bread of heaven,
> Feed me till I want no more.

It seems far-fetched when a listener says they hear Bach or Beethoven in our music, but probably they're hearing the hymns that are in the DNA of this contemplative congregationalist. There's a combination of notes you hear in the great choral music—fifths—you hear them in Bach especially. When you hear these huge hymns, you can survive any loss. You can take any amount of blows. You can make the most difficult decisions. You can march forward in your life against all adversity. It was in Edge that I found a marching music, found those huge soul-stirring melodies of Charles Wesley, Isaac Watts, and John Newton, and when I was a young man, they were exactly what I was looking for. My soul had a desperate need to be stirred.

"New Year's Day" on the *War* album came from a classical-music-like place, and later, in "Where the Streets Have No Name" or "I

Still Haven't Found What I'm Looking For," there's a certain suspension in the music, that elevated feeling in which songs take on a
hymnic quality, holding the tension between gospel and blues.

Hymns had been one of the routes that gospel and the blues
had taken on their way back from Africa and America to northern
Europe, to Wales, to England, to Germany, and somewhere in there
is our essence as a band.

An early example is Edge playing a beautiful array of notes on
a piano, which sounded like nothing I'd felt anywhere. "October"
carries the gentle power of Edge, the ache of his loneliness, that
longing to belong. The song became a location for a meditation on
impermanence.

On faith.

We all shared faith. Faith in each other. Faith that our coming
together as musicians might prove more than the sum of our parts.
It was faith that nearly broke up the band because . . .

A CHRONICLE OF OUR HOLY ROLLIN' ROCK

. . . religious faith can be a problem. Faith divides people. Faith
divides people who have faith, and divides people with faith from
those who don't. Even within the band there could be division.
Whether Adam and Paul were atheists or agnostics was immaterial, but Edge, Larry, and I became very conscious they were not
interested in all the God-bothering stuff. Paul would point out his
respect for the questions we were asking if not for our answers, and
I see now it takes a certain generosity and tolerance to live and work
in the company of these souls on fire. Paul and Adam were really
patient with our fervor.

Even while totally absorbed in all this, I had no doubt that I preferred the company of so-called unbelievers. It's not just that some
of the finest people I've known don't subscribe to any particular
faith tradition; it's more that people who openly profess faith can
be—how shall I put this?—such a pain in the arse. In a world where
it's impossible to avoid advertising, I don't want the person next to
me hard selling their take on the Big Questions. Live your love is
the right answer.

I hold to that line attributed to Francis of Assisi, who told his followers, "Go into the world to preach the gospel and, if necessary, use words." We need less to be told how to live our lives and more to see people living inspirational lives. I'm also deeply conscious that I can't live up to the badge I've pinned to my lapel. I'm a follower of Christ who can't keep up. I can't keep up with the ideas that have me on the pilgrimage in the first place.

This all started for us in the late '70s. Something curious was happening in Dublin. Depending on what you believed, you might say it was "revival," a movement of the Holy Spirit. Gatherings took place all over Ireland where people seemed to be surrendering to their higher power in dramatic ways, the likes of which no one had seen before. Worshippers would be singing ecstatically before the Spirit appeared to fall on them and the tunes would change. We found out later this was called the Charismatic Renewal, "charisma" being the Greek word for "gift," a movement that emphasized the New Testament's "gifts of the Spirit," sometimes including behavior referred to in the scriptures as speaking in strange tongues. It was particularly striking that in Ireland this was happening to both Protestant and Catholic churches. These Pentecostal sightings in our late teens had me and Guggi and others in our Lypton Village art gang very much on our guard.

The most extroverted people tended to be having the most dramatic encounters with the Spirit, while quieter, shier people, well, not so much. But if we could see through some of the melodrama, we could also see something authentic going on, and we were trying to find some kind of spiritual home outside the traditional churches.

During our time at Mount Temple, our religious education teacher, Ms. Sophie Shirley, had started some unusual prayer meetings. Because this was a nondenominational school, nobody knew if she was Protestant or Catholic, but we all knew Sophie Shirley was a special soul, and the room seemed to vibrate a little differently as she took us through the scriptures. At age fifteen, I'd found her classes an unexpected comfort, the message and the messenger disappearing into each other. That every hair on your teenage head was counted. Quite something judging by our haircuts at the time.

She had started to hold meetings in the music room after school on Wednesday, the same space the band would rehearse in not many months later. Some teachers dropped by. Donald Moxham, who encouraged us not just to read history but to try to make some of our own. A fearless questioner of orthodoxies and a man who would one day have the courage to give me a driving lesson. Jack Heaslip, another less than obvious candidate for this "charismatic" religion and initially quite skeptical but soon losing himself in the revival-like atmosphere.

A 1960s beatnik by nature, with a long beard and thinning hairline, Jack was open and understanding with students, no matter how they turned up. Angry, sad, confused, guilty?

Jack was wise counsel. Students of fourteen or fifteen engaged in risky sexual behavior? He'd find them condoms. And no subject was taboo, which meant we came to trust him. I trusted him. In particular after a few convulsive incidents where I had let my anger overcome me. Jack patiently explained to me the relationship between fear and anger and how anxiety can present itself.

As sometime housemaster, Mr. Heaslip was in charge of discipline, but he had an unusual approach. If a student who'd punched another kid or smashed a window was sent to him, he'd ask them what they thought their punishment should be. Most students, he told us later, would choose a worse punishment than the one on the books, which he took for a clue into the human condition, the role of guilt in keeping people away from their religion. The role of guilt in keeping people away from themselves. Self-loathing.

The prayer meetings became popular. Sophie Shirley, these other teachers, and maybe sixty students in this nondenominational school, all of us finding an interest in the Jesus of the Bible we'd rarely read about but who seemed to show up when we showed up. When we met, we sang simple songs and offered prayers for peace in our country, and it felt as if something was stirring. In our souls, our school, our country. And in that same music room another kind of ecstatic music was being born, the music of U2.

REVIVING THE REVIVAL

Our inner-city Christian meeting of the Shalom group, led by Chris and Lillian, lived an entirely countercultural life. They had few possessions and no desire for them. And having nothing, like the earliest Christian communities, they had "everything in common." It was entirely anachronistic and also kind of beautiful.

To Larry, Edge, and me, this way of life carried a ring of truth. It looked to our young minds like the real thing, not that we would know what the fake thing was. As Chris took us through his Bible, and talked about how God had become human in a first-century Palestinian Jew, the words seemed to come alive. We were the students, he was the teacher, but it would have been good if, just now and again, Chris had asked *us* a question or two, about the world beyond his community that we were also part of.

As we sat around their kitchen table in 1981, in the wake of *Boy*'s success, Lillian watched how Chris's answers were met by our open-faced questioning, and I sensed she understood and was sympathetic to the contrast. She could see Chris's great strengths as a spiritual guide but also his humanity. He was born of another time, the literality of his reading of the scriptures always winning out over the poetic. In that sense he was a fundamentalist with all those certainties and clear interpretations. Chris worried that our generation would not hear about the radical gospel of Jesus, that they would confuse Christianity with churchiness.

How could we help with such a problem? We tried to explain, no doubt in a clumsy, naïve way, that maybe our generation needed verbs, not nouns, needed to be loved, not lectured. That bumper-sticker Christianity was driving people away from their churches.

It was clear that Chris saw our potential as missionaries being taken over by the mission of our music. I thought I noticed Lillian smile to herself when I tried to convince her preacher man that our group could serve God better if we served the gifts we'd been given, that surely heaven would be happy if our band was a success and we'd have the means to help others a little more here on earth. But the preacher man couldn't see it. He was a good shepherd and we were his lost sheep. But actually, this sheep was starting to think that sometimes even shepherds lose their bearings.

When Edge asked her about a story doing the rounds that this charismatic couple were perhaps a little too fervent in their evangelizing, Lillian responded that she chose not to worry about her reputation. "The human heart is wayward by nature" she said, wiping down the kitchen counter. "So remember that every time you point your finger, there's three pointing back at you."

She smiled generously. Sometimes a smile or laugh is more trustworthy than any amount of seriousness.

At first Shalom had accepted how we looked and dressed. Gavin had styled his haircut on a David Lynch movie, *Eraserhead,* and he could look pretty intimidating. Some days he wore a skirt with bovver boots. And jewelry. Big exaggerated rings. At first they had been tolerant of the music we listened to, but it was becoming clear that this had been to lure us in. Over months, the questions from Shalom began to wear us down. Was our music ephemeral, transient? Wasn't the real calling to preach the gospel? How real was our faith? How ready were we to be pilgrims? Chris seemed to know the answers already.

There is no greater insult to a young man than to question his fervor. How tough is he? How serious and committed? Even if you are a slacker, you are a committed slacker. Mostly, a young man wants to be challenged to do difficult if not impossible things.

Like to give up his music.

Eventually, it became too much for Edge. He couldn't live with the apparent contradiction of being in a band finding a global audience and this humbler calling to serve a local community. He was asking himself questions about the utility of art. The Presbyterian was starting to win out over the Zen.

I drove over to his parents' house in Malahide one evening and sat down on his bed. I had a feeling he wasn't interested in talking about how this second album, *October,* was coming on, but I didn't know quite what was on his mind. I didn't know that when I arrived, I was in a band, and when I left, I wouldn't be.

"I've got a problem I can't solve in U2," he explained. "I'm not sure I want to make music this way."

Edge is not a complainer and doesn't do melodrama, but he was in some kind of agony.

"Chris, Dennis, all of them, they're asking questions that I just can't answer."

"What sorts of questions?" I asked, as if I didn't know.

"About whether we can be a band and be believers."

"Ah, those questions. Look, I'm troubled too, but there's a special feeling when we play. It's when we stop playing I feel like shit. But I won't say I'm not challenged by these people. I don't have answers to their questions either."

But Edge did have an answer, a radical one.

"There are so many problems, messy, complicated problems out there in the world, and maybe running away with the circus is not what we're being called to. Or not what I'm called to do. I've spoken to Aislinn. She understands. I hope you do. I'm out, Bono. I really am. I'm sorry."

It was a shock to hear it put so baldly, but logically, I knew what followed.

"Well, if you're out, I'm out. I've no interest in being in this if you're not there . . . who'll tune the guitars? We better speak to Larry and Adam. We better speak to Paul; that's going to be very awkward."

Heading back to Cedarwood Road in the tiny Fiat 127 I'd just learned to drive, I felt a sense of peace, though maybe that's the wrong word. There's a kind of calm that can come over you when you make a big decision, a decision that is nobler than the one you really want to make. There might be a smidgen of the martyr about it. It didn't so much feel like I was leaving U2 but more like I was joining the army and might be heading off to some unknown location with the chance of never being seen again. You tell yourself everything is okay because you're doing the honorable thing and that such sacrifice is a measure of the seriousness of your commitment. Maybe today we'd use the word indoctrinated. Perhaps that was the case, although none of us knew it.

What else could explain why, after all this time and commitment and the first signs of success? It was a question I couldn't articulate, which probably explains this other feeling that sat with me as I drove.

A huge sadness. And a loneliness.

I got back to Cedarwood Road and sat, or slumped, on the stairs to call Ali on the phone. She understood in the way you understand your friends who have made up their minds to do something courageous and difficult.

I spoke to Larry, who also understood; he had his own questions. Only Adam didn't get it. Why would he? Adam wasn't part of any fire-breathing prayer meeting like Shalom, but it's the measure of the man that he opted for solidarity with us when we met with Paul to say that there wasn't going to be a next tour.

Was it a battle between two stewards, two managers, two impresarios who both had a mission for us and were offering guidance on how we might make our way? Chris Rowe was a man of God convinced the world would be a better place if it heard the radical message of Jesus.

Paul McGuinness was a man of the world who thought rock 'n' roll allowed people to be more themselves. For one we'd be missionaries; for the other we'd be musicians.

We went to see Paul, who heard us out. There was a pause, the room quieted, and then Paul spoke.

"Am I to gather from this that you have been talking with God?" he asked.

"We think it's God's will," we earnestly replied.

"So you can just call God up?"

"Yes," we intoned.

"Well, maybe next time you might ask God if it's okay for your representative on earth to break a legal contract?"

"Beg your pardon?"

"Do you think God would have you break a legal contract? A contract that I have signed, on your behalf, a legal contract for you to go on tour? How could it be possible for this God of yours to want you to break the law and not fulfill your responsibilities to do this tour?

"What sort of a God is this?"

Good point. God is unlikely to have us break the law.

Edge agrees and argues he was always looking for some kind of signifier to go on.

Rethink.

Paul (to himself): Checkmate.

By the end of the meeting we were coming around to the thought that this tour, at least, would be going ahead.

In truth something never sat right with us about this "in or out" Christianity or the judgmentalism it came with. This was exacerbated by church people's attitude toward Adam, who didn't identify as a believer, who wasn't part of any faith.

"So you're not a Christian band then?" such people would ask Adam.

"I'm in a band with Bono," he'd laugh. "For that alone I deserve an access-all-areas pass through the pearly gates."

Larry would respond, "I don't want to be in a fucking Christian band. I want to be in a fucking great band."

Edge tried to explain that our music wished to be free from such categorization. He wanted U2's music to look and sound like the people in U2.

I, too, wanted to make music capable of carrying our own weight, even the weight of our own contradictions. To be "in the world but not of it" was the challenge in the scriptures that would take a lifetime to figure out. As artists we were slowly uncovering paradox and the idea that we are not compelled to resolve every contradictory impulse.

LATIN IS THE LOVING TONGUE

When it came to making our second album, *October,* I had no choice but to improvise because I literally had no words. At the end of the Boy Tour, I'd lost all the scribbled notes I'd made when my fancy leather bag was stolen from our dressing room in Seattle. Not just all the lyrics, but all the directions on where we should go, even what we should look like on our way.

Back in Dublin without any words for the songs, I sang myself out of it by singing about it.

> *I try to sing this song*
> *I, I try to stand up*
> *But I can't find my feet.*
> *I, I try to speak up*
> *But only in you I'm complete.*

The track "Gloria" was inspired by a psalm and by an album of Gregorian chant, ironically, given to me by Paul. Writing quickly, under pressure, I was speaking in strange tongues all right, only this time it was Latin.

Gloria
In te domine
Gloria
Exultate
Gloria
Gloria
Oh, Lord, loosen my lips.

These songs weren't the most refined or complete, but they had something that can be more important: desperation. They also had a couple of lines that captured succinctly that first phase of the band's life, the clear eyes of the innocent and the zealotry to stay unworldly:

I can't change the world
but I can change the world in me.

—"Rejoice"

Later, when the world had proved more malleable but also had more of its way with us, we all but inverted the admonition to an admission:

I can change the world,
but I can't change the world in me.

—"Lucifer's Hands"

That's my whole life, right there. In those two opposing views. But such tension was not to be enjoyed in our early twenties; in fact it was tearing us apart.

The band felt like a house built on sand rather than a church made of stone, a house about to be engulfed and swept away by the tension between faith and art. The word "kingdoms" did not seem too grandiose. We felt the whole world was underwater.

Edge was certainly underwater. I see him now, nineteen, sitting in his bedroom in Malahide, wrestling with whether he wants to be in this band or not, wrestling with the question of how he or we might best be instruments of peace in a world at war with itself.

Choosing to let go of the very thing that keeps him afloat, that keeps our band afloat, his musical gift.

In a curious way, when Edge left the band, followed by Larry and me, we got the band back. We never did answer the question about how we could be anything other than a vainglorious, egocentric artwork, but in failing to answer it, we came upon a more interesting question, about the egocentricity that would ask a question like that in the first place.

It's a pumped-up person who believes they can live a life free from worldly concerns. Perhaps sometimes you have to refuse the call of religion, to stand up to it and say no. A religion that can so punish and degrade people is likely not being honest to God. Religion can be the biggest obstacle in your path.

It was Woody Guthrie who had a sticker on his guitar that read "This Machine Kills Fascists," and in the face of all these questions Edge was finding a metaphorical version for his own guitar. "This machine makes peace." We were coming upon an answer to a question we hadn't been asking. The question wasn't whether songs could save the world but rather could these songs save us?

Music has function, it can get people from A to Z, but it won't do any of that unless, first, it gets you there—you the singer or you the player. Before music attempts its many good deeds, its first job is to save the music makers, in this case the guitar player in particular and this band in general.

Even after a successful October Tour back through Europe and America, our questions remained about whether U2 had anything useful to offer the world. The band took a short break. While Ali and I pledged to get married, Edge pledged to find the form and function of the perfect U2 song. He had an idea for a song that might be useful, a song about a small island of four million people looking at a civil war. Without knowing it, this was going to be a song that would save our band.

the morning of our wedding day, August 31, 1982 I finally left home 'I can roll cameras even now'. the toaster we couldn't train to stop smoking. the Dad shaving in our kitchen beside a boiling kettle, squinting in his vest over the sink where he kept a small mirror to clip carefully around the moustache he borrowed from his Dad. The blue disposable razor scraping across his white foamed neck before the steamy splashing was going to leave his face reddened, but they

sharp as the ~~blade~~ TWIN BLADE he does not dispose of

A + B = FAMILY

despite her discomfort Ali carried the same serenity she always did, the kind I would spend my life trying to inherit the kind of beauty that invites more of it from those around her.

Two Hearts Beat as One

They say I'm a fool,
They say I'm nothing
But if I'm a fool for you
Oh, that's something.

Not everyone in the Irish music scene was that enamored with U2's early success in America. Not even everyone in "the village." Toast of America, as The Clash had found out, appeared to break a prime punk commandment. "I'm Not So Bored with the U.S.A." was the slogan on Camden Market T-shirts, taking the piss out of The Clash anthem "I'm So Bored with the U.S.A." The Virgin Prunes were increasingly happy to be perceived as a black-mirror reflection and rejection of U2's stained glass.

BITTER TASTING FRUIT

The Prunes wanted to be an assault on the senses, journeying further and further from anything that might resemble rock or pop and embracing performance Art with a capital *A*. Punk rock had become a little bit *Animal Farm* all right, but Gavin's revenge on his overlords was not to replace them but to show them what they had done to him.

The Prunes threw pigs' heads into their audience. Pigs' heads from the abattoir where Gavin worked nine to five. Rock 'n' roll was always the sound of revenge, but this was taking it to another level.

There was some Irish hell to pay too. In their heads this political or religious satire was aimed at a country which had no division between church and state, north or south of the border. At Trinity College the Prunes were invited to showcase their "challenging" work to a more academic audience, including an installation titled *Sheep*. This featured Niall O'Shea, a friend of Gavin's, on his hands and knees in an agricultural pen. Niall loved to wear woolen sweaters from the islands of Aran in the west of Ireland. All he asked for was a sandwich break on the hour.

It was Dada that was the excuse the night I discovered my Fiat 127 was being broken into not by a car thief but by my friends, who wanted to make an art installation of it. At three in the morning a commotion on the road woke me up, and when I opened my bedroom window, I was pelted with eggs.

Although it was just me and the da left in No. 10 now, the da slept with an iron bar under his bed. For just such an eventuality as this. As well as not finding it funny to see your car entirely wrapped in wallpaper and a kind of papier-mâché made from eggs and toilet paper, I worried I would not have time to explain to the da that these trespassers were not actual car thieves. Not have time to explain before he had run out and caught one of the surrealists with his homemade truncheon. Or have a heart attack chasing after them.

These were not the best of times in my relationship with Gavin and Guggi, two of my oldest friends. We'd all been touched by the fire that was the Shalom church group, but while Larry, Edge, and I felt singed, others felt blistered and burned.

None of this was helped when Gavin announced in an interview that if U2 is God, then the Virgin Prunes are the devil. Funny. And not funny. There was also some sniggering when I mentioned I was going to get married; all of which explains why I began to turn aside from these alt families that I'd grown up with on Cedarwood Road. Now I began to look more and more to my other alt family, the one

I'd spent the last eighteen months touring with. "On the road" no longer meant on Cedarwood Road.

And so it came to pass that Adam Clayton became the best man at our wedding. There couldn't be a better man. Not that, at the time, monogamous relationships were his specialty, but Adam was the best man for a couple of reasons.

1. He would be the best at it. He'd be the best master of ceremonies and, critical for an Irish wedding, give the best best man's speech.
2. Because weddings are all about symbols, I hoped it would bring the two of us closer as, lately, we hadn't been getting on. We'd clashed a little in these early days of the band, probably ever since Adam printed up the business cards saying "Manager of U2" and started using words like "gig," "circuit," and "demo tape."

Adam had been the first person to believe this band could have a future, and maybe my teenage front didn't always appreciate Adam getting more out front. Adam knew he had nowhere else to go. From age fifteen he'd been neatly writing song lyrics in his school jotter to take him out of the boredom of being in boarding school. If his experience at the posh prep school Castle Park and St. Columba's College had done nothing for his academic credentials, at sixteen he'd been way further down the road in all the non-curriculum subjects teenagers look up to. He was a man of the world . . . the world our band was about to enter.

Plus Adam was posh.

I was not posh.

Adam had that accent. He smoked cigarettes. The more that Maeve O'Reagan, one of my best school friends, had become enamored of him, the squeakier my voice had become. He'd had that one year on me, which means nothing later in life, but at sixteen, added to all the other competitive edges, meant I was always going to have to work hard to keep up with him socially. And as the band began to find itself, there was also that Adam-Paul axis, the (British) lions that didn't want to be thrown to the (Irish) Christians.

I can't remember the substance to those early tiffs with Adam, but what I do remember is the peace that broke out for our wedding. Relationships matter, professional or fraternal. They require our attention. Especially if they're romantic.

"AND THEY SHALL BE ONE FLESH"

Ali and I were mates. Our romance was a gentle one. Friendship was at the core of the lovers we admired around us. Larry and Ann seemed like a perfect rhyme for each other. She was a true companion, as subtle as a Heaney verse. She never drew attention to herself, but if you could keep your eyes on her, she was the most perfect white rose, a long neck stem and pale perfect skin. Playful and serious. Larry and Ann always seemed to be giggling.

Edge and Aislinn were running down the road ahead of us all. So stylish apart, even more together. Talking about furniture, floorboards, tables, chairs, kitchen utensils. A pair of designers at the center of a world they were designing. Edge, the egghead, becoming an aesthete in the company of an aesthete. So much to talk about.

Sex, for example.

For all of us, so many conversations on the nature of sex and attraction. Why are people so hung up on all this?

"Isn't it *the* symbol of the union between Creator and Creation?" Is there any such thing as "casual sex"?

"Of course" comes a reply.

"Yes, if you're lucky" comes another.

"But if it goes nowhere," says a third, "girls hold on to these hurts." Ali and I find our way.

We were enthralled by the beautiful notion in the Torah: "Therefore shall a man leave his father and his mother, and shall cleave unto his wife: and they shall be one flesh." I'm sure that oneness is the direction of travel for all great loves, but I also accept that it does not happen on cue, at a ceremony, for example, like a wedding.

It can happen in all kinds of different circumstances in the middle of the night or the middle of the day, when two lovers decide they want to be a part of each other's lives more than they desire their own independence, and in continuum they pledge their lives to each other.

Ali and I really did want to uncover the mysteries that might be inside our marriage. Although I didn't like church very much, we did love its symbols. We loved the idea of baptism. We loved the concept of Communion, the symbolism of the bread and the wine, the miracle it suggested. The performer in me enjoyed the ritual and ceremony, all of which, on the surface, seems to contrast sharply with the traditional image of an Irish wedding, the messy carnival of a grand fete where the passion can soon express itself in kisses stolen round corners, a soundtrack of old family grievances shouted above the music. There's probably more sex on the outskirts of an Irish wedding than in the wedding bed of the happy couple.

GOODBYE CEDARWOOD ROAD

The morning of our wedding day, August 31, 1982, I finally left home. I can roll cameras even now. The toaster we couldn't train to stop smoking in our kitchen. The da shaving beside a boiling kettle, squinting in his vest over the sink where he kept a small mirror, to clip carefully around the mustache he borrowed from his da. His blue disposable razor scraping across his white-foamed neck before the steamy splashing was going to leave his face reddened. But hey, Bob is not embarrassed. Bob Hewson is feeling sharp as the Gillette twin blade he does not dispose of.

His son is sitting at the kitchen table scraping melting butter across the burned offering that is toast in number 10. The son is listening to his brother stomping around in the bathroom upstairs. The muffled sounds of Norman singing to himself "Come on Eileen" by Dexys Midnight Runners, number one on the charts. "Too-ra-loo-ra, too-ra-loo-rye, ay . . ."

In the vast open spaces between our occasional grunts, there was a solemn enough silence between my father and myself to remind me that I would never again spend a night in Cedarwood Road. I didn't know how to thank him for the years of shelter but I tried and he tried to accept.

"She's a great girl. I don't know what she sees in you."

"You're in here somewhere, Da, but yes, there's no explaining taste, is there?" A pause. How do I ask this?

"Iris and Ali . . . what do you think?"

"Well, your mother would have loved to see you married." Another pause.

"Just to get you out from under her!"

He's half laughing, trying not to nick his neck under the shaving foam, stretching the skin of his face over his words.

"Ali is a great girl. She's everything your mother could have asked for."

I ask him what he means by that.

"Safety," he says, staring at me.

Did I feel my heart beat a little irregularly there?

The kitchen door was open, and I could hear Mrs. Brady talking to someone over the wall. We had good neighbors, the angelic sweetness of the Blairs, the readiness to help of the Byrnes and the Williamses. It was Andrew Williams, over the road, who'd helped my father build these kitchen cabinets. I was trying not to look that interested, but the writer in me was taking notes, letting myself feel every sense and sound. The popping of the toaster, the steamy splashing of the towel on my father's red face and neck. The house looked good that morning, and my father was also going to look the part. He would dress to impress, a stylish man, "dapper" was what people said. He had a bit of style, Bob Hewson. In the next hour I would say goodbye to Cedarwood Road, to this house, to this street that I loved as well as liked. Goodbye to my childhood and teenage years. Goodbye to something else as well.

Goodbye to the aloneness of a boy who lived his exterior life collectively but kept his interior world very, very private. From now on this "one" would be half of two.

I could give myself to the ceremony, to Ali, to the force that brought us together, but could I give her the best of me when, at this stage, I hadn't really a clue who I was?

Maybe more of a quarter than a half. A band man more than a duo.

With crowds I was cocky, too comfortable in the big picture.

Wide-screen. I knew I could love at scale, but could I survive the intimacy of the close-up? As I stood in my wedding suit on the morning of the last day of summer, what would I have said if you'd asked me?

I'd have said, "I don't know how to do this, but I've found someone who can teach me."

I DO

In 1982 the band was starting to be famous, so there was a good crowd at the church when we got there, Adam and Norman having driven me and my da in my da's wine-red Hillman Avenger. All Saints' Church was originally a part of St. Anne's Park on a Guinness family estate.

My pin-striped morning suit looked as if it had rented me and I appeared to have a badger on my head. Or was it a toilet brush? It was quite a do, this protean version of the mullet that would mortally wound 1980s fashion. Even more impressive was the top of it, which was bleached blond. Nice. There were more bad haircuts inside the church and lots of people from the Monday night group, heartily singing and praising the Lord. Jack Heaslip, the teacher who saved my life at Mount Temple, now an Anglican priest, was officiating. As always he was calm and dignified, but did I detect a trace of mild panic as he surveyed the joyful noise of tambourines and out-of-tune revival singing? Jack was familiar with the charismatic Christianity of the day, and could be moved by it, but I sensed a little concern that this peaceful Church of Ireland chapel was about to be slaughtered by the Holy Rollers of Shalom.

Ali and her father parked around the corner, and when she walked into the church, she looked the kind of beautiful you can't exaggerate. But also looked, as she got closer, a tiny bit uncomfortable. I had arrived at the altar, a tiny bit late. On the day I was supposed to be signing the marriage register, I'd been explaining to people why I shouldn't be signing autographs at a church. Which took longer than signing the actual autographs. No, it wasn't my lateness, she whispered later. It was the attention, the photographers that all our friends had become.

Plus, she added, "I appear to have a flowerpot on my head."

Ali hadn't figured how to say "no" to her hipster hairstylist, who had gotten a little carried away on the horticulture. Despite her discomfort she carried the same serenity she always did, the kind I would spend my life trying to inhabit. The kind of beauty that invites more of it from those around her.

What emerges from pictures of our wedding day is a portrait of two people who couldn't be further from the rock 'n' roll culture that was bringing them celebrity. Gauche, naïve, unworldly, and completely unprepared for the challenges of their newly shared life in the world. And yet, conversely, in their raw, unsophisticated ideal-ism, two people ready for less obvious but more dangerous threats. Worldliness, world-weariness, the war of attrition the world wages on a couple as they set out to keep their union. The world licks its lips in anticipation of high-minded failure, doesn't it? Hubris. "They had it all but they lost it."

The universe may marvel at such perfectly imperfect love and the stars light your way, but back on earth, if you heed the statistics, it's as if the world stands in the way of love. I'm sure the essence of romance is defiance, and what is more defiant than two young hearts, twenty-two and twenty-one, deciding to take on the odds, to challenge the dull-thud facts around an ancient ceremony in a modern world.

As I stared a little longer into those veiled eyes, I wondered if Ali was ready to take on the life I'd chosen, even if she was ready to take me "for better or worse."

The reception was in the Sutton Castle Hotel, famous from the cover of the Van Morrison album *Veedon Fleece.* Quite quickly every-thing became a lovely mess. Despite all attempts to turn this cele-bration of a marriage into a Jumping for Jesus festival, there was just enough alcohol to keep this ecstatic moment grounded on earth. In the grand tradition the congregation set fire to themselves in their preferred manner: Holy Spirit or a whole lot of other spirits. Adam was the best man there too.

At about ten in the evening Ali and I slipped off, meandering down the Howth Road on a quick pilgrimage to the trysting places that had sheltered us as teenagers. We stopped by the school playing fields and dropped by the newsagent where on half days we'd purchase a ginger cake and a bottle of milk. Symbolically, we repeated the order to take back to our "honeymoon suite," spending our first night together in a large Victorian room laughing at the fact that the lights didn't work and we couldn't see each other. U2 had ended up playing a few songs at the reception—one with Barry Devlin from Horslips and another with Paul Brady—a jam that had me standing on the dining tables. Proud of our punk wedding band status, we had outdone ourselves by blowing out the hotel's power circuits. Alison and Paul, Ali and Bono, began our married lives in the dark.

JUST KIDS

Twenty-two and twenty-one but we could've been seventeen and sixteen. Just kids. We honeymooned in Jamaica, in GoldenEye, the house where Ian Fleming wrote the James Bond books. We were guests of Chris Blackwell, the man who brought the world Island Records. It was very fancy, unlike us. Arriving in Kingston, I'd felt as out of my depth as that first arrival in London. With no one to meet us, I found a pay phone, leaving Ali to negotiate the Kingston bustle. People generously offering to help us out with our cases. Ali talking them out of it.

"Misterrr Blackwell, Misterrr Blackwell."

Our driver turned up in a tiny Nissan van, eyes red as peppers and smoking a big spliff.

"I'm here for Mr. Blackwell."

That must be us. It was a bumpy ride along the north Jamaican coast to Oracabessa Bay in the neighborhood of Ocho Rios. Every village seemed to be painted in those bright colors that Europeans turn their noses up at, until they see them so artfully clashing on Caribbean shop fronts or in tropical town squares. Jamaicans are instinctively stylish. Our driver talks about Bob Marley without ever referring to his family name.

"Bob loved a game of cricket . . . Bob used to own GoldenEye . . . Bob was a fine footballer."

I picture the dreadlocked Marley kicking a football in his lime-green Adidas tracksuit, and I can see how the entire world converted to sportswear in his stylish wake. Our chaperone again: "You know

Bob only drive BMW cars because it spell out the name of his band? Bob Marley and the Wailers!"

An hour and a half of small talk and sign language between driver and cargo and we arrive at the first destination of our marital adventure. By now the sun is calling a truce with the day and a golden light paints the scene so that GoldenEye looks even more romantic to these tired and drooping honeymoon eyes. Seeing the singer with a bird of paradise on his head, a woman runs out of the house to greet us.

"Sting!" she screams. "It's so great to see you again!"

Violet, as we come to know her, is a welcoming fanfare of color as befits this villa, set in the wildest of well-planned gardens. The ackee and almond trees planted by Fleming himself are lit up by splashes of lime and the crimson of the poinciana, which is so flamboyant it is known locally as "flames of the forest." Violet walks us toward the sea, under a blood-orange sunset, waves crashing against the coral sand a hundred feet below.

"A moody enough sea for this time of year," she says.

A couple of rum punches deliver their knockout blows, and we're soon lying in a mild state of disbelief in our room, the kind draft of a mahogany propeller spinning in the ceiling above us. Our world is sort of spinning. We are being pulled in the drag of some tide that might just take us anywhere. Innocents abroad. Explorers, ready to explore each other.

Wherever we go, we will travel together.

BETWEEN INNOCENCE AND EXPERIENCE

It's only days since I'd left Cedarwood Road, and Ali, St. Assams Avenue, for the last time, but already we were feeling the distance between the gray-green certainties of our Irish upbringing and the more lush possibilities opening up for us. Between the pale gray skies of being home and the unflinching yellow sun of being away. Between innocence and experience.

From now on Ali and I will be looking for home in each other. But that said, though we now share a roof, I notice we are still a wee distance apart. An exciting distance. An electrically charged distance that Ali is teaching me to respect. One that sparks, flashing brightly, will leap across. The static. The kinetic. The static again. The mysterious distance between a man and a woman. She's magnetic.

We had never lived together, and we were conscious of our own self-consciousness. Is our laughter sometimes a little nervous? We had a lot of baggage and it wasn't in our suitcases. We spent a lot of every day unpacking each other. We've spent our life at the same task. All of us humans weighed down with so much stuff.

"What did you bring this for?" Ali asks, as I stretch this metaphor as far as it will go. "We don't need this."

"I didn't know I had that," I reply. "Maybe I need to get rid of it."

Already there was some yearning and learning for me. I wanted to be a better man for Ali. And in between tutorials on being wedded, in between swimming and walking, I did what I *did* know how to do. I went to work for U2.

Writing songs.

Edge was at home, writing on his own. Working on the song that might answer some of the hard questions he was asking about the band and whether we were ready to take on the very different world outside his window. He started "Sunday Bloody Sunday" without me. He had a TEAC four-track tape recorder and a black Stratocaster. With those choppy rhythmic chords I'm sure he was invoking The Clash, who in turn were invoking Bob Marley. But his fingerpicking of these same chords is the thing that cast the spell I fell under on my return.

We joke that some guitars have songs already in them. Well, sometimes that's true of chord sequences. I felt like the melody was already there. Of course it wasn't. At moments like this, Edge and I disappear into each other. Without Larry and Adam, I'm not sure how interested the rest of the world would be in finding us.

We had an album to make. *War*, we would call it. Songs of confrontation, songs of redemption, too, informed by the spirit of Jamaica. The spirit of Bob Marley. Even now when I sing a sloweddown version of "Sunday Bloody Sunday," all I can hear is Bob Marley's voice, and feel his fusion of love and rage. The three-chord strand that is his gospel: love, the longing for a loving world, and protest, the rage against present injustice.

I later discovered that Sting had written "Every Breath You Take" in that same room and, more significant to me, the exquisitely excruciating "King of Pain."

> *There's a little black spot on the sun today*
> *That's my soul up there.*

As a power trio, The Police are challenged for supremacy only by Nirvana or Cream. Sting's melodies are flawless, but like Paul Simon he allows the certainty of the melodies to recede in the lyrics. When he's exploring themes of vulnerability, he's invincible, and of course the irony is as painful as it is regal.

The greatest songwriting is never conclusive, but the search for conclusion. I had an idea for a song that would later be called "Surrender" and another called "Red Light." And one called "Two Hearts Beat as One." Some of the best titles are that obvious.

Ali and I were moving in together, and now we were beginning to move together. On paper our marriage started that honeymoon week, but in truth it didn't feel like that. We'd honored each other, made sacred vows, but the biggest moments in life may not be those we notice at the time. No fireworks, no explosions, no falling even more deeply in love now that we had time together.

We were the playwrights and the play, the actors and the critics. Excited and nervous to begin our adventure together. No idea where we'd be in ten years. Twenty. Thirty. I raise you again. Forty years.

We'll eventually figure out what was going on in that moment. Rather than falling in love, we were climbing up toward it.

We still are.

I can't believe the news today... ~· ·

all musical instruments are useful for later Exhortation only one is essential for WAR. THE DRUMS. The Drums are thin skin stretched tightly over hollow volumes mostly of wood which gives them their boominess their softness slapping what to the feeling the hand or the stick throwing across the skin & the drums ! booner a dance into a musical response

WAR

For WAR and in Particular Marching to WAR... wood was replaced (B) metal The Shield (B) its right in for good reason supplies body ARMOUR to already muscular forces CAVALRY LARRY MULLEN I don't even want to be at War But I don't even want to go to War without...

Sunday Bloody Sunday

I can't believe the news today
I can't close my eyes and make it go away
How long, how long must we sing this song?

All musical instruments are useful for love and exhortation.

Only one is essential for war. The drums. The drums are thin skin stretched tightly over hollow volumes, mostly of wood, which gives them their earthiness, their sexiness. Slapping without the tickling.

The hand or the stick bounces across the skin of the drums, throwing the listener forward into a dance, into a physical response.

For war, and in particular marching to war, wood was replaced by metal. The snare, as it's known for good reason, supplies body armor to the already athletic muscular choices available. There is a particular violence built into the snare drum, and the rat-a-tat of a military tattoo was exactly what we were looking for with the opening of "Sunday Bloody Sunday." I don't ever want to be at war with Larry Mullen, but I don't ever want to go to war without him.

From a very junior age, Larry Mullen has explained his craft and art like this: "I hit things for a living." And he does. He can hit people, too, not physically, but psychically. Most people who enter a room with Larry Mullen find him striking, in the sense that he is a stylish, good-looking member of the species but also in the sense that he can be suspicious of why you are in his gaze. Of your intentions, your being in the room, and, perhaps on a bad day, your reason for being anywhere at all.

Drummers are born, not made.

"COULD YOU TRY THAT AGAIN?"

From behind the wide-screen futurism that was the glass of Windmill Lane Recording Studios, Steve Lillywhite is producing our third album, *War,* with the patience you have to have to be a world-class record producer at just twenty-seven. Two years after our first album, we are not musical sophisticates. We have talent, but playing in tune and in time in the antiseptic environs of a modern recording studio is not a walk in the park for any of us. Scrutiny creates self-consciousness, and musical parts that were arrived at intuitively can change in subtle ways that make them less rhythmic or less locked in with the other musicians. This in turn leads to awkward moments in the control room, where words like "tightness" and "looseness" substitute for "this sounds boring" and "I never really liked this one."

It's particularly hard for the bass and drums—the foundation of any recording—and today they are under a microscope with a system of sensitive microphones that wrap their spider legs around amp and kit from every direction. This is not an environment conducive to art. The room feels more like an operating theater than a stage, surgeons conferring on how best to fix the limp in question.

Corrective surgery or amputation? The patient lies under the gaze and glare of the production team, Steve Lillywhite and his engineer, Paul Thomas. There is a lot of stopping and starting. Steve's matter-of-fact tones now a tinny voice coming through our "cans."

"Could you try that again?" is common usage for "That wasn't good enough." Is Larry Mullen cracking under the pressure? Not quite. He can just about take Steve Lillywhite's implicit criticism because Steve is famous for his dominant drum sounds. And because Larry knows this is a great song.

All of us seem to know. Steve has told us a great song can be played on an acoustic guitar with a tabletop as drums. And there was a certain completeness in the earliest, rawest expression of this song that we'd played around the kitchen table in our rehearsal room out on the beach at Sutton, where Ali and I lived. The street where Larry would make his home years later.

Steve taught us to test our material by kind of campfiring it to figure out if we had a good enough chorus or hook. Songs, said Steve, were all about the hook.

In a Bob Dylan song the hook can be a phrase, one you thought had always existed, for example "the times they are a-changin'." Nothing much in that—everybody knew the times were changing—but the emphasis, "the times *they* are a-changin'," and the tone of voice create an undertow of jeopardy.

The hook might be just a guitar line. Everyone who's ever walked into a guitar shop knows the riff from Deep Purple's "Smoke on the Water."

"No one listens to the lyrics." Edge, who is a fine lyricist, likes to wind me up. With "Sunday Bloody Sunday," the drums were the hook.

Lawrence Joseph Mullen Jr. was a member of the Artane Boys Band out of Dublin's Northside. A military silver marching band, they would perform on grand occasions like St. Patrick's Day or Gaelic football matches at Croke Park. They were there to swell the emotions, the pride in your Irishness. It was Larry Mullen Sr. who found his son a place with the Artane Boys Band so that Larry Mullen Jr. would stop drumming on the head of Larry Mullen Sr.

Looking for a reason to stay in the band, Edge had begun the bitter contemplation that would become "Sunday Bloody Sunday," taking himself to a place where music might suggest another kind of world that, according to our church group, Shalom, was broken and needed mending. Edge wanted the band to sing about "the Troubles" in Northern Ireland, troubles that were causing so much pain in our country and over in the U.K., where an IRA bombing campaign was under way.

I liked the title he came up with, via John Lennon, "Sunday Bloody Sunday," but I thought we needed to find an original way in. Could we point out the chasm of difference between people killing for a political cause and people dying for one? Was it possible, in a song, to contrast Ireland's Easter Rising of 1916 with the slumped body of a Messiah, hanging on a cross at the first Easter, AD 33? And could it sound like The Clash?

(Please.)

While "I can't believe the news today" subconsciously tipped its hat to The Beatles' "A Day in the Life," the song actually refers to what happened in the picturesque walled city of Derry, Northern Ireland, on January 30, 1972, a day tattooed on the mind of every Irish person of a certain age. A day of images we can never unsee. The chaos of a large crowd corralled and beaten by riot police, the British army stepping in with deadly force. Twenty-eight people shot, fourteen of them fatally, during a peaceful protest by the Northern Ireland Civil Rights Association. Even now I can sketch the pained face of Father Edward Daly holding up a bloodstained white handkerchief in an ambulant prayer of "don't shoot." I was eleven and I still feel the nausea.

The band talked for hours about the state of our country and what Christ would make of the religion begun in his name. Not much, we thought. Christianity seemed to have become the enemy of the radical Jesus of Nazareth. Was there any evidence Jesus even wanted a church? Our own church group, Shalom, had broken down under the weight of a certain judgmentalism. Despite emerging somewhat shaken from the immersive experience of Shalom, we were sure our faith could survive our faith. Our music, though? That was another matter. If we lost our purpose, our band was back where it began: looking for a reason to exist.

VOICE AND DRUM

On tour in 2015, I'm in the center of the venue, at the far end of a walkway stage stretching lengthways over the arena floor, dividing our audience in two. "Song for Someone" hangs in the air as I squeeze out "I know there are many reasons to doubt, but if there is a light don't let it go out." Into this tender moment breaks the muted violence of *that* drum hook.

Larry, now fifty-three, walks along the stage in my direction, repeating his snare mantra, his marching drum a gun.

How long? How long must we sing this song?

A long time, actually, already more than a third of a century. Larry has an unusual concentration; he is single-minded. He is there for the audience by signaling to them that he is not theirs. He is his own man. A protective layer, rooted in his artistic sensitivity, covers him. He is often on guard lest somebody take advantage of what could be vulnerability. There are no artists I know who are not caught in this duality, but Larry has made some cool threads out of his protective layer. I'm not far behind, but I don't cover up as well.

He is the most rock star and the least rock star that anyone could be. He likes—and he doesn't—the life that comes with it. There's something deep and primal in the relationship between a drummer and a singer, the oldest and most primitive of communications, the rhythm and the melody. Tapping and birdsong. The slow, hesitant discovery that in a great band we are both shadow and shelter for each other. "Need" is the word that comes to mind.

When Larry loves people, he loves them completely, and I am one of the beneficiaries of that love, which I trace back to when he was seventeen and I was eighteen and his mother, Maureen, was suddenly taken from him in a terrible road accident. He and his family had already suffered great loss with the death of his younger sister Mary, five years earlier. What cruel blows are meted out to the kindest hearts.

I suppose our shared grief gave us an extra bond.

Maureen was an angel. Really. An actual angel. To stand next to her, as I often did before or after rehearsal, was to feel blessed. She was utterly unvarnished, and she idolized her Irish idol son. She drove him to practice. She waited for him at rehearsals. She let Larry grow his hair long when every other mother refused, and this hair business was important because getting the right look was essential for an apprentice idol, however unconscious the apprenticeship. Glam rock had been Larry's first love, the reason he put up that notice in school. His favorite bands were Slade, the Sweet,

T. Rex, and David Bowie. Larry couldn't stand jazz, and jazz was the reason his dad let him have a drum kit. So-called serious music was never Larry's bag, and that tells you how Larry became a pop star. By pretending he was going to play jazz.

Drummers are born, pop stars are packaged, but rock stars are the self-made members of the species that is *Homo erectus* show business. I wonder if Larry loves being a rock star more than he will own up to, but I have no doubt that he is the best equipped to play Rock Star in U2. Adam wanted to be one and pulled it off—until it pulled him off his pedestal and he had to get sober. I pretended, still do, but am not fully convincing despite the bully pulpit. Edge always knew it was a folly, no job for a grown-up. Larry became a rock star by denying it was ever his intention.

There's nothing Maureen wouldn't do for us in those very first days trying to become a band. She drove us everywhere in their Morris 1300, wearing a man's anorak with a big hood, in case it started to rain while she and Larry were packing away his drums. She and Gwenda, Edge's mother, were our first road crew. Adam's mother, Jo, would occasionally turn up, but that was like a visit from Princess Margaret. Dressed like royalty, cigarette in her left hand, shaking hands with her right, complaining to Maureen that she and Brian hadn't put Adam in boarding school to have him play bass in some punk band. It didn't bother Maureen. "As long as Larry's happy, I don't mind what he does."

Larry's father was harder on him. Our prize for winning a talent competition was a series of recording sessions. In the city's Keystone Studios in November 1978, the producer—an actual, real music producer, who would become a lifelong friend—was Barry Devlin, singer, songwriter, and bandleader with Horslips, among the most successful electric folk groups on the planet. We were nervous and played badly, a little in awe of the tape-op who was so much more sophisticated than us. Her name was Mariella Frostrup. It also didn't help that a couple of hours in, there was a bang on the door. Larry's father. It was time for Larry to go home. And, by the way, this was not the jazz band he'd agreed to let his son join.

When Larry's mother died, we discovered community is found not just in location and culture but in shared experience. It's sorrow rather than joy that often glues people together, and Larry and I became close. We were bonding over something bigger than music. We were bonding over the reason music is made. How it is balm for the ache inside us, a dressing for the wounds we hide.

Perhaps the vulnerability that makes Larry a sensitive musician explains how he may also appear wary of people he doesn't know. He is the band's bodyguard, the one who senses trouble round the corner and is often right. Some days he will stand, gloves off, and as far as I can tell there's absolutely no threat whatsoever in the room. But he is the perfect antidote to a person like me who goes looking for trouble.

As a musician he has mastered the art of remaining the student.

"I'm not very good at this."

"I'm a journeyman."

"I'm not sure what all this pretentious stuff is about. I just play the drums."

In truth Larry has a much more complex view of life and music than he lets on, but as with a great actor, when he delivers those lines, they ring true. A desire for honesty is at the heart of his expression, and this honesty part charges, in an electrical sense, the U2 show. Singer and drummer in this band have very different personalities. I'm the curious one, while he's the cautious one. There are times when I will introduce him to worlds he might not have entered and times when he will protect me from worlds I should never enter.

THIS IS NOT A REBEL SONG

Once Edge had taken us across the border with his sketch of a song about "the Troubles," the band could not stop me from heading deeper and deeper into difficult territory. I feel I have a kind of perverse tic when I'm told not to say or do something. It makes it all the more attractive. "Sunday Bloody Sunday" was not just dangerous subject matter to be singing in the sense of the obvious pitfalls if you were a kid from the south. It was actually dangerous in the sense that on hearing it, some people wanted to hurt us. Some people from both sides of the sectarian divide. For unthinking unionists it was a betrayal. For unthinking nationalists and republicans it was an advertising campaign, one to awaken a sense of outrage about these twenty-eight unarmed civilians gunned down while making a peaceful demonstration.

The song arrived after the death of hunger striker Bobby Sands on May 5, 1981. Sands was a poetic soul arguing with his life that the Provisional IRA were fighting a war and that jailed combatants deserved the same status as any POW, such as the right not to wear a prison uniform. It was not an unreasonable request, but it seemed to pass their supporters by that the IRA didn't observe the Geneva Convention. Or any other convention.

When his incarcerated protest went unnoticed by the British prime minister, Margaret Thatcher, Sands took his hunger strike to the next level. Now he wore nothing but a blanket and refused to use the toilet facilities. This "Dirty Protest," prisoners smearing feces on their cell walls, was among the most anguished moments of the IRA's campaign to force the British out of the island of Ireland.

These paramilitaries didn't have majority support north or south of the border. Not even among the embattled Catholic minority in Ulster, and yet they decided who lived or died in their fight to redraw the map of Ireland. Still, Sands choosing to take his own life at twenty-seven after refusing to eat for sixty-six days caused all sorts of conflicting emotions for run-of-the-mill nationalists like me.

It was more than just a tragedy. It was also a death that became the most powerful international fundraiser in the history of the IRA, most of all in the United States, where the band felt compelled to resist any romantic ideas about the armed struggle back home. At our shows and in interviews we offered a counternarrative about nonviolence, attempting to dry up IRA cash flow, knowing that it would put guns and bombs in the hands of combatants who would maim and kill to forcibly install their version of Ireland. Unelected combatants deciding if a pub in Belfast or Manchester was a "legitimate target." Or if a parade of pensioners and World War II veterans could be blown to bits with no warning.

Sure, after every new atrocity, in the most hard-core republican communities, there'd be hand-wringing over the "unfortunate loss of life." For a week or two . . . until the furor died down and it was back to a blind eye and grunted cheers for "our lads." This duplicity incensed people north and south of the border. It incensed me, which helps explain my shrill introduction of "Sunday Bloody Sunday" from a show in Red Rocks, Colorado, a night when we would have a wider than usual audience given that it was being filmed for U.K. television.

As Edge played his plaintive arpeggiation in the rain and Larry rat-a-tat-tatted, I spewed, "This is not a rebel song!" with all the self-righteousness I could muster.

What it lacked in eloquence it made up for in brevity. It seemed the right moment to get the word out that we were not prepared to have our song co-opted to further continue the suffering of innocents like those who lost their lives or their loved ones on that dark January day.

That version took us to the top of the album charts with the live LP *Under a Blood Red Sky* and to the top of the shit list for all republican sympathizers. Things would never be quite the same for us at home.

As a band, we'd never labored our "Irishness." I was increasingly frustrated at how "Irishness" could be taken hostage by the republican movement, a movement that believed in the forceful restoration of a single country on the island of Ireland. A movement starting to appropriate generations of previous agitators and fighters for independence, drawing deeply on a wealth of poetry, folk songs, and lore whose authors would have had nothing to do with these gunmen.

To me being Irish wasn't about being a Protestant or a Catholic. Some of the greatest revolutionaries against British rule were Irish Protestants, from Wolfe Tone to Maud Gonne to Roger Casement. My da was Catholic, but he, too, wouldn't swallow the rhetoric of these so-called freedom fighters.

"I'm a Catholic," he would tell me. "And I can tell you the division of our small island was much more to do with keeping Harland & Wolff in the union than to protect the Protestants. They wanted the shipbuilding and the linen. The south only accepted the border under the threat of war by your man Lloyd George, but for all the injustice these gunmen do not represent a majority anywhere on this island—south of the border or north.

"Ignore their clichés," he would add, before reeling off one of his favorite lines from Seán O'Casey. (Except it wasn't from Seán O'Casey; he'd made it up.)

"What is Ireland but the land that keeps my feet from getting wet?"

Plus, he had himself married a woman from "another community." He was half serious in suggesting all countries were falsehoods— "They are stories we tell each other"—and he was suspicious of who controlled the narrative.

That said, he was a little shocked to see me onstage in the Rocky Mountains pursuing performance art which involved tearing up the Irish flag. A flag was often thrown at me during shows, and sometimes I would dismantle the orange and the green, reinventing it as a white flag and attempting some support for nonviolence. Later, I began to emphasize the white flag as an image of spiritual surrender, but for now we allowed ourselves a kind of militant pacifism.

This overexplaining was not always popular at home, and a growing number of people were questioning our patriotism. It was a slow dawning for some. Two years later, playing Croke Park on the Unforgettable Fire Tour in 1985, I embarked on the same flag-cutting performance, and some of the crowd couldn't stomach it. After the show, the car that Ali and I were in became trapped in a Dublin side street, an angry conflagration surrounding us, banging the roof, screaming support for the men of violence they were quickly becoming. One contorted young man, a tricolor wrapped around his fist, tried to smash the windshield beside Ali's face. Something else cracked. We were fish in a fishbowl and the piranhas on the other side of the glass had been U2 fans only a few hours earlier.

Things were changing for U2 in Ireland toward the end of the '80s. For a while it was as if we'd been the national team bringing home the silverware. We were still local heroes but there was a little bit of a mood change. In the world outside U2, the eighties felt like a fight for the soul as much as the size of the country. The border becoming more and more internalized, the island more tribal. Neither the band's mix of backgrounds nor our individual theologies fit easily into any of the tribes.

In a *Hot Press* interview, Gerry Adams, the leader of Sinn Féin, had the guts and moral candor to question "the armed struggle" he and his party had marched alongside, if not led. In the same article he chose the aromatic verb "stinks" to describe me. As an assessment of my personal hygiene maybe it was tough love, but as vituperation it sent a tacit signal to hard-core Republicans that I was, and there is no other word for it, a piece of shit.

For those already pissed off that U2's opposition to paramilitaries (of all kinds) had cost the IRA valuable fundraising in the U.S., this was a vexed signal for their growing sympathizers, some in the media, to kick U2 off their national perch. Especially the singer. Practically, we were advised to increase our security after a prosperous dentist had been kidnapped, with the tips of two of his fingers sent as ransom. When Special Branch came to see us, however, they predicted Ali was the more likely target. I still take that badly for all kinds of reasons.

The band's deep hope is that Ireland will, by peaceful and democratic means, one day become a united Ireland again. Ironically we think the biggest obstacle to that end is the weaponizing of grievances by paramilitaries.

SOME FUNNY UNFUNNY INCIDENTS

I love to be in Northern Ireland. The band playing Belfast is a highlight of any tour. We love Nordies for their gallows humor. There's always plenty of scaffolding, that's for sure.

After an early support slot with Squeeze in 1979, we were invited to an aftershow party, all pretty festive, until our car was pulled over and surrounded by British soldiers. An officer, in blunt northern English tones, ordered our hands over our heads and invited us to stand against a wall.

"What have you got in the boot of your car?" he demanded.

The answer was some expensive luggage, in the form of our bass player, Adam Clayton, who had been toasting pedestrians every time the boot of the car bumped open . . . not considering that in Belfast a car boot can be the favored hiding place of a sniper, not carpool karaoke.

Our lesson not learned, that night we were staying in Belfast's Europa, which had a reputation as the most bombed hotel in Europe—thirty-three times. Still in our teens, we were a little over-excited to be in an actual hotel, any hotel. Paul McGuinness was at the bar when we stole his key from reception, hurried up to his room, and dismantled it. Wrapping the television in the bedsheets, we upturned the furniture and scrawled a message in shaving foam on the bathroom mirror: "We know where you park your car." I suppose we must've thought Paul would find us funny, and even if he didn't, he would surely appreciate his clients' sophisticated grasp of rock-star antics when it came to hotel rooms. We were never to know. Half an hour later, key safely returned to reception and trying to hide our glee, we joined him at the bar—only to witness a complete stranger arrive to ask for the same key. Wrong room. Humblest apologies to whoever you are.

If you're going to joke about serious issues, the least you can do is get the punchline right.

THE MOST UNDERESTIMATED WORD IN THE LEXICON

"Compromise" is surely among the most underestimated words in the lexicon. If parity of pain was the essence of the Good Friday Agreement in 1998, it was only possible because, long before, extremists on both sides had been persuaded to consider compromise. In the Good Friday Agreement everyone won because no one won.

Some of the greatest words in the English language are some of the dullest, and some of the most romantic can be the most useless. The word "peace," for example, is meaningless without a framework.

THE GOOD FRIDAY DISAGREEMENT

In 1997, Tony Blair and Bertie Ahern were elected to high office in the U.K. and the Republic of Ireland, sensing a mandate from their respective electorates to try to achieve a lasting peace for Ireland. Senator George Mitchell, who was President Clinton's special envoy, became the chair of the peace talks that ensued. Eight different political parties in Northern Ireland participated, three of them linked to paramilitary groups (two loyalist, one republican), the two mainstream parties being the Ulster Unionist Party (UUP), led by David Trimble, and the Social Democratic and Labour Party (SDLP), led by John Hume. David Trimble risked his reputation with the more traditional Protestant community who had sworn never to negotiate with terrorists. Hume had lived "nonviolence" and on a few occasions nearly died for these high principles.

So many unknown faces deserve credit for compromise, but from U2's point of view, John Hume was the Martin Luther King of the Irish Troubles. Hume also set up the credit union in Derry, which helped Catholics into housing in Northern Ireland, a defiant act, as up until 1969 only property owners could vote in local elections. In August 2020, when he passed, I wrote a micro eulogy for the service in St. Eugene's Cathedral in Derry:

We were looking for a giant and found a man who made all our
  lives bigger.
We were looking for some superpowers and found clarity of
  thought, kindness, and persistence.
We were looking for revolution and found it in parish halls with
  tea and biscuits and late-night meetings under fluorescence.
We were looking for a negotiator who understood that no one
  wins unless everyone wins and loses something and that
  peace is the only victory.

You would think there would be massive support for a peace deal from regular people who just wanted to live lives free from the kind of religious apartheid that lingered in Ireland. But bitterness can be a hard taste to spit out, so when it came to the actual referendum in 1998, the vote was looking too close to call. Bitterness was holding on. Famously, Belfast's unionist-run city hall had a giant sign: "Belfast Says NO." (They had the good grace, one year at Christmas, to add an E and an L for the holidays: "Belfast says NOEL."). Unfunny, but funny. As the youth vote was not looking certain, three days before the referendum U2 were asked to take part in the Concert for Yes, along with the Downpatrick band Ash. We were delighted but only agreed on the condition that the two opposing party leaders would come onstage and shake hands. And one other thing—which sounded even more implausible—that neither the UUP leader, David Trimble, nor the SDLP leader, John Hume, would speak.

Asking a politician to turn up to a large gathering and not speak was like asking a comedian to come onstage and not tell a joke. Both men were nonplussed. We felt sure that the symbolism would travel further than any words, plus we cautioned that any politicians speaking at a rock show risked getting booed. That would be awkward, so both men agreed to walk on, one from the left and one from the right, and in a moment that signified why John Hume and David Trimble would later win the Nobel Peace Prize, they shook hands for about three seconds. When I stepped in to lift their hands high into the air, they didn't know they were copying the visual language from a Bob Marley photograph in 1978, where two opposing politicians—Manley and Seaga—came together onstage in Kingston, Jamaica, for fear of the violence engulfing that island. There again, the photograph crystallized something, an image far more powerful than words.

There would be a long way to go on the road to lasting peace, but on May 22, 1998, Ulster said Yes.

The day after the vote, Ireland began the slow dismantling of prejudice with most of the acronyms—UDA, UVF, IRA—turning away from violence and the paramilitaries promising to swap the ArmaLite rifle for the ballot box. This is ongoing.

On the unionist side David Ervine played a significant role. Gerry Adams, despite his denial of involvement in the "armed struggle," deserves his share of the credit. It takes a lot of courage to change course when the cost of your previous paths had been so high.

Martin McGuinness stepped from his paramilitary spotlight into the daylight of realpolitik. He admitted being in the senior IRA leadership, and when he also changed course, this changed the course of history . . . later becoming one half of "the Chuckle Brothers," as his friendship with his former archenemy the Reverend Ian Paisley became known.

Leaving an event in New York in 2008, I felt a presence behind me and turned around to see Gerry Adams. He'd been unwell, so I asked how he was doing and told him that I appreciated the fact that during the campaign to cancel the debts of poor countries, he'd paid a quiet visit to the Jubilee 2000/Drop the Debt offices in London. As he put out his hand, I reached out and shook it. Likely a harder moment for him than me. I appreciated the gesture.

Looking back, if it wasn't for President Bill Clinton's conscious insomnia and late-night wrangling of the various warring parties or the fastidiousness of his knight-errant George Mitchell, I'm not sure we would have peace in Ireland. I feel the same about Bertie Ahern and U.K. prime minister Tony Blair, who spent countless hours on jaw-jaw rather than war-war. Clinton and Blair were also beginning a transformation—still incomplete—in relations between the old colonial powers and the African continent. We had lobbied both of them hard on debt cancellation. No head of state worked harder on this than Blair and his Chancellor-of-the-Exchequer-next-door, Gordon Brown. Between them they would also double the U.K.'s overseas aid budget. That can sound abstract, but death by mosquito bite or dirty water is not abstract at all.

In the third term of Tony Blair's government, I enjoyed a late dinner at 10 Downing Street. We'd had a running joke about the other life he could have led had he remained as lead singer of the rock band Ugly Rumours. He had the looks, the stage presence, the top-line melody. I'd half-seriously referred to him and Gordon Brown as the Lennon and McCartney of international development, they were so prolific. Tony Blair was not a drinker, but I got him to open a bottle and he had a glass and a half. I might have had two and a half. Perhaps he forgot the time—I certainly forgot he was British prime minister—but just after midnight he remembered he was late for an important call. There was some good-humored panic on his face when he uttered a phrase of such excruciatingly common usage that I nearly missed its significance. "Could you let yourself out?"

Here am I, an Irishman, finding myself with free roam in the private residence of the British prime minister. Change arrives so casually I thought, before realizing I didn't actually know how to let myself out.

Making for the stairs, soon I'm completely lost, a child in a department store walking in and out of rooms, flicking on and off the lights. These familiar faces on the walls looking down at me— Winston Churchill, Margaret Thatcher, Harold Wilson.

And there he is, David Lloyd George, the prime minister who'd divided our island into north and south under the threat of war.

"Hello, can I help you?"

A grown-up in uniform finds me and courteously escorts me off the premises.

To advance peace in Ireland, Blair had been prepared to risk his reputation in sanctioning secret meetings with leaders of paramilitary organizations. If his early reputation as prime minister became synonymous with peace, he certainly put that reputation at risk by standing with George Bush in an unpopular war in Iraq.

The man who brought people together was also ready to divide them.

"TONY BLAIR—WAR CRIMINAL."

The headline in an Irish newspaper in March 2007, the morning after a ceremony at the Dublin residence of the British ambassador where I've received an honorary knighthood from the roundtable that was Blair and Brown and Her Majesty the Queen's Government. For services trying to fight poverty in her former colonies. Although, maybe that wasn't quite how it was put.

The newspaper headline? That was a quote from my bandmate Larry, who didn't come along to the ceremony. I doubt he and I are ever going to agree on Tony Blair. My own quote, then and now, is a more personal mantra: "Compromise is a costly word. No compromise even more so."

A BELL TOLLING

Twenty fifteen and back on the elongated walkway of the Innocence + Experience stage. "Sunday Bloody Sunday" comes to a close, and the band walks in single file toward the main stage. Larry stops and is left alone on the runway, a solitary figure playing a lonely beat in a huge crowd.

He holds his sticks over his head. His marching drum is about to introduce the apocalypse that is "Raised by Wolves" and a Dublin car bomb exploding on our screens.

He slams the snare. It's a gunshot.

GOOD , better , best . . . . .

ENO + LANOIS

GUCK PANTS Delaney
and how the best of us can
be made better or worse by
the company we keep . . . .

13

Bad

If you twist and turn away
If you tear yourself in two again
If I could, you know I would
If I could, I would let it go
Surrender.

My father, Bob, worked in the postal service. So did Brian Eno's. My da did not deliver the mail, but on his instructions I did, a holiday job in the winter of 1976. It's not easy, what with the weather, the addresses, all the different kinds of post. Brian would tell us that he could trace his lineage back to Raphael, in the sixteenth century. I thought it amazing that Raphael had a postman in his line, but Brian wasn't talking about postmen; he was talking about art school. To Brian the lineage of ideas is more important than blood. You're owned by your ideas. Although U2 never went to art school, we did go to Brian. Brian Eno was the keyboard player in Roxy Music, the great British group of the glam rock era. Albums don't come much better than the first two Roxy Music albums, a kind of blueprint for punk rock with their vivid colors, fluid sexuality, and experimentation. In period photographs Brian is wearing ostrich feathers, and when a packed theater was going off for Roxy Music, he'd usually have his head buried in the sandpit of his synthesizer, making all kinds of neon noises that might not, at first, appear very musical.

He had produced David Bowie.

He had produced Talking Heads.

It was rumored he'd been offered the chance to produce Television, which was all the confirmation we needed that he could take us to another level. In 1983 we saw ourselves as a rock band in the image of The Clash, but we were probably more like The Who. Our songs had a spiritual yearning and melodrama that The Clash were just too streetwise for. But when we spoke with Island Records about working with Brian, they were dismissive.

The dialogue went something like this.

"You're the first U.K.-signed band that might have the success of The Clash or The Who. Brian Eno doesn't like rock music. Are you out of your minds?"

"No."

"Have you heard his last album?"

"No."

"It's just out."

"And?"

"It's an album with bird noises."

The album was called *Ambient 4: On Land*.

We were a rock band, they were right about that, but that's who we *were*. It's not who we were going to be. We didn't quite know what that was yet, but we had a hunch, a slow epiphany, that Brian Eno would help us find out.

When I called Brian up, he was not particularly curious about our work. I don't believe he was pretending when he said he hadn't heard any of our songs. Evidently in a posture to turn us down, he was apologizing before the call got going, but he made one admission: a friend of his, the trumpeter Jon Hassell, had told him there was something about our band that was more than the usual colors in the rock 'n' roll spectrum. Something different, something "other."

This apparently intrigued Brian because, as he explained, in the year 2050 people will look back on the rock era with one thought: how similar everyone sounded to everyone else. The same rough beats, the same bluesy-type emotions, and the same antiestablishment stance. I found this hard to take, knowing how very different we were from, say, Echo and the Bunnymen, let alone The Beatles. I now know it to be true.

He told me that A minor to D should be outlawed in composition, before asking if we'd be interested in doing an album without any minor chords. At the very least, he said, we should make sure that the sex of the chord is not clear. He meant minor or major. I seized my chance.

"But that's what Edge does with his guitar style," I explained. "That's what we do as a band. We share a guitar chord, often a suspended chord, and try to avoid those obvious blues notes which put it in a minor key or those obvious major chords which make things jolly and smiley."

Brian Eno was becoming interested.

We were in the conversation. At the end of the call he name-checked a young Canadian collaborator, Daniel Lanois, doing exceptional work recording artists outside the normal studio environs. That chimed with our idea for where we would record this fourth studio album—in the ballroom of Slane Castle, on a famous country estate owned by Henry Mountcharles, a friend of Adam's. That ballroom was known for its unusual acoustic qualities.

"I wonder, could you work with Daniel Lanois?" inquired Brian.

"Absolutely," I replied. "If you're there."

A deal was struck and these two men, for very different reasons, arrived in our life. Daniel to develop a level of musicality that we would never have found without him. Brian, the atheist iconoclast, with a secret penchant for Russian icons and gospel music, to blow up the past. And there were to be no minor chords.

THE WIZARD OF WANDERLUST

Lord Henry Mountcharles was interested in music and also trying to figure out how to pay for his castle, which is where we came in. Anyone who'd seen the ballroom in Slane Castle could not but be in awe of its splendor. It was the splendor of the sound that attracted us; we were after the big music, in search of the operatic. It was in that ballroom singing "Pride (In the Name of Love)" where I first felt like the tenor my father never thought I could be.

At our first meeting I was struck that Brian looked more like an architect than I'd imagined a former Roxy Music man would. He wore a leather suit jacket with a leather tie and a shirt but not in the old punk way. It was elegant. Really elegant. Almost precise. And yet six months later, when he'd finished producing *The Unforgettable Fire*, he was not looking so elegant. He was a broken man, begging to be taken to the airport, routinely sleeping on the floor under our mixing desk. Despite the big billing, in the studio it was Brian's humility that struck me. Word was he'd been in trouble with Talking Heads, supposedly because he wanted to work with David Byrne as a solo artist. He certainly didn't feel like that about me; he focused on every band member, made everyone feel very special.

Larry didn't know what to make of him, but "Danny Boy" Lanois had him covered. Danny arrived with all kinds of drums and went straight into a conversation about how we could come up with a uniquely rhythmic approach to rock music without using drum machines, which we were also using.

Larry did not like drum machines. The reason Larry Mullen didn't like drum machines is that Larry Mullen is a drum machine. He has an incredible sense of timing. He could've been in Kraftwerk.

Danny and he fell into a wonderful working relationship.

"Have you tried turning off your snares? Have you tried working with timbales?"

While Danny had arrived in partnership with his comrade Brian, initially it was almost in adoration. We discovered this man was himself a uniquely gifted musician. I've never seen someone hold an instrument like him, whether it's a drum, a guitar, a slide, a maraca. Many can claim to love music, but very few, in my experience, can claim music loves them back, not the way music loved Daniel Lanois. Like King David in the Bible, afflicted with a demon that only music could quiet, when the music was going well, Danny was too. When the music wasn't, the deep well inside him appeared disturbed, and he could grumble and become tetchy. Music was oxygen for Danny; without it he would suffocate.

It was the wanderlust that drew us to Brian. We used to talk about the three primary colors of rock 'n' roll—bass, drums, guitar—but there are times when that palette feels limited and you want to stretch what's possible from a combo like U2. As a group you can be envious of solo performers, artists who can just bring in a whole new set of musicians. David Bowie went from working with Mick Ronson and the Spiders in one year to working with Carlos Alomar. He moved from arch-English drama rock to soulful American R&B. He changed the band; he changed his sound.

That's not so easy if you're *in* a band. The Beatles used orchestration and the prowess of George Martin as an arranger to get them to new acoustic and harmonic locations. In some ways we'd grown up on the electronica of the mid-1970s, not just Kraftwerk, but Can. Edge had worked with Holger Czukay. But in 1984 we were experiencing musical wanderlust. We didn't want the cold removed vocals of electronic music, but imagine what it would be like to hear Van Morrison sing with D.A.F.? What had Donna Summer been doing recording with Giorgio Moroder? In fact, Brian had brought the song "I Feel Love" into the studio with David Bowie when they were working on *Low* in Berlin, a moment when they understood everything had to change.

It was with just such a thought that our song "Bad" came into focus. Most people don't hear the similarity between Lou Reed and Van Morrison, don't realize that they mine the same arpeggiations, the same chordal repetitions. That they invoke the same spell, one with his deadpan New York storytelling, the other with his extraordinary soul and voice, among the greatest male singers, certainly up there with Sam Cooke or even Elvis. With "Bad" we were after the soulful intensity of Van Morrison and the street poetry of Lou Reed. Unfortunately, the poetry was not so eloquent.

Unfortunately, the song was never finished.

Unfortunately for the lyricist, Brian Eno loved the sound of unfinished songs.

Fortunately, for people who think "Bad" is one of our finest moments, Brian had his way. And though I'm left every night filling in the gaps of this most unwritten lyric, I see how it is mouth music, invocation, tongue singing. I see how it transports people.

I realize it is an impossibility to conjure the confused mood around intravenous drug taking, specifically heroin. Guggi's younger brother Andrew "Guck Pants Delaney" Rowen was on my mind as I splashed/smeared paint on the canvas. Impressionism, expressionism, over-reachism. It's an impertinence to imagine I could step into Guck Pants's shoes, but that's what I was doing. A conscious and unconscious attempt at empathy, it was a conversation with someone who was not there. It would be years before that could happen. Andy was impossible not to love—although a ghost looking for his body back. His family and friends were terrified of losing him to this epidemic of opiate abuse that was the scourge of so many cities and suburbs in the early '80s. But few ties are as binding as addiction. I tried. I failed. "Inarticulate speech of the heart" is what Van Morrison called such poesy.

"CAN I HAVE YOUR AUTOGRAPH?"

It was that July 1984, while we were recording *The Unforgettable Fire* with Brian and Danny, that the grounds of Slane became the venue for what would turn out to be a massive Bob Dylan show.

Bob Dylan occupied the same space to me in poetry as Yeats or Kavanagh or Keats, but he had two other qualities that had him even higher in my sky: his heavenly inquiries and his earthy sense of humor. In his earliest shows in Greenwich Village, Bob Dylan did Charlie Chaplin impersonations between songs, and there is something of the scallywag about him. Something you can't not like if you meet it. In the late 1970s he reminded the world that Christianity started out life as a Jewish sect, and he allowed it to be known that he had some vision of Christ that had saved his life. Visions are de rigueur for poets, but humor is not. Bob Dylan has had me laughing out loud at his recordings more than any other artist, and even though I hadn't got to know him in 1984, to be sleeping on the same grounds that this time-traveling troubadour was about to grace with his songs was a special gift. Such was my excitement that I could hardly speak on the day of the show, which was when a stranger tapped me on the shoulder.

"Can I have your autograph?" asked Bob Dylan.

I now appreciate that that was a very Bob Dylan thing to do, to turn the tables completely. Bumping into Bob Dylan? What's that like? It's like bumping into Willie Shakespeare. I knew I was on hallowed ground, if not on solid ground. I was not worthy to tie the laces of his moccasins, but I caught my balance and challenged him to a chess game.

That's right—a chess game.

Bob Dylan had invited me backstage, to some kind of tent where I would interview him, along with Van Morrison, for *Hot Press* magazine, quizzing them both on their love of Irish traditional music. Bob recited all of "The Auld Triangle," made famous by Brendan Behan and his brother Dominic. Not four verses, not five . . . all six. He knew, by heart, the verses that even most Irish people don't know. He told me he'd grown up listening to Irish balladeers, his time in the West Village filled with nights listening to the Clancy Brothers and Tommy Makem. He extolled the virtues of the McPeake Family. The McPeakes? I'd never heard of the McPeakes. Van said they came from the north of Ireland, which might explain why I, as a southerner, had missed them. Something was falling into place.

"How come you don't know this stuff?" Bob asked me. "This is essential for the world, let alone Ireland."

I guessed at an answer.

"I dunno, it feels like our band comes from outer space, from the suburb of a capital whose traditions are not ours, a place of pain which holds no interest for us; we're attempting to start again.

"Old farts are the enemy," I continued, graciously adding, "with a few exceptions."

At which point the most serious and important artist in my lifetime went off to apply his clown makeup.

It took the star of *Dont Look Back* to show me that it was essential to know where you were coming from before you could go anywhere. Wanderlust would have to be in both directions.

From that day on, as well as fast-forwarding into the future with Brian Eno, we would be slipping like water down a plughole into the past with Daniel Lanois, descending into the drains and out into the rivers and the ditches where all this stuff gets churned up and used as compost. That's where all the music comes from: the water. (As I write this, I'm thinking it's a very Bob Dylan thing to write.)

———

That night the mercurial one invited Carlos Santana and me to join him for "Blowin' in the Wind," but I'm not sure he was aware of the weather he was asking to share the stage with. Freak weather. The boy with no past dared to improvise/rewrite one of the most famous songs in the history of famous songs.

Since our earliest days as a band I'd been making up lyrics as I went along, but the hazards of this approach should have been obvious in front of a field full of Dylan fans who hung on every word. And would hang me on every changed one. The prettiest picture— a summer's evening, our backs to the river Boyne, a castle on a hill overlooking a crescent of assembled devotees—was about to turn ugly. At first I could sense some local pride in the audience—*that's one of our own, onstage with the great man*—but rapidly this turned to looks of puzzlement. Then astonishment. Then shame.

"He doesn't know the lyrics."

"He's making up his own."

"They're not very good."

I leaped out into the unknown and discovered I couldn't fly. I was blowing in the wind. I was blowing off in the wind, a giant fart.

Young, confident . . . and completely wrong.

"I change the lyrics all the time," Bob told me afterward, very graceful about it all. "Nothing's fixed in time."

STRETCHING THE CANVAS WITH BRIAN ENO

Brian Eno rises early, comes down into the recording studio before breakfast, and sets up a scene where creativity and risk-taking can take place. Brian is a one-off. As Danny's New Orleans friends The Neville Brothers used to say, observing him build bird noises into synthesizer parts, "Ain't that something? That's some other kind of shit." A sideways glance over to Danny: "Where'd you get that cat?"

Brian abhorred "muso" talk. We never used the word "riff," for example. He called it a "figure." A "guitar figure." He talked not about "sound" but about "sonics." Every day he wrote down his thoughts in his black hardbound diaries, sometimes words, sometimes a drawing or diagram. If one day it was some esoteric, academic concept, another it might be a lewd picture. But he took them seriously. Brian loved to talk about sex, not in any locker room way—which we thought of as uncool—but in a scientific way. For instance, a wonderful entry in *A Year with Swollen Appendices* where he describes the feeling of having an erection while swimming in the small pool attached to La Colombe d'Or restaurant in St. Paul de Vence. Brian laughing at his own eggheadedness.

The cerebral nature of our inquiries, mine specifically, may sometimes appear pretentious. Except with Brian. Hanging out with Brian was a free pass to be highfalutin. He wasn't interested in the conversation unless it was going somewhere else. For example, we talked a lot about the influence of African culture and how atonal call-and-response music was giving birth to a new form in popular culture called hip-hop. It was striking how this original African music was now arriving through all these electronic gadgets— samplers and drum machines—dreamed up by British engineers like Clive Sinclair or American designers like Roger Linn.

I'd become fascinated with the work of the Galway filmmaker Bob Quinn, who'd traced Irish music back into North Africa and the Middle East. Through the work of musicologists, old Irish melodies could be tracked like footprints across the Sahel and into the Middle East. Ali and I had just come back from Cairo on the trail of these tunes.

I use the word "inquiry" to describe this period because that's where we were at, a place of inquiry in music, religion, politics. As a band made up of two and a half Protestants and one and a half Catholics, we didn't naturally lean on traditional "Irishness," because none of us had any clear sense of what that was. Perhaps that was a good thing because if we were informing our musical wanderlust by looking in the rearview mirror, Ireland probably needed to do a little less of that.

Many of our subsequent journeys as a band began in these conversations in Slane Castle as we made *The Unforgettable Fire*.

A line that would lead to *The Joshua Tree* three years later, via stops across the United States with Amnesty International, my sojourn with Ali in Ethiopia, the Chicago Peace Museum, and making a song with Keith Richards to support the anti-apartheid movement called "Silver and Gold."

All journeys that can be traced back to a kitchen table in a castle with Brian and Danny. Perhaps this was the first time we felt like artists. In the tutorial that was our time with Brian Eno, we began to take the minutiae of our own lives seriously.

"It's all you've got," said the postman's son. "That's it. Your thoughts, they decide who you are."

I was discovering that adventures
in the wider world are often
attempts to discover who we are
when we are alone in our ROOM
with the lights off

outside its America......
inside   its America too
Bullet the Blue sky
Bullet the Blue sky

14

Bullet the Blue Sky

In the locust wind
Comes a rattle and hum.
Jacob wrestled the angel
And the angel was overcome.

You plant a demon seed
You raise a flower of fire.
See them burnin' crosses
See the flames, higher and higher.

Violence is one of my strongest memories of growing up. Violence in the north of the country, violence around the corner, violence behind closed doors, in neighbors' houses. Mental violence, the browbeating of a gay friend. Even if it wasn't true, it felt like we were always around the corner from some kind of confrontation. Bullying. As teenagers, Guggi and I discussed a twin strategy.

1. Make friends with the enemy if we can.
2. If we can't, tell ourselves we can beat the shite out of them.

Not very evolved and, of course, we didn't always follow through on this braggadocio, but by your late teens you should have grown out of such thinking. "Let's be men of the world," says my mate Carmodog, "but not this one."

But even in my spiritual life, warfare kept coming up. With a fluorescent yellow pen I'd marked a favorite Bible passage, Saint Paul's letter to the new believers at Ephesus: "Put on the full armor of God, so that you will be able to stand firm against the schemes of the devil. For our struggle is not against flesh and blood, but against the rulers, against the powers, against the world forces of this darkness, against the spiritual forces of wickedness in the heavenly places."

Great lyrics. I figured Nick Cave must have been reading them too. Maybe Shane MacGowan. Certainly the old guard, Bob Dylan and Leonard Cohen, knew their King James goth.

If it can sound a little "Onward, Christian Soldiers" now, in some ways I still see the world as at war with itself. What's different is that these days I'm more likely to try to see something off in my own behavior than in someone else's. I've slowly come to see that if we want to understand the forces we're up against, then it helps to befriend the idea in opposition to the one you're pursuing. Before you do battle with it.

The devil you know. Climbing into the ring, the best-prepared fighter is the one who has tried to understand their opponent. Especially if it's yourself.

THE INGLORIOUS SOUND OF GUNFIRE

I was discovering that adventures in the wider world are often attempts to discover who we are, when we're alone in our room with the lights off. That does not quite explain why, in the late spring of 1986, at a time when the region was in the midst of upheaval, revolution, and violence, I talked Ali into visiting Central America.

I understand "liberation" is a word to hold on to for dear life, but it's sobering to remember "liberation" is also a word that more dead people have held on to than any other. Liberation as a thought has cost so many lives. I'd become interested in liberation theology, a fusion of politically left principles with biblical ideas born in Latin America. Evangelicals in the United States would have appreciated the scriptural knowledge of these believers to the south and their radical priests, but less so the vision it gave them: a vision in which the political forces of the U.S.A. held the people of Central America in bondage.

Nicaragua had had a revolution that many in the United States feared would spread north, feared would leave the border with Mexico vulnerable to being taken by Marx and Lenin. Nearby El Salvador seemed proof of this paranoia, and with classic Cold War mentality the United States was bolstering its military junta. Simply because it wasn't communist. In fear that the good guys may turn communist, we support the bad guys who keep them down.

Across El Salvador people were going missing. Driving to a village, not long after we'd flown into the capital of San Salvador, we passed a body on the side of the road that had just been thrown out of a speeding 4x4. Pulling over, there was a note pinned to the chest of the dead man: "This is what happens to people who try to bring about revolution."

Later we were told why no one else had approached the body. Even the locals looked away. If they were identified as someone who knew this man, that might lead to theirs being the next body on the roadside. We were waking up to the nightmare of mid-1980s El Salvador.

In the midst of the horror, there was something almost comedic in the way the secret police, responsible for picking up people and disappearing them, all traveled around in the same blacked-out Japanese off-roaders. It didn't seem very secret. But they weren't as stupid as they seemed. It was a strategy of intimidation. Parking one of those vehicles outside a school or church was a warning: "We're here; we see you. We can make sure no one else will . . . ever."

So many people had been taken in early morning raids and never seen again. I wrote the lyric of "Mothers of the Disappeared" after meeting Salvadorean mothers who had not only suffered the injury of losing their loved ones but the insult of being denied the chance to recover their bodies. Ali wasn't yet a mother, but I saw her struggle with a loss she could—and couldn't—imagine. Yet the government that sponsored these secret police was the one that the Yankee, the western world, was supporting.

———

A few days later we're driving into rebel territory in the company of volunteers with CAMP—Central American Mission Partners—an American human rights NGO providing protection and aid for those receiving death threats. There was our local guide and intel, Saul; there was Dave Batstone, our group leader, along with the amiable Harold Hoyle, who had hitched a ride from Northern California with a surfboard on the roof of his battered BMW; and Wendy Brown, another idealistic American determined to join us on what you'd have to describe as a collective experiment in bleeding-heart gonzo journalism. Ali and I definitely should not have been there.

As we left our vehicles and entered the bush on foot, we heard what felt like a grumbling sky and sensed the ground tremble. We were a distance away but could see military aircraft circling a small town on the far hill dropping what we were told were firebombs on a rebel-held enclave. Government strategy was to give the town an evacuation deadline and then hope to capture or kill guerrilla fighters as they fled. If they didn't, well, who cares? They called it "the empty fish tank strategy"—empty the fish tank of water and the fish will die. This is what politics looks like far from the written orders that brought this murder into being.

The day felt extra damp and clammy; hot was turning to cold sweat, shining on our red faces. I was experiencing feelings I hadn't had since being a teenager, feelings in the base of my gut, an ominous churning. My machismo wouldn't let my mouth speak to any anxiety, and anyway our Salvadorean guides were not so bothered, apparently slipping in and out of this jeopardy every day. We walked for an hour or more along a ridge through the tropical vegetation, when a group of rebels bearing weapons passed us. Some were as young as fifteen or sixteen, and the defiant look of one of the comrades stayed with me. The weather in her eyes seemed to say so much more than I could understand, other than "I dare you not to see the fire in me." I knew what she meant.

Another day, crossing pastureland by foot, we were stopped in our tracks as rebel soldiers emerged from the bush and began firing off rounds over our heads. We froze, hearts stopping and starting, fearing the worst, until we heard their mocking laughter. As their faces emerged from the trees, their wide smiles gave way to mischievous laughter. They were just trying to scare the Yankees.

It was the first time I'd heard live rounds outside of a shooting range and it was a sound I'll never forget. A kind of "put put put" rather than "bang bang bang." An inglorious sound.

On a hillside, we find a slogan sprayed on the wall of a farmhouse: "Fuck Jesus!" Ali and I were shocked at this graffiti, bearing in mind all we had learned about how the radical priests depicted Christ as friend of the poor.

"No, no, that is not Jesus Christ," explained our guide, rolling his eyes and his *j*'s into an *h*. "That is 'Hesus,' who lives on the next corner. Fuck that 'Hesus'!" Even there it was okay to laugh; in fact it was essential. Not so different from the church itself, it seemed, there was more than one Jesus to be found in El Salvador and Nicaragua.

It's fair to say that my teenage dreaming about being a war correspondent does not adequately explain our current geopolitical coordinates, beyond supporting this small relief and development agency. I had a desire to go deeper, a need to understand the world around me, an understanding I knew would be about show, not tell, about feeling as well as seeing. A different kind of storytelling.

When I landed back home in Ireland, I explained to Edge what we'd seen and brought in some news footage to show the band, in the studio we'd set up at Danesmoate. We wondered, could Edge make the sound of those low-flying fighter planes? Larry the sound of the ground shaking? Could Adam terrorize us with the rumble of his bass? Could we tell the story of these people in this song, "Bullet the Blue Sky," that was emerging from a bass line of Adam's?

Even if we could not, we were going to try, and "Bullet the Blue Sky" became the canvas on which we would paint our Central American mural. On which I would spray my first rant.

> And I can see those fighter planes
> And I can see those fighter planes
> Across the mud huts as children sleep
> Through the alleys of a quiet city street.

You take the staircase to the first floor
You turn the key and you slowly unlock the door
As a man breathes into his saxophone
And through the walls you hear the city groan.
Outside, it's America
Outside, it's America
America.

None of us could have guessed how much improvisation that original version of "Bullet the Blue Sky" would hold. The release of *The Joshua Tree* in March 1987 and the years that followed saw the band constantly hammering U.S. foreign policy. There was no mistaking where we stood. Behind the barricades. By the early 1990s, on the ZOO TV Tour, I was lampooning the U.S. administration nightly. Behind the barricades.

OUTSIDE, IT'S AMERICA

Flash forward to a dream I had recently about the Pentagon. In dreamtime it is January 23, 2008, and I am sitting at a six-by-six oak table in room 3E880, deep inside the five-walled fortress, with the U.S. secretary of defense, Robert Gates. A phalanx of generals—not sure if they were three, four, or no star—sitting with their staff around the edge of the room having to listen to me talk. I am embarrassed. But not enough. Are these war heroes not allowed to sit at the same table as the top dog of the U.S. military? Even when he's only talking to the fella who wrote "Bullet the Blue Sky"?

In the dream the scary bit is not the combined firepower of the men from the military-industrial complex. What's scary is how comfortable I feel and how I find this man and his top brass so compellingly intelligent.

What is extra scary is that this is not a dream.

This is a memory.

Irrefutable evidence that twenty years after writing this song, it's no longer a case of "outside, it's America." Now I am inside America. Right inside. I have clambered over the barricade.

Even if I've done it to make the case—that we now make consistently with the U.S. military—that investing in USAID is investing in peace and security in far-off places where impoverishment is an invitation to bad actors and failed states, an invitation to sociopolitical chaos.

And even if the secretary of defense agrees that in the developing world it's cheaper to prevent the fires than to put them out.

This is quite a jump from Central America in 1986.

Now even a former supreme commander of NATO, General Jim Jones, leads the same chorus. And—wait for it—even Donald Trump's future secretary of defense General James "Mad Dog" Mattis rebuked his own president, I paraphrase, "If you want to cut USAID then buy me more bullets."

Even after all that, my subconscious is still concerned that this peacenik is so at home in the Pentagon. Let alone the actual conscience of the very pacifist members of U2.

I have had some fun with these apparently contradictory impulses to be on both sides of the barricade. I have worked out many of them in front of the band and our audience, and often used "Bullet the Blue Sky" as a high building to jump off.

I sing it; I perform it.

I out myself, by turning the tables on myself.

Adam Clayton's bass part is the key. Actually I'm not sure it's in any one key—no one can quite figure it out—but the band has been known to play the song for seven or eight minutes and that bass line never wears out.

It's June 2015 in the United Center in Chicago, and I'm really going at it, shouting into a Stars and Stripes–emblazoned megaphone, spewing real invective, proper abuse normally reserved for far-off ideologies or the personalities that front them. This version of the song comes out of a conversation with Irish playwright Conor McPherson. He's a jazzman as well as a dramaturge.

> This boy comes up to me
> His face red like a rose on a thornbush

A young man, a young man's blush
And this boy looks a whole lot like me
And the boy asks me
Have you forgotten who you are?
Have you forgotten where you come from?
You're Irish
A long way from home
But here you are, all smilin' and makin'
out with the powerful.

The mouth almighty is in the middle of a pitched battle between my younger and my older selves. As the younger hectors the older for being "part of the problem rather than part of the solution," it appears like an exercise in self-flagellation, but by the end of the song the present-tense pragmatist is standing up quite well against his preachy past.

I've been using this rhetorical device to capture the dialectic at the heart of *Songs of Innocence* and *Songs of Experience,* a pair of albums inspired by William Blake's eighteenth-century collection of poems of the same name. They say that talking to yourself is a mental health alarm bell, but this kind of spoken self-reflection was not only fun; it helped me see more clearly the worldliness that might have come over me in the past twenty years, a worldliness that my twenty-year-old self would likely not have had patience for. As a young man I saw the world in monochrome, black and white, with some shades of gray. (Maybe.) Most of the time it was us and them. Me and my mates, me and Ali, me and the band, against the world.

Anger is okay. As John Lydon wrote and sang, "Anger is an energy." It's certainly an energy I've been comfortable with, hoping and believing it is righteous anger. Sometimes, though, unfortunately, I'm taken with the self-righteous variant, the not-okay anger. The not-pretty anger, the not-good-at-all anger.

But righteous anger?

Let yourself seethe.

Bullies have run the world since we had one. Countries are mostly run by gangs.

"Elites" are another word for gangs. There's hardly a history of a country that mattered that was not engaged in some kind of geopolitical bullying.

And the bully can take on many faces. From the obvious villains like Putin or Stalin purging Russians who wore spectacles because people who read books were a threat to him, or Chairman Mao outlawing colored birds and flowers because they were decadent. To our western war winners who were dropping the atom bomb on Nagasaki or carpet bombing Dresden when the war was over, and in my lifetime secretly firebombing Cambodia to not win the Vietnam War. And closer to home paramilitary atrocities planned to protest regular military atrocities.

But there is another kind of bully. Circumstance.

Where sentient beings like me or you can't find their life because they can't find food.

our language remembers the word
"keening" to explain the unexplainable

15

Where the Streets Have No Name

I want to run, I want to hide
I want to tear down the walls
That hold me inside.

There is a mist lifting from the land. The red earth of Ethiopia is exhaling. The land is breathing. It is alive, only just, but alive. There's a heartbeat murmuring beneath the red clay epidermis, a rhythm under the canvas floor of a tent Ali and I have been sleeping in for the past month.

The tent is pitched in a town called Ajibar, in Ethiopia's northern province of South Wollo, at a food station and orphanage. It is the autumn of 1985, the Ethiopian famine. The world has not seen a famine like this since Bangladesh and Cambodia, ten years earlier. This is a great famine that as well as turning the lives of a great nation upside down is about to turn the tinier lives of Ali and me right side up. We will never be the same again. This morning we have been woken by a volcanic heartbeat that is now speeding into cardiac arrest.

A drumbeat so intense it is shaking the ground we're sleeping on like some wild beast being chased by boys with a machete. In fact, it *is* a wild beast being chased by boys with a machete.

Not a *very* wild beast, but a beast being slaughtered on the damp grass next to our tent. When I peer out through the front flaps, I see the bizarre bullfight come to its close, the creature falling to earth, its throat slit as steam rises from a river of blood snaking through the grass. A group of boys are laughing, their eyes the size of their appetite. Young boys with smiles as wide as their horizons might have been, had they been born anywhere else. Wider still are the differences that have torn this country apart, leaving Ethiopia in free fall with an autocratic neo-communist government doing more damage than the royal household of the emperor Haile Selassie, overthrown little more than a decade ago.

Over the last month we've encountered the laughter and defiant good spirits of many, but the shouts of joy from these young boys remind us of what kids are like in most places. Remind us that in a short period of time we've grown accustomed to the daily muted agony that accompanies the bloated stomachs of extreme malnutrition and poverty. Regularly the low hum of sorrow reaches a crescendo. All too commonplace it might have become, but death here is still significant. And grieving is operatic, not like the sobbing we're used to back home. Here it's a bloodcurdling wail, a troubling scream across the great chasm between the living and the dead. Maybe long ago in Ireland, in our own famine in the mid-nineteenth century, we, too, made this sound with our grief. Our language remembers the word "keening" to explain the unexplainable, and the sound is still heard in parts of Ireland.

But the slaughter that we observe through the tent flaps here is of a different kind.

Badly managed and poorly planned is the slow slaughter that describes the particular obscenity of famine in a world of plenty. Today, for the first time in a long time, some people in this camp will get the protein they need from this meat. It's the dawn of our last day in this small country town, whose most notable feature we can just about glimpse miles off in the distance: a historic mesa rumored, we hear, to be one of the emperor Menelik's retreats and associated in Ethiopian legend with the queen of Sheba, with Solomon, the line of David, and the Hebrew scriptures.

Some mornings in Ajibar the ground is damp and covered with a light mist, revealing eerie sights as it lifts. Weary walkers who have traveled all night to get here emerge from the low cloud like specters, ghosts in gray light. Often there are families, sometimes strangers, walking together in twos or threes. Some are on their own; they are carrying dead children, struggling to accept their child has passed. People as prayers seeking food or help of any kind. Theirs is a plight of biblical proportions. Having survived a war, now they struggle to survive a brutal peace, forcibly marching to the drum of a different dictator, one who some suggest uses starvation as a weapon to destroy resistance. Here in this corner of history, they remain a people who've never been conquered.

For the last month we've been volunteering in an orphanage, working on an educational program with theater and music. Collaborating with the site electrician, we've come up with four panto-like one-act plays with songs—then translated into Amharic—helping explain basic ideas around health and nutrition.

I am known by two names, Dr. Good Morning and the Girl with the Beard. We are here to show solidarity with the people of this country and to better understand the most important if clichéd question that has ever faced the world. A question I've been trying to answer in my life ever since: Why is there hunger in a world of surplus? How can people lack food in a world of sugar mountains and dairy lakes? And what can be done?

Some days the barbed-wire fencing in the camp conjures up images of World War II concentration camps, until we remember that this wire is not to keep us in but to keep others out. This is a food station, and at times large hungry crowds press on the gates. It's a strange and troubling visual when good people shout at the weak and the weary to back up or back off. The corrugated iron looks so out of sync with its environs. The bottom line is that we're trying to be useful but here we're not sure what that means. So why have we come?

I'M NOT SINGING THAT . . .

The level of poverty is often how we define whether a civilization is functioning, if the gains it has made are for the many or the few. With its roots in Judeo-Christian thinking, the western world has built into its foundational documents a requirement to at least grapple with the distance between poverty and privilege. To "treat others as you treat yourself" is a bit of a pothole on the road to financial or even cultural dominance.

I suppose for Ali and me this is part of a pilgrimage to better understand a landscape that has so far been out of sight—except for news reports like the BBC's Michael Buerk's coverage of the famine. I suppose the Band Aid single, "Do They Know It's Christmas?"—and Live Aid, the concert that followed it—sent us here. On the single, written by Bob Geldof and Midge Ure, I had to sing the most troubling line of the whole tune, "Tonight thank God it's them instead of you."

When Bob handed me the lyric, I said, "I'll sing any line but this one . . ."

Maybe it's that thought that got me here.

I had fun slagging off Bob, a famous atheist, for writing "a Christmas carol." It was not lost on him that one of the oldest Christian churches in the world was founded by Ethiopian Copts in the fourth century who very definitely *did* know the date of Jesus's birth—incidentally, being Orthodox, January 7, not December 25.

I suppose there was some religious inquiry here, too, on our part, even if we weren't entirely conscious of it. I remember hearing the American evangelical Tony Campolo explaining that there are 2,003 verses of scripture that relate to the poor, that poverty is second only to redemption in the priorities of the God found in the Old and New Testaments. It's a theme you can trace from Moses to Doubting Thomas, from the Torah through the beatitudes. Strikingly, only once does Jesus speak about judgment, and when he does, it's about how we treat the poor:

> *And they too will reply, "Lord, when did we see You hungry or thirsty or a stranger or naked or sick or in prison, and did not minister to You?" Then the King will answer, "Truly I tell you, whatever you did not do for one of the least of these, you did not do for Me."*

And yet for some reason even now people of faith think that what's going on in their—or other people's—pants is more important to God than, say, what's happening to the homeless. The lives of the poorest people are at the heart of Christianity, but sometimes religion seems to be what happens when Jesus, like Elvis, has left the building. It becomes a bless me club for the Holy Rollers and navel gazers.

"THE LOVE THAT DRIVES OUT ALL FEAR"

Wembley Stadium, July 1985. Live Aid. A gigantic moment in the life of U2. In the life of so many musicians. A transformation in how to think about pop music being of practical help in the world. For the record I don't think pop music has any obligation to be any more help than a three-minute rush of pure joy, an unexpected kiss of melody, a sung and swallowed capsule of truth telling. Sweet or sour coated.

Music for me has always been a lifeline in times of turbulence. It still is. That's enough to justify its existence; the sacred service of getting a soul from there to here is not to be underestimated. Just giving someone a reason to get out of bed in the morning counts for so much. Music as the love that drives out all fear. Music is its own reason to exist.

All that being said, there is also a history of music in service of the greater good, a magnificent testament to the ideals and steeliness of musicians like George Harrison organizing a concert for Bangladesh. But never before had there been a gathering quite like Live Aid, raising money to support Ethiopians in another famine. A global audience, a stage on two continents, and an unprecedented superstar lineup that would ensure sixteen hours of high ratings.

A LICENSE TO MAKE STUFF UP

What are the odds of two antipoverty campaigners being born a few miles from each other and both in rock 'n' roll bands? The truth of it is that Bob Geldof opened the door and I walked through. He showed me, as an Irish person, that ideas get more authority the better they are described.

We knew him first not as an activist but as lead singer in the

Boomtown Rats, Southside posh boys pretending to be rough while we, the younger upstarts, were Northside rough boys pretending to be posh. Well, two of us were anyway.

Bob Geldof was as gifted with words as any virtuoso offering their talents to the main stage on that day in London's Wembley or Philadelphia's JFK Stadium. He was Miles Davis, Eric Clapton, Ginger Baker, and that was just in conversation. His was a genius of vocabulary and communication. Words would do anything for him. It was as if the words knew how much respect he had for them and decided to give him special permission to improvise. The man could puke language and it remained eloquent. He had a license to make it up as he went along. And if he was a master of bellicosity, he always had a point to make. His jabs were aimed at finding the weak defenses in a body politic that had become inured to the hemorrhaging of human life. On-screen and in print Bob would let off language like a hand grenade, the more explosive the better. Jagged consonants breaking up the dull thud of vowels landing on some dumbfounded pundit.

"Fuck the address. Go to the phone number. Give us the money, there are people dying now so give me the money."

Bursts of static electricity that cracked and fizzed across a table, always energetic, always energy releasing. I can't imagine I will ever experience such excellence in the spoken word, and when I have occasionally tried to follow in the footsteps of his invective, I've usually ended up sounding childishly rebellious and inarticulate. A runt student at the foot of a colossus. But the real expletives, as Bob told anyone who tuned in to Live Aid, were the statistics of how many people were dying unnecessarily.

As for the show itself, influential though it was in the arc of our band, I confess that I find it excruciating to watch. It's a little humbling that during one of the greatest moments of your life, you're having a bad hair day. Now, some people would say that I've had a bad hair life, but when I am forced to look at footage of U2 play Live Aid, there is only one thing that I can see. The mullet. All thoughts of altruism and of righteous anger, all the right reasons that we were there, all these flee my mind, and all I see is the ultimate bad hair day. Business in front, party at the back, as it has been aptly put. Just as a man should never be thought of as ironing his leather jacket, so he should never be thought of as ironing his hair. And if you think that sounds like the vanity of the performer, well, on my head be it.

Live Aid, Band Aid, and their successive spin-offs raised a quarter of a billion dollars for people whose lives shouldn't depend on charity. Years later we discovered that the continent of Africa was spending that much every week paying back old loans to rich countries who'd force-fed them cash during the Cold War. Every fucking week, as Bob might have said. These numbers would move from the soft focus of charity toward a much more hard-nosed discussion of how injustice was disguising itself as bad luck.

If it was charity that had brought me and Ali to Ethiopia, fifteen years later it was justice that would send me back. The Drop the Debt campaign would return me to a geography where I had to unlearn so much of what I thought about "poverty." Land and cityscapes that would transform my view of human potential and its squandering. A magnificent continent that would lift me out of myself, and teach me so much.

A COUNTRY OF THE IMAGINATION

While we're on this journey in Ethiopia, some other snapshots come to me. Literary snapshots. In my notebook I've written down a phrase that I know is the title of a song. Even though I don't know what the song is about. "Where the streets have no name" is the phrase, and on reflection I suppose I want to write about that "other country," the country of the imagination. I want to break free from my own self-consciousness; I want to run out of hiding, to tear down the walls that hold me inside myself. I want to touch the flame.

In one way it's a teenage lyric, but in another the song is about something more adult. In my notebook I write slightly preposterous declarations, how, for example, our shows will "reveal rather than conceal." Some of it is hard to read now, but heartfelt all the same. If I've little idea what some of these notes are about, back home in Ireland, Edge is working on the music that will become "Streets." He has no lyrical reference at all. Edge is in a different world, enjoying the rush of a new dance music breaking in clubs around Europe, trance music, whose optimum tempo is 120 beats per minute. While I'm writing notes that I don't understand, Edge is building an engine room that will transform a concrete stadium on the outskirts of a town into a spacecraft that can transport an audience into another universe. The music on "Streets" is way more sophisticated than my sketch of a lyric, but together they will become more than the sum of their parts, and for anyone at a show in the decades that follow, this song will become an invitation to take a metaphysical journey into the possibilities of rock 'n' roll.

If ever a song got to live up to a ridiculous billing, "Where the Streets Have No Name" is that song. We must have played it a thousand times, and no matter how shite a show, how off form the band or, more likely, the singer, to this day when we play "Streets," it's as if God walks through the room.

> *The city's a flood, our love turns to rust*
> *We're beaten and blown by the wind*
> *We labour and lust*
> *Your word is a whisper*
> *In the hurricane*
> *Where the streets have no name.*

If the lyrics were born in a feeding station in famine-ravaged Ethiopia, all the more bizarre that fifteen years later a car company offered us $23 million to use "Streets" in a commercial. I won't say we didn't agonize. But not for that long. It was a preposterous amount of money to turn down, especially as we could have given it away, but turn it down we did based on one comment out of the side of the mouth of a great friend and champion, Jimmy Iovine. "You can take the deal," he said. "But you just have to prepare for that moment when you say 'God walks through the room' being known instead as 'Oh, they're playing that car ad.'"

Best to arrive at her feet defenseless
to have half a chance at challenging her
own almost unbroachable defense system
Its the only way over that drawbridge

inscrutable but not unknowable All will let her soul
be searched only if you reciprocate and she is
ready for the long dive

there is in my way a kind of the clan
romance to a desarted sea side town in the
winter. I do I tour hearts opera scored by the sound
of the tide crashing on/of a storm really shushing
gray tiny on the waves say to make up their mind whether
they are leaving or staying while waves kissin black stones

white waves kissing black stones
shushing all around them . ssh ...ssh

16

With or Without You

Through the storm,
We reach the shore
You give it all
But I want more.

The walls of the Martello tower were made of granite and seven feet thick. It was a fort containing three circular rooms, two bathrooms, and a kitchen built into the walls. The living room was like a granite igloo with a proud hollow for a fireplace, another opening onto a solid-stone winding staircase leading to what can only be described as the lookout we slept in. A lighthouse. A glass room from which we could look out over the promenade of the seaside town of Bray.

I'm not sure you would call it a house, but it was the first dwelling Ali and I owned and lived in, and it felt wildly romantic after having previously been holed up in the band's rehearsal room on the beach in Sutton. In their day Martello towers like this were serious military technology, a line of nineteenth-century defense against Napoleon, who was always expected to invade England through Ireland. The idea was that each watchtower could see the next one down the coast and, if an enemy was spotted, raise the alarm by lighting a fire in the battlement we had turned into our bedroom. There had previously been a large cannon where the bed was, some humor here for the honeymooners.

Blue-eyed boy meets a brown-eyed girl
The sweetest thing.

—"Sweetest Thing"

Being kindly and graceful, my brown-eyed girl surprises people with her forthrightness and humor; polite, but absent of politesse, you might not be prepared for her tough-minded reading of the world or the people around her. Inscrutable but not unknowable, Ali will let her soul be searched only if you reciprocate and she is ready for the long dive. Best to arrive at her fort defenseless to have half a chance at challenging her own almost unbroachable defense system. It's the only way over that drawbridge.

Ali would have been happier with a life that was simpler than the one we've ended up with, and it wasn't long into our marriage that I began to sense she was becoming distant from the life we were living. Though not demanding in any selfish way, Ali had never been "just" my girlfriend, and now she was never going to be "just" my wife. Neither of us knew what the word "wife" meant anyhow, nor had any sense of how valuable this relationship was going to be for each of us. We were equal partners in an adventure we hadn't figured out. Our path.

Naïve but kinda not. When we promised "till death do us part," we understood both its literality and its poetics, that this marriage thing was a grand madness: jumping off a cliff believing you can fly. Only in the air to discover you might actually be able to do this. We flaunted the odds, made ourselves dependent on the miraculous, and didn't have far to look to see that though marriage is a great analgesic, it can also be the source of the pain. We were up for the ride, but there were air pockets from the beginning, like, say, my immaturity. Married at twenty-two going on eighteen.

The thought was dawning that one of us would take longer than the other to work out how to be married and that the one of us was not Ali. She was also realizing that there were three other men in her marriage. Men whom she was more than fond of, but men who were taking her man away, not just in his wild imaginings, but physically, all over the world.

"If you want a friend, get a dog," as the thirty-third president of the United States, Harry Truman, famously didn't say on his arrival into Washington, D.C. Returning home after another tour, I wasn't laughing at that old nugget on discovering Ali had actually gotten a dog and I hadn't been involved in the decision. She looked longingly into the eyes of this border collie called Joe, and I was left wondering why *I* wasn't a woman's best friend taken on long walks to yap at her heels.

Incident 1. Ali was a vegetarian, so I was moved to arrive home one evening to a kitchen scented with Irish stew. She explained it was not for me; it was bones she'd picked up at the butcher's. For Joe. The dog. I muted a laugh and ate the dog's dinner.

It wasn't two years into our married life together, and I could see Ali in prolonged moments returning to the vast silence she holds inside her. Our weekly walks along the promenade could be tinged with melancholy.

There is anyway a kind of off-color romance to a deserted seaside town in the winter, your heart's opera scored by the sound of the tide crashing over a stony beach, shushing everything as the waves try to make up their mind whether they're leaving or staying. White waves kissing black stones, shushing all around them.

Shhh . . . shhh.

We would heed the invitation of the waves to silence and reverie, allowing ourselves to get lost in adoration of this old Victorian lady of a promenade, watch her before our very eyes slipping into the sea. A remnant from another age of romance, Victorian England might have held many hypocrisies, but the marriage of Victoria and Albert wasn't one of them. She spent forty years dressed in black after his death, the two of them inseparable across time. Had she come to Bray, she would have found a perfect rhyme for English seaside towns in Bournemouth or Blackpool.

Holiday capitals of courting. But the glory days of promenading were long gone, because the Irish, like the English, discovered the hot climes and cheap cold beer of the sandy beaches of Spain. The dances and teahouses of early Victorian flirtation now replaced by the more salt and sugar pleasures of fish and chips, Mr. Whippy ice cream, and trips with the kids to the dodgems and one-armed bandits. In mid-1980s Bray the only couples promenading in their finery were ghosts from another time. If we didn't want to join them, we'd have to reinvent our own romance, lest our love go the way of these boarded-up grande dame hotels.

Ali was also having to live with Keats, Shelley, and Byron, the romantic poets I was reading, who might not have been the best company. I'd read *The Tower* by W. B. Yeats, and now we were living in one. Spare us the furrowed brow of earnest men reading and writing poetry.

It was on one walk around Bray Head to Greystones that, considering her loneliness, I started to understand something about my own. Ali was moving behind the battlements to protect herself from me. She saw that the writer's life was not just one of mental wanderlust but physical too. She would rather not be there at all than me not be there when I was home. With the band taking off, she would fight for her independence, enrolling in University College Dublin to study social science and politics and—having always wanted to fly planes—heading out regularly to Weston Airport in Lucan. We were beginning to understand how complex is the search for home, especially if you have pain hiding there. And that the small things are often the big things.

Incident 2. In March 1986, working on *The Joshua Tree* at Danesmoate, I noticed Ali wasn't speaking to me. This observation was followed by some sign language in which it emerged that I had forgotten her birthday. Oh, dear. This was not good for any young couple, but for a man applying for the job of romantic and living in a round tower, it was deaf and dumb. My apology—and belated birthday gift—came in the form of a song, "Sweetest Thing," and one weekend I slipped into the studio to record it when the only other person around was Pat McCarthy, our studio-tape-op-cum-assistant-engineer who would go on to mix Madonna and produce R.E.M.

Baby's got blue skies up ahead
But in this, I'm a rain-cloud,
Ours is a stormy kind of love.
(Oh, the sweetest thing.)

I'm losin' you, I'm losin' you
Ain't love the sweetest thing?

All sour irony was accepted, and "Sweetest Thing" went down like a spoonful of sugar, but Ali was not as convinced by another gift, of a painting, called *Easter.* I'd tried to capture Jesus in the style of a religious icon with a load of scratching of paint and canvas contributing to the feel of an old relic.

"You've even worn Jesus out."

Unimpressed, she forgave me my sins, of which forgetting her birthday was only an emblem, and I was let out of purdah. Neither of us wanted to lose what we had, even if we weren't quite sure what that was.

"If the song is a gift, then I presume I actually own it and can do what I like with the proceeds, right?"

"Of course," I replied. "But I'll need to clear that with the band."

"Why?" she chided. "Is it not yours to give? I thought it was a gift from you?"

She was messing with me but not about the proceeds, which to this day continue to be directed to Chernobyl Children International.

ART SCHOOL'S OUT

At the same time she surprised me by noting that I am most myself when I am painting or drawing. Surprised perhaps because when I'm painting or drawing, I don't notice anything else. It's a meditation. And it's fun. I find myself able to be in two worlds at the same time, totally absorbed by the canvas and totally absorbed by the music I'm listening to. I also laugh a lot, something my mate thought was missing in these earnest times, as we pushed the rock that was U2 up the hill. Which explains why Ali encouraged my return to painting in 1986, a time when I was trying to fix up a wounded relationship with some of my childhood friends.

I think I mentioned, or did I, that neither Gavin, Guggi, nor any of the Virgin Prunes had been invited to our wedding. The various slagging matches between the two bands had taken their toll, but Ali figured that that's what I was missing, being slagged by my male mates, the surreal humor that had given us joy as teenagers. I missed the closeness we'd once had. If common ground couldn't be found in music, maybe it could on canvas, which is how our Wednesday night "paint the town any color you want group" became a fixture through the recording of *The Joshua Tree*. As we painted, we allowed ourselves to surrender to the playlists of the highly regarded northern Irish painter and draftsman Charlie Whisker and tuned in to his blues, gospel, and old folk field recordings, which were in perfect sync with the ode to America the band was making.

After putting down our brushes, we'd hit the town, where, after eleven p.m. in the Dublin of 1986, there was very little to hit. We ended up in lock-ins, country bars or dodgy nightclubs where Guggi's joke du jour when people recognized me was "Hi, I'm Jim Bowie, David's brother." It wasn't funny the first time.

The teenage drinking stuff had passed us by—Adam apart, no one in the band had drunk that much—but now we relaxed a little, heading for what Ali referred to as "fun trouble." When I was nine years old, Guggi and I had made a pact to never grow up, to never become part of the adult world because, well, our fathers were adults and we were sort of at war with them. Being in a rock 'n' roll band turned out to be the perfect excuse for such stunted growth.

I had to accept Ali's admonition that if we didn't need security, we certainly needed someone to get us home. Enter Greg Carroll, a handsome and elegant young man from Auckland who'd met us on the Unforgettable Fire Tour in 1984 and stayed with us when we returned to Ireland. Greg became a kind of personal manager to us, including nocturnal transport responsibilities after we made the mistake one night of rolling the car in Adam's drive.

Teenage kicks in our mid-twenties. Delayed adolescence catalyzed by the missus wondering if it would cure the poet of his earnest romantic phase. It did. Sort of.

Recording *The Joshua Tree* was a purple patch for the four of us, a time when I could hardly sleep for the excitement of the work I'd wake up in. It wasn't work. It wasn't even a recording studio.

Danesmoate was—and is—an imposing Georgian villa, just across the wall from Columba's, one of Ireland's poshest public schools. Once owned by the playwright Tom Murphy, it was pretty spartan when we found it, a sprawling country squat, a little river winding through forested grounds. The name Danesmoate suggests "fort," and it became our own musical citadel up in the mountains, looking out over the entire city.

The city we were looking over in our heads was imaginary. Probably American. It was not to be a concept album, but we had a vague concept in the background guiding both lyric and music that I was calling "The Two Americas," which was to be a clashing, contrasting vision not just of North versus South, rich versus poor, native versus nativist but maybe more important of real versus imagined America.

The Irish saw the U.S. the way that the U.K. saw Ireland—ours for the taking. A colony like a migration of birds or, in our case, pilgrims. A promised land to enter. There were more Irish in America than in Ireland went the boast. It was ours to play with, a landscape to get lost in, and its literature was now colonizing my imagination the way its movies once had. In San Francisco's City Lights bookstore I'd found an army and navy of poets and novelists, storytellers like Flannery O'Connor and playwrights like Sam Shepard and poems like Allen Ginsberg's "America." Sam Shepard had written the screenplay for Wim Wenders's wide-screen/close-up *Paris, Texas*, which you could have put on in the background while we were recording the songs for *The Joshua Tree*.

Brian and Danny were back on our campus, professors of very different departments, though I'd be careful not to characterize Brian as "the intellectual" and Daniel as "the instinctive." Brian had great "feel" and Danny wonderful musical ideas. Brian operated the studio as if it was a single instrument, and in his college of art we were still students.

Whatever piece of plywood Danny held in his hand became a sacred object when he played it.

Our engineer, later producer, was Mark "Flood" Ellis. Flood had the look of the engine room about him and often quoted Scotty from *Star Trek*. Even when he warned us that "the dilithium crystals are packing up," Flood would still get the starship *Enterprise* home. If, like Flood, you are intimate with the opening of that '60s sci-fi TV show, you might just hear a hint of it in the eerie guitar sound that opens "With or Without You." The Infinite Guitar.

As always Adam brought some wild innovation in the form of some time signatures that none of us had heard before; then he would ground us with his single-note, single-finger minimalism on something like "With or Without You." Larry brought the joy of discovery, with Danny bringing new drums and percussive toys as they renewed the partnership they'd made on *The Unforgettable Fire*. The timbale is a shallow drum he had used on "A Sort of Home-coming," but it was going to take over drum shops everywhere on "Where the Streets Have No Name."

While we made the music, the bohemian spirit Mary Gough was running the house, preparing meals, and mostly delighting in our delayed adolescence. The Blue Light was the pub where we'd head for a drink at the end of a long recording session. Two drinks if it was a great session. Or three. We were becoming good at drinking before understanding that some things you shouldn't get too good at. We were becoming good at motorcycles, too, a tendency of adolescent rock bands, a love rooted in America, the open road, and leather pants. Guggi liked Japanese bikes as well as the Harley-Davidsons that Larry, Adam, and I enjoyed. Edge, a new father, wasn't allowed a fast bike.

It was the biking that saw our new comrade Greg Carroll and Guggi become firm friends, all of us on the road together. While Ali and I were on our way to Texas for Farm Aid, the pair of them rode to Waterford to meet with members of an outlaw bike group called the Freewheelers. When they were returning to Dublin, near Don-nybrook, a driver, not seeing Greg, did a U-turn on the main road and Greg went straight into him. Greg never recovered from the impact, dying in the hospital early the next morning. It was like the death of a close family member. I can still hear Guggi's voice, normally so male and assured, sounding strange and weedy as he broke the news down a squeezed telephone line to Ali and me in Austin.

Our small community at home was traumatized by the news, but then we had to call Greg's family in New Zealand and try to explain the unexplainable. It's impossible to tell someone that somebody they love no longer exists, in this life at least. We decided we should not leave Greg's body to travel alone on the great distance to his New Zealand home, and so a group of us took him on the long journey to Kai Iwi outside Whanganui. The Māori have a very evolved view of how to bury their dead. Their version of an Irish wake is called a *tangi*. In a traditional Māori *tangi* you speak directly with your lost loved one, laugh with them, say sorry for when you let them down. It's a powerful immersive experience, where you let waves of anger and grief, rage and laughter, break over you. I had never seen Ali in such pain. I didn't again, until the death of Michael Hutchence in 1997.

A few weeks later, in the studio at Danesmoate, Brian Eno was working at his Yamaha DX7 keyboard, on which he could create unusual rhythms. "Two Tribes" was a beat of his that felt to us as if it had a Tahitian or South Seas feel, and it became the foundation of a song we called "One Tree Hill," after the place overlooking Auckland where we had spent such a special time with Greg. The song could carry the grief we could not.

> *I'll see you again when the stars fall from the sky*
> *And the moon has turned red over One Tree Hill.*

THE GAVIN FRIDAY AGREEMENT: FIONÁN HANVEY

It's the yearning for love, or the loss of it, that is the subject of great love songs. I was in love and becoming terrified that I would never write a truly great love song because my heart was full, not broken. Fissures but no fractures.

Yes, there was the occasional electrical storm blowing in from wherever but nothing more threatening than the tension caused by Ali and me wanting to be the best we could be for each other but fearing we couldn't. The tension in my mind was a choice between artist and family. Could I do both well? Had I to surrender to the cliché of settling down and becoming domesticated or the cliché of "the wild colonial boy," the insouciant and selfish life of the artist?

"There is no more sombre enemy of good art than the pram in the hall" is how the English critic Cyril Connolly summed it up. Unless, that is, you want to write about the contradictions of your new life. Unless you dare to write about that pram, the push or the pull of it. My breakthrough was realizing that I had to write about the moment I was in. The tearing. The tension. This fear of either losing creativity or mistreating creation. There's nothing any man can make—can imagine, write, draw, or sing into being—that is as beautiful as that child in that pram. And yet the artist lives in fear of it. Why? Because it is truly creation. Ultimate creativity. The woman has this on the man.

I began to learn that with Ali not only could we both be ourselves. Together, we could be all our selves. It was never a binary "him outdoors," "her indoors" situation. She was all the women I needed but fortunately/unfortunately not all at the same time. We would have to wait on each other. I had to accept she could never be known. There was something unfathomable about her. She was a mystery that deserved better than some straightforward rhyming couplet, and I should never commit the crime of sentimentality to honor her. I'd better write her a sexy song, an erotic hymn. Well, yes, but . . .

"With or Without You" is a song that could not contain her but at least captured some of her dark beauty and our bittersweet duality. It was also the product of listening to too much Roy Orbison. We were trying to write a song like Suicide's "Cheree," a classic underground electronic moment of intimacy, darkness, and romance. Something with the melody and opera of a Scott Walker song. When I was fourteen, my own heart breaking, Harry Nilsson's "Without You" seemed to explain me to myself: "I can't live if living is without you."

But containing all these thoughts in your head leaves your brain a cocktail shaker, and when you pour out all the stuff you've poured in, it becomes something completely unique. We wanted a sound that no one had heard before, and we got it. Except for one thing. We overshot the runway and landed in a place called saccharine. It became that dreadful thing that a real group of artists could never own up to. An ugly pop song.

Pop was kind of a swear word at the time, and if someone bumped into an easy emotion or a too-obvious chorus, it was as if they'd brought a bad smell into the room. And with Brian Eno and Danny Lanois around nobody dared own up to the fart. "Oh my God, can you smell that? A pop song!"

We abandoned "With or Without You."

The person who pulled it out of the trash was Gavin Friday, more indie than all of us and equal in sedition to the art insurrectionist that is Brian Eno.

"What's wrong with pop music?" he demanded. "Listen to the melody; it's a classic. It's like a Scott Walker."

The only reason it's not working, he insisted, is that it peaks too early, that you don't believe the singer can get to the emotion of that huge chorus so quickly. It's an arrangement problem, he said, not a song problem.

The song that became one of our most well known opens with a whisper, slowly building to the opera of a big chorus, which only happens once at the end. Over time Mr. Friday has found a role as a kind of midwife to our albums, arriving late, when everyone knows everyone else's opinion on everything and can't stand the sight of each other. Gavin will walk into the room with fresh ears and a pair of forceps.

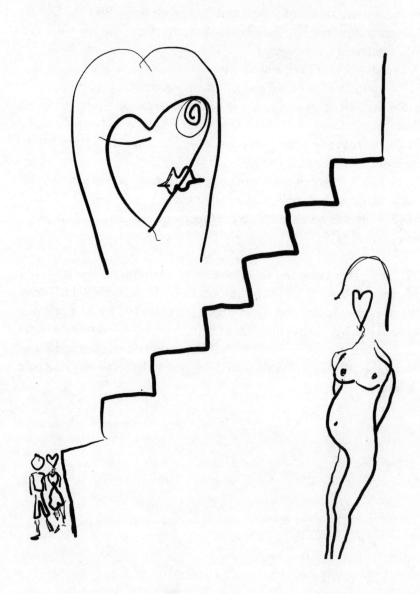

17

Desire

Lover, I'm off the streets
Gonna go where the bright lights
And the big city meet
With a red guitar, on fire
Desire.

Los Angeles. More people live off their imagination in this city than any other. I have loved Los Angeles since the moment the band and I arrived here in 1981, when it felt farther from home than any other place I'd ever been. I reveled in that distance. The shop fronts looked like stage sets, there was no center of town, but looking up to the hills, I glimpsed an architecture that fascinates me to this day. Modern buildings that look fresh sixty years later, evidence of a city where mid-century architects had their way more than any other city outside Brasília. Neutra, Lautner, Meier, Niemeyer. If it's true that since the turn of the millennium the world is pivoting from a western orientation to an eastern one, then these cities on the Pacific Rim are closer to the center of things than we Europeans. Sydney, Hong Kong, and Beijing share the circumference surrounding this new center with Vancouver, San Francisco, and Los Angeles. Former frontier towns facing away now face right into the action.

People will tell you Los Angeles is insincere, but I always found L.A. people easy to read and honest. It was as if the assholes or scammers or con jobs carried a big sign announcing they were "coming to rob you." It was and is a city of signs, of billboards, even Tower Records on the Sunset Strip was made famous for its gigantic album covers, promoting the music of the day. The whole city felt young and of the moment.

That first time, in March 1981, we stayed in a proper rock 'n' roll hotel called the Sunset Marquis. Out of the door, we could walk up the hill and around the corner to the Sunset Strip, where, for all its supposed worldliness, the neon—like us at twenty years old—felt naïvely drawn. I know the underbelly was there, but we hadn't the eyes to see it.

"GLASNOST" AT THE CLUBHOUSE

There's nothing like the flattery of a megalopolis to blind you to its dark undertow. Our first show was at the Reseda Country Club with six hundred people, one of whom was the *L.A. Times* critic Robert Hilburn, a genius of compression known for terse, melodrama-free analysis. The band, manager, record label, and agent couldn't have asked for a better welcome to the country/country club, and his rave review that appeared on the front page of the Calendar section. A few months later we were back, playing the Hollywood Palladium, a year later the Sports Arena, and by 1987 the Coliseum. From six hundred to eighty thousand in seven years, and because L.A. had started to feel like home, after touring *The Joshua Tree*, we decided to make it home.

Moving to the city was a good way to be on hand during postproduction of Phil Joanou's concert film of the tour, *Rattle and Hum,* and to work with Jimmy Iovine on new songs for the soundtrack. Edge and his family took a house in the Beverly Hills Flats, while Adam, Larry, and I moved into a house in Bel Air, soon to be torn down. A house we could treat like a clubhouse. A house where we began our own "glasnost," named after the term Mikhail Gorbachev used to describe the new openness he was promoting in the Soviet Union. We'd always harbored a certain self-protective wariness, maybe in fear of losing our hometown values, but perhaps we'd frozen certain people out of our circle of trust. Had we been so suspicious of being changed by success that we ran the risk of staying exactly the same? Could we get over our imported Calvinism and make peace with success? We could try. It was time to thaw this slightly frozen public image. After all, as Paul McGuinness reminded us, "it would be a shame to look like a band too stupid to enjoy being at number one."

> She's the candle burnin' in my room
> Yeah, I'm like the needle
> The needle and spoon
> Over the counter, with a shotgun
> Pretty soon, everybody's got one
> I'm in a fever, when I'm beside her
> Desire
> Desire.

And so it came to pass that in Los Angeles in 1988 we began to live it up a little, entertaining some new experiences, expanding our tolerance of acceptable behavior. The clichés were only too happy to see us. Riding motorcycles and drinking tequila, occasionally at the same time. Riding with no helmets—which would soon be illegal—to late-night bars along the 101 and returning to the clubhouse only as the orange sun came up over the eastern mountains. It was a kind of stupid fun I was looking for. When Ali arrived, she was initially aghast at this extended late adolescence but after consideration decided it might be a "necessary phase." She might even have joined in, albeit after striking the compromise of a driver and a car with which we explored the city's restaurants and bars, heading for the netherworld of downtown Los Angeles, the Flaming Colossus or WWIII. It was a romantic time, cruising along Mulholland Drive looking out over this city of tiny lights and meeting Michael Hutchence of INXS and his beautiful Australian film director pal Lian Lunson. Ali and I were starting to accept that our marriage could handle the challenges we would face as the band became increasingly popular.

> She's the dollars
> She's my protection
> Yeah, she's the promise

In the year of election.
Oh, sister, I can't let you go
I'm like a preacher stealin' hearts at a travellin' show
For love or money, money, money . . .
And the fever, gettin' higher
Desire.

ATTITUDE AND ALTITUDE VIA QUINCY JONES

Kids were a different matter. Even after six years of marriage, at twenty-eight I was not sure I could be so ambidextrous as to be band leader and father. I was frightened of such responsibilities and of blowing them.

One night, driving home through Bel Air in a long black car, Charlie, the driver, stopped off to get some cigarettes. On his return, he confessed he'd overheard our conversation about the producer Quincy Jones and, because he was a friend of Mr. Jones's, he'd called him to see if we could drop by. What? Our feelings were mixed. From several levels of embarrassment that our driver had foisted us on our hero to, well, a little delight. We'd been invited for a late-night drink at the home of *THE* QUINCY JONES! Before we could object (as if), we were pulling up outside a very fine Bel Air mansion, and on the sidewalk to welcome us was *the* Quincy Jones. Last time we'd seen him we were sitting behind him at the Grammys, where *The Joshua Tree* had surprised us and everyone else by beating Michael Jackson's *Bad,* which he'd produced, for Album of the Year. It was a historic night for a bunch of Irish people, who left with a Grammy each and had an evening of such fun that I'm left with only a few mental Polaroids. One of the most vivid was the dignity of Quincy, looking like a cross between the snappy bebop conductor he was and the natty Afro jazzman professor of pop he was becoming. This same untouchable talent, now bringing Ali and me into his glass-framed living room overlooking the whole of Los Angeles, pointed out landmarks on the skyline. We walked by a hardwood sculpture of what looked like an African man, his jaw jutting forward in some imaginary storm.

"That's called *Attitude*," explained Quincy. "You need some." We talked until the sun came up and learned that Quincy Jones has never been to bed before the sun came up. He keeps jazz hours.

"It's great to be alive," we cooed.

"Great to be alive?" he came back. "It's crucial, man!"

By four a.m., we were a little jazzy ourselves, but there began a friendship that has endured, in which this genius of American music made his wisdom available to us and one other thing, which none of us would have anticipated. Describe the gifts of Quincy, and not a lot of people would put parenting near the top of the list. We discovered he had six kids from four relationships and seemed very close to them. His ex-wives appeared to live on the same street. Very jazz, and quite a long way from Ireland. His cool teenage kids were climbing all over him, biting their father, tickling his ears. I asked the youngest, Rashida, who would later become a successful actor and director in her own right, if she minded that her father wasn't like the other school dads.

"No, no, no. I love that he's different. Maybe one year, around when I was eleven, I wished for a more regular dad, but I grew out of it."

"How old are you now?"

"Twelve."

GIVING BIRTH TO YOURSELF

As Ali and I walked back from Quincy's one night, an invisible switch got flicked. We were talking about kids and how the conventional life is not the only route to parenting, how people who live in their imagination can also live in the real world of parent-teacher meetings, school drops, and being there for birthdays. Even if being there doesn't always mean physically being there. There was a scent in the air, and as we turned past our gate into the clubhouse, a deer ran across the road.

It felt as if the sky had come to meet us halfway, that we could have touched the stars.

We lay outside in the summer humidity and let them touch us.

———————

A month later and Ali was pregnant. I was swinging from the stars. Actually, more like hanging from them. I was terrified. Ali had taken the test into the bathroom, and I sensed the result when she came out. I felt her emotion. I felt mine. Panic. I pretended to be asleep. It was only five minutes, but in an act of cold cowardice I left her on her own again. I was trying to prepare myself for a whole new life. If I wanted to raise children, I still had some growing up to do myself.

What was I so afraid of? The clue might have been in my father's reaction, when we returned to Dublin to tell him.

"Revenge!" he kept repeating. "Revenge. Revenge."

He laughed in our faces. He wasn't trying to be unkind, but his laughter hurt my feelings. Somewhere deep down I was afraid that my father was right, and I would give birth to someone like me. Ah, bang on cue, the self-loathing of the performer making itself known.

Ali told me that she loved all of me, that even the troubled parts of my soul were her delight. That she loved me when I was four and eight and twelve, that she loved me before she met me aged thirteen, when she heard about this boy who could make everyone laugh but could also throw a dig. She didn't need me to be anyone else. She loved me.

I wrote her a song called "All I Want Is You," but I put her as the protagonist. She is the singer of the song. It became one of our most enduring songs and the opposite of pretty much everyone's reading of it.

> *You say you want diamonds on a ring of gold*
> *You say you want your story to remain untold.*
> *All the promises we make*
> *From the cradle to the grave*
> *When all I want is you.*
>
> *You say you'll give me a highway with no-one on it*
> *Treasure, just to look upon it*
> *All the riches in the night.*
> *You say you'll give me eyes in the moon of blindness*

A river in a time of dryness
A harbour in the tempest.
All the promises we make
From the cradle to the grave
When all I want is you.

Rattle and Hum sold fourteen million copies, but because it was a double album, we used to tell ourselves it was a twenty-eight-million seller. Which is a clue to both our competitive nature . . . and our Irish bluster.

The reviews were less exhilarating. People didn't think it was as original as *The Joshua Tree*, and they were right. How could it be? This was a live album, and while we'd written new songs, some critics claimed we didn't understand the roots music we were genuflecting toward. Ours was a superficial trawl through the Great American Songbook. I took solace in the critical response to an earlier homage to American music, when the Rolling Stones' *Exile on Main St.* led to their worst-ever reviews. Maybe Americans have a right to be more demanding custodians of their own mythology.

DREAMING IT ALL UP AGAIN

The film, directed by Phil Joanou, really worked. The black-and-white aspect was shot as if the band were four Robert De Niros in *Raging Bull*, while Jordan Cronenweth's wide-screen colorscapes were like nothing ever seen on MTV. We were now mainstream, just at a moment when punk was resurging, all set to become grunge, and when electronic music was being reborn in Europe, the children of Kraftwerk about to remind rock how to dance. I knew that mainstream wasn't where we wanted to be, but I wasn't interested in returning to punk—been there, done that. I was interested in what was going on in Europe. In particular, in Berlin.

"I think we're done with America," I told the band.

"I think it's done with us," replied Larry.

Things began to crystallize on New Year's Eve in 1989, playing our hometown at the Point Depot and trying to recall the point we'd had when we were first making music in this city. B. B. King was onstage with us, his wonderful brass section accompanying us, and for a band born from punk who boasted about coming from year zero, we found ourselves with more roots than ever. But some nights it felt too rooted, earthbound, the ecstatic and airborne element in our music constrained and weighed down. I blurted out some kind of apology.

"This is just the end of something for U2; we have to go away and dream it all up again."

It was a few months later, at a noisy house party, that I found myself grumbling to Adam, his big smile a little dimmed by the stain of red wine on his teeth.

"You need to relax. We've made it . . . here. We're not on our way. Who else has been here?"

"What do you mean 'made it'?" I asked, testily. "What is *it*?"

" 'It' is getting to do what we've always wanted to, while selling a boatload of albums. 'It' is all these Grammys. 'It' is living this life."

Adam was laughing. Why was I not?

Was it because I had the killjoy suspicion that at our most successful we were at our most vulnerable? I couldn't shake an irritating question about what was next. The irritating thought that we hadn't arrived at all.

Is this why we'd started our band? Why we'd crawled out from under the table in Larry's kitchen and run away from all the God botherers? Just to be rich and famous?

"If only we'd been that smart," Adam mutters, under his breath. Is he smiling? I'm not.

Maybe Adam was right.

Paul McGuinness's warning came back to me: "It would be a shame to look like a band too stupid to enjoy being at number one." If I was stupid—and I have been—I also had a fear that when you think you're at the top is when you find you're at the bottom. I was starting to feel it was time we cut down the Joshua tree, before someone else showed up with their chainsaw.

PART II

I can change the world,
but I can't change the world in me.

—Sydney Cricket Ground, January 1994

18

Who's Gonna Ride Your Wild Horses

You're dangerous, 'cos you're honest.
You're dangerous, 'cos you don't know what you want.
Well you left my heart empty as a vacant lot
For any spirit to haunt.

STS Studios were above Claddagh Records on Crow Street in an area of Dublin known as Temple Bar. Today this is a noisy, messy marvel of a place with music spilling out of pubs onto streets, buskers, and drinking songs, a kind of a local spin on the French Quarter of New Orleans. But in 1989, it was a sprawling area of old warehouses and ramshackle retail awaiting compulsory purchase and eviction orders from the government, which wanted to turn the entire area into the city's bus depot.

Claddagh Records was a legendary folk emporium that sold everything from the popular protest of modern folkies like Moving Hearts to rare old recordings like Seamus Ennis and his famous pipe album *The Pure Drop*. It smelled of thrift store as the four of us climbed the musty carpeted stairs to the hidden attic of a recording studio, the place where we made demo tapes for some of our most popular songs. With a small bathroom and kitchen, it was all a little bedsit romance, the exact opposite of the sleek sci-fi modernist aesthetic of Windmill Lane. Maybe that's why we felt so at home. It was the dead space of a very alive musician and time traveler by

the name of Paul Barrett who'd built STS Studios as a sort of tree
house in the city. Paul had some birdlike qualities himself, including sitting on an unusual seat he'd designed, which he described as
a perch.

"It forces alignment in my spine," he explained. "I will get around
to a patent."

There was something of the inventor about Paul, which is why
we called him the doctor. Not Dr. Who or Dr. Why, but Dr. How:
Are we going to hear what this song would sound like with a brass
section? Or a marching band? Dr. How, what would a saxophone
solo sound like on here? Paul was the Brian Eno of Middle-earth,
giving a group of young musicians the impression he could conjure
any sound at all from his state-of-the-art MIDI-interface keyboard,
a little Fairlight CMI that was probably more valuable than the
building.

A time traveler, too, because the good doctor was able to take
our music to and from the 1950s, which is how we found the Buddy
Holly–like simplicity of "Desire" in 1988. How he could take us on a
visit to the country music of the 1960s and discover a song like "All
I Want Is You." The STS TARDIS could take us anywhere from the
1970s bombast of "Bullet the Blue Sky" to the 1980s and "Pride (In
the Name of Love)" and out into the future-facing "Unforgettable
Fire."

It was okay that the doctor was not of this world; we, too, were
looking for a music we had yet to hear. Now and then our heads
might turn to pilfer from the past, but our feet were mostly marching into a future we hadn't yet heard. We never recorded better
together than in STS; the bass and drums in particular seemed to
bond at a chemical level. Was it because it was so cramped? We were
almost recording on top of each other, just as we had been in Larry's
kitchen or Edge's garden shed. It was like going back to the womb.

Speaking of which . . .

FORESIGHT AND FORCEPS

It was a call from a more earthly doctor, on May 9, 1989, that made
me suggest canceling that day's session at STS. It was four days

before Ali's due date, and her doctor had suggested it was time to come into Mount Carmel Hospital to consider having the baby induced. I covered up my anxiety by suggesting to Ali that maybe being induced is a kindly eviction notice for a child getting too comfortable with its temporary accommodation. Even now that isn't funny. I'd cancel the session and drive out to pick her up. Ali wouldn't hear of it. She would rather drive herself to the hospital and pick me up on the way. I feigned hurt but accepted my driving was not something Ali had ever fully relaxed into. I had wrapped my first car around a lamppost on Willow Park Avenue. When I drove, Ali would commentate, offering helpful suggestions: "Traffic signals are not advice; they are commands."

She packed an overnight bag including Walt Whitman's *Leaves of Grass* and the blues poems of Langston Hughes, copies of *Q* and *Rolling Stone,* and a flask of whiskey.

Presumably to wet the baby's head. Foresight. Forceps. Forthright. Ali has long endured my inability to see her in any discomfort, no matter how necessary. As if she didn't have enough on her mind, she was already questioning how the whole thing was going to play out with my Neanderthal "If you make my partner cry, I will make you cry" attitude.

Does a man ever feel any more useless than when he's watching his partner give birth? At best you're a pipe player as she goes into battle; at worst you're the reason she's at war.

Does a man ever feel more in awe of womankind than when she faces the trauma of childbirth and risks her own life to bring life? I had with me a small battery-operated Sony system that I used to record thoughts and melodies, and I busied myself making a recording of the baby's heartbeat, a low but significant rhythm being picked up by ultrasound. Maybe I'd write a song to the heartbeat one day. A creative thought designed to hold off my growing terror. The last time I was in a hospital with a mother, it was my own, and I had had to say goodbye to her. Unconsciously, I was fearing the worst.

Then the worst happened. The baby's heartbeat was slowing. At first it was minuscule amounts, just mild arrhythmia, but as I was recording, I could tell it wasn't keeping time. I pointed this out to one of the nurses, but she didn't seem concerned. It slowed again, and this time I pointed out that I knew tempo better than most. Larry Mullen Jr. was my teacher. I knew if this beat was speeding up or slowing down, and right now the drummer in our baby's heart was slowing significantly. This time my alarm was taken seriously, and there was a change in the tone of dialogue. Another nurse and then a doctor arrived in quick succession, and before I knew it, Ali was taken away from me.

Thank God for science. For medicine. For doctors and nurses. They brought our baby girl through a raging storm, the men and women in white coats and plastic gloves quieting the choppy waves with their miraculous calm.

Peace be still.

Jordan Joy Iris Still Water Hewson was born at 9:36 p.m., to close a bright and beautiful tenth day in May. On my birthday. And at just five pounds five ounces, what a delicate gift. We named her after the river Jordan, the river of the gospel song, where the sweet chariot swings low, and a band of angels are coming for to carry me home. After she was moved from the incubation room, a nurse suggested she might be a wee bit traumatized by her stressful entrance into this world and that she might benefit from sleeping on her father's chest.

"She doesn't yet know she is separate from her mother, so your heartbeat will be a sound that soothes her."

With this poetic thought I started to feel useful. When she's twenty-one, I'll be fifty, I thought. As I write this she's thirty-two.

The reason I didn't really sleep for the next few weeks had little to do with me harmonizing with Ali's feeding patterns and all to do with my terror at turning over on a five-pound baby girl as she slept on me. Jordan and me. I sensed our connection as I lay there. Cosmic twins, our hearts totally beside each other. She's still right there.

If Jordan was born in a storm, her sister, Eve, *was* the storm.

In July 1991, she stormed the Bastille that was our home, Temple Hill, with a shock of black hair and a sense of comedic timing that she can't shake even when she's melancholic. She was born at seven fifty-nine on the seventh day of the seventh month, so we called her Eve because "Eve" is at the center of "seven."

———————

Eve's birth came with an intrusion we would never have expected when a gossip column reported her gender a month before we knew ourselves. One of Ali's regular scans was leaked to a tabloid journalist notorious for digging up dirt on whomever she could. It was known that people lived in fear of turning up in her column, but the extent of her ruthlessness was revealed to us one evening when an aide of hers whispered in my ear that unless Edge cooperated with her column by releasing information about his divorce, things would not go well for him. Should he agree to cooperate, he'd be "looked after."

Mostly.

Fame is not so famous in Ireland. Rather like success, Irish people have their doubts about it. One of them is Catriona Garde, who has worked with me for twenty years. Garde by name, guard by nature, fame appears to her as a hot air balloon that needs to be burst. She has a sharp needle. We all know deep down that doctors and nurses, teachers and firefighters, are the real heroes of any story. Maybe that explains why we never decided to relocate to London, to New York, or to L.A., which would make more sense for a band needing to stay in touch with the art and commerce of music. But we were never not going to raise our childer in Dublin. There's no better example of the natural respect and meritocracy of Ireland than *The Late Show,* our highest-rated talk show, which is an unlikely mix of those who are famous on-screen and those who are famous in their local community. All culture, not just celebrity culture. A woman in Cork who's had a vision of the Madonna along with, say, Madonna.

In the 1990s its host, Gay Byrne, was the most famous man in Ireland. Whenever our kids were getting a little too much attention or too recognizable, we'd remind them that no one would ever be as famous as Gay Byrne. Like everyone else in the country, they wouldn't miss his toy show special at Christmas. But if he's not a singer, an actor, a comedian, how come he's so famous? He was famous, I would explain, because he had real values. He's been there for our country in our moments of need. He lets people feel heard and seen, and more than most, I believe, he talked whole communities down from civil war.

If you're going to be famous, sure, be funny, be irreverent. Listen to the shouters as well as the whisperers. But above all, be useful.

That was his modus, it always seemed to me, a modus that became a prayer in our family. Simple. Direct. Make us useful, dear God. We're available. How can we be useful in this world where we find ourselves?

PLAYFULNESS: CHILDLIKE AND CHILDISH

Your kids take you back to being a kid. As they grew, I found myself singing to them, melodies and words of songs I hadn't known I remembered and can't explain how I knew them. They must have been sung to me. Returning me to childhood was good because I was learning that not only must you "enter the kingdom of heaven as a child" but it's also how you access your creativity. Adultism is the enemy. My hunch is that the stunted growth of many a creative figure can be explained by the domination of their adulthood, how they forgot to play, stopped messing around in the sandbox with images, music, or words.

After my initial fear of having children, as the girls grew up with us in the 1990s, I knew I could surrender to adulthood.

It's true what we're told that kids teach us to grow up, but ours also taught us not to go too far. They inspired a certain playfulness, childlike and childish. Eve was playfulness itself. A performer from two years old, she did not surprise me when, at the time of our Elevation Tour in 2001, when she was barely ten, she was stepping into the spotlight with the band, walking onstage for "Mysterious Ways" and dancing with her father.

Playfulness was where the lyric of "Elevation" came from, the playfulness that kids can have. The kind fathers can have driving their children to school . . . in my dressing gown, just out of bed, singing along to the radio. "Embarrassing" was the word I wanted most from their mouths. I wanted them howling and hissing because being a nob is sometimes the job of being a da. I was no longer concerned with the looks of other drivers with other kids in other cars. Self-consciousness was the only enemy because if I could be free, then maybe so could our kids. I let them dare and provoke me into some stupid fun, like getting out of the car in the middle of a traffic jam and dancing to the Backstreet Boys' "Everybody."

I had some of their moves down, having taken lessons from the girls. It was a time when moments like that achieved permanence only through memory. A time before smartphones made us look stupid.

Jordan reminded me of my own early imaginative life, and I was envious of her surreality. She sparked the writing of "Staring at the Sun" on our *Pop* album. One summer day in France, I watched her explore every corner of the swimming pool as if it was her own consciousness. Her eyes, wide open under the water, the color of a jacaranda, utterly at home in this Atlantis. She was dreaming her self up, even then writing her own story, a writer being written. I wonder if writing is a kind of life underwater; you have to surface, but if it's going well, you don't really want to.

The girls attended DSP—the Dalkey School Project National School—where the buildings, windows, and doors were painted in primary colors, all designed in a contemporary structure that looked as if it were built from chocolate bricks. The DSP was a nondenominational free school, with all the right values, and a wonderful place of learning. The school protected us as a family and made sure our kids were treated the same as anyone else's, and this was essential because, as Seamus Heaney would point out, "creeping privilege" can start early.

In school Jordan met a teacher who would explain to her (and us) that even in primary school the key was to get her teaching herself. A love of books, reading, he explained, will do much more than I can for her education. If she loves books, there is nowhere she can't go; she can splash about or deep dive. The attention of this man was a great gift and set her on a path to study poetry and political science at a fine university. Her teacher's name was Iarla Ó Lionáird, a man whose singing I have studied and learned from, with his role in both Afro Celt Sound System and the Gloaming.

I learned a whole other level of determination from Eve. She was even disciplined about discipline. It's a talent to be able to turn that side of yourself on and off. A glad eye for mischief, from early on she put a premium on fun, ferreting it out if it wasn't easily accessible or if the general good mood had been stolen by the too serious. Eve had innate physical comedy to work with. Age four, when the adults were getting boring, she would cycle by the dining table on a toddler's trike wearing a full-size crash helmet. The more you laughed, the straighter her face. No explanation offered. Performance art.

Method acting started age five, when after watching the movie *E.T.*, she began to wear her hoodie over her head indoors and only answered to the name Elliott. Thumb-sucking her way to the green planet.

Two last talents were present from the get-go. Eve could really dance. Eve could make you laugh even if you didn't want to.

A scene to replay: Christina Aguilera's "You Are What You Are (Beautiful)" was coming over the speakers one afternoon when I noticed Eve's face contort.

> *Every day is so wonderful*
> *Then suddenly it's hard to breathe*
> *Now and then, I get insecure*
> *From all the pain,*
> *I'm so ashamed*

It's a beautiful lyric of Linda Perry's, the video championing teenagers who feel like outsiders. I ask Eve if she's okay, if there's anything we might talk about. "It's hard to explain," she says. I wonder if it's the life I've brought her into that's hard to explain.

I hope I have been a good parent, but others will have the better view. I'm not proud of the times when I wasn't a good parent, when I lost my temper, when I couldn't control my anger. The girls have seen that. The boys more rarely. Was that going back to my father and my relationship with him? I was conscious that I did not want the kind of relationship with my kids that I'd had with my father and maybe it was the silliness that saved me. These were happy years in our family and dropping the kids off at DSP before heading out to walk Killiney Hill or the beach with Ali was about as good a way to start the day as I could imagine.

Creeping privilege can hit adults even harder. We learned in the '90s to have some fun. Looking back on it, I might have gotten a little too good at the good life, a little too free with the freedoms, but we didn't let the spoils of success spoil our family life. The girls were our priority, and even if U2 took me away from home more nights than most fathers, when I was back in Temple Hill or France, I tried to make up for it. Now I could be more available than most professional parents or even ones who commuted for a 9-to-5, which was often 7-to-7, and might only see their kids in the evening or at weekends. Plus we had all kinds of support over the years. Ali was the A team. I was more often the only B on the A team.

We who love what we do, and would do it for free, should never forget that we are 1 percent of the 1 percent of people who have ever lived. In history we hardly exist. To be this free of financial worry is the gift our audience gave to our band. To be free. To do what we love, to love what we do. Hardly anyone has lived like that. History has been a hard climb for our ancestors and getting up on two legs in black plastic pants doesn't really compare, but I don't want to forget that U2's story is a freak of nature. A black swan event. Worlds have come crashing around the ears of more talented people than me, but since success first arrived for this band in the late 1980s, freedom has been our story and the story of our families. We owe a lot of that to you, whoever you are, reading this book.

The 1990s had its darkness at times, too, and some was not of our own making. We discovered that a famous gangland leader in Dublin had been planning to kidnap the girls, that his people had been casing our house for several months and developed an elaborate plan. Years later his daughter wrote a book in which she talked about hearing her father discuss the plot. That was the kind of news that messed with your sleep patterns.

As one by one the kids reached twelve years old or so, I've had a conversation with all four about how they are now supposed to become troublesome teenagers and how that's fine with me.

"You torture me. I try to control you. We fall out. We don't speak, and then we go through difficult years. You come out of those years, and then we meet up in your twenties, and then we get close again."

That's how it often goes, I explain. On the other hand I will add, "We could just, say, skip all that."

And all of them went, "Yeah, let's skip that." And they did.

Although, of course, if you talk to their mother, who didn't go off on the road like their father, she might tell you a different story about how the girls might have missed out on me being there to torture and how I might have missed out on that too.

UNtil the end of the world
where Edge and I take a train into
a subway / bomb shelter
in the capital of ukraine AND
Mikhail Gorbachev once leader of
the 'UNFREE world' knocks on our
DOOR in DUBLIN to offer a
teddybear for a picnic

19

Until the End of the World

Haven't seen you in quite a while
I was down the hold, just killing time.
Last time we met it was a low-lit room
We were as close together as a bride and groom.
We broke the bread, we drank the wine
Everybody having a good time
Except you.
You were talking about the end of the world.

The train lays down a rhythm track. It's spring, 2022, and the click and the clack reminds me of the journey Ali and I took into London forty-five years ago with my "demonstration" tapes of U2 songs, my mission to score a recording contract and a life yet to be lived.

Ali is not with me on this trip from Poland to Ukraine. Edge and I stare through pockmarked glass at the rocket launchers lined up as far as the eye can see, pointing toward Russia. These sci-fi slings remind me of the cranes on the port in Dublin, giant stick insects hosting a swarm of cruise missiles.

Our twelve-hour train ride to Kyiv takes a detour as there's been "trouble up the track," a euphemism for the constant shelling endured on this route.

"The Russians should try Google Maps, because with their own tech they keep missing us," jokes Oleksandr, who's in charge of the railway today.

Oleksandr, fearless, is certainly older than the fourteen years he looks.

"No need to worry, now we've antibomb filters on the windows. The windows have been blown out a few times . . ."

Cool.

Edge and I nod, like we're on our daily commute. I'm always struck by how humans in ridiculously abnormal circumstances hold on to normal like it's an old friend they've just spotted at a party where they know no one else. I look across the carriage to check if our shadow is with us. Our shadow is Brian Murphy, who for twenty-five years has been running U2's security operation, sunup or sundown.

Tomorrow, May 9, is Victory Day in Ukraine and Russia, victory of the Allies against the fascists in 1945. In Moscow, Vladimir Putin will parade the huge Ilyushin Il-80 Maxdome aircraft that in the event of a nuclear attack will become the "Kremlin in the Skies." Parading, too, will be some of Russia's own cruise missiles and a couple of WMDs—weapons of mass destruction—pointed back toward the rest of the world.

Edge, U2's own WMD (weapon of mass devotion), is holding his usual form of protection, his guitar, and strumming it now, trying to remember chords to songs we haven't played in a while. Douglas Alexander, a former U.K. cabinet minister who's been in a few war zones, offers some battle-weary foreign policy advice as we strap on the compulsory body armor. "Arriving into Kabul by helicopter they told us to sit on our body armor . . . more likely we'd get shot at from below."

We laugh harder than we might. Douglas, advising me for the last five years on pretty much everything, volunteered for this mission, as did Martin Mackin, who consults for the Irish government. Brian takes our phones away because traveling into a war zone with a cluster of foreign numbers is easy surveillance and we're supposed to be on a secret trip.

These two train carriages have earlier moved 320 refugees to safety, and with their chintz curtains and elegant dining chairs they feel like a 1940s throwback, where characters like Roosevelt and Churchill and Stalin will rendezvous to argue war and peace. As they did in 1945 at the Yalta Conference, on the southern coast of Crimea, a part of Ukraine occupied and annexed by Russia. It was at this conference, historians argue, that the Cold War table was first set.

Our journey is at the invitation of President Zelenskyy, who I met in Kyiv in the days when he was an actor and comedian. In the days when he hadn't imagined he'd be leading the defense of his country with unbowing intelligence and valor against a Russian invasion. He epitomizes the courage of the thirty-five million Ukrainians who remain to fight, and focuses their purpose with daily communications, reinforcing their personal as well as their country's territorial integrity. It's a dramatic defense, their creativity forced into combat. Warcraft. Who would mess with these people?

Zelenskyy's second-in-command, Andriy Yermak, is a former film producer, and I feel that these are our kind of people, storytellers who want the Victory Day story to show and tell that their spirit is not broken by this brutal bombardment. Music is what we do, that's what Edge and I say. That's how we bear witness.

FOUR SCREENGRABS FROM A WAR ZONE

#1: In the subway, deep underground, a nuclear bunker created by the Russians in 1960, we're joined by local band Antytila and frontman Taras Topolia, now soldiers. I introduce a new take on "Walk On" by explaining how "we're all used to world leaders who turn out to be comedians but what a revelation to have it the other way round."

> And if the comic takes the stage and no one laughs
> And dances on his own grave for a photograph
> This is not a curtain call this is the greatest act of all
> A stand up for freedom . . .

We busk through "Sunday Bloody Sunday," "Angel of Harlem," "Pride," and "One." This crowd of a hundred is impersonating a crowd of a thousand by the time we've turned Ben E. King's "Stand by Me" into "Stand by Ukraine."

#2: Standing by the towering statue of Taras Shevchenko, the country's most famous poet and painter, a journalist asks Edge if there's a role for musicians and writers in this kind of situation. "Well," he replies, looking up at the giant statue, "the Russian empire seemed to think so. Isn't that a bullet hole in the poet's head?"

#3: The lights are off as we are led by torch through an endless series of corridors to meet President Zelenskyy in the war room. He and his right hand, like the whole country, appear in casual camo, in contrast to the dull gray men of Putin and his next-door neighbor Lukashenko. The Ukrainian leadership are like some art-directed life force calmly presenting the case for freedom as Putin nervously whispers in the direction of the four horsemen of the apocalypse.

At a small round table the president talks to us about storytelling, how to outflank the Russian disinformation machine, which in India and parts of Africa is now stealing the narrative. He wonders why half of the countries who abstained in a UN vote criticizing the Russian invasion were African. We're told Ukraine will soon have 120 million tons of grain but the Russian blockade means they won't be able to get it onto the ships and away to feed the world. Ukraine supplies about a third of the world's wheat, barley, and corn and half of the world's sunflower oil. All of this left to rot while the poorest countries starve. The president discusses how to get this to places that will be at risk of famine without it. That his country is under siege and he is thinking about all this gives you a clue as to who he is. Who his people are. Their morale is moral but also strategic.

#4: In Bucha, we witness firsthand how the Russian military have engaged in a massacre. In the days ahead I will try not to remember these scenes. I cannot describe them to you without risking my own mental health. I ask the local Orthodox priest about the Orthodox patriarch of Moscow. Why has he colluded with the lies spewed out daily, lies that mutilate the truth, that mutilate a people.

"What God does he pray to?" I wonder.

"Vladimir Putin," he replies.

HER OR HISTORY

It's impossible to conceive the weight of history that some can carry. We read about them. They write us. The earth revolves around the sun but may spin on the actions of a few. Mostly these are terrible men with names like Putin, Stalin, Mao, or Hitler. Sometimes, like Alexander the Great or Napoleon the Tiny, dangerously flawed individuals who through wily strategy and force of will outwit all rivals, leaving a mark on history we would notice were it gone.

Others seem to have been shaped by the history they were shaping. It's as if the greatness of their task made them great and overpowered their flaws. They have names like Winston Churchill, Nelson Mandela, Martin Luther King, and . . . Volodymyr Zelenskyy. Like Aristotle or Marx. Like Muhammad Ali, Beethoven, or Oscar Wilde. History being written by men about men, there are fewer names like Joan of Arc, Julian of Norwich, Rosa Parks, Mary Robinson, Marie Curie, Malala Yousafzai, or Greta Thunberg. History being too rarely herstory.

In my lifetime no one person has had the impact on the world of Mikhail Gorbachev. Though Vladimir Putin would attempt to pull down the digital blinds, the rolling back of the Iron Curtain is right next to Neil Armstrong's walking on the moon in my cosmos, the most awe-inspiring event I witnessed on a television. But unlike the moon, the world Mikhail Gorbachev landed on was one I walked on myself. Two epoch-making events: one signaling human ambition to challenge the boundaries of where we might live; the other redrawing the boundaries of where we actually do live.

MIKHAIL GORBACHEV AND THE WHISKEY STREAM

Our house, Temple Hill, on a Sunday is a train station where the trains do not run on time and you're never quite sure who will alight at the platform. Guest preacher or seer, traveling musician, author on a book tour, any configuration of friends and family. Open house, open minds.

The doorbell rings on this particular day in January 2002, but before I can climb the stairs Ali is on the way. Pulling open our big navy-blue front door, she comes face-to-face with a life-sized stuffed toy bear. On closer examination the bear is being held in the arms of a modest figure that history will judge a great one.

I'd forgotten to tell Ali that Mikhail Gorbachev might drop by. In Dublin, along with some other earth movers, to receive the Freedom of the City, he'd shown some interest—politeness, I'd guessed—in some downtime with our family.

"No need to arrange anything," I'd said. "It's open house on a Sunday." Accompanying him was Nina Kostina, his translator; a good translator makes conversation between foreign tongues not just possible but somehow more enjoyable. After a while your brain has tricked you into thinking you speak each other's languages. Or was that the whiskey? With everyone around the table, no question was off the table.

Question: "In the darkest days of the Cold War how real was the nuclear deterrent of mutually assured destruction? Put it like this: Was MAD mad or serious?"

Answer: "I could never consider such an option. Even as a younger man with all the bluster I knew if fate brought me there that I would not exercise that option."

Question: "Where did your moral compass come from? Does the state encourage this kind of centeredness?"

Answer: My mother and grandmother were religious. On one table in my grandparents' house were my grandmother's Ortho-dox prayer icons. Next to it, on another table, my Communist grandfather placed his portrait of Lenin.

"It's important people don't forget that the revolution in Rus-sia began with the most noble ideals; my grandfather believed in those ideals."

Question: "Do you believe in God?"

Answer: "No." (Long pause.) "But I believe in the universe."

At which point the Universe interrupted.

Noisily, on prosthetic legs, a little girl enters the room. This is Anna, Ali's goddaughter, who is staying with us for the weekend.

Ali had first met Anna on a visit to Belarus.

That's right. Belarus.

Formerly known as the Belarusian Soviet Socialist Republic. Of the Soviet Union.

The last leader of which was Mikhail Sergeyevich Gorbachev.

Anna had been born with severe physical disabilities due to the radiation poisoning of her parents, following the nuclear accident at Chernobyl. Only she and the former head of the Soviet Union were unaware of the irony of this moment.

Around the table, one by one, we sensed the poignancy of this unexpected meeting. Maybe the great man picked up the shift in mood and overcompensated, directing his whole attention to Anna.

"Hello and what's your name, young lady?"

Anna approached him, and he lifted this little girl onto his knee.

"Anna," she says, in a broad Cork accent.

"Short for Annastacia," explains Ali, perhaps a little paler. "There's a story you should know, Mr. President." She hesitates. "This might feel like a setup." But it really isn't. "You should know that us Irish have long had an uncomfortable relationship with nuclear power."

The president checks in with his translator and his glass, kind of squinting back at Ali.

"In some east coast areas, just down the coast from Dublin, the unusual incidence of Down's syndrome births and cancer cases has raised a lot of suspicion about a radioactive plume after a fire in 1957 at the U.K.'s Windscale nuclear plant."

Gorby can sense the next move, but has no clue about the one after that. Another guest looks as if he's not sure where this conversation is going at all. The whiskey is being poured.

Quickly.

"Mr. President, days after the catastrophe at Chernobyl, radioactive contamination was detected in Ireland from water in water filters and even samples brought in by local people. It was nothing, of course, like what your people had to put up with, but in our country people were so keenly aware of the dangers of nuclear power from the Windscale fiasco that they paid special attention to Chernobyl.

And in Ireland people responded generously to the plight of dis-
placed Ukrainians and Belarusians, people whose lives were turned
upside down for years. Even now we keep in contact."

It was a little surreal observing Ali explaining her connection with
the U.S.S.R. and with Russia to the man who had the ultimate power
over that power plant. My wife is the quietest storm that ever blew
into town, and for her to speak like that requires some psychic concentration. But if she was nervous, she was not unnerved. For a quarter century Ali has worked with an Irish NGO, Chernobyl Children
International, since its founder, a whirlwind of a woman called Adi
Roche, persuaded her to narrate a TV documentary, *Black Wind,
White Land.*

Ali has made regular journeys to the region, joining convoys of
Irish trucks and ambulances stuffed with supplies, taking the wheel
on the two-thousand-kilometer journey from Dublin to Minsk. It
is both humbling and invigorating to notice all the ways in which
your partner is tougher than you. Along with other Irish volunteers,
Ali has slept in asylums and cleaned up the mentally ill whom they'd
found chained to walls. Having fallen in love with the Slavs while
railing against the conditions that people had to live in, on one trip
to Belarus she met Anna, who later became one of several thousand
children brought to Ireland for surgical procedures.

Anna had since been adopted by the Gabriel family in Cork, and
as the universe would have it, it was on this weekend that Ali had
invited her godchild, Anna, to stay with us. Now with this little girl
on his knee, the voice of Mikhail Gorbachev quieted to a murmur
as he explained that it was that 1986 nuclear disaster at Chernobyl
that convinced him the Soviet Union could not continue as it was.

"I thought to myself if the state cannot control a nuclear power
plant of this significance, then the state is no longer functioning as a
state. The state is kaput.

"Morale was low. We were finding it difficult to pay the wages of
our armed forces, let alone our scientists, and we were not keeping
the reactors to the standard they require.

"When we see the devastation that splitting an atom can cause,
then this is untenable; this cannot ever be acceptable. The Soviet

Union was no longer viable; it has to find a new path—a path that must include rapprochement with the West."

So this had been a moment when Mikhail Gorbachev changed his own history and ours. We discover history doesn't have to shape us. The world is more malleable than we imagine, and things do not have to be the way they are. History is clay and can be pummeled or punched, corralled or even caressed, into a whole new shape.

FOUR SCREENGRABS OF MC ANGELA MERKEL

Angela Merkel is a woman whose policies are a lot more classical than rock 'n' roll, polka even. The chancellor turned out to be one of history's most disciplined and deft corrallers. She grew up east of the Iron Curtain and once it was drawn back walked through to lead a united Germany. I hold in my mind four standout pictures.

#1: G8 Summit in Heiligendamm, 2007

With the ONE Campaign, I am pushing Angela Merkel hard on why she won't promise more German overseas aid. She looks me straight in the eye and quotes her father, a Lutheran pastor from East Berlin: "My father taught me never to appear more than you are and always to be more than you appear." By the time she has left office, Germany has more than doubled the money it sends abroad to help the poorest.

#2: Midnight in Berlin, August 2012

Our van stops at a light.

"You'll never guess who's pulled up beside us," says our driver. "It's Chancellor Merkel."

I look out the window expecting a motorcade, but it's just two cars, and in the back of the first, face lit by the glow of her laptop, sits the German chancellor.

"Has she no life to go to?" I joke.

"No," replies our driver. "That's why we vote for her."

#3: Munich railway station, 2015

Among the images of the twenty-first century that will endure are those pictures of Syrian refugees arriving by train met by Germans holding parcels of clothes and children's shoes. Images to counter those from seventy years previously.

Germany now, a reason for many of us to believe the European Union was a thought that had become a feeling and Angela Merkel had become the head and heart of Europe.

#4: Bundeskanzleramt building, 2018

I am about to introduce the chancellor to fifty ONE ambassadors from across Germany.

Angela Merkel to me: "Have you heard 'This Is Nigeria' by Falz?"

"Chancellor, are you turning me on to new music?"

"I'm surprised you haven't heard of it, apparently it's very popular."

With that, MC Angela reached for her iPad and found me the video, a West African homage to Childish Gambino's "This Is America."

"It's really a kind of dance."

And so is politics, a dance.

You find the steps that take you to common ground. It's choreography, and I am being moved by it.

Oh and a fifth screengrab, which will never decorate our fridge door: Post-Fukushima disaster, 2011.

Chancellor Merkel agreed to dismantle Germany's nuclear power grid. You might think I'd be punching the air here. I'm not.

You see, almost two decades on from Gorbachev's visit, it's January 2020, and though I am still sleeping with an antinuclear campaigner, my wife is not.

I've gone over to the dark side.

I'm in a Seattle office building where Ken Caldeira, an atmospheric scientist from the Carnegie Institution for Science, is explaining to me that essentially a city is made by or from carbon.

"Look out the window, but before you do, look at the window. Making glass requires energy—a window emits two-thirds of its weight in carbon. Notice how many buildings out there are made of glass . . . and concrete. Concrete is basically one part concrete, one part carbon—because making a hundred tons of concrete means a hundred tons of carbon."

Ken points to the street, to the vehicles, to the restaurants and supermarkets, their supply chain of food. He points around the room we're in. "The table, the chairs . . . even this carpet has a carbon footprint."

Ken is working with Bill Gates, who's good with numbers and says the climate emergency comes down to two of them: fifty-one billion (tons of greenhouse gases we annually add to the atmosphere) and zero (tons we need to add to avoid climate disaster). A growing consensus suggests it's not possible to get to zero solely with renewables, with solar, wind, or wave power. Battery storage for these breakthrough energies looks likely to fall well below requirements in most geographies, but especially among developing populations in India and in countries across Africa where new and reliable power sources are essential. Even alternate fuels like hydrogen require an evolution in science that's decades away.

Thirty years after U2 joined Public Enemy, Big Audio Dynamite, and Kraftwerk in an antinuke Greenpeace show to protest the U.K.'s Sellafield nuclear power plant, the inconvenient truth may be that the same splitting of the atom that weaponized uranium into fissile material and threatened human extinction post–World War II may now be an essential stepping-stone if we are to avoid our latest extinction event.

Ali, for one, is not convinced.

Ali thinks of Anna, her goddaughter.

Some days I am on the other side of the barricades. Even in my own kitchen.

ONe

in which, in Berlin, haunted by the ghosts
of HANSA, the U2 group fall out and
nearly become history ourselves until
I am eventually reminded that I am
one quarter of an artist without
Edge Adam and Larry.

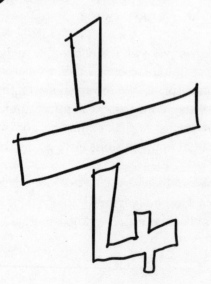

20

One

You say love is a temple, love a higher law
Love is a temple, love the higher law
You ask me to enter, but then you make me crawl
And I can't be holding on to what you got,
When all you got is hurt.

October 3, 1990. Arriving in Berlin to record *Achtung Baby,* the British Airways captain came over the speakers to tell us we're on the last flight to land as the wall is finally being demolished.

We stepped off the plane into history and like good Irish rebels went straight to find the party. This was going to be one of the greatest street celebrations of all time; only it wasn't. The atmosphere was downbeat, people's faces more stunned than exalted.

"Oh, dear," observed Adam. "These Germans don't know how to have a good time."

"Shite party!" Larry shouted.

Slowly it dawned on us that we were not at the party at all. We were at the protest. Support for the old Soviet ways had not been entirely extinguished, and we were marching in step with recalcitrant communists who wanted to keep the wall. "U2 Protest Wall Coming Down." Some headline that would have been.

———

That night I slept in Brezhnev's bed. No, it wasn't a dream. I was actually sleeping in the bed of Leonid Brezhnev, the man who led the Soviet Union for longer than anyone except Stalin. Dennis Sheehan, our tour manager, told us the rent on the house is a bargain. "It's in East Berlin, a very upmarket neighborhood, if you're allowed to say that word here. It's where the politburo *used* to stay."

I wake with a bang next morning. The sound of my head, deprived of oxygen and H_2O. Getting up, I root around the basement in search of a glass of water. The kitchen, I later discover, is across the road. There is nothing in this basement except for a rock star clutching his head, wearing a T-shirt and no underwear. Another bang, this time not in my head. The front door. I gingerly climb the stairs and stick my head around the corner to find a medium-sized family in the hallway. Mother, father, children, grandfather. They are not embarrassed at the state of my undress. But they are annoyed.

"Who is living in zis house?" inquires the granddad.

"I am," I reply, squinting in the bright morning light. "What are *you* doing in here?"

"ZIS IS MY HOUSE!" comes the reply, volume turned up to eleven. "ZIS IS MY HOUSE AND ZE HOUSE OF MY FATHER. YOU DO NOT BELONG HERE AND YOU NEED TO GET OUT!"

A picture was emerging, and there seemed little point in explaining Dennis's rental arrangement. There was no denying the emotional connection between this man and this place, and to this day I have no doubt he still believes he met a squatter. These people hadn't seen their house for fifty years. A wall had been in the way.

BALLROOM BLITZ

Number 38 Köthener Straße. From the wide windows on the higher floors in Hansa Studios you could look along the Berlin Wall and over the no-man's-land that formed the demilitarized zone on either side of the scar that crossed this old and soon-to-be-new capital of Germany. The west side had been occupied by an unusual mix of alternative lifestyles with their caravans and small-scale farming.

Chickens ran around the epicenter of Berlin. Imagine London's Trafalgar Square as a caravan park for a community of travelers.

The room we were recording in had been an SS ballroom in the 1930s, its mahogany panels a reminder that we were a long way from the future and just a stone's throw from a dark past. Our fanzine eyes swept the herringbone wooden floors for any clues that our musical heroes might have left for us. An unused lyric in the trash from Nick Cave? An early 808 drum machine with some programming by Conny Plank? A leather jacket left behind a couch by the Thin White Duke himself?

Recording at Hansa in Berlin with Brian Eno was an invitation to hubris. At Hansa, Eno had already made some of the greatest recorded music any of us had heard. It was an arrogance to imagine we could create anything on a par with David Bowie's *Low* or *"Heroes,"* or other Hansa occupations like Iggy Pop's *Lust for Life* or Nick Cave & The Bad Seeds' *The Firstborn Is Dead.*

But some arrogance is essential to the creative process.

The very idea that your private thoughts or feelings are worth sharing with anyone outside your family or friends is already a kind of arrogance. Arrogance is the exit and entry point to the humiliation that art requires. Not unrelated is a dubious courage that when you find yourself out of your depth in troubled waters, you will discover how to swim. Another daft but true idea that creativity seems to depend on.

Along with Brian, we had Daniel Lanois and Flood, like Eno, artists in their own right. What could possibly go wrong?

How about everything?

There was something important missing. The songs.

Our promising demos were just that. No "Sunday Bloody Sunday" or "Pride," no "Desire" or "Angel of Harlem." They weren't bad. They just weren't that good. All of which begged the question: What exactly are we doing here? That was a shitty feeling.

We had one or two sketches of songs and some parts of what might make one or two others. A bit of "Mysterious Ways" here, a piece of "Even Better Than the Real Thing" there. And that? That will become "Until the End of the World." Lots of bits, but no hard drive. Bits and pieces and beliefs.

We'd believed that this storied place, haunted with the ghosts of some of our favorite living artists, would be where these presences would become present again, inside some great new songs. We believed the occasion would make up for what we were missing.

Wrong.

What happened was entropy. The old ballroom that was to be filled with song was instead filled by self-consciousness, a kind of embarrassment. That accusatory voice in my head repeated the question, "What are we doing here?" It wasn't just in my head; I could see it in the eyes and occasionally read it on the lips of Larry and Adam. If Larry was skeptical of the drum machine, Adam, too, was unconvinced by some of these new grooves. Why tear up this tone that we own? "We've become the biggest band on the planet with the collection of sounds that you're now saying we can't use. Because? What? They're too successful?"

"Too familiar," I would retort. "Too much of the same. What was once striking becomes cliché."

Danny too. After shepherding and sheepdogging the famously freewheelin' Bob Dylan on the acclaimed *Oh Mercy* album, he'd much rather we headed home to our folk roots than off and away to electronica. I wanted both, as always. Less is more but more is even more. Edge got it intellectually. He was up for it as an art experiment, in the way we'd approached writing the score, a year previously, for the RSC stage production of *A Clockwork Orange*. He also had a similar interest in dance music, but Edge was more reverent than I about the limitations of our band. He saw our limitations as a positive, not a negative. Wise, I thought, but wise is for later in our life.

The joy of exploration and the delight in getting lost in unfamiliar territory were replaced by drudgery and begrudgery. The wall might have been coming down between East and West Germany, but in our little musical nation the walls were going up. If the Cold War was ending outside the windows of Hansa, inside it was just starting.

It was cold in Berlin in the winter of 1990, really cold, but some days it was colder in the studio than on the street. Even the hot food in the restaurant beneath Hansa was cold, although one particular waitress warmed to us. Warmed to Edge, especially, now a single man again.

"How's it all going, Edge?"

"It's not going anywhere. You need to be somewhere long enough to get to know the girls."

After the longest-held breath, Edge asked the waitress out, a bit of a moment for all of us with our furrowed brows. Edge mutters: "In this kind of work a lad can end up feeling as if he were on a North Sea oil rig."

DUMPING BALLAST TO GET AIRBORNE

The Team. Flood, he of the single name and singular focus, was always good company. Flood had previous experience operating on remote rigs like this and always managed to discover oil when no one else thought there was any. His habit was to line up cigarette packs at the start of the session—Marlboro Reds—and by the end of a session step back and measure his time at the mixing desk by the amount of packs he had stacked up. Could be a hundred packs. Could be two hundred. In Hansa Studios, he might as well have been sucking on the exhaust pipe of one of the East German Trabis that littered the city.

Flood, like Brian, was a kind of talisman for the sound we were looking for. His work producing Depeche Mode was both radical and accessible, a combination we would need if our work was not to be taken hostage by self-indulgence. Flood was the man behind that drum sound on Nick Cave's version of Bob Dylan's "Wanted Man," a sound so primal it demanded we come hear the room for ourselves. He understood the balance between what we could create by playing live in a room in a traditional way and creating music that was electronically generated and processed. We wanted one foot in the analog world and one foot in the digital world. One foot in the past, one foot in the future.

And on the days when the work became a bit grim, Flood was the man to inject the moment with levity, notably one session when we performed naked. Except for gaffer tape over our bits and pieces. All in the cause of art, you understand. The audio engineer Shannon Strong revealed that under her oil rig uniform of black military shirt and cargo pants she was wearing some vivacious red lingerie.

"I know you guys think of me as a tomboy, but I'm much more than you think," she said, laughing, as the hirsute Danny Lanois shrieked in pain while attempting to de-gaffer himself. A Colorado girl who loved the avant-garde, it was Shannon's brilliant ear and explorer's instinct that had brought her to Berlin. She didn't tell us she was a closet performer, too, later formally changing her name to Bambi Lee Savage.

Whether it was the difficulty of moving out of our comfort zone, the bad food, or just the cold, dreary winter days of Berlin, the four of us began to get cranky. Success was not a given: it's hard to leap a ravine with one foot in the past and the other in the future. It was not made any more likely by someone's voice, just as we were about to jump off the ledge, saying, "You know, I don't know if we can get across there."

It was Brian who understood that we needed to dump the ballast to get airborne and that this might be courageous.

Despite the city's mythology there wasn't a lot going on at night, unless your idea of fun was hanging out with real estate developers or lawyers, now deciding who owned what, after the fall of the Berlin Wall. It was like the Klondike, hotels full of people coming in to make deals. Not so much the Wild West as the Wild East. Danny took a shine to a staff member at the Palasthotel who explained that she used to work in the secret police. So did the doorman.

"All the rooms in this hotel used to be bugged," she said. "All the special rooms."

They'd been part of the Stasi, but with the Stasi gone, everyone was out of a job. So many people in the GDR had turned informant for the secret police, a story later dramatized in the Oscar-winning film *The Lives of Others*. Everyone spying on everyone else. Paranoia was now part of our palette.

THE NECESSARY SUSPENSION OF DISBELIEF

Is there a price of admission to enter a studio like Hansa?

There are certainly some tolls to pay, simple stuff like preparedness. In our defense Edge and I don't want to overprepare the demos, because it's through improvisation that Larry and Adam get to shape the songs. But it can be hard playing songs without lyrics. Or melodies. Especially for Larry, because he really listens to the lyrics and plays to the singer. It takes a great leap of faith to improvise, to build your house from the sky down.

When it works, it's a thrill making stuff up on the spot, but it's frustrating when you jump off into the unknown and there's nothing there to meet you. The other price of admission is willingness. Willing to be there and willing it on. You have to will it on.

Suspension of disbelief is not just crucial for appreciation of an artwork; it's necessary for its manufacture. It's not about rolling your eyes when something goes wrong, as if to say "I told you we shouldn't be here." But likewise it's hard to fake excitement going to work with friends, when the friendship is proving a struggle. We were an hour into a session one morning, tuned up and ready to play, when we noticed Larry's empty drum stool and realized he hadn't shown up. That no one remembered if they'd seen him that morning was the most hurtful aspect, suggesting we were not keeping an eye out for each other. It was a low moment.

This was a band, as Larry observed, coming the closest we'd ever come to breaking up. Since our last crisis of faith in 1982, almost ten years before. Which goes back to the reason we were here in Berlin. In that decade we'd asked our music to do so many things that by the end of the eighties it felt as if it were exhausted. As if it were in danger of being weighed down by its own seriousness—a point made by some of the harsher critics of the Phil Joanou–directed big-screen rockumentary *Rattle and Hum*. Perhaps we needed to release the music from some of its purposefulness, however subtle. From its utility and campaigning, its self-importance. We'd come to play with the ghosts of this hallowed studio—Nick Cave, David Bowie, Iggy Pop—and the ones they themselves had been possessed by, Conny Plank, Kraftwerk, Neu!, and Can. But was the quality of our own communication betraying the shadowy presence of some still earlier patrons? When this place had been a Nazi ballroom.

For many years I'd had a recurring dream about breaking and entering the house I'd grown up in on Cedarwood Road. I was attempting not a robbery but rather to break in without being noticed by my da. That had been a regular enough routine in my teens, when I might have forgotten my house keys and didn't want to wake the ol' man up. Scaling the drainpipe and entering through the first-floor bathroom window, it wasn't exactly rock climbing, but there was always one moment of vulnerability. That was when I had to leave the drainpipe, find the bathroom window with my left foot, and reach for the fly window, usually left open. Then I could reach in, open the window proper, and scramble into the house. It was all the more awkward attempting this in the dark, after a drink or two, exhausted after the walk home from the city center.

One night, mid-operation, as I was half-in and half-out, the da woke up, wondering if he was being burgled.

"Paul! Paul?" he yells. "Is that you?"

"Yeah," I shout-whisper back, trying to impersonate the muffled sounds of someone not hanging outside the bathroom window. "I'm in the bathroom."

"What time is it?" he goes.

"I don't know," I reply, still muffling. "About one."

"Get to bed."

"Okay, Da."

In Berlin, I have this dream for the first time in years. But this time it's not my father who shows up as I stretch from the drainpipe to get my foot on the bathroom window ledge. This time it's my mate Guggi appearing from inside the bathroom, reaching toward me and pushing me back so that I fall down and down onto the clothesline in the garden below.

I wake up under the pillow and, lying there in a cold sweat, wonder what my subconscious is bothering me about. It's not a dream about Guggi. It's a dream about friendship. It's a dream about the fear that your dearest friends might let you down when you need them most. At the moment when you are vulnerable, attempting some precarious leap in the dark.

In the studio in Hansa, I figure it comes down to this.

"Has everyone got my back or not?" (How pompous have I become?)

And if not, my not-so-sophisticated self wants to know, who has a better idea of what this band should be doing right now? Who can draw it and who can write it?

I stretch Edge's patience and imagination to the limit regarding our capability, but he's always figured that if he puts our friendship first and my survival instinct second, things will probably work out okay. Which in long-lasting relationships is an increasing likelihood. My frustration is down to the conviction that now is the very time I need my friends the most, just as we're about to take this huge leap of faith. My deepest fear is that they're not there for me. Am I scared, deep down, that this shape-shift in our sound and attitude might be a struggle for our audience too? Or that the band's hesitation might be a product of the songs themselves not being up to scratch?

Was I aware that I might be the one pushing the band to the brink of breakup? It's not as if I didn't remember how close we'd come to ending it all that last time, when Edge decided he couldn't go on. Why would I put everything at risk again?

What's got into me? What gets into me?

Why am I prepared to bet the house, or at least the band, on these intuitions, this instinct that if we step into the dark as artists, we'll depend more on the light. That somehow we'll find an open window. Because there is no manifest destiny. There is no guarantee that this will all work out.

LOVE AND IMMORTALITY

In Berlin we were pilgrims on a holy journey to the source of some sacred music, and among our hosts was the great film director Wim Wenders. This bohemian cinematic auteur explained that on the shoot for *Paris, Texas,* the crew had been listening to our album *Boy,* and now he repaid the compliment, becoming our spirit guide during our stay. Wim's *Wings of Desire,* in which an angel falls in love with a mere mortal, had become my favorite film. So torn was I by the idea of having to make a choice between love and immortality that it began to preoccupy my own work. I saw the film a dozen times, coming to understand both the director's probing cinematic eye and the influence on him of the angels in the poetry of Rainer Maria Rilke. A collision of many of Wim's concerns: the instant and the eternal, the frozen image and the entropic life. Questions that kept me awake at night: Could you give up eternal life for a moment of actual love? But isn't a moment of love always eternal?

Wim arranged for us to see an early cut of his new film, *Until the End of the World,* and beguiled by the title, I took it home and wrote a completely different story, a conversation between Jesus and Judas. Reading *The Book of Judas* by the poet Brendan Kennelly, I'd noticed how powerful it was to put yourself in such a mythic conversation.

> *I took the money*
> *I spiked your drink*
> *You miss too much these days if you stop to think*
> *You lead me on with those innocent eyes*
> *You know I love the element of surprise.*
>
> —"Until the End of the World"

Because I couldn't find a memorable melody for the verse, the song ended up in the conversational mode, allowing for this kind of lyric. The pitch of your voice determines the kind of vocabulary you can use in a song. Tenors should learn Italian because the tenor was invented in this most romantic landscape—the landscape of the vowel. Sono. Eeo. Alto. Opera is not the same for singers in German; it's harder to find vowels there, harder to hit the big notes. While we were working on *Achtung Baby,* I made a note to self: "Sing lower, use technology if you have to." On "The Fly," for example, I used electronic distortion to get to a different personality, but on "Until the End of the World" I used a conversation. With Jesus.

> *In the garden I was playing the tart*
> *I kissed your lips and broke your heart.*
> *You, you were acting like it was the end of the world.*

There were days when making this album felt like it was the end of the world for us. Are you not laying it on a bit thick, I hear you ask. It's not as if you're going down a coal mine every morning. Okay. I'll grant you that. I know. It's male egos rubbing up against each other. But we're a band, a foursome. Unlike a solo artist we're trying to realize a shared vision. That can offer unparalleled exhilaration . . . or a kind of dreadful torpor.

Fortunately, there are moments when the agony turns to ecstasy.

In our final week in Hansa we're making a song that will be called "Love Is Blindness." I am standing beside Edge, encouraging him to tell the story of his life, right now, through the instrument he best expresses himself with. It is a story he must tell, but a story he can never tell with words. A story too painful even to tell himself. The story is about his marriage, which is over, and how he is splitting up with the mother of his kids, these three girls whom he loves more than life. He loves their mother, too, but they can no longer make it work for each other. In the studio Edge has no place to hide from his friends, and with his guitar he has no place to hide from himself. As we stand, he begins to exorcise these demons, but then to exercise them. It's not enough to say he is losing his temper; it's as if he's taking out all this pent-up rage and grief and sadness on his guitar. Fighting with his feelings by punishing the guitar in his hands, smacking it, trying to rip strings off it. To the rest of us it feels as though the world is crashing down on this man and his guitar, that they are disappearing into each other, man into inanimate object or the other way around.

And in the midst of this electrical storm, I notice some furious beauty, a tiny tunefulness that appears among the dissonance, a melody emerging that no one who hears this song will forget. It's a powerful thing to be present at the act of creation, and I count myself fortunate to have been present at a moment such as this in Hansa Studios.

It's always the tone first with Edge; the tone is as important as chord progression, as the hook, as the lyric. The sound itself is what Edge occupies, and what occupies Edge is the sound.

A KIND OF SUMMONING

We had a breakdown in trust at Hansa, and it started to become wearing. We were one but, well, you know the rest. *Achtung Baby* had a difficult birth. We almost lost her. But when the baby arrived, we soon forgot the pains of the labor. The waiting, the wanting, the longing for the music, imbues the final songs with something other. It's a kind of summoning.

A key component to greatness is that the work has to answer a deep personal desire to make it. The song you are writing and recording has to be, above all other criteria, a song that you want to hear yourself. "One" was such a song. We wrote it because we really needed to hear it. It was made up of two discarded chord sequences that Edge came up with for a middle-eight breakdown section in "Mysterious Ways." When he put them together, it became an invitation to sing a brand-new song.

The Dalai Lama had written to us, not long before, asking us to be part of the Festival of Oneness. I hadn't a lot of knowledge of what the Dalai Lama was about, but he struck me as a poetic figure in a tragic situation. I replied, politely, explaining why we couldn't make the festival, and, after "respectfully yours, Bono," added a P.S.: "One, but not the same."

I was, and still am, suspicious of the idea of oneness. I don't buy into the homogeneity of the human experience. I don't think we're all one. We can be one, but I don't think we have to see things the same way for that to be so. An anarchic thought: We're one but we're not the same. We get to carry each other, not that we've got to, just that we get to.

Now I improvised a lyric about a son telling his religious father he was gay. About a lover who had been discovered finding sex outside a sexless marriage and explaining how she'd got there. Part of its drama is that it starts in the middle of an argument: "Is it getting better, or do you feel the same? Will it make it easier on you, now you've got someone to blame?"

You're overhearing conversations, and you draw your own conclusion, just like that woman at the Palasthotel who used to listen in to the rooms she and her Stasi friends had bugged. All the intimacies from different rooms entwine into one story about how people are more the same than they are different. But still, they remain different. *We don't have to pretend we're all the same, and we don't have to carry each other. But in truth, like it or not, we do get to carry each other.*

Great comradeship is at the heart of a true band. And when the comradeship leaves, the muse is usually running down the street after it. I'm someone with an inordinate desire for company and specifically for collaboration. If I cherish time on my own, my inclination has always been to take what I learn on my own and double or quadruple it in partnership.

Without the band, I can't make the music I hear in my head. Without my partner, I can't be the man I aspire to be. I succeed only through collaboration.

THE SONG WE NEEDED TO HEAR

Nearly thirty years later, in November 2018, and onstage in a very united Berlin, I found myself explaining this period in this city to the crowd. Explaining it to the band, to myself. It's the last show of the tour and Brian Eno is here, along with Flood, and I've explained how the two of them and Danny had been so vital to us in that period. With Larry stock-still at his drums, Adam and Edge prepping for the next song, it all came back to me: not just how we fell out big-time while we were recording *Achtung Baby*, how we ran out of love for being in the band, but also how "One" was a song that saved us.

We wrote the song that we needed to hear.

How I understood that in the end I am one quarter of an artist without Edge, Adam, and Larry. How I am one half of a person without Ali. Exit signs flickering up in the stands, I looked around the stage at my co-dependents and noticed my own gratitude. We're one and for a split second we're the same.

The Fly

in which I begin to get out of my own way
by discovering the importance of not
being earnest... and start channeling
Elvis before Elvis turns up, in my
chicago hotel room hoping to
become the leader of the free world

21

The Fly

It's no secret that the stars are falling from the sky
It's no secret that our world is in darkness tonight.
They say the sun is sometimes eclipsed by a moon
Y'know I didn't see you when she walked in the room.

Holding on to your first true love feels like no small victory against the world and the unlikely odds placed on such a bet, but it turned out that's not a good enough reason for two people to stay together. When Edge and Aislinn lost their marriage, there was a loss of innocence all around. Our whole community got a bit skittish. They were the first to have kids, in a way the first to be grown-ups. If they couldn't make it, who could?

Ali and I stared harder at each other. It was as if we were standing outside our selves, hovering over our own relationship, staring down at it. Had we committed to each other too early or made promises that we didn't understand the cost of keeping? The answer to both of those questions was likely yes, along with a loud no to the idea that we'd made a big mistake. True, now raising two little girls, we were having our own Achtung Baby moment, and I saw that our music had to be capable of telling more interior stories like these.

Whether real or imagined, sexual or spiritual, infidelity is a subject you can't ignore if you think of yourself as a diarist of the heart.

"The Fly," the first single released from *Achtung Baby,* was not just an image of a man's insignificance up against his unconfessed libido but an acknowledgment of how annoying that libido can be.

> *A man will rise, a man will fall,*
> *from the sheer face of love,*
> *like a fly from a wall.*
> *It's no secret at all.*

Here sex is the fly spray, and why would I not fully embrace a subject that, if Sigmund Freud was even half right, is close to the center of personhood? "The Fly" gave me license to be licentious in U2's work if not in my play. But if you imagine that watching the father of your children onstage wearing the glad-eyed face of a thirteen-year-old might be alarming for the partner of the über-rockstar persona you'd be . . . wrong. Ali had never forgotten how that thirteen-year-old had made her laugh. She delighted in the delayed adolescence we were both enjoying as lovers, too. And knew deeply and surely that mine was a single-sun universe. If, on occasion, she figured she was being eclipsed by whatever moons were mooning, she was there, minutes later, to reset gravity. And me hers, but that was rarer.

BIRTH OF "THE FLY"

Moving to Los Angeles to make *Rattle and Hum* in the late 1980s, we'd begun unfreezing those four serious-looking men on the sleeve of *The Joshua Tree.* Now *Achtung Baby* raised the temperature, giving us more freedom not to be dragged down by the weight of our own moral baggage. It was time to release some ballast. The balloon that could so easily have burst instead fizzed and squealed and crackled its unpredictable trajectory toward fun.

"The Fly" we described as the sound of four men chopping down *The Joshua Tree.*

At the moment when I was looking for a chance to out myself as a too-serious artist, Ali was right by my side telling me she missed the bold face I had as a teenager. But in loosening up, I was also fearful of being called a hypocrite. The answer was staring me in that bold face.

The answer was to declare myself a hypocrite.

In song, onstage, and on camera I had to find a character that could own up to my worst excesses. A fantastical rock star. An über rock star. So what if I'd never really felt like a rock star, only ever played it part-time? "The Fly" knew how serious silly can be, understood humor as a weapon, knew that comedians have more chance than songwriters of saying the thing that no one wants to hear.

Tall Tales, Short Rock Stars

1. Singers are short. Bryan Ferry is an exception. Nick Cave is an exception. Okay, there are others, but as a rule singers are not tall. The stage is our platform shoe.

2. Insecurity is our best security.

3. Frontmen are often out the back door when it comes to paying the bill.

4. The only thing rock stars are more interested in than ourselves is other rock stars.

Part Dada, part art attack, part Shakespearean fool, I loved the freedom I found as I stepped into my role as contrarian court jester. Gone was old and earnest Bono, taking a finger in the eye from his shadow self, the importance of not being earnest Bono.

Plus, the getup was great! I stole a bit from all my heroes and a lot from Elvis's *'68 Comeback Special*. The Elvis leather jacket, the Jim Morrison leather pants. Offstage the shades were Lou Reed's Ray-Bans; onstage I'd found these spectacular, funkadelic, bug-eyed goggles. Actually, our wardrobe man "Fightin' Fintan Fitzgerald" had found them, in one of London's secondhand markets. During recording I'd kept them in the studio, having fun with them when the music wasn't having any. I put them on and told the production team I could see into the future. "So what does the final mix sound like?" asked Flood. "Are Fulham going to get promoted?"

Previously I'd had to ask Edge, who everybody knew was from the future, what it was like. He would think for a moment before his answer, which was always the same. "It's better."

SLEEPWALKING WITH THE MUSE THAT IS DAVID BOWIE

I was twelve when I first saw David Bowie perform "Starman" on *Top of the Pops*. He was vivid. Luminous. Fluorescent. In terms of impact David Bowie was England's Elvis Presley. There are so many similarities: the masculine-feminine duality; the physical mastery of being on a stage; how each created original silhouettes, stark cutout shapes now seen as obvious that did not exist before. Bowie borrowed the famous flash symbol from around Elvis's neck, the so-called TCB—taking care of business—dog tag for his face makeup on *Aladdin Sane*.

They were cosmic twins, born on the same day twelve years apart, and they both had an otherworldliness. With Bowie, you had the sneaking suspicion that if you hung around him, you would find a door into other worlds. In my teenage mind "Life on Mars?" was really about life on earth. Are we really alive? Is this really all there is?

On a spring day in dirty old Dublin while we were recording *Achtung Baby*, David arrived up the river Liffey, dressed as a ship's captain. He had indeed come from his yacht even if we might have preferred a spacecraft. This was our "stealing from the thieves" period, so we were unembarrassed to play him an album so obviously influenced by him. He told me he thought "The Fly" needed work but was reassuringly reassuring about some of the other songs . . . quite generous of him, considering he was being plagiarized. He recognized some of the similarities as the influence of Eno on both of us, rather than just him, and reminded us he'd been a bit of a magpie himself.

He'd covered the subject with the song "Fame," written with Carlos Alomar . . . *and* John Lennon.

> *Fame (fame) what you like is in the limo*
> *Fame (fame) what you get is no tomorrow*
> *Fame (fame) what you need you have to borrow*

As he was spending more time in Dublin, he wanted to know about local bars and clubs, and maybe because he was dressed as a captain, we thought he might like our local Dockers, on the Liffey, at the back of Windmill Lane Studios. Maybe he imagined it was some kind of Marlon Brando *On the Waterfront*–themed bar? Because the next time the man from Mars turned up to see us, he asked to meet in Dockers, but seemed puzzled that the place was filled with actual dockers. And the families of actual dockers. To add to the surprise, his and theirs, David was wearing a brighter-than-day electric-blue suit that I thought looked as if it had a spotlight that came with it, and for a long moment he pulled off the impossible. He created silence in a noisy Irish bar. A dumbfounded silence followed by the inevitable crescendo of lip and laughter, compliments and crass jeering, which the Starman was graceful enough to pretend not to hear.

Another Sunday and Ali caught the crush, while he fawned over our little faun Jordan. When his better-self manager, Coco, was leaving him to stay with us overnight, she passed Ali some instructions.

"David can be odd during the night. If he sleepwalks into your bedroom and stands at the end of the bed, just tell him to go back to his bed. He usually does."

"What if he doesn't?" questioned the missus.

"Call me."

David slept well, but Ali, up in the night with two-year-old Jordan, did not.

When she walked by David's room, the door was open and so she closed it. An hour later, same drill. Next morning I asked her about the sleep patterns of the man who fell to earth.

"What a beautiful creature, like one of Blake's angels," she said. "Only just anchored to the ground."

Platinum chains. We rarely notice how lucky we are to be in the orbit of certain people until their presence is no longer present. How blessed we were in that moment to have such a bright light around.

We would see a lot of David in the years ahead, but there'd also be periods when he'd go missing. Toward the end of his prolific life, I tried to keep in touch, but he went quiet. On the release of his song "Blackstar" at the end of 2015, Jordan and I took a winter walk over Killiney Hill, sharing a set of earbuds to listen to his new communication. A chilling ache of a song, "Blackstar" (named after an unreleased recording of an Elvis track) was more jazz than pop, more Miles Davis than Michael Jackson, but four minutes and twenty-five seconds in it swivels to his 1970s purple period. Suddenly it could be something off *Hunky Dory* and I was fifteen again—walking with my twenty-six-year-old daughter, whose favorite artist had always been David Bowie. I slowed on the brow of the hill with tears in my eyes. I held Jordan so tightly she realized it was her holding me, hot teenage tears from my eyes on her crimson cold cheeks.

On his birthday a couple of months later, I wrote David a longer than usual note to tell him how we felt and included Michael Leunig's beautiful poem "Love and Fear":

There are only two feelings.
Love and fear.
There are only two languages.
Love and fear.
There are only two activities.
Love and fear.

I included a selfie of Jordan and me toasting him, and three days later we woke to the news that he had died. Some part of so many of his fans died too. The poster fell off the wall in 10 Cedarwood Road. U2 owed him so much. Even his folly, the Glass Spider Tour, we took as an inspiration for our own ZOO TV Tour, which Robert Hilburn of the *Los Angeles Times* called "the 'Sgt. Pepper's' of rock tours." A fine accolade from a fine critic who certainly knew that it had been David Bowie on our minds all along.

It was "zoo radio," the term given to shouty, manic DJs broadcasting from anything-might-happen-next radio studios, that sparked the thought of us taking our own station on the road. A TV station.

We could do outside broadcasts, take live satellite feeds, channel surf. We could make prank phone calls to the White House. We could do it all during a show. We could call the tour ZOO TV.

So we did.

The building of U2's live shows had long demanded the assembly of a whole other band backstage. The sound is the most important, and for that we have Joe O'Herlihy, who first met us at the Arcadia Ballroom in Cork, his hometown, in 1978. And never left us again. At the time he was an apprentice wizard, but somewhere along the line he became a grand master, some kind of diviner, who listens less with his ears than with his gut.

The central architects who shape and build the show are few. Many designers have contributed, but only a few stayed with us, including Mark Fisher and his team. But no one has had as significant a role as Willie Williams, who arrived with us as our LD— lighting designer—on the War Tour, in 1983. I remember him early quoting his friend Steve Fairnie, from the post-punk art-house band Writz, who used to declaim from the stage, "I have a vision, a television." Willie had televisions too, and for ZOO TV he put them all over our stage. Not to mention hanging those East German Trabants above us.

Willie has a voice that seems to go through its own public address system. A voice he can turn up or down at will but that is always clear and audible, regardless of background clatter or roar. Raised in Sheffield, England, and, like us, diverted from university by punk. If we were fans at a Clash show who decided to climb up onstage and be the band, Willie was a fan at one of our shows. And instead of invading our stage, he decided he might as well design it. A stage dive in reverse. Now our show designer and absorbed in every detail of our productions, he lives for the lighting, and if sound is Joe's force, light is Willie's. Willie's long been tripping the light fantastic in arenas and stadiums, but just as important in a touring band, where morale is everything, he's the great entertainer, happy to make a show of himself when he wants to.

Florida, opening night, February 1992, and MTV's Kurt Loder is asking me what's happened to the "normal dude, wearing normal clothes."

"You didn't like me when I was me, so I found somebody new."

The startling Technicolor sleeve of *Achtung Baby* offered a stark contrast to the monochrome aesthetic of earlier albums, and it was time for our stage show to ring the changes too. Although "going to a rock show and watching television," as Larry put it, did not sound like a whole lot of fun, in the age of grunge the idea proved counter-cultural in a nicely argumentative way. This was the era of Pixies, Pearl Jam, and Nirvana, of music stripped back to the bare bones. The songs of Kurt Cobain sounded like bare-knuckle fistfights, while Eddie Vedder performed open-heart surgery nightly, minus the fluorescent light show. Were we so out of sync with the cultural spirit of the times, with the raw back-to-basics rock 'n' roll of grunge? Yes, we were. And loving it. We were fans of this new crop of bands, but we enjoyed the friction with some of the more bogus ideas of authenticity that surrounded the scene. We asked Pixies to tour with us, and it was a perfect stylistic fit.

Sure, they were brutish primary-color rock 'n' roll, but lyrically? They were sci-fi.

Our own colors were now Day-Glo—ultraviolet and electric blue—and there was a chaotic energy in the ZOO TV nightly production. Fast jump cuts and hard edits between comedy and tragedy, between what was real and what was not. The duality of *Achtung Baby* was writ large on banks of TV screens, illuminating our stage. A playful phony futurism that was captured by one of our guiding literary lights, the cyberpunk prophet William Gibson, who wrote, "The future is here. It's just not widely distributed yet."

Each night "The Fly" would crawl up and onto the wall that was our stage before visibly falling back and down in front of the puzzled crowds. Each night the show closed with "Love Is Blindness."

> *Love is blindness, I don't want to see*
> *Won't you wrap the night around me?*

Oh my heart,
Love is blindness.
In a parked car, in a crowded street
You see your love made complete.
Thread is ripping, the knot is slipping
Love is blindness.

ENTER ELVIS, STAGE LEFT . . .

Most nights onstage we'd been calling the White House of George Herbert Walker Bush. We always had a few questions. I'd leave some inane message like "Watch more television." All a little Dada-esque: maybe we picked that up in Germany too.

It was more mischief making than political point scoring until September 1992, when we first met the then Arkansas governor William Jefferson Clinton. The rule in the band is if you have the big suite, you have to host band meetings and the aftershow. But this particular meeting was after the aftershow. Some hours after the after-party. We'd arrived at the Ritz-Carlton in Chicago after traveling from the show in Madison, Wisconsin, and by eight a.m. the room, which happened to be mine, looked as if a poltergeist had been staying in it, not a gaggle of rock stars and a giggle of friends and crew. Apprentice lounge lizards in fact.

Edge and I had been up until the wee small hours working on a song to pitch to Frank Sinatra. When I listen now to "Two Shots of Happy, One Shot of Sad," it feels like an homage to Frank's classic "In the Wee Small Hours." But hanging with Frank Sinatra, we were not prepared for Elvis to appear.

Elvis was the nickname some in the governor's team gave their fearless leader, and with his swaggering gait and smile as wide as Tennessee, it wasn't hard to see why. We should have been prepared because discovering, the previous evening, we were staying in the same hotel, we'd invited the Democratic presidential front-runner to join us. There might have been some alcohol involved, but as our very sober tour manager, Dennis Sheehan, stooped to put an invitation under the candidate's door, he had been dissuaded by the Secret Service.

"They know each other," Dennis explained. "The band once spoke to the governor on a radio phone-in."

"I'll pass your note to the governor in the morning, sir. He'll be sleeping now; we just flew in."

Dennis, undaunted, saw his opening.

"We just flew in too," responded the man from Dungarvan town, sure that the touring logistics of a presidential candidate's entourage might not be so different from those of his own charges. "We who move through the air when everyone else is sleeping," said Dennis with a smile.

The Secret Service remain unmoved.

"The boys were only offering pizza. Nothing funny going on."

Well, maybe a little bit of funny going on. After we had spent six months touring in excessive rock star parody mode, the clothes were beginning to fit a little too well. The late nights had been getting later, and as the governor walked through the door into our after-party aftermath, even we knew this was not going to be his greatest photo op. As for all the would-be president's men and women, they were thinking only damage limitation, how quickly they could move along from this unscripted diversion into rock 'n' roll Babylon.

But not Bill, from Little Rock, Arkansas. The future president saw four Irish fellas having a little fun, four fellas he had the power to make his best friends. We would discover that this special superpower was as deadly as any ballistic missile program in ensuring a president gets his message through. Charm at scale. Nuclear charm.

Laughing out loud as he surveyed the wreckage of empty wine bottles and pizza boxes, he turned to his advisers with his hands out.

"Well, I guess this is what a rock band is supposed to look like . . ."

Then he sat down to discuss the Irish peace process, Miles Davis, and Frank Sinatra. There was such an easy inclusiveness at the heart of this man and, it was clear, there was no one he couldn't talk to. No one.

"You been to a Bears game?"

"Governor, we've never been to a football game."

After he invited us to piggyback his motorcade to a Chicago Bears game, our friendship was sealed, so when Bill Clinton won the election a month or so later, his new best friends were a little deflated not to receive an invitation to the January inauguration. Surely, some mistake.

MTV was throwing a Rock the Vote party, and Larry and Adam formed a hybrid tribute band called Automatic Baby with R.E.M.'s Michael Stipe and Mike Mills to play "One." It was a special moment for these southern musicians to have a southern president in the White House. But Edge and I? Not even asked to the afters. Still, one of the president's advisers, Mike Feldman, did stay in touch, and a few years later, when I needed to get a meeting with my new best friend and now leader of the free world, I finally got my invite.

LESS IS MORE . . . MORE IS EVEN MORE

ZOO TV crossed the Atlantic with confidence. Though assembled in America, it was built for the crisis and opportunity that was the new Europe. Since the wall had come down and the Iron Curtain been pulled aside, anticipation had been building for a larger, more unified free Europe. A place where many different voices could speak with the same voice. Or none.

Brussels was sometimes the capital of eurobabble. Was this babbling tower of globalism just going to bring the nationalists out onto the street? Yes . . . and no. Yes, the neo-Nazi gangs were on the rise, and the first all-out military conflict in Europe since World War II was breaking out in the Balkans. But also no. Many of us loved, loved, loved, this most romantic idea of a new Europe. Like America, but more of a mosaic than a melting pot. Cultural origins and palimpsests preserved, traditions and languages protected.

This dramatic static was the stuff of the ZOO TV tour, now prompting us to write new songs collected under the name Zooropa, as that's where we were headed. Zookeepers and circus animals all aboard. Could we record an album in the break between the U.S. and the European legs, the break between the indoor shows and the "outside broadcasts."

Translating an indoor production into an outdoor one is difficult enough, but a new album too? Maybe. If we let go to the grand madness of it all. Which we did. More mad than grand.

As I write, I note a tendency toward the preposterous can often be traced to my fizzy head and that this can be a challenge for everyone around me. Especially Edge, who is likely not going to sleep for the next couple of months. (Unless it's facedown on a mixing desk.) If it were not for some of the material he had prepared going into *Zooropa,* despite our in-studio improvisations with Adam, Larry, and Brian Eno, there would be no album.

It would be comedically costly but we would try to magnify the ZOO TV multimedia onslaught for a stadium setting. Now even more over-the-top with the giant TVs and a vintage collection of East German Trabant motor cars, installation art to hang high up in the rigging. Repurposed as spotlights. More is more, as we came to say. Maximalism.

I love stadiums for a simple reason: the punters on the terraces can see the stage. I love the big, round roar of the crowd in these concrete crucibles, in contrast to the open field, where the sound of a crowd singing floats away into the night. I grew up watching rugby matches with my father and brother, and we particularly loved the Ireland versus Wales games. The Welsh choral singing from the stands takes you to a whole other level and has the hair standing up on even their opponents' necks. True, crowds gathered for communal purpose are vulnerable to orchestration and manipulative suggestions. Good and bad.

Of all the judgments history lands on Adolf Hitler, the crimes of showbiz rarely make the list. But Hitler had an instinct for sound systems and stadium rock was part of his lethal playbook. With Joseph Goebbels he harnessed spectacle to power the dark specter of the Nazis. Albert Speer, his favorite architect, was commissioned to build the towering backdrop for the Nuremberg rallies, and advised on the new stadium constructed for the 1936 Berlin Olympics. The Third Reich—on point, on style, on design. All designed to show the world their aesthetic of superiority. All for murderous intent. Filmmaker Leni Riefenstahl's *Triumph of the Will* and *Olympia* celebrated Hitler's vision of *Herrenrasse,* the master race.

Our plan was to satirize all this with ZOO TV. "Mock the devil" as C. S. Lewis suggests in his *Screwtape Letters.* To use this multimedia monster to stand up to the neo-Nazi upsurge in Europe was just too tempting to pass up and our whole art attack of a show was designed to be a tragicomic antifascist rally. The night opened with me goose-stepping onto the stage.

"Achtung, baby!"

We'd decided to appropriate footage from *Olympia* for our ZOO TV overture long before we knew that in June 1993 we'd be playing the Olympiastadion itself. What a moment, nearly sixty years on, replaying the footage back into the very stadium where it was filmed. Life imitates art. Art irritates life. And the risk of offense? Sure. Political satire had been such an effective tool of the dadaists and the surrealists that they were some of the first to be persecuted by the Third Reich Nazis. The neo-Nazi expects to be met with violence on the street; this is the language of their mollified machismo, the sex appeal, especially for young men. Mockery can be a delightfully dangerous weapon. Dada unzips the fascist male and pulls down his combat pants, exposing him to ridicule. A journalist asked us if the band was afraid the physical structure of the Olympiastadion would oppress us. No, I replied, but if Berlin was fearful, they should paint the stadium pink. Was I getting a little flip? That ended abruptly as the tour rolled into Italy, where it became clear that the war in Bosnia was revealing genocidal tendencies on the Mediterranean Sea, long thought to have been banished.

ART IMITATES LIFE . . . AND DEATH

Bill Carter was a maverick American filmmaker and relief worker. He was living in Sarajevo during the Bosnian War, at the height of what would become the longest city siege in modern times, almost four years from the spring of 1992. A dashing young man of twenty-five, Bill had a fearlessness that allowed him to risk life and limb and run the gauntlet of Serbian snipers to escape the siege and cross the border into Italy. Just to see our show in Bologna. He was a fan. And as resourceful as he was broke, Bill was on a mission to deepen the relationship between his favorite band and his adopted hometown of Sarajevo. He'd heard us talking about the war in the former Yugoslavia and how Bosnians were facing near genocide; and how it shamed a disunited Europe that had failed to respond. I'd mentioned how snipers were firing on former neighbors from hills around the city, like shooting fish in a barrel.

Some fourteen thousand people would be killed during the siege, the population of the city falling by as much as a hundred thousand. This was hell and the devil had a special place in his heartless heart for Sarajevo, not least because it had once been known as the capital of tolerance in the region. For a thousand years Muslim, Christian, and Jew had lived peacefully alongside each other.

Backstage in Italy, Bill told us of life just across the sea, right on the edge of Europe, where Bosnians were hiding in shelters from the constant shelling. They played loud music to drown out the sounds of destruction, he said, and they were watching MTV, including our band, protesting as Europe turned its back. He played us messages of love from fans trapped in the siege and asked if we'd come and play for the embattled city.

"Sure," I said, without looking around, not good behavior in a democratic institution like U2.

And could we get out the story of how harmonious this city of many traditions had been, before the Serb right wing set about trying to destroy it? How Sarajevo is proud of its unique mix of Muslims and Jews, Catholics and Orthodox Christians? How they all used to feel safe here?

"Yes." Again.

The first "yes" was irresponsible. We'd heard news of people queuing at a bakery opening that had led to mortar strikes, so a band turning up might spark mayhem. But the second "yes"? How about we organize a live satellite connection? To every European show? If Bill in Sarajevo could gather a collection of people of different faiths and ethnicities, I would speak to them live every night from the stage.

With a show called *The Real World*, MTV had developed a format that would become known as reality TV, where viewers were invited into the apartment and daily lives of a posse of cool young people. All good fun but a highly regulated and heavily edited version of reality.

The reality TV entering the structured chaos of our ZOO TV

production would be unedited and unregulated. Anything could happen, and some nights it did. At London's Wembley Stadium, for instance, the mood quickly went from sweet to sour, when, after a few innocuous questions from the singer, the three girls on camera from Sarajevo sensed a brush-off.

"What are you people going to do about our situation here in Sarajevo? Nothing, is the truth!

"You people are going to get back to your night out, to your nice lives, and forget about us. We're going to die, and it might be better for us and you if we died quickly."

There was no response to that. No segue. Just nothing to say.

Seventy thousand people and four band members eviscerated by a brutally real juxtaposition. A transcendent night of rock 'n' roll crashing back down to earth. There was barely any applause as the now fugue-like keyboard of "Bad" began, a song, at least, that always found room for sorrow.

The reviews of the show were dreadful, accusing us of exploitation, but in our defense, when we began these live broadcasts, the siege of Sarajevo was not getting the headline news it merited. By the time we got to London, the war in Bosnia was on every cover, making it appear that we were riding a bandwagon rather than supplying some extra wheels.

Still, one person at least was inspired to respond to what he'd witnessed at Wembley Stadium that night: Brian Eno went to work for War Child, determined to better serve his bullied European neighbors. A year later we'd work together with him on it, forming a band of convenience called Passengers. On our only album to date, *Original Soundtracks 1,* we released the song "Miss Sarajevo," with a libretto and aria sung by Luciano Pavarotti.

Another song that came out of these London shows was "The Ground Beneath Her Feet," a track written with the novelist Salman Rushdie, who broke cover after several years in hiding to join us onstage at Wembley Stadium. Salman had needed round-the-clock protection following the publication of his novel *The Satanic Verses,* which some believed portrayed the Prophet Muhammad in a disrespectful way. Iran's Ayatollah Khomeini decreed a fatwa—granting permission and encouragement to "all brave Muslims" to kill Rushdie and his publishers without delay for blaspheming the name of Islam.

This being ZOO TV, at the moment when the great writer courageously stepped out onto our stage in front of eighty thousand people, I was in full Mr. MacPhisto regalia, dressed as the devil, and now face-to-face with the author of *The Satanic Verses*. His perfectly arched eyebrows arched farther, and I uttered my one good line in my best slo-mo luvvie timbre, an affectation I'd developed since witnessing Steven Berkoff all those years ago play Herod in Oscar Wilde's *Salomé*.

"It's inevitable that one falls out with one's biographer, isn't it?" The rub of art on real life . . . and real death threats.

Even better than the real thing

in which, in Australia, ADAM loses
the plot and we nearly lose ADAM
the band is degenerating until
ADAM learns to breathe underwater
(BELIEVE IT OR NOT!)
and Friedrich Nietzsche comes to
the rescue with the right turn of phrase
and we discover the FLAW is
sometimes even better than the
perfect thing

ADAM ♡ SYDNEY

22

Even Better Than the Real Thing

Give me one more chance, and you'll be satisfied.
Give me two more chances, you won't be denied.
Well, my heart is where it's always been
My head is somewhere in between
Give me one more chance, let me be your lover tonight.

The mischief maker who streaked through the school corridors in Mount Temple was now streaking the halls of grande dame hotels in Paris, New York, and Sydney. The high Adam Clayton got off oxygen and cigarettes in Mount Temple had long since been replaced with stronger stuff. We'd always laughed at stories of Dennis trying to wake him up after a couple of days out, all day and all night. Pouring water on his sleeping head.

Emptying an ice bucket over him to make sure he didn't miss a plane or train. "Yes, I'm on my way."

That rare ability he developed to answer his hotel phone. While asleep. "I'm just getting into the shower." Sure you are, Adam.

Crew members sought out hotel master keys, even, on one occasion, climbing scaffolding beside his window and breaking into his room to break him out of it. Never less than professional, he would eventually begin his bleary-eyed day with a bucket of coffee around his neck, but the fire he was playing with was starting to play with him. The drinking, once his playmate, was now his boss. Drugs had prolonged his ability to stay up late and still halfway function— enough to drink more.

He was the life and soul of the party right until the moment he wasn't. Sydney marked the moment. It might have been the end of Adam's youth, but that was better than the alternative. The end of Adam. It was very nearly the end of U2.

ADAM AT THE BOTTOM OF THE SEA

In November 1993, Adam Clayton was so excited to be in Sydney that he forgot to go to bed the night before the first show. There was a particular reason to be excited to be back in this country we all loved. Over two shows we were making a film for broadcast to mark the end of our ZOO TV Tour, a big full stop at the end of a long graphic novel.

We love a big ending. We were putting to bed a tour that had not just redefined touring for us but pushed the parameters of what was thought possible in arenas and stadiums. Now the tour was going to bed, but the bass player was not.

Having overshot the runway with drink and drugs, Adam ended up in the company of some party people whose job was to keep him at the party. A binge of such epic proportions that he couldn't recall what happened until a lot later, when he read the accounts of those who could remember, the memories they'd sold to the press.

Adam had been out on the town attempting to seduce one of the most seductive of cities. Sydney, her head popping out of the water like a movie star. Sydney, a city where everybody is going somewhere in a land that couldn't be farther from anywhere. Sydney, her outstretched arms a long-span bridge too far if you wanted them to be. And yes, our hero wanted them to be. And so he had his head and heart stomped on, not by the great beauty that is Sydney, but by an adolescent version of freedom far away. Sydney is where Adam Clayton ran out of his youth and all the excuses as to why, at thirty-three, a part of him was still thirteen.

He had the best of times; he had the worst of times. And the first any of us knew about it was when he didn't appear at sound check at the first show at the Sydney Cricket Ground. Band and camera crew were onstage blocking stuff for the filming when Paul McGuinness walked straight out onstage to where we were confabbing with a deliberateness that suggested something was very up. A summoning on his face, half whispering, half shouting: "Adam is a no-show."

ME: "Sorry?"
PAUL, as if speaking to a child: "I said Adam is a no-show, as in he's not going to be showing up here."
ME: "On time? For this sound check?"

Sydney, I assumed, had gotten the better of my best man and he was sleeping off a big night.

LARRY: "What time did he make it back to his room?"
EDGE: "We'll just have to cover the camera blocking. Stuart can stand in." (Stuart Morgan was/is Adam's guitar tech and well up to the task.)
LARRY, coming closer, philosophical look on his face: "Hmmm. Is he okay?"
PAUL: "No, he's not okay. He'll survive, but none of you are hearing me. Adam is not just not coming to the sound check. He's not coming to the show tonight."

Silence.

PAUL: "You'll have to go on without him."

The words landed like a slo-mo horror-movie sequence. Voices slowed as well as pitched down, as if you were hearing someone speak underwater, which is where Adam was, which is where we all were now. Submerged in the brown silty, salty water at the bottom of Sydney Harbour. He'd been found locked up and unconscious in a Sydney hotel room after a massive blowout. The practicalities of a TV shoot were suddenly irrelevant next to the well-being of our bandmate, but Paul assured us he was going to be okay. Just not tonight.

Words none of us ever thought we'd hear as long as we were in this band.

"What are we going to do?" asked everyone. All at once. Cancel the show? Or play it without Adam? People were already en route to the venue; the camera crew was set up. Stuart Morgan wasn't only a fine bass guitar tech; he was a talented bass player. Only Adam knew the bass parts for our songs better than Stuart. Maybe he could stand in for the whole show.

Maybe Adam would show up halfway through. Quite a lot of "maybes."

LARRY: "If we put the ZOO TV uniform on him, nobody will know."
EDGE: "That's not gonna work on TV, Larry."
LARRY: "I was making a joke."
ME: "Will he make it for tomorrow night?"

"I think so," says our tour manager, Dennis Sheehan. "I've seen worse."

Well, we figured, because it's a television event, maybe we could make it work. Two nights to make one concert film. "We'll choose the best bits of Adam from tomorrow. If he makes it tomorrow."

When we walked out that night, in front of forty-five thousand Australians, it felt as if our superpower was gone. We had never been onstage without being the four of us, not since Larry broke his foot in a motorcycle accident in 1978 and the good-looking, leather-jacket-wearing Eric Briggs filled in for him. I've been onstage a lot on my own. I've been onstage with Edge. It's a different feeling without the four. We got through. We recovered. Adam has been in recovery ever since.

GENERATE, DEGENERATE, REGENERATE

Reflecting on it, I wondered if part of Adam's problem was exhaustion. The band had released two albums in two and a half years while doing an indoor and outdoor world tour over three years.

Even for us, it was on the busy side. Adam had questioned the necessity of the constant reinvention, the dreaming it all up again and again. He wanted to enjoy the view from the top of the world. Who would question such instincts? Well . . . that would be me. His bandmate pointing out to anyone who might listen that there was another, more interesting view, higher up or lower down or round the corner. Anywhere but here in the comfort of comfortable success. I was paranoid U2 could fall for the entitlement we had heard of with 1970s rock bands who lost their songwriting chops but felt their very presence onstage was reason enough for the crowd to bow. We were going to stay students and refuse the invitation to be rock gods. Unless we could be ironic rock gods, which was the central motif in ZOO TV.

Because selling a boatload of albums is no proof of anything except your popularity. If you have a shot at greatness, you'll need a different measure from having some of your songs in the pop charts. All I could hear was the songs U2 hadn't recorded yet. All I could see were the shows we hadn't staged. If we kept going, we could do that thing that no one else has done. But only if we kept moving, kept together, and kept a kind of humility. Only if we kept breaking up the band.

And putting it together again.

In the cycle of this band, like in all creative cycles, there is birth, death, and rebirth.

Making a band, breaking a band, remaking a band.

Generate, degenerate, regenerate.

And right now, in ZOO TV, we are at the degenerate part of it. And Adam's journey was kind of emblematic. But I had to ask questions of myself too. What was my drug of choice?

This envelope pushing, where was that coming from? Was it some kind of dysfunction? That I don't know when enough is enough? Was I singing to myself in a song like "Lemon" from our 1993 record, *Zooropa*?

A man builds a city, with banks and cathedrals
A man melts the sand so he can see the world outside.
A man makes a car, and builds a road to run (them) on.
A man dreams of leaving, but he always stays behind.

And these are the days when our work has come asunder.
And these are the days when we look for something other.

Is it obsessional? That I keep feeling our reach is far from our grasp? We hit a vein with *Boy* at twenty. We hit another one at twenty-six with *The Joshua Tree*, but we discovered a whole other seam to mine at thirty with *Achtung Baby*. We weren't writing pop songs that everyone would remember in a hundred years like The Beatles, but we were creating a special feeling in our music and bringing into the open subjects that hadn't been in rock 'n' roll. And when we played live, something happened in the chemistry of band and audience that was pretty rare.

We were on a roll and this was no time to stop.

I have come to see the band as a relay race. There are times when one member of the band seems to be striding forward faster than anyone else. Adam had it in the beginning, by far the more advanced. On our shared marathon, in Sydney he ran out of road, but he also started a new one. It's not a flat road; it's a hill, the endless one that he's still on. A hill that the philosopher Nietzsche used to climb, the man who wrote that for anything great to take place in your life, there has to be "long obedience in the same direction."

That's been Adam's steep climb to recovery, his personal regeneration, for three decades. I've never been to AA, but I get a sense of the spirituality of the 12 Steps in the idea of "breathing underwater," a phrase I heard from the Franciscan friar Richard Rohr. Taking responsibility for yourself is one of the most important steps, along with surrendering to your higher power.

Adam surrendered to his higher power. He'd never been a religious person, he'd opted out of Shalom when the rest of us were in its thrall, and he was annoyed by our Christianity. But he ended up on his knees with the three of us, looking to save himself from himself.

Looking for help from something bigger than himself.

It's an extraordinary thing, the moment of surrender. To get down on your knees and ask the silence to save you, to reveal itself to you.

To kneel down, to implore, to throw yourself out into space, to quietly whisper or roar your insignificance. To fall prostrate and ask to be carried.

To humble yourself with your family, your bandmates, and to discover if there's a face or a name to that silence.

Mysterious ways

in which I wonder what is really going
on with my ma and my DA and muse
on the mysterious distance between
a man and a woman while Edge's
muse takes me on a game where we
all fall in love with the supermodels
but my own super muse isn't falling
for it ..

23

Mysterious Ways

Johnny, take a walk with your sister the moon
Let her pale light in, to fill up your room.
You've been living underground, eating from a can
You've been running away from what you don't understand.
(Love)
She's slippy, you're sliding down.
But she'll be there when you hit the ground.

In July 1969 everyone is talking about the moon. Neil Armstrong has just stepped out onto it, and President Kennedy has done it, says my da, "not because it was easy but because it was hard." It's an image that will stay with me through the years, an image for the impossible made possible by faith and fearlessness, by science and strategy. The moon became mine in a different way ever after, a symbol of romantic pursuit, pushing and pulling the tides of our human nature. Sometimes even a bit of a bully, if you believed the people who worked in the mental institute at the top of Cedarwood Road.

"On a full moon the mad go really mad," it was said. "Sure, aren't we made of water?" as one nurse put it to Gavin's mother, Anne Hanvey.

The moon smiles on the harbor bar tonight, and in a noisy, smoky

SURRENDER

room my da and Barbara talk about Apollo 11's dusty landing in the Sea of Tranquility.

"It's not been a sea for a billion years or so."

"Sure, Bob, it's only a few years ago they figured out that the moon wasn't itself a little sun. You know? Like a little sun for the night. Rather than a reflection of the sun."

"What planet are you on?"

My da shoots a look in the direction of my uncle Ted. Now they're talking eclipses, and I, the student in the midst of these great minds, am wondering how our big yellow fireball sun can be obscured by the most petite of ice-cream moons. I'm wondering also if that's what's happening to my mother as my father seems so focused on this most cerebral conversation with my aunt. It's all about the maths, he says, about the angles involved in an eclipse.

IRIS RECOGNITION

I'm only nine but I have an angle, too, a grasp of what's going on. Later, back at the caravan, I am watching my mother, Iris, as she washes the sand off her feet in the sink, her dark locks wet from swimming. In this moment she is the most beautiful woman in the universe.

The chatter of my girl cousins playing outside the caravan is always more interesting than that of the boys. Boys grunt, girls sing. Boys like my company, but, Guggi or Niall Byrne apart, I prefer the company of girls. For someone who will spend a life on the road and in the studio in the company of men, I am already trying to even things out with the company of women. Women in songs, women in film, women in magazines. Girls on our street. I love to draw or paint women, particularly to paint on top of photographs, like my father. Watercolors. I watch him lovingly drop rouge onto black-and-white lips and soft greens onto my mother's eyes. I love him loving her in these moments. He paints over the photographs of my aunts, too, and my appreciation of womankind grows.

THE ADVANTAGE OF NOT KNOWING YOU CAN'T DANCE

In the 1990s we didn't just take to clubbing; we built one. Owned it. It was called the Kitchen. It was at the bottom of the Clarence Hotel in Dublin. But actually it was house parties that became our thing. The kitchen. Again. We listened to Prince, George Clinton's Funkadelic, James Brown, the Undisputed Truth. We listened to U.K. indie dance like the Happy Mondays and New Order, like Massive Attack and Soul II Soul. Our appreciation for American music moved beyond blues, country, and rock 'n' roll into the urban expressions of hip-hop and the music those rappers were listening to like Wu-Tang Clan, A Tribe Called Quest, N.W.A. And then there was Lauryn Hill. After which nothing else can be said.

During the days we listened to American garage and grunge— Pixies, Nirvana, Smashing Pumpkins, Pearl Jam, Hole. We loved the Brits' bounce back of Oasis with their hip-hop attitude and splash melodies. What great years for music, what a voice that Liam Gallagher was given, and what songwriting at his service. His brother Noel raising the bar for anyone who had one (Liam standing on it).

And yes, Radiohead, you'd almost want to take your shoes off to listen to such sacred talents. Radiohead ruled certain hours in our house parties, usually at the end of the night, when people were more meditative, ready to calm down. Their music tended to be in more minor keys.

But mostly it was Black artists, old classic funk like Sly and the Family Stone that Edge and I became preoccupied with, not just because late at night we were dancing around our kitchen to it, but because, as Edge pointed out, it was groove-based music with very few minor chords. If Edge wasn't up all night dancing, he was up all night in his home studio dissecting dance, exploring the anatomy of what made these grooves and beats so sticky.

Maybe that's why it was called a home studio: he was living in it. It was our house he was building. These new demos had the joy that we looked for in our music but with a funkier bottom end. They gave us our sexiest song. They gave us "Mysterious Ways."

The lyrical genesis of this song had been a conversation with Jack Heaslip where he mused on the idea that the gender of God is not clear in the original biblical Hebrew. In fact one of the names of God, El Shaddai, means "the breasted one." If the greatest creative force in the world is a woman giving birth, then of course the greatest creative force in the universe is likely to be a feminine spirit.

"In the beginning God created the heaven and the earth" is how the Bible opens. "And the earth was without form, and void; and darkness was upon the face of the deep."

Until God makes her move. "And the Spirit of God moved upon the face of the waters."

"The world moves on a woman's hips." David Byrne. Sex can be awkward.

Writing about it, that is, if you want to avoid the clichés. Our band was never much about "sex and drugs and rock 'n' roll." There'd been sex, there'd been drugs, there'd been rock 'n' roll, but none of us were really taken in by the entire three-part cliché. Even Adam, who, to be fair, had genuinely applied himself. As a songwriter, though, I loved the playfulness and flirtation of some of the groove-based songs of the time. Tracks like Prince's "Sexy M.F.," Dawn Penn's "You Don't Love Me (No, No, No)," and Soul II Soul's "Back to Life (However Do You Want Me)" had a lightness of touch that I yearned for. Gravity was getting a little too heavy. I longed for weightlessness.

By the 1990s, our teenage imaginary world of Lypton Village had developed into a wider community based on a similar surreal silliness. We were becoming grown-ups but not quite. Trashing the house takes on a whole other complexion when it's your own house being trashed. If we were now supposed to be adults, some of us appeared to be declining the role. Guggi and I had promised each other as kids that we would not turn into our parents, that we would retain the fun and keep the playful . . . for which read a joyous bacchanalia. Mainly it was innocent fun, but out clubbing, some of our people did get hurt by alcohol and the drugs.

Coming out of our twenties, into our thirties, we were high on each other's company.

We expressed a lot of that through dancing, and in our heightened state we had the great advantage of not knowing we couldn't dance.

I used to say that the Irish are like Brazilians except for three damning differences: we hardly ever qualify for the World Cup; we avoid our own nakedness; and you might not always recognize our dancing . . . as dancing.

This period worked better for some of us than others. Edge certainly found his groove. The Zen Presbyterian turned out to be very much in touch with his funky self, and the nature of the band's music came to reflect that. And it also introduced Edge to his dance partner for life.

THE MUSE THAT IS MORLEIGH STEINBERG

It was in 1992 that we first met Morleigh Steinberg. We're on the ZOO TV Tour. Adam is in full-flight rock star grand madness. I've put my toe in. Larry's holding on for dear life. And Edge has become a wingman, not just for the singer, but for the bass player. It's Adam's bass part that gives up the show's sexiest moment.

> It's all right, it's all right, it's all right
> She moves in mysterious ways.
> Johnny, take a walk with your sister the moon.
> Let her pale light in, to fill up your room.

Edge is dancing onstage with the woman in the song. Isn't he? Surely the song must have been written for this woman. Except that this belly dancer on this stage has pretty much everything, except a belly. Morleigh Steinberg occupies the position of muse at the center of the song because she has an innate understanding that the muse is often controlling the artist who is painting her. This muse is in control.

Morleigh Steinberg had first caught our attention for having what the band referred to as the most attractive oxter on earth. Witness the collective gasp when she lifts her arms up in Matt Mahurin's film inserted into the video of "With or Without You." Born to a California arts family, Morleigh was co-founder of ISO, an avant-garde dance troupe that would hang themselves from ceilings, carry each other over the stage on skates, throw each other at props with Velcro. For surreal theatrical experience, it's hard to compete with ISO, dancers dressed in ball gowns, gliding over the stage as if it were an ice rink. On their knees, roller boards concealed by the gowns. The soundtrack playing Debussy's *Danse Sacrée et Danse Profane*.

We'd become more theatrical with ZOO TV, and the question of choreography had been raised, not something we'd previously been noted for. Morleigh proved the answer, a great help to Willie Williams, Catherine Owens, and to Gavin, our guiding lights for these huge traveling productions. We'd met a belly dancer in Busch Gardens in Florida, and a week before we opened the indoor version of the tour, we talked this woman, who also danced with snakes, into joining us. She proved a wonderful moment in the show, but, admirably in retrospect, she left the tour complaining about our use of plastics backstage and opining that we weren't idealistic enough. Morleigh stepped in. As slim as a daffodil, she was not an obvious choice for the belly dancer role, but there was something in her chemistry with the band that was out of the ordinary. The dance in "Mysterious Ways" started out with me but ended up with Edge, the real funky member. Life was to imitate art.

A quarter century later, after two children with Edge and several tours that could not have existed without Morleigh's choreographic gifts, I for one couldn't walk across the stage without her. I'm a natural person to be on a stage, but I'm not a natural performer. There's a difference. It takes some thought and preparation for me to be centered in my body. I'm not a dancer, but Morleigh taught me how to move. And, harder still, she taught me how to stand still.

Choreography or dance was never part of our lingua franca.

Leaping, thrusting, pushing, preening, jumping into the crowd, and climbing speaker stacks? Yes. Staying in a groove? Less so.

The opening of ZOO TV featured me being shot in the back or overpowered by the electrical charge in Edge's guitar bursts at the start of "Zoo Station." Then there was the goose-stepping.

Telling me when to calm down and stay on the back of the beat. None of this was natural to me.

Edge has always said that I look at my body as if it were an inconvenience. I can be out of touch with my physical self, and I've had to learn to understand how your body moves through time and space if you're going to be onstage. Morleigh started with me by just breathing, feeling my body. Early yoga, I guess. Stretching. Early Pilates. I was never going to take part in "I am a tree" improv dance and cannot see myself ever roller-skating across the stage, but I began to like feeling connected to my body. And happily, when I let go of some of the tension that had kept me so taut onstage, my voice improved. It stretched and relaxed and became more capable of hitting the high notes than when I was forcing them through my larynx. Morleigh has a gift for understanding the physicality of being onstage, hard earned after a life devoted to it.

TAKEN BY THE SUPERMUSE

When you invite the Muse to come in, she may bring her sisters. Into the rolling improvisation that was the ZOO TV tour swept Christy Turlington, Helena Christensen, and Naomi Campbell. Three women we treasure to this day. The supermodel was the closest thing our generation had to silent movie stars. The glamour that beguiles. On camera mute but off camera eloquent beyond words. And never acquiescence, only authority. Feminine authority. We fell for these superwomen; one of us fell head over their heels.

It was on a flight across the Atlantic that I found myself sitting next to "Naomi Fucking Campbell Soups" herself, as I explained to Adam Clayton when I helped persuade her to meet him that evening in New York City. For several years, Adam had had a massive crush on Naomi to the point where a few months later he asked her to be his bride. She accepted. It never got more exciting than that, but that . . . that was pretty exciting.

Naomi didn't just break the glass mirror on the ceiling of fashion in the most spectacular way, she shattered it into smithereens of costume glass. Her very presence and personality on such a high catwalk changed that world for women of color, like no one before her except Iman, who took her serenity on strike to protest the structural racism in fashion.

As gifted as Naomi, Christy, and Helena were in the world of fashion, they continued to evolve and revolve the roles they were supposed to blithely accept. They had more than agents; they had agency, actual power, not just superpower. These were women who were not going to be pushed around by the gaze of men nor dazzled by the glare of being in the gaze of women.

It was after experiencing complications with her own childbirth that Christy set up Every Mother Counts, turning the gaze toward mothers in the developing world, women who die in childbirth. Ninety-nine percent of maternal deaths happen in the developing world.

Helena took that gaze and turned it back on itself by becoming a sought-after photographer in her own right. She collaborated with UNHCR, with ONE, and with EDUN, subverting the stereotypical images of the world's most vulnerable people.

THE MUSE IN MANAGEMENT

When Ellen Darst, who'd run our operation in the United States since our earliest days, moved on in 1992 I realized that she'd bequeathed us a particular ethic that goes some way to explaining the strong tradition of powerful women who have kept our show on the road ever since. It's the ethic of the mentor, and Ellen had become the mentor of so many gifted women who would both inspire and challenge us. Something of the academic about her, serious in her specs, she was the source of a great river of wisdom. Mentoring is foundation, pillars, and roof of any successful organization.

There'd always been something of the muse in our management team, which since the early days had been led by a succession of dynamic women. Without such women in power positions the music business becomes a male domain, a boys' club, a load of men barking orders at each other. Think about it. We started out as four musicians and one manager, all men. We took the band on the road with men and went into the recording studio with more men.

This wasn't good for anyone.

I wish I could say it was an intentional effort to improve gender balance in the industry, but I think it was just that Paul hired women who were smarter than many of the men swaggering around.

If the band was intense, I was probably the most intense, even in my thirties still feeling I had so much to prove. But these women were like air in our sails, and in their company I lightened up. It was on my thirty-fifth birthday that the women of our tribe organized a trip on a double-decker bus round some of my old familiar neighborhoods, including one of my favorite pubs, the Grave Diggers, beside Glasnevin Cemetery. Larry, Adam, and Edge were out of town, but when we arrived at dinner, they were represented by people wearing outsized papier-mâché heads designed by the giant puppet troupe Macnas.

I think of Larry's soul mate, Ann Acheson, in particular at birthdays. Ali and Ann have always had a very close bond. Like Ali, Ann is part of our origin story, someone who's been on the U2 journey since the beginning. And always great at birthdays. Did I mention that dancing is not one of my gifts? It was Ann who made it a gift, in the shape of a pair of dancing shoes in a blue box, and ten salsa lessons with a Cuban dance teacher. More than that, in order to make sure I took the time to follow through on the gift, Ann promised to do the classes with me. Week after week we'd meet up in town in the old Factory rehearsal studio, and I did the cha cha cha to her sa sa sa salsa.

We've been lucky to be part of a rich and enduring community, maybe because we'd go to any lengths to make each other laugh.

THE MYSTERIOUS DISTANCE BETWEEN A MAN AND A WOMAN

While dancing on the table when it's in your own kitchen may not sound like rock 'n' roll Babylon, in the 1990s we were finding again a mischief and flirtation we'd had in the 1970s and mislaid in the 1980s. Ali and I laughed a lot with each other and at each other. Dancing is flirtation. The last drop of romance the century had to offer before sex could rob a silly moment and turn it into a serious one. Flirtation is part of the static electricity of some friendships. It's essential with my first love.

"I wouldn't trust a man who didn't find you attractive," I say to her.

"I wouldn't trust a woman who found you interesting," she replies.

Superwomen Inc.

I spoke to Anne-Louise Kelly daily through the 1980s and
well into the 1990s. Looking after the band across Europe as
well as Australia, New Zealand, and Japan, she had IQ and
EQ and enough energy to power Dublin.

Her protégée Barbara Galavan would go on to run a hefty
music publishing business—her most famous charge, Bill
Whelan and his *Riverdance*—while Suzanne Doyle ran my
own world for a while, before establishing a management
company with a roster of traditional Irish legends like Finbar
Furey and contemporary songwriters like Declan O'Rourke.

Working with Ellen in the United States was Keryn Kaplan,
our Jewish mother long before she had her own kids, a
brilliant strategist who'd be looking out for us for thirty
years.

Across in London, the keyboard player of our old rivals
the New Versions took on our PR and never stopped. With
acute psychological insight and the eye of a novelist, Regine
Moylett decided early we were a story she was interested in
making happen.

Sheila Roche arrived like an advert for the 1980s, her Olivia
Newton-John–style headband segueing into power suit and
shoulder pads. Few colleagues have mirrored our times like
Sheila—from dating Adam to marrying Aileen Blackwell,
from the music business to political activism with (RED) and
setting up WRTHY, a social impact agency run by women.

Sharon Blankson we'd known since we were teenagers, first
working with Stiff Records, next with Regine's operation, and
later—and ever since—our stylist, managing the wardrobe
department, keeping us à la mode, if not quite in vogue. We
nicknamed her Shaker, not noticing the phonetics of the word

"Sheikha" suggesting "Princess." Shaker was elegance fallen into rough company.

Cecilia Mullen, Larry's sister, who ran our first fan club, was the point person for so many U2 fans, and family enough to not just read through our mail but to redirect it to us: "It's not just fan mail."

stuck in a moment you can't get out of
in which a sort of sabbatical summons us
to Matisse's chapel and paradise in
the south of France but the laughter
of our carnival is thrown into darkness
and I realise that I love my heroes
even more for growing old... and
then Matisse offers illumination

24

Stuck in a Moment

And if the night runs over
And if the day won't last
And if your way should falter
along the stony pass
It's just a moment
This time will pass.

It was part reverie and part revelry, part rosary and part rosé. The day I fell asleep in the Chapelle du Rosaire de Vence, the mesmerizing little church designed and constructed by Henri Matisse just after World War II. Was it an excess of humidity or a lack of humility?

Either way I got a poke in the ribs from a visiting priest who thought it disrespectful to drop off in the pews. I thought it respectful to be so comfortable that I could fall asleep in the arms of this place. Other times when I've found myself alone here, I've sung in this chapel. It felt right. But the real show in Vence is what Matisse called "the music of the light reflections," which play on the white Carrara marble floors. Even when you look down, you feel uplifted.

For twenty-five years I've been drawn to the peace of this place. The combination of the cold monochrome of Matisse's portrayal of Christ on the cross, single line drawings on white tiles, and the riot of color in his defiantly nonfigurative stained glass has me coming back again and again.

I tried to explain to the priest that stained glass is the birth of cinema and how these are the first examples of the use of a projector.

"It's the sun that propels each narrative; the glass is the film. Catholics are great storytellers, even when it's just pure color, like these greens and blues and yellows."

It reminds me, I continue, of the stained glass of St. Canice's Church, where I used to go as a boy with my mother.

He wasn't having it.

Driving through Val d'Enfer in Provence and down along the south coast of France for the first time in 1986, I felt I'd been here before. But I hadn't. Cézanne had taken me there in his paintings, which I've studied and even copied as a teenager. Ali and I loved it and kept coming back.

In May 1986, I spent the night alone on the azure water of Nice. I was writing the lyric of "With or Without You." I was not lonely; I had the company of torment. At least a song about torment. I was also finishing two other songs, "One Tree Hill" and "Walk to the Water." It was a lovely old lady of a hotel, the Cap Estel, "une grande dame," read the blurb. I was a baby in the arms of an old aunt. I couldn't believe the turquoise sky or the chiaroscuro light, bouncing back off the turquoise water, onto the jagged cliffs of the Maritime Alps, roads like the Grande Corniche, beaches with names like Petite Afrique.

I could never get used to this. The light had hold of me.

It made sense that painters would search out its clarity, especially in the winter, when there's no humidity and the lower-hung sun creates sharpness across the features of a face or a scene. Nor could I believe the way the French lived. *La belle vie.* Some kind of balance. How come no one seemed to be overweight when every other shop was a pastry shop? The French like a little of what they love. Except cigarettes.

And if you're starting to wear a famous face, as we were by the early 1990s, the French put a premium on privacy. In truth they're not that interested in anyone else—unlike the Irish, who flatter everybody else. I watch the warm interactions between locals as they kind of sing to each other across the counter in the chemist or newsagent and how, when a stranger arrives, they act as if they can't see you. How in bars or cafés they give you the "What do you want?" look. "To give you money," I reply. I'm not complaining. It's oddly refreshing to be recognized but ignored.

All of us fell hard for the south coast of France, and Nice became a lifelong love affair. All four of us began holidaying here in the 1990s. Together. At the same time. I talked everyone into viewing a sprawling, run-down pink ruin on the sea's edge.

"This is a big job," said Edge.

"This is madness," said Adam.

Edge and I walked the property, sensing it would be a life's work to restore its former grandeur. So it has been. Thirty years now, making music, raising our children, holidaying with friends. Long, lazy summer lunches, segueing into Cannes for the evening and dance clubs with names like Opéra and Bâoli. Sometimes sleeping out overnight on a beach. Ali and I grew into our marriage in the 1990s and though new parents, still found time for the fun that freedom brings. We were fortunate to have our nanny, Saoirse—which means "freedom" in the Irish language—and more fortunate still that she took fun as seriously as she did looking after our kids. We'd been working hard for fifteen years, and with the end of the ZOO TV Tour in 1994 we fell into a kind of extended sabbatical. "Ready for the laughing gas . . . ready for what's next." Ready for experimentation. For late nights and early mornings. Looking for light and to be a little lighter. Finding light everywhere, even in a home-made disco ball dancing into the dawn. Next day waking up with our children. Holding on to them as if they were our youth. Ready for the romance.

"Life's too serious to be so serious." That was Ali's line.

IMPRESSIONISTS: MICHAEL AND HELENA

I always felt a bit of a sham as a rock star, a bit part-time. I've known some real rock stars, and Michael Hutchence was one of them. A proper rock star, he had some essential equipment for the job. He was extremely masculine and extremely feminine. Tick. He could live large but travel light. Tick. The name of his band was INXS, which was a bad pun like The Beatles. Tick. He had a supermodel girlfriend from Denmark. Tickety tick. He lived up the hill from Cannes with Helena Christensen, who was a force in front of the camera and behind it. They lived on a piece of land with an olive grove, and as the sun came up after our first night staying there, Michael was wandering around naked after a swim in the understated slate-gray pool in their garden. A proper rock star.

Eight or ten of us—Ali, Edge, the musician Andy Gill from Gang of Four, his partner, the author and activist Catherine Mayer—had resisted the return journey, after the party the night before.

"You know olive trees don't necessarily die." This is Michael speaking; we're all waking up.

"There are olive trees still around from the time of Christ in Israel. They look better the older and more contorted they get. Just like us."

"Get some pants on!" This is Helena, but Michael ignores her and instead grabs a towel to serve us an Irish breakfast. He knows, like the rest of us, that it will fall off while he serves us breakfast.

"I'm a vegetarian," says Ali.

We'd often lunch at the Colombe d'Or, an old inn at the entrance of the medieval town of St. Paul de Vence, not so far from the Matisse Chapel. Diners in the restaurant are leered at by the art hanging from the wall. Art, so the rumor goes, provided by former patrons in lieu of large bills—patrons like Matisse, Picasso, Miró, Chagall, Léger, Braque. When you eat under the shade of fig trees, it's not long before you start to feel you're a still life.

It felt fated that Ali and I would become close friends with the supermodel and her rock star. The Great Dane was laugh-out-loud company with a Modigliani-like sad face when not laughing. Which was not often. Laughing *at* you as well as with you. We took revenge by naming our feisty pup after her so that when she came around, she'd have to hear, "Get down off the chair, Helena!" or "Outside now, Helena!"

"H-Bomb" was our nickname for her. That was some kind of fusion, Michael and Helena.

For the great seducers it's not just every woman in the room they want to seduce; it's also every man. Also every living creature. Michael was a ladies' man, a man's man, and an everything-in-between's man, and yet, when you were in his gaze, you were the only other person in that moment. On the town he was great to go out with.

He was less great when it came to going home. Over a long weekend he could set fire to himself and everyone he was with, but waking up on your couch on Monday morning, he'd be smiling through his self-harm.

"You," he'd say impishly, "have destroyed my life forever." Elegant in every situation, with pockmarked skin you never saw in photos and the tiniest lisp, which could leave women still weaker at the knees. How annoying.

"Are you exaggerating that lisp?" I asked him one morning.

"Don't be thilly," the world's sexiest man mocked me.

OUR OWN NIRVANA

A late night in 1994 and Michael and I are lying on a stony beach watching the moon dancing on the water. The conversation drifts from sweet to sour, to talk about Kurt Cobain, who has taken his own life. We're mumbling. I'm smoking. Smoking in the way people smoke who have drunk too much, clumsily, ash falling on chest.

"Don't you think if he'd just hung on," Michael says, "he'd have gotten through it? If he'd glimpsed the life he could have had."

I'm listening. He's talking.

"I hate people saying he couldn't cope with being famous, it's such a cop-out."

"Fuck that," I reply. "Who can stand a whinging rock star? Kurt Cobain was too great to be in that club. His real story offers real clues, about some real issues. Those songs have a lot of real despair in them, along with the pure joy of the band's playing. Hard to fix a problem that's paying everyone's bills."

"Yeah," replies Michael, staring into the blackness of the Mediterranean, flat as a pond. "This stillness here. If he'd just have waited, mate, he'd have found a way out of whatever hole he was in. Didn't need to be a grave."

I watch him skimming a stone across the bay as morning peeps over the hill of St. Laurent. Helena interrupts.

"A night like this would save anyone's life? What are you on about? You boys are great fun, aren't ya?"

Like a great actor the H-Bomb has perfect timing, knows when to drop the right line for maximum effect.

Carole Lombard to his Clark Gable. She's got rhythm; just don't let her sing. Too late. Now she's singing. Helena has a habit of singing in your ear while you're listening to music. Completely flat.

"How do you like my singing? Has it gotten any better?"

"No."

She sings louder.

Michael said the greatest starfuckers in the world are other stars. Stars are fascinated by each other. It must be a kind of narcissism. Trying to figure out how somebody else is dealing with fame. How much they rely on security. Will they sign an autograph if someone interrupts a family meal? Bruce Springsteen will always sign someone's autograph—if they're happy to wait for him until he's leaving the restaurant. "It's surprising and a little hurtful," he smiles, "how many people don't wait."

It was in the summer of 1992, in Copenhagen with Helena, that Michael had an argument with a taxi driver while riding a bike. The taxi driver smacked him on the head, knocking him off his bike, and as he landed, he cracked his head open and never completely recovered. He lost his sense of smell and taste—even kissing became different—while his ability to control his moods seemed to dissipate, which may explain why mood-altering substances became a bit of a crutch. The great lover's insecurity went up a few notches.

Helena and Michael's relationship was over when Paula Yates, the wife of our close friend Bob Geldof, fell hard for Michael, and he fell further for her. Sharp as a stiletto with a deadly wit, she was someone I'd known since I was eighteen, and I learned from her something about the importance of not being earnest. But here we were, earnestly upended as this magnetic couple, Bob and Paula, dismantled before our very eyes. And this other magnetic couple, Michael and Paula, appeared. Paula worshipped Michael at a time when he needed all the adoration he could get, things not going well on- and offstage for INXS. Ali and I had a sense that this was going to go wrong and that this intensity could not last a lifetime. Neither of us dreamed they'd both end up dead so soon. Michael taking his own life in November 1997, Paula, after a drug overdose, less than three years later. Even now, I can't believe I've just written that.

As their behavior changed, our friendship became strained, and we grew uncomfortable during their visits. It should have been the greatest honor, that day, in 1996, when Michael and Paula called on Ali and me to ask us to become godparents to Tiger Lily. But we were wigged out. They were in free fall, spiraling down the vortex of a recreational drug use that had become hard work for everyone, especially their family, especially the younger ones.

Paula had been such a great mother, and Michael, with his attentiveness, would have been such a great father. It was too much for friends to bear and ignore. Ali was out of her mind with worry about how this was affecting a newly born child, so we nervously tried to explain that while they were in the condition they were in, we'd rather not play the role of best friends. We'd rather *be* best friends, and that meant being truthful. Friendship is not a sentimental business.

This was a hard moment, and we both felt queasy. Would our rejection make them think again about where they were at? No. It only made them think again about us. We regret this decision. Not just because it didn't work. That we can half live with our conscience is no substitute for the fact that we can't live at all with our friends. They are gone.

> Two worlds collided
> And they could never tear us apart
>
> — INXS, "Never Tear Us Apart"

PARADISE LOST

I confess to an unforgiving aspect in my personality which can take me by surprise. I had an intolerance for what I perceived to be self-generated problems. In the past I've rushed to wrongheaded judgments. I could get angry if I saw people in corners of the world begging for a breath, fighting for their life through hunger or illness, and then see privileged people throwing their life away. I know this is deeply unsound thinking. I know people can be in such a dark place that they'll do anything to escape it, including escaping this life itself. I know it's not a loving response, but that was the furious me writing the lyric of "Stuck in a Moment You Can't Get Out Of."

> *I will not forsake, the colours that you bring*
> *The nights you filled with fireworks*
> *They left you with nothing*
> *I am still enchanted by the light you brought to me*
> *I listen through your ears,*
> *And through your eyes I can see.*

In the song, I cast the lyric as a one-sided conversation where I let the singer be intolerant and not as forgiving as he should be. I still hate the death cult that loves to raise its head in rock 'n' roll. It was in the mid-1990s that I wrote "Hold Me, Thrill Me, Kiss Me, Kill Me" about how, if you don't die on a cross at thirty-three, people start asking for their money back. It's not completely untrue. Chrissie Hynde, one of my very favorite singers, a performer who made the intimacy of her recordings more punk than punk rock, a lyricist who can so deftly deliver the heaviest of heavyweight punches, once said to me, "Bono, we don't want to die stupid, choking on our own vomit, falling asleep in a swimming pool."

Chrissie spoke from nauseous personal experience, she'd lost two of her bandmates in the Pretenders, Pete Farndon and James Honeyman-Scott, and it still hurt.

"I like my heroes to be alive," she told me. "I like them to grow old."

I, too, admire my idols more for the lines on their faces, for the bumps and bruises, the cuts and scar tissue. Every year that goes by that I have Bob Dylan in my life, I admire him more. And although she's a lot younger, same goes for Chrissie Hynde. Now we've lost Johnny Cash, Frank Sinatra, Aretha Franklin, and B. B. King, but not before we discovered them discovering their older selves.

Living well, as someone put it, is the best revenge. Come to think of it, just living will do.

On the day Michael was discovered dead in his Sydney hotel room,
I remembered what he'd said to me about Kurt Cobain. "If he'd just
hung on." It felt as if our whole world had been crushed. Paradise
lost. All those eternal summers we would never spend together.

We mourned. While I was on the PopMart Tour in the U.S., Ali
was at home in Dublin, brokenhearted. She traveled with Lian Lunson to Sydney for the funeral—Lian, who had brought Michael into
our life ten years before. Nick Cave sang a new song.

> I don't believe in an interventionist God
> But I know, darling, that you do
> But if I did I would kneel down and ask Him
> Not to intervene when it came to you
>
> —Nick Cave & The Bad Seeds, "Into My Arms"

The 1990s had been a kind of carnival, but after Michael's death I
was reminded that in a carnival you've got to know when to leave.
Had we been getting a little too good at the good life? We all have
to ponder our navels now and then, but too much of it and depres-
sion is around the corner. In my case, perspective is the only thing
that can fix that. If this was a period that I spent exploring my id,
unveiling my inner Dionysus, I think I knew that I had to return the
gaze on the outside world, the real world outside our little paradise,
before more paradise would be lost.

I ended up back in the Matisse Chapel, this time staying awake,
this time looking for illumination. Illumination is the experience we
all reach for in chapels and churches, in mosques and synagogues.
We search for a light without which we only half see ourselves. My
mind takes me to the apostle Paul and his letter to the early Christians in Corinth and why he thinks love is more important than
faith and even hope.

"For now we see through a glass, darkly; but then face to face:
now I know in part; but then shall I know even as also I am known."

Wake up Dead Man

in which, Andy Warhol leads us
on a quest for making the instant
eternal but we get lost en route
and lose our album and the tour
opening flops and failure introduces
herself and our friendship is under
threat (AGAIN!) Note to self
maybe I'm the one who needs to
wake up

25

Wake Up Dead Man

Jesus, I'm waiting here, boss
I know you're looking out for us
But maybe your hands aren't free.

Andy Warhol was more religious than the art world understood.
When he was a boy, one of his first sketches was a Child of Prague
figurine, Jesus as a child. In 1986, among his last works was *Sixty
Last Suppers*, some black-and-white reflections on Jesus's last meal as
seen by Leonardo da Vinci.

I'm seventeen when Gavin, eighteen, presents me with a book
called *The Philosophy of Andy Warhol: From A to B and Back Again*. It's a
series of conversations, some quite ephemeral, nonsensical, a friend
with a friend. "'For me to think about nothing is just about impossible,' said B. 'I can't even think about it when I'm asleep.'"

A: Should we walk? It's really beautiful out.
B: No.
A: Okay.

I'm drawn to conversation because in the best kind you don't know
where you're going, only that you will get somewhere good. I wondered at what Warhol was saying, how everything that happens is

valuable depending on the way you see it. You're gossiping with a friend over someone you know, but look twice and there's some kind of dance happening, something compelling in the way we talk. The book touches me. It's 1977. Gavin and I are walking out of the cinema and arguing about Andy Warhol. We've been to see his film *Bad* and are having a serious disagreement over its value. Which I can't see. But we're agreed on one thing: Andy Warhol, Lou Reed, Patti Smith, the Velvet Underground are more and more a part of our conversation.

The conversation will be lifelong, and twenty years later, in 1997, ten years after Warhol's death, U2 will name an album after him, calling it *Pop*. Andy is synonymous with pop art; we would go so far as calling our tour PopMart.

Acknowledging how consumerism is at play in his art. And now ours. And art in consumerism.

"All department stores will become museums, and all museums will become department stores" is how he put it.

There'd be no shortage of people to inherit his pop art mantle, but fewer actually wanted it. Jeff Koons didn't want to wear that crown. While he was taking objects from pop culture into his work, he was way more classical in his adaptation of them. I loved his daring and kind of biting humor, and he agreed to meet us, to talk about a proposal for the album cover of *Pop*. He couldn't have been less like Warhol in his demeanor, entirely absent of any trace of the counter-culture. Perhaps his analytical approach and clipped conversation reflected his time on Wall Street. His presentation to us might have been someone delivering their PhD thesis.

"I'd like to put four kittens in socks hanging from a washing line," he says, speaking in precise, academic tones. "For you are individuals. Each of you is represented by a kitten, looking out from a sock, hanging on a washing line."

We wait for him to laugh. The signal that we could. He doesn't. He's dead serious.

He gets that these four suburbanites want to lighten their image, lay down some of the heavy baggage and serious themes they've lugged around for twenty years. From the washing machine of his imagination out pop four baby cats, freshly sudsed. He's not joking.

He gets it and we don't. It's we who miss the sedition in his suggestion, as radical an image as the music we wanted to make.

A brilliant idea that we didn't use. It nearly happened, but it didn't.
This turns out to be the story of *Pop*. Nearly. Not quite.

BEATLES OR STONES?

If you're a rock band that formed in the late 1970s, you have a Beatles view of the world or you have a Stones view. Though Mick Jagger was the greatest frontman ever, we wanted to be The Beatles
more than we wanted to be the Stones, in the sense that The Beatles
changed their sound on pretty much every album.

Sometimes their producer, George Martin, brought in orchestral
players or quartets. Sometimes the band would solicit guest musicians like Billy Preston and Eric Clapton. Other times the four of
them swapped instruments: Paul McCartney playing drums or
Ringo singing "With a Little Help from My Friends." Who knew?
Wow! A strategy to keep things fresh for them and their audience, a
strategy that spawned some of the greatest songs in all of songland.

By contrast, the Rolling Stones. If you know their work well,
close your eyes and listen to them play in your head. Above any one
single song, it's a single sound that you hear. It's their sound. They
own it. Its signature is a certain holler, a weave of guitar, a rhythmic
gait that's as Black as any white boys have been. A sexy, uninhibited
sound that encouraged suburban boys like me to check out more
urban influences like the Meters, the Isley Brothers, the blues in general, and, yes, the thrill I still have listening to some disco.

The Rolling Stones have had many faces and facets over sixty
years, but critics tend to overlook the sonic innovation of "2000 Light
Years from Home" or the exotic hook lines that Brian Jones brought
to a song like "Paint It Black." Unfathomably great, the songs of the
Rolling Stones have endless dimension, but mostly they work with
a similar palette of sounds.

After all, it's the same people playing the same instruments.

If a solo artist like David Bowie can use different musicians to create different sounds, how does a band like ours, a band of the same

four people, create enough variety to keep an audience interested? To keep ourselves interested? How do we do this over twenty years?

Over forty? Do we stay in our lane or swerve across the road in search of a new way that no one has discovered? *The Unforgettable Fire* and *The Joshua Tree* answered this question for us in the 1980s, and *Achtung Baby* and *Zooropa* answered it in the 1990s. But as the millennium approached, the question returned with a new insistence as rock looked less and less likely to translate to an era when a more rhythmic-oriented music would dominate. The zeros would present a digital world of ones and zeros where rap would revolt and electronic dance music (EDM) would be the only other format to challenge the rule of hip-hop. This digital world allowed lots of white acts to access a blacker, more polyrhythmic sound through an algorithm.

Listen to Joy Division, the great Manchester band of the late 1970s, then listen to New Order, who all but conjured up the rave scene in the early and mid-1980s. Joy Division, however experimental, still sounds like a rock band. New Order is an electronic act and with their song "Blue Monday" began to change the concept of what a rock band would be. They are mostly the same band as Joy Division, minus the gifted singer Ian Curtis, who took his own life in 1980. Adding a new member, Gillian Gilbert, New Order, inspired by electronic innovators like Kraftwerk and The Human League, began laying the foundations of what would define pop music for thirty years—certainly the EDM that surged in the early years of the twenty-first century. Suddenly any artsy teenager in their bedroom could buy or rent a synthesizer and drum machine or, in time, dial one up on their laptop. They could discover original sounds or grooves without going to a music academy. It was as liberating as punk rock except that the digital nature of this music meant the rhythm section had a tightness that even ten thousand hours of practice would not offer. No speeding up or slowing down. The grooves, at first quite simple, soon became more sophisticated, and it was no surprise when Black artists entered this digital fray and took this innovation to a new level.

All of which helps explain why, in 1996, the four members of this very white Irish rock band were still trying to find our take on this phenomenon. What would The Beatles do? As the world changed outside Abbey Road Studios, so would The Beatles, not always creating those vectors of change, but certainly riding and amplifying them. Why, even the Stones had success with "Miss You," their punk take on disco.

We'd already had some luck with remixes from *Achtung Baby* and *Zooropa* that hit dance charts on both sides of the Atlantic, with "Lemon" going to number one in the U.S. In fact, a little further back, the "Hollywood" remix of "Desire" had seen us waving the 1980s goodbye from club dance floors. But one part of the process would always upset the status quo, of both fans and band. In a remix, sometimes the guitar but certainly the rhythm section might be replaced by machines. The analog bass and drums replaced by digitally created or enhanced grooves. (There goes Adam or Larry.) Now, this might be fine on a remix, when another artist has their take on your melody and words, but on a stand-alone U2 album?

Problematic. The album has to be our self-expression, so if we weren't all up for the experimentation, if we weren't all up for taking charge of the machines that will transform the human interaction of music, well, the next decade might be a strain. The next thousand years, even.

THE INSTANT AND THE ETERNAL

Pop was supposed to be the album where we explored our New Orderness, returning U2 to the mainstream with a new 12-inch spin. There was one other problem. By definition, *Pop* was supposed to be popular. Lowbrow enough to be fun, highbrow enough to keep you there.

Pop was to be popular music. Contemporary. Like Andy Warhol's take on news events and celebrity. The big questions right next to the little ones. Our attempt to make the instant eternal. A series of Polaroids of this moment. To keep forever. But as long days in '95 turned into long days and nights in '96, it's evident that we are not very good at the instant and that the eternal is nowhere to be seen.

I'm starting to feel that the band is not quite buying into it, which explains why the music is not quite happening.

Great work doesn't happen unless you commit completely. Making this album *Pop* is when we begin to understand the elastic limit of our band. As stretched as this elastic band can be, there's two points where it snaps. The point where the band forgets about the tunes or the point where the tunes forget about who's in the band.

Now, Edge, according to the blues progenitor B. B. King, is "the greatest rhythm guitar player in the world." And Edge, as anyone on any weekend might have noticed, is more interested in dance music than any of us. But Edge is not convinced that dance music is who we are. To compete in dance music, he says to me, you have to use machines to create the music, so why would you use a band to create music?

I speak of New Order. I speak of another Manchester band, the Happy Mondays, who have transformed into the ferment of Black Grape and, while not all about drum machines, are all about digitized loops and samples. Edge is not convinced.

"Flood thinks Larry sees drum machines the way someone on death row sees a rope. In his mind you're asking him to replace himself."

"It's not about replacing," I respond. "It's about multiplying."

"Adam is starting to think you see us dressed up as Kraftwerk and pretending to be German futurists. You know our drummer is Larry Mullen, not Larry Müller."

"Very funny," I say. "You're quite the wag, but . . ."

I can't leave it there. I'm having trouble imagining why a rhythm section can be challenged by the advent of electronic music, but I guess this might be a failure of my imagination. I pick up the argument again.

"I think you're wrong. Adam is mad for the groove, and he's made to experiment. He's always saying he's fed up with those driving four-four bass parts that's he's made so famous.

"Look, Adam and Larry love dance music. Larry loves Prince. Have you seen him listening to Cameo's 'Word Up!'? He knows every word. Adam loves Massive Attack, Soul II Soul, dub. The drum machine is just another tool in their box, like your echo machine or fuzz box or foot pedal. They're in charge of the machine."

Anyway, I add, we're not making an electronic album. It's just a few tracks. "Did The Beatles think they were being replaced by George Martin's string arrangements?"

Edge looks at me. "When Paul McCartney started playing the drums, Ringo did.

"Look," he continues, "what's unique about U2 is the handmade analog experience. If we go too far away from that, we won't be playing to our strengths.

"And one other thing," he says, pausing. "This dance music you're talking about, this music that is inclusive by nature, it needs inclusive lyrics." He looks at me before revealing the ace in his hand. "Have you got any?"

That silences me. For a moment.

"Okay, what are you trying to say? Go, get it all out."

"This new song, 'Discothèque,' the lyrics. Kind of abstract. What exactly are you on about?"

"Love," I respond. "Love." It's so obvious. To me.

> You can reach, but you can't grab it.
> You can't hold it, control it, no
> You can't bag it.
>
> You can push, but you can't direct it
> Circulate, regulate, oh no
> You cannot connect it—love.
>
> You know you're chewing bubble gum
> You know what that is but you still want some.
> You just can't get enough of that lovey-dovey stuff.

"And the bubble gum?" he asks.

Well, that's the rave scene, drugs as junk-food transference . . .

"Right, great, that's cleared that one up then. The charts won't be able to get enough of that."

This is one such conversation among many. Too many. I wonder why we are not on our A game. Is it about the idea or the execution? Is it the kids? The interior designers? Is it the fun and frolics of these lazy French summers? Is it the distractions that success offers you to keep you away from it? Has all this softened our original resolve "to fuck up the mainstream by staying in it"?

"Or is it . . ." I suggest out loud, returning to the conversation. "Is it, dearest Edge, that our relationships have become hardened, to the point where we won't challenge each other to make anything other than 'interesting' music?"

"Probably all of them," replies Edge, now as earnest as me. He knows the pejorative I've made of the word "interesting." That word had been the most stinging criticism of the Passengers album we'd made a couple of years before, when Brian and Danny joined us to make up an alternative band. The idea had been to confuse a rock audience and bypass commercial success. It was a triumph on both counts.

We had recorded "Hold Me, Thrill Me, Kiss Me, Kill Me" for the *Batman Forever* movie. The track was produced by Nellee Hooper, who was so decisive, smart, and fun that we brought him in when we started making work on *Pop*. But for all his discipline even he couldn't stop our continuing swan dive into the world of "interesting." Even on an album called *Pop*, where we wanted to capture the snap and crackle of the moment.

Leaving the studio one night, he turns to me. "It's not exactly *Thriller*, is it?"

And with that the producer of classic albums by Björk and Sinéad O'Connor quits. "I don't think I can help you anymore."

YOU CAN REACH, BUT YOU CAN'T GRAB IT

Michael Jackson's *Thriller* was a pop album with seven top ten hits, but we had yet to find one. *Pop* is not living up to its title. "Generous" was the word Jeff Koons had used to describe our instinct to make popular music, but we were a long way from anywhere accessible or memorable. I was feeling lost and losing the will to compete. Not just with the pop charts, but with the band. I daresay the feeling was probably mutual.

I'm speaking to Morleigh in New York. We're on the soundstage of a video shoot for "Staring at the Sun," directed by Jake Scott, son of Ridley. It's a hustle and bustle of creative professionals on a dead-line, which is when a conversation can take its chance. When it can turn into a deep dive about something more important than the thing you thought you were talking about. We find we are talking about Edge, Morleigh's man, who is also my man.

ME: "Does Edge understand the danger we're in?"
MO: "No, because you're not in actual danger."
ME: "The danger of being irrelevant?"
MO: "What is relevance? You mean popularity?"
ME: "Sort of, but more about being in the moment you're in, being in the cultural moment."
MO: "Bono?"
ME: "Yeah?"
MO: "You're not happy."
ME: "No. The band didn't buy the vision, and even Edge seemed to disappear down a rabbit hole. We mixed 'Discothèque' a hundred times. Edge knows the permutations are infinite, and this time it felt like he wanted to see what infinity looked like."

Mo says nothing. Stares ahead.

ME: "We haven't got the big songs. Just interesting ones."
MO, now looking at me, choosing not to roll her eyes: " 'Staring at the Sun' is a big song with a beautiful melody. Didn't Edge write that melody? What are *your* big melodies on this one?"
ME: Says nothing. Stares ahead.
MO: "You're not happy with yourself. Maybe go a little easier on yourself. And on everyone else?"

Me saying nothing, feeling as if I should have gone harder. On myself. On everyone else.

I'm melancholic and frustrated. Am I right in my analysis? Who cares, I'm definitely wrong in my expression of it. This is my worst side, the side of me that doubles and trebles down in an argument. The side of me that uses cold dispassionate truthfulness as a blunt instrument, a bludgeon. What am I so scared of? I'm scared of breaking the promise we made to each other as kids, that we wouldn't sell out our vision of music for an easy life. I'm scared we're becoming the enemy of who we used to be. It's not even the fear of being a has-been. It's the fear of having been and gone and not deserving your place.

I take up the conversation again. This is what I do. I get carried away. And this is the me that you wouldn't want to be in a band with. Thank God it's Morleigh who has to listen to me. She's an art-ist in her own right. She understands entropy and the dark, swirly stuff around art.

"Look at us raising our kids in our fancy houses, sleepwalking into our forties. Getting ready for life in the rearview mirror. Tired and retired but not yet ready for superannuation. What happens when we discover we've pissed away our chance to actually be great as opposed to pretending we are, which is what I'm doing right now?

"You know who we'll blame? We'll blame you and Ali because emasculated men feeling the loss of their power find scapegoats."

Now I'm ranting. This is not a conversation with my friend and collaborator and fellow artist but a row with myself. I'm arguing out loud.

It doesn't matter if you're right in a moment like this, because you're wrong.

Artists are the worst for blaming the exterior world for their inte-rior failures. It's the radio programmers, the record company, the press. It's my gallery, my agent, my partner. It's the artist's dilemma: the problem isn't out there but in here. We confuse our self-esteem with our self-expression. We confuse our life with our work when the work isn't working out. The painter rarely blames the canvas. It's the muse that takes the blame for disfiguration.

Who am I trying to hurt here? What's got ahold of me in my late thirties? The diminution of the ego or a sense U2 is about to become a cliché and, as the song we've just written goes,

> Referee won't blow the whistle.
> God is good but will he listen?
> I'm nearly great but there's something missing.
> I left it in the duty free,
> But you never really belonged to me.

You're not the only one staring at the sun
Afraid of what you'd find if you stepped back inside.
I'm not sucking on my thumb, I'm staring at the sun
I'm not the only one who's happy to go blind.

—"Staring at the Sun"

Morleigh and I are despairing but not for exactly the same reasons. My good fortune is that we're great friends who are going to be great old friends. My good fortune is that she will forgive me.

THE MOST EXPENSIVE SET OF DEMOS IN MUSIC HISTORY

In March 1997, the album *Pop* enters the charts at number one in twenty-seven countries.

It doesn't matter to me.

We're in this band that became as big as bands can get, and we're still here. It's like a football team still winning the Champion's League after all this time.

Same fucking manager. Same fucking four players. Not even any transfers. But everything has to end, doesn't it? Have we peaked? Do you, Edge, at thirty-five, want to be in a group that used to be famous? It doesn't happen to a novelist or a filmmaker or a painter, this idea that your best work has to be done while you're young. Why should it happen to a rock band? (That's my speech from the dock, Your Honor.)

U2 was never going to be Michael Jackson. In subject matter we're closer to the gospel-singing great Mahalia Jackson.

Lookin' for to save my, save my soul
Lookin' in the places where no flowers grow.
Lookin' for to fill that God-shaped hole
Mother, mother-suckin' rock an' roll.
Holy dunc, space junk comin' in for the splash
White dopes on punk staring into the flash.
Lookin' for the baby Jesus under the trash
Mother, mother-suckin' rock an' roll.

—"Mofo"

Nirvana is a pop band, Kurt Cobain used to say; "Smells Like Teen Spirit" is a pop song. He was right. The great rock bands are pop bands, really. We would come to love some of the songs on *Pop*, almost as much as we would love to have had the time to finish it. But there's no time to finish it. The tour is booked and tickets for the PopMart Tour are on sale. Somewhere along the line our priorities changed. Jimmy Iovine corners us; he says that the moment an artist changes is the moment they stop putting the recording first. He thought *Pop* might be the most expensive set of demos in the history of music. The demo didn't deliver.

Not quite. Nearly. It's all nearly. No one cares about nearly. When it's finished—and it was never finished—*Pop* is not the party we were looking for. It's the hangover after the party.

POP. THE SOUND OF A BALLOON BURSTING.

"Following a rock band is like following a football team." Paul McGuinness usually has a theory, and in 1997 this is his theory. "You want your team to win trophies, but in music, unlike football, neither artist nor fan will admit it."

The Pink Floyd fan says, "Give us new music; we don't want to hear *The Dark Side of the Moon* again." Really? The Pink Floyd fan *loves The Dark Side of the Moon.*

That's the record that stays on the charts for them. You can't force everyone to love your experiments.

Critically and commercially, we've been at the top since *The Joshua Tree,* but now we might be running out of road. Maybe these new songs will find their life played live. Maybe PopMart the tour will turn things around. Maybe not. Barbara Skydel, our agent in America who had so carefully minded us since we signed with the great promoter/impresario Frank Barsalona, is worried that the world has moved on. People don't get our pop-art signaling.

"This is the time for grunge, the Seattle sound, everyone's wearing plaid shirts and torn jeans and making earnest rock, while U2 are dressing up in muscle suits and playing under a McDonald's arch. People don't get it, and radio's not playing the record. The band might be in for a big fall. Look at the genius that was Peter Frampton. The scale of his success was only matched by the backlash."

But still, the tour.

PopMart could change the narrative. Couldn't it? If we deliver on the road, we can turn things around. And the idea for the tour is bold, paying homage to pop art, performing alongside fruit sculptures like those of Claes Oldenburg and huge animations of paintings by Roy Lichtenstein and Keith Haring. And what's more, because the capital of pop is surely Las Vegas, we will open the tour in Las Vegas.

How great is that?

Hmmm. Not quite as great as anticipated.

The only place in the world where PopMart the show is going to look normal is in the entertainment capital of the world, Las Vegas.

For all our supersized art, this is a city that can outrun any rival for larger-than-life irony. This is a capital of pastiche. Our PopMart will be parked right next to the Pyramids.

The one city where our production will look humdrum. And it does.

And we hadn't had time to rehearse properly. Did I mention that?

And our daughter Jordan, traveling with us, gets bitten by a dog on the day of the opening.

And if you're allergic to desert weed (the tumbleweed variety), which I am, this is one of the few places in the world where you might lose your voice.

Which I do.

And everyone turns up for our big opening night, and we can't quite play our new songs.

It's a kind of humiliation. And that's just the start of it.

We were losing money as well as momentum. We were losing our way. And in some geographies playing to half-filled stadiums, which wasn't particularly pop-ulist of us. Turns out, *Pop* was the hangover before the expensive party that was PopMart. Still, by the end of the tour in 1998, we'd managed to pull some kind of victory from the jaws of defeat, in part by reinventing some of the songs—"Please,"

"Last Night on Earth"—so that they were close to how they might have been if we'd ever finished the album.

By the time we got to the end of the tour, we were just about ready to start it. The shows in Mexico City were amazing. The film, directed by David Mallet, remains one of my favorite U2 moments.

But still, the sound of this album was the sound of a balloon bursting. Pop.

Our balloon. The carnival of the 1990s was drawing to a close, and while the masks would always have a place, there was a danger we looked like those people walking home from the party in fancy dress. Having forgotten they're dressed as a chicken. Or an egg.

Having the serious talk and looking ridiculous having it.

Enough of the navel-gazing. We needed to go back to the reason we were in a band in the first place. There were bellies out there to feed, but they weren't ours. It was time to wake up to what we really were, beneath the experimentation and the face paint. A not-half-bad rock band with some big old tunes. When we're on our A game.

WAKE-UP CALL

Andy Warhol went to Mass every Sunday and volunteered in New York food kitchens all through his life. He never talked about God, but his first work and his last work were religious. In the art dictionary, you find that pop was about the death of God because if there's no eternal, then we must live in the instant. But the job of art is making the instant eternal.

There's no contradiction.

Pop. Making the instant eternal. Nearly. Not quite.

That last album we'd make in the old millennium was less about the death of God and more about the death of an idea—the idea that the four of us in this band were unstoppable, indestructible, that we could do anything. It became the birth of a kind of humility that wouldn't always suit our art, but might be necessary for us as people. We were discovering that the elastic limit of this band is the elastic limit of four people, four friends whose friendship is under threat when any one doesn't feel valued in the creative process.

———

The song "Wake Up Dead Man" could hardly be further from the Polaroid aesthetic of the original record we set out to make. I thought it was a song we'd addressed to Jesus in the tomb, but maybe it was a letter from Adam, Larry, and Edge to me.

Maybe I was the one who needed to wake up.

> Listen to the words they'll tell you what to do
> Listen over the rhythm that's confusing you
> Listen to the reed in the saxophone
> Listen over the hum of the radio
> Listen over the sounds of blades in rotation
> Listen through the traffic and circulation
> Listen as hope and peace try to rhyme
> Listen over marching bands playing out their time.
>
> Wake up, wake up dead man
> Wake up, wake up dead man.

I got just enough low self esteem to get me where I want to go

26

The Showman

The showman gives you front row to his heart
The showman prays his heartache will chart
Making a spectacle of falling apart
Is just the start of the show.

A spectacle. A show. Making a show out of yourself. A curious thing to be doing with a life. Showbusiness. Shamanism. All kinds of reasons we turn up in the stalls or on the stage.

Something to know about performers. In pursuit of truth we are capable of more untruth than most. In many ways we are not to be trusted. We may convolute emotion. Appear aroused by the person next to us, when they make our skin crawl. We can make you cry, while laughing inside. Marlon Brando described acting as lying for a living. "Deceit" is not a word you associate with a great artist or a great anyone, but I confess my part in this deception is ongoing. Almost as much as honesty, deceit is a key component of being a performer, and the greatest deceit of all is authenticity. Like the rock 'n' roll star who turns up to the photo shoot in his oldest jumper, ripped just so.

The hardest thing to do on a stage is to just walk across it is how the great acting coach Konstantin Stanislavski put it. We are changed by the eyes of our audience. The Stanislavski method, which Brando learned, was about how to be your true self whilst stepping inside the character you're playing. In rock 'n' roll the different kinds of performers range from those who are just so pleased to be at the center of attention (where we're meant to be) to those whose shtick is that they'd rather be anywhere else. On film this reluctance can be an advantage because the camera is drawn to performers who don't like the camera and suspicious of performers who love to be its focus. Those who are too big or too grand in gesture.

That would be me.

A lesson I learned after one of our early appearances on the U.K. TV show *Top of the Pops,* then the pinnacle of pop attention. We were not quite ready for prime time, or, to be precise, I wasn't ready. "Hysterical" is a word you might use looking at the footage. I moved like a bad puppet, a jack-in-the-box with a look of constant surprise etched on my face. This may explain why U2 are a member of that small but perfectly formed group whose song went down the charts after appearing on *Top of the Pops.*

The camera may pursue truth, but more often it's distorting it.

"My advice to you," mused Paul McGuinness, "with a piece of architecture like that in the center of your face, is never be on the outside of a wide-angle lens."

I hadn't yet found out how to be on the TV. I wonder if Brendan Behan's wisdom applies: "My head's too big for the telly." Some people are naturals, but even the naturals have been in training because the hardest thing to be on a stage is yourself. I have only managed that in moments. It's hard for me to turn myself off. I have to really step inside the song in order to step outside of my head. Self-consciousness is the enemy. Insecurity is not. On an unconscious level, an audience needs to know you need them.

It is what it is but it's not what it seems
This screwed up stuff is the stuff of dreams
I got just enough low self esteem
To get me where I want to go.

Enter one of the great showmen of all time: Frank Sinatra. Not on the charts or streaming so much these days, but on New Year's Eve in 2008 he's right there with me in the crush of a Dublin pub. Glasses clinking, clashing, crashing in Gaelic revelry. Swinging doors, sweethearts falling in and out of the season's blessings, family feuds subsumed or resumed. Malt joy and ginger despair are all in the queue to be served on this, the quarter-of-a-millennium mark since Arthur Guinness first put velvety blackness in a pint glass.

There's a voice on the speakers that wakes everyone out of the moment: it's Frank Sinatra singing "My Way." His ode to defiance is four decades old this year, and everyone sings along for a lifetime of reasons.

It's an interesting mood he occupies tonight in bubblin' Dublin. A financial crisis. The new Irish money has been gambled and lost; the Celtic Tiger's tail is between its legs as builders and bankers laugh uneasy and hard at the last year, and swallow uneasy and hard at the new year they will survive, although the country nearly didn't, nor the people who borrowed the money to buy or rent their homes pay the highest price. Oddly, Frank is here for everyone, the accusers and the accused.

I am struck by the one quality his voice lacks: sentimentality.

In the midst of uncertainty in your business life, your love life, your *life* life, why is Sinatra's voice such a foghorn—such confidence in nervous times allowing you romance but knocking your rose-tinted glasses off your nose, if you get too carried away.

A call to believability.

A voice that says, "Don't lie to me now."

Fabulous, not fabulist. Honesty to hang your hat on.

As the year rolls over, the emotion in the room tussles between hope and fear, expectation and trepidation. Wherever you end up, this voice takes you by the hand.

Back home from the pub, I'm uncorking some wine, ready for the vinegar it can turn to when families and friends overindulge. As I am about to. Right by the kitchen door, I look across to see a vision in yellow: a painting Frank sent me fifteen years ago after I sang "I've Got You Under My Skin" with him, on his *Duets* album. A painting from his own hand. A mad yellow canvas of violent concentric circles gyrating across a desert plain.

Francis Albert Sinatra, painter, *modernista*. It's a new year and I allow myself a drop of melancholy, to rewind the reel as the projectionist in my head plays back memories of a man I pretend to know from some special moments shared. A man I actually know from his songs.

UNDER THE SKIN OF SINATRA

Edge and I had spent some time in his house in Palm Springs, looking out onto the desert and hills, no gingham for miles. Plenty of miles, though, Miles Davis. And plenty of talk of jazz.

That's when he showed me the painting. I was thinking the circles were like the diameter of a horn, the bell of a trumpet, so I said so.

I said I had heard he was one of Miles Davis's biggest influences.

"The painting is called *Jazz* and you can have it."

(That's how come I'm staring at it now, hanging at the bottom of our stairs in Temple Hill.)

"You know, kid, you're the only man I ever liked who wore an earring."

Mrs. Sinatra walking down the stairs in a glorious crimson dress, elegance personified, Frank with a big smile: "Barbara, you look like a blood clot!"

"Miles Davis never wasted a note, kid—or a word on a fool." Then this.

"Jazz is about the moment you're in. Being modern's not about the future; it's about the present."

To be present is the thing, isn't it? I was with Frank Sinatra the moment he forgot the present, a moment he was no longer present. It was earlier that day, and we'd met up in the California desert to shoot a video for "I've Got You Under My Skin." With the director Kevin Godley and his crew on our tail, we shared a limo ride to a Palm Springs bar, run by one of Frank's friends. The idea was that Frank and I would shoot the breeze, and Kevin would shoot the film. The opening scene was Frank at the bar on his own waiting for an

Irish crooner to arrive, which I did the first time. But when Frank was asked to repeat the opening shot, a camera failed, leaving him on his own at the bar for ten minutes too long. The director's "take two!" didn't just take him out of the moment; it took him out of the bar and out of the video we were shooting. He disappeared. Alarmed at being left for so long, the showman shimmied off, leaving me and a film crew sitting in the bar, half a duet short of a full video shoot.

Later a call from Barbara. Some kind of misunderstanding. How about we come over to their place that evening, a few friends, a little whiskey. Edge paces himself. I don't.

Now, if I'm drinking whiskey in this version of America, I would usually drink JD straight up without ice, a Tennessee sipping whiskey, so why did I go and blow it by ordering ginger ale?

"Jack and ginger?" asks Frank. "A girl's drink."

As he takes me in, I sense he is looking at my two earrings and making his judgment. Pretty sure the word he is looking for, the word he is not saying, is "effeminate."

I drank quickly to compensate and worse I mixed my drinks. Over dinner—Mexican, not Italian—we drank tequila in huge fishbowl glasses. "Never drink anything bigger than your head," I thought to myself as Frank pushed his nose up against the glass.

And as he carefully folds a turquoise napkin, Edge overhears him saying under his breath, "I remember when my eyes were this blue . . ."

For real.

Later there were some movies shown in Frank and Barbara's screening room, where, asleep on their snow-white sofas, I had a fright. I woke up to a damp sensation between my legs. Dreams of Dean Martin gave way to panic.

First thought: I have wet myself; I have urinated next to Sinatra. Second: don't tell anyone. Third: in this land of white, don't move; they'll see the stain, the yellow on white. Fourth: make a plan.

So I sat in my shame for twenty minutes. Mute. Waiting for the movie to end, wondering how I would explain this Irish defeat to Italy. This sign that what was once just verbal incontinence has matured and grown to conclusive proof that I didn't belong here. I am a jerk. I am a tourist. I am back in my cot at four years of age, before I know how to fail.

"Mama, I need to change . . . I've peed my pants."

Well, I hadn't. I'd spilled my drink. I guess I was drunk, high on Frank, a shrinking shadowboxing short-ass following in this giant's footsteps.

"WHAT NOW, MY LOVE? NOW THAT IT'S OVER?"

We went back to the hotel. Turn left on Frank Sinatra Drive. I knew I would never drink in the company of the great man again. I would never be asked to. Wrong. Twice. Next year and I'm at the bar in the manager's suite upstairs in the Shrine Auditorium in Los Angeles. It's the Grammys, and Frank has asked me to introduce his Legend Award.

He's a little angsty. I'm a little angsty.

To the bartender: "Make it worth my while."

We're ordering the bar staff about instead of ordering each other to be on better behavior.

I don't drink to get drunk, do I? I drink because I like the taste, don't I?

So why am I doing an impression of a drunk once again? Frank has just fixed me another stiffy, that's why. Jack Daniel's, this time straight up as he suggests, and in a pint glass. I'm talking to Susan Reynolds, Frank's publicist and patron saint, and Ali, my wife and patron saint. Paul McGuinness asks Frank about the pin on his lapel.

"It's the Medal of Freedom, the highest civilian award, given by the president."

"Which one?" inquires Paul.

"Oh, I don't know, some old guy. I think it was Lincoln."

Cool, I think, wondering if you have to be American to get one. Wondering if my legs are starting to go. Wondering if I should have prepared something to say in case our album *Zooropa* gets the gong for Best Alternative Album.

Remembering that we won't. Until we do. My legs take me out to the mic, and I tell a couple hundred million people that "U2 will continue to fuck up the mainstream." It's not that funny or smart, but back at the bar Frank turns to the room and offers, "I thought I liked this kid. I love this kid."

I'm thirty-three years of age.

Over a coffee we prepare for the main event. When I make it to the stage, I've become a seriously annoying John the Baptist preparing the way for our Italian messiah. Swaggering, with a lit cigarillo at my lips, I do the smirk thing I do when I'm really, really nervous. I smoke; therefore, I am agitated. I cough. I speechify.

As I walk offstage, the set opens to reveal the mayor of any city he likes, Frank in his classic dinner suit, walking out to a standing ovation in the city he made more famous than anybody. That's what everyone here thinks anyway. He looks into the crowd, straight-faced, and gives out about the barman backstage, makes a few jokes. He's truly moved then, in a flash, removed. Not lost in the moment, lost to the moment. Just lost. The Grammys cut to a commercial. The present had left Frank for a showbiz minute and the producers and his management panicked and pulled the plug.

Being modern's not about the future, he'd told me; it's about the present. To be present was the only thing Frank demanded of himself and his art, and when his grip of it waned, it must have been terrifying. The years will always steal your glory as they offer you longevity.

BLUE EYES OR RED

Back at Temple Hill the morning after the New Year's night before, I put on a recording of Sinatra singing "My Way" that he made for a duet with that other master and maestro, Pavarotti. The duet doesn't quite become them. These are the greatest of the greatest voices, but there's a part of me that will only let one of these Italians sing in English. But underneath the bluster, I discover an aspect to Frank's performance that so moves me, I had to get hold of a copy of the take without Luciano. That take uncovered the most remarkable vocal, revealing a whole other view of the lyric. What was a boast when Frank was fifty-four had become at age seventy-nine an apology.

The first was recorded in 1969 when Frank told Paul Anka, who wrote the song for him, "I'm quitting the business. I'm sick of it. I'm getting the hell out." "My Way" here is more kiss-off than send-off, embodying all the machismo a man can muster about the mistakes he's made on the way from here to everywhere. In the later recording, the Don Costa arrangement is the same, the words and melody are the same, the tempo, the key . . . but now all to an entirely different end. Now the song has become a heartbreaking song of defeat. The singer's hubris is out the door.

How did he do that? The song has become an apology. Truly. The genius of interpretive singing. Duality. There were two songs in there all the time.

This "kid" from Cedarwood Road got lucky enough to duet with a man from Hoboken who understood duality, who had the talent to hear two opposing ideas in a single song, and the wisdom to know which side to reveal at which moment. Blue eyes or red.

Like Bob Dylan's, Nina Simone's, or Mavis Staples's, Sinatra's voice is improved by age, by years spent fermenting in cracked and whiskeyed oak barrels. As a communicator, hitting the notes is only part of the story. Singers, more than other musicians, depend on what they know about the world, as opposed to what they don't want to know. While there is a danger in this—the loss of naïveté, for instance, which holds its own certain power—interpretive skills generally gain in the course of a life well abused.

If, like Frank, you sing it as if you'll never sing it again. *If*, like Frank, you sing it as if you never have before. *If*.

CASE STUDY TWO: A VOICE BIGGER THAN THE WORLD

Among those who had noticed the rollout of our ZOO TV Tour as it tumbled through Europe in the early 1990s was someone famously familiar with the grand gesture. Being Italian, Luciano Pavarotti was acutely aware that the region in flames was in his neighborhood. You could almost see the war in Bosnia and Herzegovina from his seaside home on the Adriatic coast. Pavarotti was deeply troubled by the war going on "over his garden wall" and felt compelled to help. He could offer up his singular vocal talent in a couple of ways: as a performer expressing and releasing the contorted emotional life of the conflict in song, or as a fundraiser talking people into doing stuff they didn't necessarily want to do and building some kind of war zone relief package. In the end this man who possessed a voice bigger than the world decided to do both.

A world-champion emotional arm wrestler, Luciano must have called Temple Hill twenty times in the mid-1990s to check if we'd written him the song that we had definitely not said we would write for him. The answer was always no, because, as I had tried to explain, we were struggling to finish one of our own songs, let alone one for him. We had already embarked on Passengers, a new musical experiment with Brian Eno. Not everyone was convinced this experiment would lead to any artistic discoveries. Pavarotti had good English, but there was one word he never seemed to understand.

The word "no."

He kept calling, talking to our housekeeper, Teresa, or to Ali, to anyone who picked up. Eventually, it was my bad luck/good fortune to answer. To my surprise he asked not about the song but about me, about the family. We were looking forward to an Easter break in France, I said.

"Wonderful. So you have time with your lovely wife and children . . . without pressure."

"Yes," I said. "I'm worn out."

He said, "Perfect, so you have time to write the song then."

I coughed and said I'd do my best.

"God will find a song for this most religious of festivals," he said. "It will rise up within you. You will find it. I am sure."

He was right. We did find the song.

There was an improvisation during the Passengers sessions that needed words and a melody and maybe a guest singer. The lyric idea came from a story I'd heard about how the people of Sarajevo were defending themselves against the siege with everything they'd got, including a surreal sense of humor. Under cover of darkness, a concert cellist was playing sonatas in the rubble of bombed buildings. A group of defiant women had pulled together a Miss Sarajevo beauty pageant. Their sashes were inscribed with phrases like "Do you really want to kill us?"

The film of the parade was a powerful testimony to women who refused to give up their femininity to hate.

We recorded the backing track of "Miss Sarajevo" and went to visit the lead vocalist at his villa in Pesaro. This legend lived in a more bohemian way than I'd imagined. He'd told us he had a studio in the house, but who knew that we'd find the microphone at the end of his bed. He sang in his bedroom. But he only sang after eating, so we waited while the food was prepared: a bowl of pasta the size of Italy. Then he had to sleep. He only sang after he slept.

After he ate. So we waited. We continued to eat and drink until it was time for him to rise from his hammock and address the microphone.

We were all a little bit on our holidays.

SOME THINGS ABOUT OPERA THAT CRITICS WON'T TELL YOU

Opera singers are not simply athletes whose high jump is a top C, or circus performers whose freakish genetic advantage we applaud. Opera singers are above all communicators of emotion.

Empathy.

Making unbelievable tales understandable to the listener is their gift, because there is no such thing as an ordinary life for anyone. So opera singers' voices are made better for the life they've lived; the more life they've lived, the better the voice.

Empathy.

No matter how confusing the life, the human voice reveals the emotional contours and the spiritual landscape, not just of the music, but of the singer who takes you through it. That is what opera is about. That is what Luciano Pavarotti was about. Within a few takes it was evident that Luciano Pavarotti had lived enough of a life to sing for people who were losing a grip on theirs. He made the surreal sorrow of Sarajevo understandable.

Empathy.

I was mistaken in thinking that this song would mark the end of his harassing me or our house. Within a week he was calling again. We had to perform the song with him in Modena at his annual charitable concert. I kept telling him no; he kept telling me yes. I talked to the band. Collective eye rolling.

"Tell me one good reason why you are not going to play Modena for me?" he asked.

"We are in the studio," I said. "Even if I wanted to, the band don't want to."

"If I speak to the band, I know they will say yes."

I explained that I knew them quite well and this was not negotiable.

"Will you speak to them one more time?"

"Okay," I said, to end the call. "I'm with them in the studio to-morrow."

"In Dublin?" he said. "In your hometown they will understand. A chance to do what's right, not only for me, but for humanity. Tell them I said that."

Okay.

He rang the studio the next day. "Are you there?"

I said, "Yes, I'm in the studio."

"Hold on, I'll be there in thirty minutes."

"What!"

"I'm just getting out of the airport, and we are on our way to see you."

"You're not in Dublin?"

"I am in Dublin. I want to speak to your band. You told me they were here. I am coming. We will talk."

The band doesn't like being railroaded, and I couldn't see how this could end well. I broke it to them that Pavarotti was passing through, wondering if he could say hello.

Larry: "Who's he with?"

"I think just Nicoletta, I'm not sure."

It was a big deal to have such a global superstar come to visit, but I was more worried than flattered. I put my reputation within the group on the line and explained that we should be polite to the greatest singer on earth should he come calling. Eventually, we reached an agreement, which held until the moment he arrived.

With a television crew.

We were being played, but not everyone in the band could see the funny side. Luciano Pavarotti arrived, and we surrendered. Well, half of us. By the time the opera that was Pavarotti took his TV crew and left, Edge and I had agreed, on camera, to play Modena, and in September 1995, joined by Brian Eno, we debuted "Miss Sarajevo" at the annual Pavarotti and Friends concert in support of the charity War Child.

THE THREE TENORS: GARVIN, BOB, AND LUCIANO

Life is marked by unlikely transformations, and it was in Modena where I witnessed the transformation of my father. Who would not bring their father, the tenor, to meet Luciano Pavarotti, one of the Three Tenors? Edge brought his own Welsh tenor father, Garvin, and at some point Bob, Garvin, and Luciano sang "Happy Birthday" to Brian Eno's wife, Anthea. Garvin Evans took it to the top note, really and truly trying to outgun the crack shot.

"We're the three tenors, are we not?" he quipped. "We don't shortchange an audience of a top C!"

No drama until the arrival of a radiance who could even outshine Pavarotti. Diana, Princess of Wales, was a giant star, made larger by her demureness. Edge mentioned that because his parents were going to meet her, maybe my father would like to join them. I knew the answer, but decided to give him a chance anyway.

"Da, do you fancy meeting the Princess of Wales, Lady Di? Gwenda and Garvin, being Welsh themselves, are going to meet her with Edge."

"What? What? What's she doing here? She's bloody everywhere! Do I want to meet the royal family? That's like asking me do I want to meet the winner of the lotto. Why is the winner of the lotto interesting? What could possibly make me interested in that?"

"I know, I know," I said, a little wearily. "I know. It's okay. I was just asking."

"Not at all. Don't be ridiculous."

An hour later in our dressing room Luciano Pavarotti brought the Princess of Wales to say hello, and the first person she met on entering our trailer was Bob Hewson. Approaching six feet in her heels and wearing the most beautiful coral-white dress, Diana was something else. The da melted. The shock of a close encounter with the British royal family quickly became a teenage crush.

"How do you do?" she inquired.

"Lovely to meet you," he said, quivering. "I'm very well, thank you for asking." Eight hundred years of oppression disappearing in eight seconds.

If you've ever wondered about the usefulness of royals, I would always point to this incident. Eight hundred years in eight seconds.

> Here she comes, heads turn around
> Here she comes, surreal in her crown
>
> —"Miss Sarajevo"

Pavarotti stole his own show in that first live performance of "Miss Sarajevo." Just how he got there doesn't matter; he willed the material into existence, and it willed him to be his best. The song, released by Passengers on *Original Soundtracks 1* later in the year, remains one of my few recorded favorites, probably because I'm not carrying the emotion of it. The big man with the volcano voice was doing all the heavy lifting, and here he is now lifting the crowd with a promise to build a music center in Mostar for Bosnian survivors of the war who'd found themselves left with little but the ruins of their grief. The great arm wrestler had his way with us, and we his audience just had to give in. Who could not be moved by the grand master's endgame? The middle was kind of sublime, too, but it's his opening that still makes me laugh, common enough but classic—the Sicilian. His knights, his bishops all around, and of course his queen— Princess Diana. Suspension of disbelief was now a royal decree. In the court of high drama we were pawns.

It's easy to lampoon a character the size of Luciano Pavarotti based on the sheer scale of the man, his personality, his talent, his unparalleled gift. But underneath that volcano was a hot molten, magnificent outrage.

> *It's no secret that a conscience can sometimes be a pest*
> *It's no secret that ambition bites the nails of success*
> *Every artist is a cannibal, every poet is a thief*
> *All kill their inspiration and sing about the grief.*
>
> —"The Fly"

Opera is never too far away.

Not all great singers are great performers. Is it honesty? Connectivity? Is it when the performer needs the song more than you, the audience?

"Honesty" may be the wrong and the right word. Insincerity is a lie badly told. I'd rather the lie than the insincerity. The performers who enthrall me are the ones who mistrust the stage or find it too confining. They are constantly breaching the fourth wall, that moment when an actor speaks directly to the audience or, on film, straight to the camera. These are the performers you feel might jump from the stage and confront you in the crowd, elbow you out of the way, wrestle you to the ground with their song. Follow you home. Make you a cup of tea. (Sugar?) Or mug you. Feral thespians like Iggy Pop or Patti Smith. The kinetic performer despises the distance between them and their audience. Not just emotional proximity. Sometimes it's physical.

Performers who make a light show of their emotions and a pyro of their rage. Those who dazzle you in the special effects of their thinking. People don't think of Bob Dylan or Miles Davis as the most theatrical of showmen because they don't put on what we think of as "a big show." They just let you in on their mood. Which, to those of us who love them, is the most generous thing they can do. Then there's just the really great showmen that you can't keep your eyes off. As I said, Mick Jagger, the most mesmeric of all.

Connectivity? In our band we've always tried anything to get our music to where you are. Technology was our friend in this pursuit of connection, from in-ear monitors, which allowed us to build satellite stages at the back of the venue and not be thrown off by time delay, to screens as art installation rather than just video reinforcement.

Even if you're at the back of a stadium or a festival crowd, still we want your complete attention. I'll try any trick to stop you wandering off. From stage diving to climbing to the top of the PA. If I see people going to get a drink during a particular song, I take it personally. Now I am a dog left out in the rain. A bathroom break during this song? Really?

At the Los Angeles Sports Arena in 1983, I climbed up onto a balcony with a white flag to make some point about pacifism, and when someone tried to pull the flag out of my hand, I started beating him off with my fists. In the name of nonviolence. Then I jumped off the balcony in what one critic called one of the most stupid stunts he'd ever seen.

You could call it showboating. It is, but I also call it the search for a physical symbolism. That's how I rationalize it. All experimentation to the same end, breaking down the barrier between performer and fan. Like inviting fans up onstage to play guitar or to dance with us. Or just to hang out. At a show in Montreal in 2015, I invited a hundred people up onstage, built to hold a band of four. I get carried away.

Edge, or Larry, or Adam . . . or someone in management . . . will periodically intervene, extracting a promise that I will not get carried away like this. But that's the point. Music carries us away. Why else would a man approaching his sixties still jump into the arms of a big strong lad or lassie and have them carry me across the stage? It's a symbol of what is really taking place, which is that this audience are still carrying this band after forty years.

PUTTING THE MESSY IN MESSIANIC

Over the while I've understood that even showbiz is rooted in shamanism, that the most superficial of arts holds the memory of much older and deeper questions: immortality, the death and resurrection show. The pseudo-religious part of being a rock star, how we put the messy in messianic.

It was reading Rogan P. Taylor's *The Death and Resurrection Show: From Shaman to Superstar* when I understood that show business is not a branch of shamanism. It *is* shamanism. From pulling a rabbit out of a hat to the Indian rope trick to the pyro of the rock show, deep within us we have this need for a belief in magic and ritual and ceremony. We have some unconscious desire for performers to have an otherworldliness, to have traveled to that "other world." We want to see through them. We want them to be our seers.

From Elvis to Jim Morrison, from Beyoncé to Umm Kulthum,

these superstars regenerate our need to believe in the supernatural, which goes back to ancient mythologies. In Ireland we had a super creature in our mythologies called Cúchulainn who could smack a ball with a hurling stick and then run fast enough to catch it. Superpowers: Marvel mags and rock 'n' roll, the teenage diet of which we never tire.

You see, in all this show-and-not-telling business something still keeps me going back to the dressing room, back to the familiar rented furniture, the deli tray of sweating cheese and dry cold cuts. Back to the anxiety of how high the notes are or how low the energy is.

It's not a miracle or a trick.

It's both. And when it happens, everyone knows the transubstantiation has occurred. What is the shaman doing during the show? Apart from wrestling with the technical issues and whether I can hit those high notes? Apart from wondering if the house is sold out and the set list is right? When all that noise quietens, the moment I know a show is really working is when I feel that the song is singing me, rather than me singing the song.

That's a great night.

On a really great night you are the crowd and the crowd is you. That can really happen.

Question: What do you call a person who before the magic trick sees the rabbit being placed in the top hat and is still surprised when the rabbit is revealed?

Answer: A magician.

That's the magic.

In our band the show is where we finish our songs because without our audience they feel incomplete.

The shaman who previously thought he was conducting the audience is humbled by the realization that he is the one being conducted. Not simply transmitter, but also receiver. There's a lot of static out there. All those attachments. Everybody living their own unique life in any given song. Magic again. Think about that too much and you'd never go there.

Owning up to being a showman is probably what saved me. When I put the makeup on and assume the character of Mr. MacPhisto in our show, I am able to speak the words that wouldn't normally trip off my tongue. Give someone a mask, as Wilde put it, and they will tell you the truth.

Taking the mask off is also revealing, as I found on tour in 2018, wiping my face of clown makeup live onstage and staring into the camera while talking to Ali at home in Ireland. In front of twenty thousand people I regularly discovered a moment of vulnerability verging on frailty. Emptying rather than filling the moment, awkwardness as dramatic gesture. If there is such a thing as honesty for the showman—and remember I've said there's not—this is as close as we come.

A moment on the way to surrender.

It's the song's instruction that matters most, the lyric and melody. If you obey the song, you will get to that place that all of us singers live for.

The experience of being sung. The experience of not carrying the song but being carried by it.

This doesn't happen to order, but when it does, the technical, physical, and spiritual effort just falls away. It is effortless. I am weightless. As unselfconscious as a child in a playground. It's a make-believe which is truer than true and that everybody's in on. It is a freedom which is contagious.

Somewhere there is science in this magic. The high-tech bricks and mortar of a sporting arena built for the roar of rivalry is now a unified field theory of we are one and the same. The audience and Edge, Adam, Larry, and I have disappeared into each other. There is No Them, Only Us. This space-age concrete craft that someone landed on the outskirts of a metropolitan town is now lit up and taking off to some unknown address. People who didn't know each other or didn't like each other are singing the same song. An audience that arrived separately is leaving together, the community gathered for one purpose has found another.

When this happens, I know we have inched beyond entertainment to something else and it's as plain to the singer as the nose on his face.

Even in wide angle.

PRIDE (in the name of love)

in which the millennium turns and I accidentally start a new band - NOW PLAYING - the white house and World Bank as I finally understand what our visit to Ethiopia fifteen years ago was all about. and we try to make 'DROP the Debt' a hit SONG and my days of disorientation are about to be reorientated...

27

Pride (In the Name of Love)

One man caught on a barbed wire fence
One man he resist
One man washed up on an empty beach
One man betrayed with a kiss.

You can't help feeling that to enter the Oval Office is to enter history while it's being written. You don't really want to enter looking as if you've broken in. On March 16, 1999, I walked through the cream oak doors looking more like a cat burglar than the serious activist I was pretending to be. I'd thought a black cashmere coat would suit the occasion, but on the journey from New York to D.C. the sun came out, the temperature rose, and I had to discard my respectable Crombie, entering history wearing a black T-shirt and black combat pants. A roadie in the orbit of a real rock star but maybe not so inappropriate. I was hoping I might be able to "assist" William Jefferson Clinton, the forty-second president of the United States.

I was used to being part of a collective of four, but now I was also becoming part of a collective across the globe, a tenor singing the rallying cry of antipoverty campaigners, a song that was growing louder as we neared the millennium.

In the pale splendor of this revered room, the president seemed faintly amused by the dressed downness of his 2:30 appointment. A very different look from the crushed-velvet hangover I'd been wearing the last time we met in that Chicago hotel room. His mildly puzzled expression was less at my attire and more at the wind-up I'd inscribed in a volume of Yeats poetry that I handed him: "This fella writes some good lyrics too!"

A smile breaks like a wave on that beachhead of a face as the president wonders aloud as to whether my handwritten scribble was faux arrogance or the real deal. He was clearly familiar with the poetry of W. B. Yeats, flicking through the pages, then placing it carefully on the Resolute Desk. "This desk was sent by Queen Victoria," he explained. "But President Kennedy liked to remind people it was Irish oak."

I thought I remembered seeing this famous piece of furniture way back, on a magazine cover, a three-year-old John F. Kennedy Jr. crawling out from under it. On the desk today is a photo of the president and Hillary with Chelsea, looking wise at fifteen years old. A biography of Robert Kennedy. A Bible. A bust of Jefferson. My brain was atomizing, but my first reaction was to try to slow down the molecules in the air.

Bill Clinton had made the first substantial presidential visit to sub-Saharan Africa in twenty years and needed no convincing of the strategic importance of the continent, which in fifty years would have twice the population of China and be home to a third of the planet's youth.

Slow down the tempo enough to make a non-simple pitch for a complex idea that could transform life for millions of the world's poorest people. An idea building momentum among a panoply of antipoverty campaigners I'd been introduced to who were gathered under the sobriquet Jubilee 2000. I'd rehearsed my pitch with them, so now I went for it, methodically describing how the richest countries held the keys that could unlock the prison of poverty for the poorest countries. Then I turned to how it was time to get serious about writing off the historic and unpayable debts of the poorest countries and that January 1, 2000, could be the symbolic date to allow them to restart their own clocks.

The president was gracious, but I couldn't help noticing his eyes. Coming and going. I was getting the sense there were other things on his mind. How could there not be. Wars and rumors of wars. Rumors of rumors. An attempted impeachment a month earlier that Democrats called a coup d'etat. From the get-go with the First Lady he'd entered one of the biggest fights anyone could remember, the pitched battle for health-care reform. Hard for us Europeans to figure out how access to health care could be so controversial, but the politics in the capital was becoming increasingly personal. The most powerful man in the world was discovering how much power he didn't have. As if he didn't have enough on his plate, here was a poorly turned-out rock star trying to heap on some more. If only I could get him to tune in.

"The turning of a millennium, Mr. President. What a moment to be leader of the free world."

"That's true."

"You must have planned some great announcement?" My impertinence doesn't seem to bother him.

"Hillary's heading a White House Millennium Council; we're planning a whole heap of stuff across the country."

"Anything that involves the rest of the world? Such a historic occasion, bit of a one-off, I mean . . . one of those only-comes-around-every-thousand-years types of situation."

Of course I'm laughing as I say this, but apart from my embarrassment at stating the obvious to one of the cleverest men anyone has ever met, I thought I heard the sound of silver entering a slot machine. Or maybe a whirring sound as his big brain jolted. This idea is landing on him just like it had landed on me. Were those blue eyes getting bluer? Was the president sitting up a little straighter? I watched him returning to his body, to the room, to the conversation and now leaning forward toward me. "Tell me more about this millennium idea. We're already doing debt relief. With the World Bank."

"With respect, Mr. President, the World Bank process looks dead in the water, and they're the words of its own president, Jim Wolfensohn. What we're talking about is bigger, demanding the richest countries mark the millennium by announcing a new start for the poorest countries. Abolishing what those countries see as 'economic slavery' caused by old Cold War debts."

I had his attention.

"Who would be the 'we' here?" he asks.

"There are all kinds of campaigners around the world working on this, mainly churches and NGOs. Only one rock band so far, but they're working on that too."

"Go on."

"Economic slavery, it's a spiritual concept, Mr. President, tackling an injustice the western world has exploited for hundreds of years. 'Redemption' I've discovered is an economic term."

Bill Clinton started unpacking the idea with the enthusiasm of a child at Christmas. A child from the South who'd grown up in the era of segregation. Bill, from Little Rock, Arkansas, understood racial injustice. He was also a master of political symbolism. A few more questions and he sent me down the corridor of the West Wing with instructions to speak to some of his closest advisers, the people who could get things done.

I was starting to have a sinking feeling, that I was standing on quicksand and about to get sucked under. That I was completely and utterly out of my depth and the only way to survive was to adapt. It's a feeling, weirdly, that I crave more than most.

THE CURRENCY OF FAME AND HOW TO SPEND IT

Jubilee 2000 was not just another NGO. It was a social movement and one of those rare moments where religion made some practical sense to people who didn't care much for religion. It wasn't about charity; it was about justice. These people were using phrases like "Sabbath economics." I've always revered the concept of a Sabbath, even if it's just a Sabbath hour. And on a Tuesday. I'll always try to make some time in the week that is sacred. A time to stop doing and start being.

Jubilee, I learned, was a biblical idea: "a year of Jubilee," described by the Hebrew prophet Isaiah as a year of the Lord's favor. In Jewish tradition every seventh cycle of seven years you must write off people's debts and release them from their bondage. It's how Jesus started his own ministry, "to let the oppressed go free." Redemption songs. Isn't that one of Bob Marley's?

A debt write-off had first been proposed by Desmond Tutu and the All Africa Conference of Churches, but it was two Brits, Martin

Dent and Bill Peters, who thought to peg it to the millennium. I got a letter from one of Jubilee's lead campaigners, Jamie Drummond, who had a moral indignation and the kind of buzzy brain that kept up an argument with himself and all around him that felt familiar. After a call I met with two of the people he worked for, Ann Pettifor, whose clipped conversation and shrewd intelligence cut through the crap, and her quiet but wry sidekick, Adrian Lovett.

The more time I spent in the company of these Jubilee activists, the more I sensed this might be more than just a side project; this might be a band I could join. I knew I was not going to make a solo record or have a solo career, but I had a passion to harness this fame and use it for something more useful than getting a table in a busy restaurant, though this is not to be sniffed at. "Fame is currency," I told anyone who'd listen. "I want to spend mine on the right stuff."

As the grassroots campaign swelled on its way to a record-breaking petition of twenty-four million signatures from 155 countries (including some thumbprints), Jubilee were on the hunt for spokespeople. To get America on board, the campaign needed salespeople. The United States itself was owed lots of debt and also had a big say at the International Monetary Fund (IMF) and World Bank. The U.S. churches had gotten organized, but the campaign had yet to break through in Washington, D.C. I was put in touch with the attorney Bobby Shriver by his mother, Eunice, sister of John F. Kennedy. She suggested that I study the arguments for and against debt cancellation. "Get to understand every side of this."

I needed to go back to school. Bobby hooked up a meeting at Harvard with the liberal economist Jeffrey Sachs. Following Eunice's advice, I asked Professor Sachs to lunch with Robert J. Barro, the conservative economist. This was to become our model for twenty years, trying to get the left and the right on board before they took up entrenched positions. Barro was skeptical, but gave way a little at the thought that canceling debt could be tied to reform and tackling corruption. He stated his position in *Business Week:* two restrained cheers for debt cancellation.

Professor Sachs, however, was all in, writing op-eds, making speeches, and putting the campus of Harvard's Center for International Development to work on it. At times it felt like I was moving in with him and his wife, Sonia. They, too, didn't just suffer my stupid questions but encouraged them, before painstakingly answering them. They, too, were outraged at how the poor often paid the price for the bad strategies of the rich.

As I crash coursed on economic policy—Ali raising an eyebrow at World Bank and IMF reports piling up on the bedside table—Bobby schooled me in American politics.

"Even if the president writes the check to cover debt relief, to get it cashed by Congress? That's a whole different ball game. Democrats can't get that done. We need Republicans. I'm a Kennedy, and you're a rock star. We'll be lucky if they return one phone call."

Bobby was right. Capitol Hill would have to become our second home.

MY NEW NEIGHBORHOOD: THE CAPITAL

One of the greatest characters in my life over the last twenty-five years has been the capital city of the United States of America. Washington, D.C. I've spent weeks and months there: days that felt like years, loathing some of its hierarchy and protocols, but loving other days that stretched out to meet a new horizon of the possible . . . if politicians could get past the politics.

The original plans for the city were drawn up by a French engineer going by the moniker of "the Child." Pierre Charles L'Enfant got the big job at the request of George Washington. The city was to be arranged around two institutions: the president's house and Congress. Two great axes crossing at right angles so each could keep an eye on the other. The neoclassical buildings would deliver an ode to the Enlightenment, the orders in Roman and Greek. The Greek columns hold up the biggest idea anyone ever had for a country. It's as if the capital were screaming one word to the world: "Greece." This is what democracy grew up to be.

But how grown up?

Part of me would have to grow up there, too, to rise to meet the challenge of putting my own ideas second to the collective.

I've always seen myself as a kind of salesman—selling songs, selling ideas, selling the band, and on my best day selling, well, hope. If

we could get this drop-the-debt song on the charts, this was a different kind of hope, maybe for millions of people.

In order to do this, though, I would have to join a new band,
while not getting booted out of the one I was already in. Booted out
for double jobbing, for moonlighting. I told myself this was part of
our history as a band, that since 1982 the four of us had promised to
see beyond ourselves, to a world of other, more dire needs than a hit
record. Which, in fairness, we had also promised ourselves.

Still, my usual certainties did not look so certain. I was about to
make friends with people I'd always presumed were the enemy. And
to fall out with people I thought would be friends. I was to discover
that the left does not have a monopoly on compassion for people
living in poverty, that there are compassionate conservatives just as
affronted by this kind of inequality.

Our drop-the-debt tent would need to be big enough not just
for nuns and punks, for football moms and trade unionists, but for
those on the right as well as those on the left. And with this strategy
we could double the size of our campaign and double the pressure
on the politicians.

Whatever room I was in, I would remind myself that the success
of U2 had me over-rewarded and over-regarded and that I must not
forget how much these people had given up, working long hours
and living far from their families. Trying to make the best of their
lives and for their constituents.

MAKE ONE POINT NOT TEN

All that being said, I had a pretty good intuition that taking up with
this new band of activist ball breakers might not receive an entirely
warm reception from the manager of my usual band of ball breakers, the ones who paid my way here. Fame as currency is one thing;
U2's credibility as currency is another.

Paul McGuinness was a genuine student of American politics and
immediately sensed danger. He'd been telling me for some time
that these noble notions of bridging the political divide in the United
States were—candidly—preposterous.

"What is this 'Mr. Bono Goes to Washington'? You think you can be the glue in a politics that has become completely unstuck, if not unhinged?"

I read it as tough love, but I wouldn't be moved.

"There's a line in one of Martin Luther King's sermons in *Strength to Love*," I told him. "Courage faces fear and thereby masters it." Paul looked at me, Churchillian eyebrows raised. "Even with one eye open . . ." I added.

"Maybe it helps that I come to this city as an outsider," I continued. "Anyway, I'm a good student. And I've got some great teachers."

In the capital I found myself in the Potomac home of JFK's sister Eunice and her husband, Sargent, the Shriver family coming to have a formative influence in my life. As Bobby and I began to take our arguments through the choppy waters of the U.S. Congress, his peerless parents helped hone our pitch. For a pub-rock speechifier like me, it was a little surreal to sit around the kitchen table with Eunice and Sargent reviewing my stumbling efforts.

"Make one point, not ten!" "That doesn't make sense." "You've lost me."

Their critique had authority because they'd worked on the speeches of JFK himself. In another time Eunice Kennedy Shriver might herself have run for president. As it was, this beautiful soul did something no less influential, founding what became known as the Special Olympics, offering millions of young people with intellectual or learning disabilities the chance to excel at sport. With her passing, her family captured her perfectly. "She was a living prayer."

RAT HOLES AND WATER HOLES

It would just be a drop by, but at least it was a meeting. Lawrence Summers, who had just taken over as Treasury secretary, was not prepared to "waste precious time meeting a rock star with one name who sang with a group named after a spy plane." He arrived in the company of two beyond-smart young women, who chipped in during my pitch and steered things back on track when their boss occasionally impatiently drummed his fingers. Sheryl Sandberg, who would go on to be second-in-command at Facebook, was then the youngest chief of staff at the Treasury Department, while adviser Stephanie Flanders would later become the BBC's economics editor.

I was conscious I was not doing the arguments justice. "Need to speak in sentences and paragraphs" was my note to self. "Consider full stops and commas, even in conversation." Larry and the two Valkyrie women left, leaving this mini-Thor nursing my wounds until Sheryl returned: "That couldn't have gone better. The secretary is in." Okay. Maybe forget the punctuation.

If we had the Democratic administration on board, how were we going to win over the Republican-controlled Congress?

"Not by hanging out with a Kennedy," says the Kennedy.

Bobby thinks his brother-in-law, later elected governor of California, Arnold Schwarzenegger, may have some suggestions.

"Go see John Kasich from Ohio," Arnold tells me. "He has a heart as well as a brain."

Congressman Kasich throws me in our first conversation. The subject is U2's music peers Radiohead.

"Bono, what's your favorite: *OK Computer* or *The Bends*? I was a *Bends* man, but I'm changing."

I later tell Thom Yorke, the "Sufi"-like singer and writer in Radiohead—who as well as being a sacred talent has bothered his arse enough to be protesting alongside us—that John Kasich was asking after him. I do this partly to wind him up. I just couldn't be in the room with people like that. "Isn't he the budget cutter? Don't they call him 'the scissors' or something?"

Yes, I answer. "He's a fiscal conservative with an economic view of the world that our crowd usually don't agree with."

Thom gives me one look that says, "This is not something you and I are ever going to agree on."

I'm reminded that I'm already a long way from my home base and that I've deprived myself of a core weapon of the most combatant of political activists: animus toward the enemy. It's not so easy to go into battle without one.

It was a fact that the U.S. Congress was controlled by conservatives who did not warm to this idea of $435 million in debt cancellation for countries they saw as led by corrupt governments. (This cash was a down payment and was only America's part, but if we didn't succeed in the U.S. capital we wouldn't succeed in any other.) And bipartisan agreement would not emerge sufficiently until people like Kasich took off his gloves in a floor fight in the House of Representatives. Which he did.

"We blow more money than this in Washington just leaving the lights on at night; so to spend less than a billion dollars to help people improve their economies and to help people dying before our eyes is just the right thing to do."

Equally combative, but not at first on our behalf, was Sonny Callahan.

The Republican congressman from Alabama is swiveling on a leather chair in his office in the Capitol. As chairman of the House Appropriations Subcommittee on Foreign Operations he holds the purse strings for the world's poor. He is speaking rhetorically to the assembled visitors and avoiding my eyes because, in some honest way, he wants to talk about debt cancellation behind my back. Even though I'm standing right in front of him. He has the way of a county sheriff about him, inspecting the scene of a crime. He has acid. His stomach is grumbling and so is he.

"This money on debt relief is going down a rat hole," he tells everyone. "I'm just gonna say it straight. Bonio here [that's me] may have priests in the pulpit working for him, may even have the pope in Rome, may be riding a wave of popularity with some of our friends, but I'm standing up for the U.S. taxpayer, and there ain't nothing good coming from this for them."

He takes a breath . . . but he hasn't finished.

"He [me again] may try to roll me in some late-night hoo-ha stitch-up, but I'm here to tell ya why I'm tryin' to stop him [and again]. I know these dollars are not going to the people they're intended for. So I'm standing in his way."

Bonio [still me] is not just in Sonny's way; he's in Sonny's office. He repeats the mantra over and over, like he's Van Morrison in a song. "This money is going down a rat hole.

"This money is going down a rat hole."

"These crooks that call themselves presidents and prime ministers, these people are buying goddamn Gulfstream jets like they're Nike sneakers."

"Congressman," I reply. "As angry as we all are about corruption, the people who are promised these resources are even more angry and better organized than ever at tracking the cash."

In the end Callahan didn't stop Kasich. He just got out of the way. John, who would go on to run for president, was aided by fellow conservatives Jim Leach and Spencer Bachus, who worked with Democratic pugilists like Chris Dodd, Teddy Kennedy, and Joe Biden.

I can confirm Joe Biden was quoting Irish poetry even then and not just to Irish people, and yes, he sometimes wore green ties so fellow Hibernophiles would feel more at home. Disarmingly warm, he could be disarmingly blunt when talking about the hardships faced by people he worked for in his district at home and on his travels abroad. "Catholic" as an adjective as well as a noun.

TOP OF THE POPES

If the drop-the-debt song was climbing the U.S. charts, what we really needed was a worldwide hit. In the summer of 1999 in Cologne, Germany, Youssou N'Dour, Thom Yorke, and I joined fifty thousand Jubilee supporters to surround a World Leaders Summit in a human chain. A few days after, Jubilee's ever more impatient boss, Ann Pettifor, called me with another idea.

"We're making progress, but not quickly enough. I think we have to find a way to meet the pope."

His Holiness John Paul II and the Catholic Church had been heralding the Jubilee idea from the beginning, but we needed some kind of public proclamation. And in September 1999, we got it.

One hundred days before the new millennium, Pope John Paul II enters the room in the Palace of Castel Gandolfo, the papal summer residence, on a Zimmer frame. He is fighting with his own frailty to be with us. But he is with us. Present. Giving his public blessing to the Jubilee 2000 campaign. More than his blessing. He gives the proposal an intellectual charge more radical and urgent than any of us expected.

Our party on this September day in 1999 includes Quincy Jones,

Bob Geldof, Ann Pettifor, Jeff Sachs, the Nigerian economist Professor Adebayo Adedeji, Mayor Francesco Rutelli of Rome, and Laura
Vargas, leader of the Jubilee 2000 coalition in Peru. Castel Gandolfo
is as labyrinthine as the Vatican, and we move from one room to
another in a kind of video game in which every next room may be
our destination. It gives us time to take in the frescoes, to marvel at
the Renaissance paintings.

"So totally hip-hop," says Quincy.

Bob Geldof has the giggles because Quincy can't stop sneaking
sly comments out of the side of his mouth about the surreality of the
situation. Thirty of us in the room with the pope, whose oxblood
Gucci shoes are peeping out below his cassock.

"Those are some pimp loafers," says Quincy, not as quietly as he
might have. "That is some funky footwear."

You don't want to laugh in church, but you can't help yourself.
Until you notice how seriously the pope is taking our mission. How
determined he is to be alive and with us, to be reading out this statement on behalf of the world's poorest communities.

"The law of profit alone cannot be applied to that which is essential for the fight against hunger, disease, and poverty," says the pope.
"It is the poor that pay the cost of indecision and delay."

His presence quiets our nervous laughter. Even Bob gets a little
teary.

Is he looking at me?

I'm sure he's looking at me. His Holiness is looking at me.

I quiz my own narcissism, give it a thorough interrogation. Yes,
he definitely is. He's looking at me. I move. His attention moves
with me. Then I get it.

My glasses.

My blue-tinted D&G shades.

Does he think wearing sunglasses is disrespectful? I sometimes
encounter that, but it's usually too complicated to explain about
the migraines that will eventually be diagnosed as glaucoma. I take
them off and hold them at my side.

Now he's staring at them in my hands.

"I'm pretty sure he's staring at my shades," I whisper to Quincy.

"I'm pretty sure I'm staring at his loafers," he replies. "This is one stylin' pontiff." Maybe that's what gave me the thought as Diarmuid Martin, a bishop from Dublin, introduces me.

"Holy Father, this is Mr. Bono, and he is a singer and has done a lot with Jubilee."

As I approach the bishop of Rome, I present him not only, as planned, with a copy of Seamus Heaney's *Collected Poems* but also with a bonus gift.

My glasses. My pale-blue-tinted glasses.

He reciprocates with a gift of his own, a crucifix on rosary beads.

"This is a great swap," I say, not sure if the Polish former actor, goalkeeper, and cold warrior will see the funny side. No worries. He does. More than that, he evidently understands the power of a symbol because now he takes these blue-tinted Fly shades and puts them on. Looking through them at us, he makes what can only be described as, excuse my language, a devilish grin. And as the camera of the Vatican press photographer flashes, I know we've just got "Drop the Debt" on the cover of every newspaper in the world.

Result!

I smile, kiss the papal ring, and, looking up, notice Jeff Sachs smiling back at me. It's the church campaigners and the stealth of Jubilee HQ that has got us through the door, but Jeff, more than anyone in the room, has helped shape what the pope will say today.

The ceremony over, His Holiness departed, I can't stop thinking about the power of the photo when combined with the power of those words. This will go viral, and we've never even heard of going viral.

"Can I see one of those photos?" I ask of anyone left behind. "Can we approve one for the press?"

The reply comes in a now familiar Irish timbre. "Bono," says Bishop Martin firmly, "you will never see one of those photographs. Ever."

Understanding how this imagery could travel—the posters, the T-shirts—the clever soon-to-be archbishop is shutting it right down.

Of course the next day we got plenty of coverage, but it was not until John Paul II died, six years later, that one of the Vatican photographers, now retired, let that particular image be seen. I would never forget the wonderful mischief of this pope, and many a time I have held on to his crucifix.

THE DEVIL WEARS PRAYER BEADS

The papal blessing gave the Jubilee campaign the moral propulsion of a billion Catholics, just when we needed it. Next day, the team and I were on a plane back to Washington, D.C., preparing for the annual meetings of the World Bank and IMF. After some badgering, I got an invitation from Gene Sperling. Was I free on Sunday to pop by the West Wing for a discussion when there'd be no one around and he could concentrate. Gene, an unusually warm-blooded economist, explained he'd recently been invited up to the master cabin on Air Force One, where he found the POTUS all but yelling at him and holding out a letter.

"Gene, can you give me one good reason why we cannot get this debt stuff sorted out? I mean, really? Just explain to me why we can't do the right thing here?"

I'd worked hard on that letter. Sometimes a single letter is more effective than hours of face-to-face argument.

The letter had led to this unexpected invitation and why the man who—with Secretary of the Treasury Larry Summers—has to make the maths work has today given up his Sabbath to get under the hood of the politics as well as the economics.

> GENE: "If we do this, who—apart from the U.K.—is going to
> follow our lead in Europe? Jim Wolfensohn at the [World]
> Bank is pushing hard, but what about [Michel] Camdessus
> at the IMF? Have you spent time with him? I'm not sure he
> agrees with how you guys want to do this."
> ME: "I met him yesterday actually, and the head of the IMF
> is not the devil I thought he was. I'd imagined him in
> a big office instructing a bunch of postgrads on how to
> push sovereign states around with structural adjustment
> programs."
> GENE: "It's happened. To be fair . . ."

ME: "He's a Catholic so I pulled out my rosary beads—the ones His Holiness gave me in exchange for my Fly shades."

GENE is not sure whether to believe me: "Go on."

ME: "He pulled up his jacket sleeve, and around his wrist he wore beads of his own. Buddhist prayer beads given him by the Dalai Lama. He's a humble man, nothing like the Lucifer I was expecting."

GENE: "Humble? Or just humbler than you?"

Did I mention I liked Gene?

GENE: "Listen, thanks for your work on this. The president really wants to help more, it's just that I'm not sure we can get it into the budget this year, but we're trying to figure something out."

ME (sensing the brush-off): "Gene, we're in September of the year 1999, and in the public mind—and the mind of the pope—the whole argument hangs on the millennium. Miss this budget cycle and we miss the moment. If you're worried about Congress, I promise you we'll help you get it through Congress."

We end the conversation with a wonky discussion about the difference between canceling the 90 percent of the debts owed to America that the Treasury is comfortable with and the 100 percent that Jubilee campaigners are asking for. I reiterate, as we've done so many times in the past year, that while 90 percent might sound like a lot, that is pretty much all the debt that is never going to be repaid anyway. That won't free up new resources for the countries; they'll be paying the same just to cover the remaining 10 percent.

I try one final thing on my way out. "The president seems to want a melody line. 'Canceling 90 percent of the debts of the poorest countries' is not a melody line."

A few days later I flew back to Nice, where the kids and Ali were on a school break with my brother, Norman, his children, and my father, Bob. Back from the airport I pulled up a seat beside my da.

"Well, fair play to ya, I hear Clinton's done the right thing. I thought that was a mad idea, but looks like you lot found someone mad enough to run with it."

I'm perplexed.

"What are you talking about?"

"Yeah," Norman chimes in. "It's all over the radio this morning. Bill Clinton announcing debt forgiveness for thirty-six of the poorest countries."

I must have looked very surprised. "You knew, right?"

"I didn't. Last I heard, a few days ago, they were telling me it was unlikely." I excused myself to check in with the Jubilee team. I got Bobby.

"We've been trying to contact you . . . WJC has really pulled it off. Listen to this: 'Today I am directing my administration to make it possible to forgive 100 percent of the debt these countries owe to the United States . . . when needed to help them finance basic human needs and when the money will be used to do so.'"

I was to learn that on the morning of September 29 William Jefferson Clinton, forty-second president of the United States—with the help of Gene Sperling, Larry Summers, and Sheryl Sandberg—made his mind up to run with debt forgiveness. He rewrote his speech in the motorcade on the way to the World Bank meetings. Which is not a long journey. I mean, you could walk it.

AS THE CREDITS ROLL . . .

Just in case you've forgotten Congressman Sonny Callahan.

Two years later we would return to his office, this time with a sheaf of photos, evidence of what had happened as a result of the money being freed up following debt cancellation in Uganda. Local campaigners, led by Zie Gariyo, were the key. The slightly overcast Sonny brightens up as we take him through a list of educational projects, and I explain the cash was all independently tracked to make sure it got where it was meant to go. I show him pictures of newly built water holes.

"Congressman Callahan, we've come back to thank you for appropriating that $435 million to the 150 Account. Despite your reservations. Sir, I'm proud to say that those U.S. tax dollars went into water holes, not rat holes. You should be proud too. It went differently than some of your staff predicted."

Congressman Callahan looks up, looks directly toward me, his Ulster Irish eyes smiling.

"What's different about this," he says, "is not the good work. People in this building are at that all the day long. It's not often people come back to say 'thank you.' Fancy people love to ask for money, but they never tell you how it was spent. It's not often one of you do-gooders ever came back like this."

Bobby Shriver starts to laugh. "Congressman," he says, "can I also say thank you and how much I enjoyed you hurting Bono's feelings?"

"How'd I do that?" he exclaims.

"Calling him 'fancy people.'"

Everyone is laughing. Except me.

A SOUNDTRACK FOR CHANGE

It was not impossible to measure the effectiveness of the coalition of organizations that Jubilee 2000 brought together. Though it took until 2005 for the full promises to be made and met, most economists agree that without Jubilee 2000 and its millions of supporters the cancellation of more than $100 billion of debts owed by the poorest countries would not have happened. The World Bank estimated that an extra fifty million children went to school on the savings that governments made once they no longer had to service old Cold War debts.

This maths was music to me. And this turn in my life set something stirring within me. In giving my time to this movement for justice, I was getting a lot more back. In spending time with people I would otherwise never have met, I was coming to understand myself better. I was grateful. But it amplified that nagging question: Did our band want to create a soundtrack for change or help create the change itself?

I ran from this question.

I have always looked to the songs to tell me what to do. It was

"Sunday Bloody Sunday" in 1983 that had us sing to the sectarianism in Ireland and "Where the Streets Have No Name," four years later, that took us out of Africa. In 1984 it was "Pride (In the Name of Love)" that took us to race relations in the United States. Jim Henke from *Rolling Stone* gave me a copy of *Let the Trumpet Sound,* the story of the life and death of Martin Luther King Jr., by Stephen B. Oates. Jim had been traveling with us on the War Tour in 1983 when we were becoming known as activists for nonviolence and when I was acutely aware that my walk might need to catch up with my talk. (Just how effective can a singer with anger issues be in the cause of nonviolence?)

Let the Trumpet Sound led me to dig deeper. I returned to the scriptures. I read Tolstoy, Gandhi, the speeches of MLK, people who closed the deal on my conversion to nonviolence. Still, fifteen years later, there was something that didn't quite sit right about my new role. And what would this all mean for U2?

Was my new band swallowing my old one whole?

Paul was concerned I was getting distracted. Edge, Larry, and Adam supported my new direction but also worried about the time I was devoting to it. And how unhip this line of work could get.

Bob Geldof told me that after Live Aid people used to throw money at him as he walked down the street. Pennies, not contributions. Rock stars in this kind of enterprise are an invitation to lampoonery.

Could I take it? I could take it.

I wasn't sure the band could. Or if I should be asking them to. They've always had my back, but maybe this drop-the-debt stuff was pushing them too far.

My mind took me back to the Joshua Tree Tour in the 1980s when we were part of the campaign for Martin Luther King Day, a national holiday to honor his life and the African Americans who built America. Some states were refusing, including Arizona, led by a recalcitrant reactionary governor, Evan Mecham. Having agreed to play Phoenix before we'd realized what was kicking off, we'd inadvertently broken the cultural embargo, contradicting our own position. What to do? Ahead of the show we decided to campaign against Governor Mecham and the racism in his state, and in our news conferences I stirred the pot. The show would be the crescendo of this troublemaking, but on our arrival we discovered we'd received some death threats—and maybe not just from pranksters—that if we performed "Pride" in the show, I would not make it to the end of the song.

I had pretended I was not that bothered by the intel and I trusted our security team would be extra diligent and put in additional measures. The venue was swept for firearms and explosives, and we made the decision to go ahead as planned. If we started "Pride" defiantly, by the third verse I was losing some of my nerve or at least losing concentration. It wasn't just melodrama when I closed my eyes and sort of half kneeled to disguise the fact that I was fearful to sing the rest of the words.

> Shot rings out in the Memphis sky.
> Free at last, they took your life
> They could not take your pride.

I might have missed the messiah complex at work in my own anxiety, but it was only when I opened my eyes that I realized I couldn't see the crowd. Adam Clayton was blocking the view, standing right in front of me. He'd stood in front of me for the length of the verse.

PART III

We started out from here as four fairly innocent
boys from the Northside. Tonight we return
as men daring to believe that at the far end of
experience with some wisdom and good company,
it might just be possible to recover that innocence.

—The Point, Dublin, November 2018

28

Beautiful Day

The heart is a bloom
That shoots up through the stony ground
But there's no room
No space to rent in this town.

"Anything strange or startling?"

That's how my da opens our conversations. We meet in our "local" pub in Dalkey.

Finnegan's is its own country with its own laws and customs. Time is said to change shape on crossing its door. I have experienced that. It's a constitutional monarchy with Dan Finnegan the head of state, his sons effectively running the government with his eldest, Donal, the prime minister. Donal is six feet four but, depending on the hour and the state of the state, can appear six feet seven. I would not want to mess with Donal Finnegan. The Finnegans are fine people, but there is a code. A strictness. Understandably, Dan does not approve of children in the pub for too long. There have been occasions when Dan has had to resort to unusual tactics to protect his principality from the upstart republicanism of an eight-year-old wandering from their father's legs to bother staff for some salt and vinegar crisps. For their da. Having spilled some cold water on the child, Dan returns him to

the table with a roll of his eyes. "That could have been boiling."
Bang on.

Dan sits astride a democracy and a meritocracy, and the more
famous our band became, the more I was treated like everyone else.
This is how it should be. And only grated when he treated people
he didn't know as well more cordially than me. Like my da. Dan
Finnegan loved my da. They shared a love of opera and stage musi-
cals, and Dan recognized when another prince was present, one
who could actually sing. On the occasion when my father silenced
the place by singing "The Way We Were" followed by "The Black
Hills of Dakota," Dan looked over at me with something like pity,
and I imagined him speaking under his breath, "Think how far
you'd have come if only you had your father's voice."

Sundays at midday used to be quiet in Finnegan's, the light coming through the frosted windows and revealing something more
akin to a golf club than the *Star Wars* bar of the night before. The
dark oak and the blue flame over the gas-burning coal fire flickering
in the corner. Not a "snug" in the literal sense of a closed-off area in
an Irish pub, but it might as well have been. It drew us closer to each
other, Bob and I. A long way from a snuggle, but, heh, we were all
working on being men now. Bob liked the ambience of a golf course
and played most of these Sunday outings as if any minute his son
would have the ball in the bunker.

"Anything strange or startling?"

The Catholic orders Bushmills Black Bush, a Protestant whiskey
from County Antrim in the north of Ireland. We stare at each other.
Talk around each other.

Occasionally, we talk to each other. Bob is going through some
personal stuff that he is here not to talk about. He is also not well. I
didn't know how not well.

I was also having a little scare. They caught something in my
throat and wanted to biopsy it. It turned out to be nothing important, but it was a sobering experience. I was crossing the fortieth-
birthday threshold, the halfway mark of a good life, and, for the first
time, noticing my mortality. And those of the people I loved. Like
Michael Hutchence. Like my da.

That was in the background when I was writing a song called
"Kite."

Something is about to give
I can feel it coming
I think I know what it is
I'm not afraid to die
I'm not afraid to live
And when I'm flat on my back
I hope to feel like I did.

The da had become proud of the band's achievements. He still played the hard man, but the pride was there. Like the smile on his face when he was waving his fist at me from the mixing desk in Houston on the Unforgettable Fire tour in 1985. I had turned the spotlight on him from the stage. "Ladies and gentlemen . . . appearing for the first time in these United States, more importantly, his first time in the Lone Star State of Texas . . . will you please welcome my father, Bob . . ." The sound of the crowd like a 747 taking off over his head. A sound the size of Texas. It was a big moment.

We were left on our own in the dressing room after the show. He reached out his hand to me, looking up with blood orange eyes. Could this be an even bigger moment, I thought to myself. Am I about to receive a compliment from my da?

"You're very professional," he says, very professionally.

Over time he'd become comfortable with his son being loved and loathed, which is the price of popularity in Ireland. He'd virtually annexed another family, the Lloyds, so as not to be too dependent on his sons. He had his own friendships.

He had the musical society. He had golf. He found it amusing that I'd done so well because it was Norman, my ambitious brother, the entrepreneur, who was always going to do well. And he thought it hilarious that I was throwing cash away as fast as I'd earn it. And that I kept making it.

"When are you going to get a real job?" he asks me with a wink. He still gives me a fiver for Christmas.

Are we becoming friends? At least we're meeting. Talking. I turned the tables one Sunday in 1999.

"Anything strange or startling?" It's the first time I've asked him his own question.

"I have cancer," he deadpanned.

———————

Huge boulders fall on your head just like that, from some unseen mountain when you're not looking up. When you're not looking anywhere. The change in someone else's life will utterly transform yours, even though your life is not quite the point here. Is it? This is the moment when Bob Hewson describes his own situation as "the departure lounge." I am not ready to give up on the man I'm just getting to know. I'm not ready to be orphaned. Is anybody? Let me cut away as quickly as I did in Finnegan's that day. Surprising for a singer, but when things get really emotional, I can get quite heady. I don't know if I was much help to Bob Hewson that day, though, self-reliant as he was, I doubt he was looking for help from me.

What is the relationship between sex and death? The instinct to pro-liferate our DNA is at its strongest when we fear the end of our line. A partner passes, a parent, a child, and the next thing you know your own body screams for life. Through Bob's illness, Ali and I opened two new chapters in the book of Bob: his first grandson, Elijah Bob Patricius Guggi Q, born in 1999, and his second, John Abraham, born in 2001.

WHEN RECORDING IS A DAY OFF

I'd thrown myself into politics and campaigning, economics and finance, a world of suits and sandwiches and fluorescent lamps. To be a convincing advocate, I'd had to learn the facts, to absorb the tedious detail that is the price to be paid for political change. Not sloganeering. Not sound bites. Just serious homework. At the same time as recording our first album in four years.

Unexpectedly, there was one sublime knock-on effect. It turned music, once again, into what I did on my days off. The studio became the playground that it had been in the early days when we had limited time to rehearse together. When recording time was so expensive we had to sprint through the sessions to get everything down in a few weeks. When you were in the studio, you had to be so sharp, so completely present. No lying around a greenroom watching afternoon TV, no time for the torpor of exploring every permutation of another mix. To be back in the studio became something I craved.

It was a throwback to being a teenager working in a petrol station during the 1970s oil crisis, my elbows angling to be anywhere else as I looked down a long line of queuing cars. Bored and begging to be back at band practice, where the sound of amps was louder than car horns, the bass deeper than the rattle of the trucks passing on the airport road.

I was not bored as an activist, but they were long arduous days looking for top-line melodies in folders of statistics. Flights to and from D.C. were spent cramming, with back-to-back meetings on arrival from breakfast to bedtime, while days back home became a stream of calls and notes on my daily to-do list from Suzanne Doyle, my assistant, who found herself under fire from Jubilee.

"You lot are supposed to care about human rights," I heard her say to Jamie on a phone call at the end of another long evening. "You could start by showing a little consideration for mine!" She blinks, then winks. Funny.

Our music became a place to escape to again.

Perhaps that explains how we wrote a song as joyful as "Beautiful Day" and why *All That You Can't Leave Behind* is often judged in our top three albums, along with *The Joshua Tree* and *Achtung Baby*. It must be the joy. The joy of being back in the studio. The joy of friendship and family. The joy of being alive. Life is short. Ali shared in this uplift. She'd gone back to college and emerged with a degree in social science and a similar ambition to serve. But our kids were her first port of call. I told myself that I was there for them as much as any father who was building a business. Any father away putting food on the table. And Ali told the kids. Your father is away putting food on other people's tables. People not so fortunate.

Looking back, I see the selfishness in that act. I got to fight injustice abroad, which left Ali at the kitchen table. The world of advocacy had me on loan from my wife. She had a right to expect more of me in the raising of our children but consciously decided to not exercise that right and let me go. Those years belonged to her, and she gave them away to me because she believed in the cause we were all working on, the people we were advocating for.

But still. It doesn't sit easily with me.

THE HEART IS A BLOOM

In relationships, I've observed that a partner can start out as a friend, then become a passion, then a co-parent, a mother or a father of your children, and if you're really fortunate, the partner remains—or returns as—a friend. It's a lower-temperature take on a romantic life, but it's enduring. I have been so fortunate.

Great friendships can survive most of the crap thrown at them. They thrive on the manure of shared disappointment and drama. It's hard to imagine a force as great as romantic love, but friendship comes close. Someone once argued that "friendship is higher than love," and I understood what they meant. It may not be as melodramatic or grandiose or passionate as love, but friendship is often deeper and wider. Great friendships explain why we hold on to this life so tightly because it disappears so quickly. Just as Ali and I were becoming best friends, I was aware of the wider web of deep friendships we had both grown up in, this sacrament of friendship from the band to the community around us. Relationships we had chosen, not ones chosen for us by blood. Pandemics aside, I still embrace people when I meet them, which goes all the way back to the days of Shalom when that's how we would say hello. I don't know that I've ever shaken somebody's hand without having to think about it.

My instinct to hail a friend is to hold them.

The recording of *All That You Can't Leave Behind* was a joyous time and not dogged by our periodic "musical differences." Maybe this was because we'd decided to make a more straightforward U2 album, thematically as well as musically. The band is rooted in friendship, but as these pages witness, we're not always on form for each other. These are deep and lasting relationships, but more than most they're put under strain. Difficult decisions in art and in business are made by standing over a position and allowing your three closest friends to kick the shite out of it. It can be bruising. And I recognize my own role in all this. How I can be over-the-top in standing up for what I believe in, how very wearying that must be.

I have a habit of playing to U2's weaknesses, trying to make these weaknesses our strength. Was that what our 1990s had been about? Now it was time to make a record which played to our strengths, which did the things we can do that no one else can do. The things I can do that other people find a little difficult. A certain emotional candor, the uncool stuff. Brian Eno above all else believed that U2 should never surrender to cool. In terms of our emotional temperature, he told us, our music was hot, more southern than northern European. Yours is like Latin music, he'd say, the Mass, the opera, the ecstatic.

Eno had been over in Dublin.

"Let's make one more album together, Brian."

"Why would we do that?" he responded, not unreasonably.

"Let's make every single song something you can't live without," I replied. "Let's not be heady, let's only make a song if it has to be sung, let's make an album of essential communications."

For such a great talker, Brian Eno is also a good listener. Did you know, I asked him, that there isn't a song of any note called "I Love You"? How about we make a song like that with no angle or irony, no twist or subterfuge? Almost to the point of embarrassment. Not the usual rock 'n' roll take on love.

Brian wonders aloud, "There has to be a song called 'I Love You.' I know there's 'Ich Liebe Dich' and 'She Loves You.'"

I throw in "I Will Always Love You" because Brian loves Whitney Houston; Eno the atheist loves church singers.

He's turning away to look out the window of the living room in Temple Hill. I am not convincing him.

"I love you?" He's thinking out loud.

I push him. "You think it already exists?"

"Sorry, no, I was wondering if you could cover fresh subject matter and still use the word 'love.'"

I'm listening.

"Could you write a song about your father?" he asks. "You were talking about the memory books people who have HIV put together for their loved ones, for when they are not around. An album as a memory book is an idea."

I'm thinking.

The conversations you can't not have, the pictures you must take with you when you leave, our interpersonal relationships. I'm thinking about my da and that polyp in my throat, the lingering thought that I could have cancer too. The ol' man is dying and now his young fella is no longer young. No longer indestructible, how inconvenient. I'm thinking about Ali and our kids. About age and mortality, about friendship and family. I knew we could write songs like that, but the trick would be not to give in to melancholy, to write with defiance as well as honesty.

The first time I thought we might have pulled it off was recording the song that would become "Beautiful Day." It wasn't "I Love You," but it was as innocuous and joyous a phrase. We were looking for some ecstatic quality. To sing a chorus like "It's a beautiful day," we'd need some clouds parting, the sun coming out, some kind of road rising. Edge found it with that repeating echo of his that he made famous in the 1980s, but stumbling on the part this time, he was immediately embarrassed. We all were.

"Oh my God, that sounds like U2."

"The problem is," I ventured, cautiously, "it sounds like the Edge in U2." To which Edge offered the perfect response.

"I *am* the Edge in U2. I can sound like this if I want."

I think we might all have stood up and whistled. Edge's modesty is part of the construction of his music, and occasionally I remember he is the most influential guitar player of not just his generation. Ask any guitar players.

The song had liftoff and lifted us out of wherever we were in our lives, brought us into orbit and back to earth in four minutes and five seconds. Because what's the use of liftoff if, being that high above yourselves, you don't get the advantage of perspective?

The middle section of the song is a play on astronaut Neil Armstrong's line from Apollo 11's mission to the moon: "It suddenly struck me that that tiny pea, pretty and blue, was the Earth." Everything and everyone that mattered to him he could cover with one thumb.

All that you could leave behind. All that we are leaving behind. If we don't fix the climate crisis.

> *See the world in green and blue*
> *See China right in front of you*
> *See the canyons broken by cloud*
> *See the tuna fleets clearing the sea out*
> *See the Bedouin fires at night*
> *See the oil fields at first light.*

Then Noah's release from quarantine after forty days of rising sea levels.

> *See the bird with a leaf in her mouth*
> *After the flood all the colours came out.*

And yes, after the confusion of everyone speaking in their own tongue in the story of the Tower of Babel comes "the rainbow" that is still the motif for how we might embrace our diversity and not just ecologically.

> *It's a beautiful day.*

The world will wake up to its beauty. It's not just the natural or even the supernatural world. It's us.

But Edge brought us back to earth too. Our man can build sonic landscapes that we haven't heard before, like the chewing gum sounds of "Elevation," but he can also revel in the non-extraordinary.

Like his guitar part for "In a Little While." This bluesy accompaniment will never get old because it's never felt new. The chords are classic gospel from Brian Eno. I sang it in a few takes after a big night out. The big head I had on me was ready for bed, but still . . .

> *Man dreams one day to fly*
> *A man takes a rocket ship into the sky*
> *He lives on a star that's dying in the night*
> *And follows in the trail the scatter of light.*

"When I Look at the World" has a similar perspective.

I'm in the waiting room
I can't see for the smoke
I think of you and your holy book
While the rest of us choke.

I always think that last verse was courtesy of my da.

This album of mostly ecstatic music won some ecstatic reviews. It went to number one in thirty-two countries and would win seven Grammy Awards. Gavin Friday had come up with the symbol of a heart in a suitcase for the artwork, which became the emblem for the subsequent tour. We built a stage in the shape of a heart and invited our most ardent fans to step inside it. The Elevation Tour was like playing two venues at the same time—a club, inside an arena. Our band had liftoff again, airborne with a joyful defiance. But now it was getting harder to leave home, knowing Bob was in an altogether different departure lounge.

During his last days we were touring Europe, and after shows I would fly home and be the night watchman at his hospital bed, sleeping in his room on a mattress the staff set up for me. Beaumont Hospital was so close to the airport that often I'd be sitting there in silence an hour and a half after the roar of an encore. Next morning we would chat with our eyes or with words, depending on how sick he was. On these hospital night shifts in his last days, I drew him while he slept. It helped me to stay close to him, wriggly writing as prayer. To draw someone's face, you really get to know them. It sounds uncomfortable but it wasn't.

When Norman arrived to take up his shift, Bob and I both knew everything would be okay. Even if it wasn't.

My brother was more helpful to my father in these dark, difficult days. Even had I been able to be there more, I don't know if I was equipped for the messiness of somebody dying in front of me. Not as useful as my brother, full stop. Since I can remember, Norman had always fixed everything. Toys, train sets, bicycles, motorcycles, radios, and tape recorders. Not this time.

Bob Hewson was a recording of many lives lived, and now we were losing the chance to access a library of information that might help us explain ourselves better. To listen for answers to so many questions. Questions about our mother. About long-ago family trips where the family hadn't seemed to be the reason we were there. About the back pain that had Bob surly and disengaged. The guilt he held inside his singer's head. About all the rage this appeared to raise in his younger son.

We would not press play anymore. The right-hand reel was emptying and the tape set to flap about until someone finally pressed stop. Norman couldn't fix this. But Norman was a constant; he made things better by being there.

AND IT'S YOU WHEN I LOOK IN THE MIRROR

When the da started slipping away, we were close enough friends for me not to feel abandoned, but there was always a hint of that in his independence. Patricide is what they call the son's killing of the father, but what if, as my friend Jim Sheridan—film director and psychological genius—suggested, "the son, deep down, believes the father was responsible for the untimely death of his mother? It's ridiculous of course, but emotions don't have to make sense; they just have to make themselves known!"

Then that rage is a roar, all right. A rage that first fills up the lungs, then gives tempo to the pulse as blood begins to sprint through veins. A roar that can fill stadiums, fill thousands of hearts while emptying its own. A rage that can break bones and promises. Grab teachers and students by the throat. A rage that will bully bullies and thump photographers who are just earning a crust by trying to steal one of your moments. A rage that can throw itself off balconies and into the arms of a crowd. A nuclear rage that can power a rock band or leave it in meltdown. *How to Dismantle an Atomic Bomb* we called an album a few years later.

Good question, Jim.

I've spent a life trying to understand my own rage and if it's possible trying to rewrite it. Some of it had to do with depending on other people, but some of it had to do with my father. Some of it is righteous, but some of it is volatile and extrusive.

After Bob passed away, Ali thought my agitation was getting worse and I was becoming a little more aggressive in my relations with people. Perhaps I could do with the cross-questioning of a ther-apist. I dodged that suggestion, but, perhaps unconsciously, I opted for another kind of inquisitor. I hadn't anticipated, when I signed up for the *Rolling Stone* interview with its legendary editor and publisher, Jann Wenner, that I would be lying on the psychiatrist's couch, but, heh, his interviews with Bob Dylan and John Lennon had changed me as much as some of their songs had.

Wenner evidently researched the pressure points of his "patients," and he really dug deep into my relationship with my father. At the end of a few long sessions he surprised me with an insight that all my prayer and meditation had missed.

"I think your father deserves an apology," he scolded me. "Can you imagine this story from his perspective? Your father loses his wife and he's left to bring up the two kids and one of them is charg-ing in his direction, coming for him all guns blazing. One of them is going to take him out by achieving all the ambitions he was afraid to have."

Okay then . . .

A BARITONE WHO THINKS HE'S A TENOR

Easter 2002. Ali and I visit the little chapel in Èze, France, a fisher-men's church with a hilltop view that has seen it all. Blood has run down these steep rocky routes to the shore for millennia, a com-munity defending itself against pirates, against armies and navies. And now against tourists like me. From the baroque pulpit a lone arm sticks out of the wall holding a cross, and a fishing boat hangs from the ceiling. After the service—sometimes improved, I find, if you don't speak the language that well—I returned to the pews on my own. I sat there and apologized to my father, Bob Hewson. I had forgiven him for his own crimes of passion, but I had never asked his forgiveness for mine.

> *Tough, you think you've got the stuff*
> *You're telling me and anyone*
> *You're hard enough*
> *You don't have to put up a fight*

You don't have to always be right
Let me take some of the punches
For you tonight

Listen to me now
I need to let you know
You don't have to go it alone

And it's you when I look in the mirror
And it's you when I don't pick up the phone
Sometimes you can't make it on your own

We fight, all the time
You and I, that's alright
We're the same soul
I don't need, I don't need to hear you say
That if we weren't so alike
You'd like me a whole lot more

Listen to me now
I need to let you know
You don't have to go it alone

And it's you when I look in the mirror
And it's you when I don't pick up the phone
Sometimes you can't make it on your own.

—"Sometimes You Can't Make It on Your Own"

I'll never know if it was related to me asking for his forgiveness in that little chapel, but after my father died, something changed. I've heard of people walking away from the confessional without the weight they carried in. What changed for me was my voice. I felt I got an extra couple of notes on my range; I felt I was becoming a real tenor as opposed to a pretend one. I could ring those high notes like a church bell, as I had never hit them before. It makes no scientific sense of course, but I've heard it said that when somebody close dies, they leave you a kind of passing gift, some invisible will where you inherit a special blessing. Bob Hewson's final gift to me was to enlarge the one he gave me long before. I was now a true tenor, no longer a baritone who only thought he was a tenor.

And when I get that lonesome feelin'
And I'm miles away from home
I hear the voice of the mystic mountains
Callin' me back home.

When Norman and I proudly carried Bob's coffin out of the Church of the Assumption in Howth, the congregation of old friends and family were singing "The Black Hills of Dakota." At the reception in the Marine Hotel a truck pulled up outside from County Antrim and off-loaded a hundred miniature bottles of Black Bush whiskey. At first I thought it was a promotion of some sort, but no, it was nothing other than a random act of kindness north to south, Prod to Catholic. The universe of Bob Hewson behaves like that.

the door through which

NO. THEM there's ONLY US

OPEN

things fall apart
the centre cannot
hold...
mere ANARCHY
is loosed upon the world.

Right now we are his mirror as he tightens the belt of his trousers and locks us both in. He gives one eyebrow raised suggesting a collegial questioning to my appearance but with no contrast in the reply

we are another mirror. History baffle's me now in his reality society has been fighting injustice since before we were born

our movement will pass

29

Crumbs from Your Table

From the brightest star
Comes the blackest hole
You had so much to offer
Why did you offer your soul?
I was there for you baby
When you needed my help
Would you deny for others
What you demand for yourself?

I am sitting on Harry Belafonte's bed. There is only one chair in this small hotel room, and Bob Geldof is sitting on it as we watch our host get dressed. I recall the old French proverb "No man is great in the eyes of his valet," but Harry Belafonte is great even when he's pulling on his pants.

What am I doing here? Harry Belafonte's backing band once included Charlie Parker and Miles Davis. He is the king of calypso; he sang the "Banana Boat Song (Day-O)," a track released on the first-ever million-selling album. He's also a lifelong troublemaker for equality. And so good-looking he probably never had to check himself in a mirror.

Right now we are his mirror as he tightens the belt of his trousers and locks us both in his gaze, one eyebrow raised suggesting a collegial questioning of his appearance, but with no interest in the reply.

We are another kind of mirror. Belafonte, now in his early seventies, has been fighting injustice since before we were born. With his combination of charm and admonition he has written the playbook for every artist-activist who came after him. In the 1960s, he reminds us, he marched in step with his friend Martin Luther King Jr. in the civil rights movement, and as he bends to tie the laces of his shoes—which I would gladly have done—he tells us a story that has shaped every day of my life since.

From Irish writers in theater—Wilde and Beckett, Synge and Behan—he segues into the Irish in politics, where we anticipate similar thrall with the arrival onstage of Irish royalty, the Kennedys. Not quite. Harry Belafonte rounds on Bobby Kennedy as a heel dragger, an obstacle in the way of the charging civil rights movement. I want to object that this was not how I'd seen it. But then I remember I'm not Black, I wasn't there, and, anyway, Harry has the floor. He also has a speaking voice that sounds as if a fuzz box were attached to his vocal cords, lending melodrama to his simplest expression. And with this stage whisper he transports us back in time.

"When Jack Kennedy appointed Bobby to attorney general in '61, it was such a setback to our struggle that it caused one of the most heated debates we ever had at the SCLC [Southern Christian Leadership Conference].

"Everyone in the room was sounding off about Bobby Kennedy. How he lacked the inspiration of his brother John, the president. That he was known to have warned JFK off trying to reconcile our agenda with that of the Democratic Party. Bobby was sure that if the White House got too close to the civil rights movement, it would cost the Democrats dear in the South, where holding the highest office in the land as a Catholic was already a stretch." By all accounts, he confessed, "Scratch the surface and many who carry the banner of the Democratic Party would not exactly be antislavery."

As the conversation grew more heated, Harry recalled how he turned to Martin Luther King, who he could tell was growing tired with the bitchin' about Bobby Kennedy.

"Martin slams his hand on the table to snap everyone out of it. 'Does anyone here have anything positive to say about our new attorney general?'"

"No, Martin, that's what we're telling you," comes the reply.

"There's nothin' good about this man; he's an Irish redneck, got no time for the Black man's struggle."

Dr. King, said Harry, had heard enough and adjourned the meeting. "Gentlemen, I'm releasing you into the world to find one positive thing to say about Bobby Kennedy, because that one positive thing will be the door through which our movement will have to pass."

If I hadn't been sure what I'd come looking for at the feet of Harry Belafonte, suddenly it was all clear. The search for common ground starts with a search for higher ground. Even with your opponents. Especially with your opponents. A lightbulb moment for me and a conviction that's informed my life as a campaigner ever since. The simple but profound idea that you don't have to agree on everything if the one thing you do agree on is important enough.

But, hold on, school isn't out.

Harry Belafonte hasn't finished our lesson.

"Years later," he continues, "when Bobby Kennedy lay dying on the kitchen floor of a Los Angeles hotel, he'd become a civil rights hero. A leader, not a laggard, in our movement, and I ask myself to this day if we got him wrong in those early days. I'll never know, but I still grieve his loss."

"So did you find it?" asks Bob, raising the question we were both thinking. "When the meeting reconvened, did you find that one positive thing Dr. King was looking for?"

"We did. Bobby was close to his bishop, who was in turn close to some of our clergy from the South. We found a door to move through."

GEORGE BUSH'S FRONT, BACK, AND SIDE DOOR

In 2001, when George W. Bush became the forty-third president of the United States, all of our contacts in the previous administration were replaced. The women and men who replaced them had no reason to think of us as friends. Worse than that, they had good reason not to think of us at all. Not just the new faces around the cabinet table, but the commander in chief, the president himself. It wasn't just that I was seen as a friend of Bill and Hillary's. It was worse again. Only a few years before, on the ZOO TV Tour, the band had walked onstage to a mash-up of the State of the Union address of his father (President George H. W. Bush), reimagined as a parody of Queen's "We Will Rock You."

Night after night I crank called his da from the stage. Well, crank called the White House operators.

"Tell the president to watch more TV."

I was calling so frequently that one night I realized the same operator was answering the White House phone.

"Tell me," I asked her, "what's your name?"

"Operator Two," she replied.

Operator Two became my favorite. I even invited her to a gig. She said, "I work evenings."

I said, "So do I."

But Operator Two never showed up, and although I often asked for her, we never spoke again.

My phone number was not going to be in the Filofax of anyone in the new crowd moving into the West Wing. Not even Operator Two. And that was a problem because the movement we were part of would need this new administration on our side in order to complete the job of canceling the debts of the poorest countries. And then there was AIDS. The rapid spread of the HIV virus through Africa and Asia was now threatening to undermine the benefits of debt cancellation in developing economies. Kofi Annan captured it: "AIDS is far more than a health crisis. It is a threat to development itself."

But how to make friends with George W. Bush? What was the door we might move through? And, anyway, what kind of movement were we now part of? The big tent coalition that was Jubilee 2000 had promised to put itself out of business at the end of the year 2000 . . . whether or not all the debts had been canceled. Which they had not. But as that disbanding was discussed, it dawned on me that I loved being part of this new band. I didn't want to let go of my new comrades.

I drove Jamie Drummond mad, but as mad as he got, he drove me sane. He was deeply briefed on any subject we had to talk about, and he made sure I was too. When people came out of meetings thinking I was smarter than they'd expected, they were really talking about Jamie. A faucet of data and hard-won analytics that you just couldn't turn off. Except when we got to talking about County Mayo making it to the All-Ireland GAA final. The faucet would stop dripping, and the pints of Guinness would slowly start pulling our "evidence-based activist" away to a different kind of chatter. Without Jamie there would be no band.

Bobby was a political strategist of the highest order, I guess that was partly DNA, but he seemed to prefer backstage to front of house. If you ask him, he'll tell you it was the death of his best friend, the photographer Herb Ritts, of HIV that fired him up.

Lucy Matthew, a Jubilee campaigner who'd worked in Zambia, was the grown-up, reminding us not to confuse our access with success. She had a talent to make big problems appear a lot smaller than they were. It's not a sunny disposition, it's steelier than that, but its brightness kept us going when our lights were occasionally punched out.

I invited them and Bob Geldof to Dublin in August 2001 to decide whether we should continue. Everyone gathered in my kitchen the morning after we'd played Slane Castle. Ali, too, swaying from side to side with our newborn son, John, wrapped around her neck and a two-year-old Eli wrapped around her leg. She looks at me as if I'm a child about to start a new school. I need to know she'll be there when I come home. I have a fleeting moment of doubt about the decision we're about to make. Fleeting.

Bobby, Jamie, Lucy, and I not only liked working together but we also had a strategy we believed in, of not playing the left off the right or the cool off the uncool. We were inhabiting a space where it didn't feel like we had much company, a space critics might dismiss as a compromised middle, but I imagined as a radical center. We stood up from the table deciding this band still had some work to do . . . but first it would need a name.

We might have called the band WONK.

Luckily we didn't. Geldof suggested DATA, drawing on three pressing issues that kept coming up with African activists: "debt, AIDS, trade." Lucy and Jamie argued for a kind of DATA deal, where action on debt, AIDS, and trade had a flip side, a commitment to democracy, accountability, and transparency for Africa.

In the years since, I have often regretted that we didn't stop to think a little more carefully about what right we had to take on this work, to barge our way into the corridors of power. We took it for granted that because the problems of global inequality were mostly created by the Northern Hemisphere, it fell to those of us in the north to solve them. I recognize now how arrogant this position was. I learned a little late the wisdom in a Senegalese proverb, "If you want to cut a man's hair, be sure he is in the room."

DIRTY LITTLE SECRET

"It was the Catholics who got Bush elected." The radical center had some natural allies. James Carville was a star of Bill Clinton's so-called third-way strategy to win the White House. Now, post–war room, he remained a force as a Democratic consultant known as the Ragin' Cajun, his insights delivered in Flannery O'Connor southern gothic style, all raspy voice and semiautomatic phrasing. With a head like a bullet, Carville was a political animal who knew there were hunters hiding in every wood because he was one of them. A Louisiana native who could charm the birds out of the magnolia trees before catching them in his net, Carville coined the mantra— "It's the economy, stupid"—that helped get Bill Clinton elected.

Bobby Shriver tracked him down because no one knows political strategy like Carville—how it has to be rooted in the deepest understanding of your opponent, almost to the point of empathy. "Compassionate conservatism is what Bush believes got him elected," explains Carville. "You want an in with Bush? You got to make friends with the Catholics, and you got to make friends with the evangelicals."

Oh, and one other thing, he adds. "There's a dirty little secret about elections and their promises."

A beat.

"Most presidents want to keep those promises. They really do."

Perhaps the door through which our movement would pass could be the same one MLK found. Perhaps religious commitment might again be the key to the door.

On a more prosaic level, I might need to sharpen up on the dress code if we were to get ourselves into the White House again.

The word was that the forty-third president had reinstated the formality of the fortieth president, Ronald Reagan, and the golden age he represented for conservatives. It was said that the former governor of Texas wore a jacket and tie in the Oval Office, that the rangy collegiate style of the forty-second president was so 1999. In preparation I bought a tie, but I still failed to get a meeting with the big boss. How about Paul O'Neill, his Treasury secretary? The man who signs the very U.S. dollar bills we wanted to reassign from fighter jets to classrooms and clinics, a better kind of defense, we argued.

Another polite refusal. We asked again. And again. This time in person to Tim Adams, the secretary's discerning chief of staff. I can't remember if I wore the tie, but we finally got our breakthrough.

Tim would give us twenty minutes with the secretary to say hello, "just to be courteous."

"HAVE YOU EVER EVEN BEEN TO AFRICA?"

Paul O'Neill had a special way with words. He spat words out of his mouth as fast as possible, with as little fuss as possible. "Direct" doesn't capture it. But stripped of the usual politesse, he came across as disarmingly honest and trustworthy. He also came out fighting. Like a lot of great fighters, he had a teeny-tiny lisp.

"Have you ever even been to Africa?" Quite a few times, Secretary.

"Okay, okay, you've been, but have you actually ever worked on the continent? You know, I worked all over the place with Alcoa. You heard of Alcoa? You heard of Guinea? Well, if you think this administration will give you an extra dime to waste on some of the most corrupt countries in the world, you're crazier than I already think you are."

Okay. Starting to see where you're coming from, Mr. Secretary. He wasn't finished. "These tin-pot dictators rob and steal from their own people. You know, we don't even believe the accounts of our own government aid agency about how they spend the money we pour into these countries, so why would we believe you?"

I remembered my mantra and began to look for some common ground, some kind of door. Corruption, you're right, Mr. Secretary, that's as big a killer on the continent of Africa as any disease. "But that was true about all of our countries at different stages of development, including Ireland."

Bobby Shriver chimes in, suggesting new leaders were emerging in Africa with more principled positions than just being our friend or enemy during the Cold War. "There is a new Africa rising," I heard myself saying, "from the ruins of colonialism and the proxy wars between West and East."

"Nonsense."

Did I mention Paul O'Neill was direct?

"Absolute nonsense, you're reading the wrong newspapers."

Our time seemed to be up—was this the fastest twenty minutes of my life?—but as we were firmly niced out of the office, I put my foot in the door long enough to catch Secretary O'Neill's eye.

"If I could show you ten African countries moving in the direction of good governance and accountability, would you reconsider?"

"If you could show me five, I'm happy to talk more, but I don't think we'll be seeing each other again. Thank you, Mr. Bono, good day."

"SON, LET ME PUT MY HANDS ON YOU"

We would have to seek out the "compassionate conservatives" that President Bush believed had elected him, and we would have to make the case to them that debt relief and sending U.S. taxpayers' money overseas to fight HIV/AIDS was both compassionate and conservative. Polling suggested the opposite. When asked in 2001, more than half of evangelical Christians said they "probably or definitely would not help" even AIDS orphans. They believed this "new plague," as it was sometimes called, was not something they should be concerned with. Many put its rise down to sexual immorality; some even claimed it was divine judgment for sinful lives. The idea that Jesus might have died for everyone, not just those who saw themselves as morally upright, had passed them by. Along with any parallel with the so-called untouchables of Jesus's day, those with leprosy, the ones he sought out to welcome and heal.

As I started visiting influential religious leaders, I reminded them of those 2,003 verses in the Bible relating to the poor and that, after personal redemption, concern for the poor is the dominant motif in the whole book. Not who is having sex with whom. In a Washington meeting with three dozen prominent evangelicals I quoted Jesus, himself quoting an earlier prophet, Isaiah.

"The Spirit of the Lord is on me, because He has anointed me to preach good news to the poor. He has sent me to proclaim liberty to the captives and recovery of sight to the blind, to release the oppressed."

Not exactly rock 'n' roll . . . but then again.

I was coming to see that the Bible was a door through which I could move with people who might otherwise stay put.

Love thy neighbor, I used to say, is not advice. It's a command. Right? Whoever our neighbor is. Wherever.

Cut to a meeting in Senator Jesse Helms's office in the Senate. I am putting out of my mind that he is one of the characters behind the story of our song "Bullet the Blue Sky," a Cold War warrior who argued for U.S. intervention in Central America in the 1980s. This is the archconservative senator from North Carolina, the nemesis not just of AIDS activists—he'd talked of "the gay disease"—but of artists, too, thanks to his attempts to censor the National Endowment for the Arts. He'd also tried to filibuster the bill making Martin Luther King's birthday a public holiday. In 2001, Helms sits on a powerful throne as the chair of the Foreign Relations Committee.

And here he is, putting his hands on my head.

"Son, I want to bless you. Let me put my hands on you."

He has tears in his eyes, and later he will publicly repent of the way he had spoken in the past about AIDS. As big a shock to the left as to the right. It was the leprosy analogy from the scriptures that moved him. He had to follow his Jesus there. Still, at times like this I feel as if I've turned up in someone else's drama and one day I'll meet the writer.

Edge is particularly upset to hear about this meeting. I'm stretching the patience of the band and of our audience. I'm about to stretch it some more.

A VERY ODD COUPLE

Cut to Kotoka International Airport in Accra, Ghana. I am now part of a military operation. From the moment "Air Force America" touched down with my new best friend Secretary of the Treasury Paul O'Neill, it was as if we were an invading army. Rock singers know a thing or two about the traveling circus, but nothing compares with traveling with Uncle Sam's stagecoach. Talk about "wagons roll." Yet for all the logistical hoopla, this motley crowd of economists, bureaucrats, and media seemed genuinely committed to challenging the clichés that we'd all harbored about the continent. Paul O'Neill was up at five a.m. and, on the dot of six a.m., sitting in the motorcade. (Not having got to bed until five, I was occasionally a little late. And usually forgiven.) "The Odd Couple Tour," as it was dubbed, rapidly caught the imagination of a media determined to see if there was any substance in George Bush's claim of compassionate conservatism.

We'd asked local organizations to set up meetings with sex workers, doctors, AIDS educators, and activists. The Treasury organized visits to the stock exchange, a dental records processing office, a Ford car manufacturing plant.

But as the days passed, I began to observe something paradoxical but also encouraging. If the perspective of Secretary O'Neill and his team of monetary theorists was being changed by the stories of heartbreak that the AIDS pandemic placed in our path, my perspective was also shifting as I began to see the role of domestic industry and commerce, and especially infrastructure, in bringing people out of extreme poverty.

While I started paying more attention to the kind of economic data that lets you know what's really behind the poverty of a country, Paul and his wife, Nancy, along with Julie, their daughter, ended up spending longer than planned talking to nurses, doctors, and patients in clinics and hospitals.

I can still recall how shocked they were, visiting a clinic in

Soweto, to discover that while the United States funded the drug nevirapine for pregnant mothers to prevent them from passing HIV to their unborn children, there was no funding for ARVs (antiretroviral drugs) to save the life of the mother herself. If I wasn't in tears, the O'Neills were. We were all changing.

> *You speak of signs and wonders*
> *I need something other*
> *I would believe if I was able*
> *But I'm waiting on the crumbs from your table.*

As the secretary and I hugged and went our separate ways at the airport, I knew that despite our differences we now had an ally in the Bush administration. We left the continent starting to believe that the Bush White House might make a serious move on AIDS in Africa, and I was excited back home in Dublin to tell Edge all about it.

Over a Guinness in Finnegan's, I'm describing the transformative facts of "regional integration" and some of the finer details of the stock exchange in Ghana. My pulse quickens at the memory of flying in a twin-engined Cessna over the port of Dar es Salaam to get a better view of container ships and rail links.

"Well, we need to get you back to the studio as fast as possible," says Edge, lifting a pint of Guinness to his lips with a perfectly straight face. "The poetry is just pouring out of you."

Not so long later and we're getting ready to go back into the studio with producer Chris Thomas to write songs for *How to Dismantle an Atomic Bomb* when I hear the news.

Paul O'Neill, the man who held the purse strings of America, had been sacked.

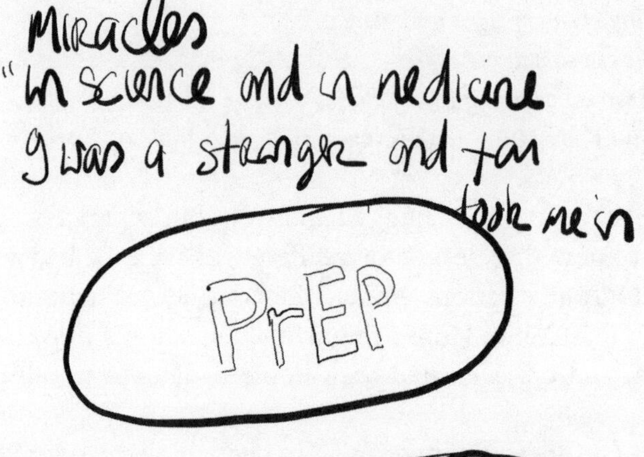
Miracles
"In science and in medicine
I was a stranger and you took me in"
PrEP
ARV
GOD BLE$$ AMERICA

30

Miracle Drug

Beneath the noise
Below the din
I hear your voice
It's whispering
In science and in medicine
I was a stranger
You took me in.

You know when you're in a hospital? That scent in the corridors? The smell of detergent. Of hygiene. Except when the hospital has no supplies. Then another odor. Then the odor is of people who have not been able to wash, who have no access to a shower. People who smell smoky from the fires they've made in the hospital grounds on which to cook whatever they can find to eat. This is the smell that fills my nostrils in the hospital in Lilongwe, the capital of Malawi. This is the smell of a hospital itself on life support, where there is no way to treat the invisible killer that stalks the wards.

A THREE-ACT PLAY OVER TWO YEARS. NINE SCENES
FROM THE LIFE OF AN AMATEUR AIDS ACTIVIST

Act 1, Scene 1: On the Wards with Sister Anne
in Lilongwe, Malawi (The Saint)

In early 2002, I am in Africa in the company of Professor Jeff Sachs and his wife, Dr. Sonia Sachs. Today we are meeting Sister Anne Carr, who tells me she was born in Dublin and raised in Cork and has spent her life as a medical missionary, working in maternity units or mobile clinics in remote villages.

We meet at the city's overwhelmed 750-bed hospital run by Dr. Mwansambo, who tells us it's at 300 percent capacity. It looks more like a multistory car park, floors stacked up on each other, outside walkways running the length of each floor. Outsiders are not invited into the hospital, but I am quickly through the doors, no questions asked.

"I told them you were my nephew," Sister Anne tells me.

I like this woman immediately. The nun whom everyone recognizes walks the rock star whom no one has heard of past queues of patients who line the corridors. They are newly diagnosed, explains Anne, HIV positive. They are waiting to be admitted to an anteroom where they will learn from a health-care worker that there is no treatment for their condition. Here they must prepare to die.

On the wards the scene is still more troubling. Three or four patients to a bed, sometimes two on top, head to toe. Sometimes two more underneath. Everyone preparing to die.

As we walk, I risk a glance at some of the faces waiting in line, anticipating their despair, anger, or rage. Why wouldn't you be furious when you know that if a white westerner like me contracted this disease, it would not be a death sentence. I would get treatment. Yet there is no rage in the faces that look back at me, only acquiescence. These people who are being told they're going to die are almost apologizing for their situation.

There is no rage on view, only good manners. They hide their embarrassment; they are polite and graceful. They disguise their hurt with gratitude to the caregivers who have given them the worst news possible. While they wait to die, they must also live with stigma—the stigma of having been tested, of being HIV positive.

The anger is in other eyes looking at me. In the eyes of the hospital staff. What does it feel like for a health worker who can diagnose but not treat, who must tell their patients that nothing can be done for them? This anger is muted. It is not screamed, not even spoken. But I see it. More than that I feel it, and I want you to feel it now, you reading these pages. The anger is behind my eyes too. I am enraged that the world is allowing this to happen. When my family and my friends wanted to know why I spent so much time in the corridors of power, meeting all these suits, shaking all these fuckin' hands . . . I just had to paint this picture.

This hospital in Lilongwe.

Twenty years after HIV was first identified and five years after citizens of wealthy countries gained access to life-transforming drug therapies, there is still no treatment affordable or available here. Why would you bother getting tested, even if you could? East and Southern Africa in the early years of the twenty-first century are the epicenter of the epidemic. In Botswana, 38 percent of the adult population are HIV positive. Over a third of adults are going to fall ill and die. You could look around a crowded market and imagine the vanishing. It was no exaggeration when their president, Festus Mogae, declared, "We are threatened with extinction." This virus is not just killing the young and vulnerable; it's killing nurses, doctors, teachers, farmers, accountants, lawyers. Mothers and fathers. If no treatment reaches them, the hopes and dreams of the whole region will perish.

Sister Anne is not as angry as me.

I am sitting in her office, and all I can take in is the overwhelming stink of shit. Her office is over a drain.

"How can you get used to this?" I ask.

"Get used to what?"

"This smell," I say.

"What smell?" she asks, a look of total disbelief. And then she winks at me.

Sister Anne deals with death by telling it off or holding its hand.

She laughs a lot, but there is no one more serious about transforming the lives of the poor. This is her service; she sees the face of her God in these people she lives with. I remember that verse from scripture, how whenever we serve those who are judged among the least, we are serving God. Whether we know it or not. Perhaps if I stand close to Sister Anne, I am standing close to God.

But still, the stink.

Act 1, Scene 2: South Africa
Don't Waste Our Time, Mr. Bono (The Professionals)

Malawi and South Africa, these were the visits that radicalized me. Radicalized all of us in our team at DATA. It wasn't enough to get angry; we had to get organized and get answers to difficult questions. Questions about the cost of the therapeutics and how to make universal access to ARVs a reality. We believed that HIV was a battle beyond arguments about compassion or good development, beyond a conversation about rates of return on investment of resources. I'd met Treatment Action Campaigners (TAC) fighting with their lives for universal access to AIDS medication, and to this day I've never experienced an activism propelled by such force as theirs. Their anger was not muted. It was as loud and insistent as a fire alarm. The formidable Prudence Mabele (who died of pneumonia in 2017, aged forty-five) was one of the first women in South Africa to make her HIV status public. She looked me straight in the eye as she explained she was missing a family funeral—a death from HIV—to be at this meeting with me.

"I hope you are not wasting our time, Mr. Bono," she said. "Because some of us don't have any to waste."

Médecins Sans Frontières had donated ARVs to TAC, but there weren't enough. This led to unthinkable decisions about who would receive this lifesaving medication and who would not. Among colleagues. Among families. Among siblings.

Cofounder Zackie Achmat was on a drug strike, refusing to take ARVs until they were available to all South Africans. TAC had been battling Big Pharma in the courts for refusing to allow cheaper, generic versions of their medicines to be made, and would win landmark victories like that in Pretoria, which forced the state to provide nevirapine to all HIV-positive pregnant women.

That these expensive pills were prolific in the rich world but denied to the poor world seemed to physicalize inequality. To actualize global injustice.

Act 1, Scene 3: Kampala, Uganda
Find a Family Who Will Care for Your Children (The Instructions)

When I met women from TASO—the AIDS Support Organization—a few days later in a concrete block building in Kampala, Uganda, this reality could not have been clearer.

Understated and matter-of-fact, the women described their situation as if they were explaining the rules in a classroom, which went something like this.

THE RULES OF PREPARING TO DIE

Find a family who will care for your children. Prepare a memory book for them full of love.

Educate those in your community who do not have HIV. Embrace and pray for those who do.

Look after each other.

The women are composed as they explain, as they show us the memory books they are gathering for their children: photos, mementos, family history, letters for future occasions, advice. Messages of undying love. In his office after the visit, Dr. Alex Coutinho, the director, chokes, telling us that he is often the one who has to decide who will get the few available ARVs.

Holding these three pills in my hand, I felt the gelatinous surface that contained life or death, and the showman/salesman in me knew that we had the visual props to win the argument. As with Jubilee 2000, this was an argument about justice rather than charity. If access to ARVs really came down to your geographical address, "an accident of longitude or latitude," as I used to put it, then I believed we could win that case in the court of public opinion. If we could do that, we could win the politics.

I would put the thought in "Crumbs from Your Table," which we recorded a couple of years later:

> Where you live should not decide
> Whether you live or whether you die
> Three to a bed
> Sister Anne, she said
> Dignity passes by.

> —"Crumbs from Your Table"

But the idea was a hook in my life even before it was a hook in a song. A hook we needed to get played on the radio—of public opinion.

"Where you live should not decide whether you live."

Act 2, Scene 1: Midtown Manhattan, NYC,
News Corp HQ with the Kingmaker or Scaffold Erector

For politicians to make bold decisions that would benefit people thousands of miles away, we had to engage with opinion shapers as well as lawmakers. Which explains why a few months later I'm with Bobby Shriver in the corporate headquarters of News Corp in midtown Manhattan, around the corner from the newly Disneyfied Times Square. Nothing special about the office at the time, though looking back, I see that it was special: this is where a right-wing revolution will be stealthily nurtured, one that will shake the foundations of American democracy.

We're sitting with Rupert Murdoch, who, only a few years before, has launched Fox News, which is already anointing the bellicose TV anchors and right-wing firebrands who will weaponize the disgruntlement of a whole set of U.S. constituencies. People who feel the regular news media are a liberal intelligentsia talking down to them, oblivious to their pain or fear. In the years ahead, as globalization no longer seems to work for many Americans, more and more will find their fear turning to anger. Joined with the rise of the internet, the cost of the war in Iraq, the financial crisis, and mass migration, these people will feel their pockets emptying as their bills pile up. They will become Donald Trump's support base as he bids for the White House—not that there's any evidence he's ever seemed too bothered about their plight in the past.

Rupert Murdoch is mostly not like Donald Trump. A sophisticated thinker, camouflaged by colloquialisms. Australian. But there is a similarity. Rupert Murdoch likes to say the thing in the room that some people want to say but won't. There's something in him of his Presbyterian preacher grandfather, but the latest version of fire and brimstone is a headline in *The Sun* or the *Post*, a headline he believes reveals another establishment cover-up.

The establishment?

Anyone powerful or political, rich or famous. (Including, eventually, himself. A few years later he will fall on his sword in the wake of the U.K. phone-tapping scandal that his *News of the World* was caught up in.) You might think the methods his empire employs to uncover this reveal a morality deficit worse than the hypocrisies they expose. Rupert Murdoch doesn't think this. What do I think? What I think is less important right now than that News Corp's newspapers are on our side rather than against us.

How far can I push this strategy once described as "We have met the enemy and they are partly right." This is certainly a toxic environment for anyone who might care to be on the cover of *Rolling Stone*. Curiously, I'm encouraged to take these risks by that magazine's ultra-liberal publisher (and my erstwhile therapist) Jann Wenner, who laughs while reminding me of the old proverb about "picking a fight with a man who buys ink by the barrel."

"You or him?" I respond.

Sitting next to Rupert is Roger Ailes, who will be forced to resign as CEO of Fox News, but not before he will help transform Donald Trump from a reality TV star in *The Apprentice* . . . to a reality TV star in the White House. Next to him is Murdoch's fellow Australian Col Allan, editor in chief of the *New York Post*, which in this city is like the *Daily Bugle*, if you're a fan of Spider-Man. I'm ready for the usual skepticism about the efficiency of aid and try to explain why Americans should care about a health pandemic in Africa. Then I await the judgment of the man who makes presidents and prime ministers, the kingmaker or scaffold erector. Rupert Murdoch's face is an unmade bed held in two hands and then one.

"Thank you, Bono, for visiting with us today and for presenting your case on HIV/AIDS, which we recognize is destroying the lives of millions of people. But . . . but . . . but . . . if you're asking can News Corp involve itself in that campaign by attempting to influence the president of the United States on the matter, the answer is no. A definite and nonnegotiable 'no.'"

I felt like a fool on a fool's errand and nodded to Bobby as we prepared to thank everybody for their time.

"But . . . but . . . I haven't finished."

The unlikely revolutionary isn't done.

"I want you to know that *should* the president of the United States take up a historic AIDS initiative of the kind you are arguing for, then we here in this building will come on like the tide."

No sooner were we out the door than Bobby was calling Karl Rove, President Bush's chief adviser.

"Hey, Karl, here's a surprise: Rupert Murdoch has just told us that if your guy goes big on the AIDS emergency, he'll be all over it with his support. Come on, man, you can do this."

Act 2, Scene 2: Washington, D.C.
Falling Out and Falling in with Dr. Condoleezza Rice (The Ferry Woman)

Two people in the administration who consistently held open the door for us and were genuinely interested in what DATA was up to were Josh Bolten, a senior economic adviser who was to become President Bush's chief of staff, and Dr. Condoleezza Rice, his national security adviser. "The president," she said, "has given me permission to try and understand what you're doing."

That explained her confidence in letting Bobby, Lucy, Jamie, and me into her office. Meetings that would end up with the content of Jamie's and Lucy's backpacks spread all over Dr. Rice's desk, all across her office floor, while she pored over Christian Aid or Oxfam analytics. This was not a picture most people would reconcile with the stiff and upright image of the Bush administration, but it was inspiring that Dr. Rice was open to any relevant information. She just wanted verification and insight. Ordering us coffee, she also asked us hard questions about whether these numbers really added up. They did, which is why she kept asking us back.

Turned out that the Bush administration was a lot less interested in Africa and an AIDS pandemic than in the march of freedom, from Afghanistan to the Gulf states, especially Iraq. Freedom is fundamental to progress is their argument, so that American-style capitalism can turbocharge these economies. Crudely put: if only these tin-pot dictators and religious extremists would get out of the way, then commerce would do its job and the ingenuity of the people in these countries would do the rest. There might have been a kind of coherence to the argument if it had not completely ignored both the depth of ethnic and religious tribalism and the devastating impact of HIV/AIDS. A successful commercial sector is generally not one where the workforce is lining up in a hospital corridor, or dying, two or three to a bed.

After 9/11, the administration was starting to take the continent of Africa very seriously, at the very least as partner—or protagonist—in the war against terror. That said, it was the transformative power of commerce that continued to guide the president's thinking on development. Treasury economist John Taylor and South African ambassador Jendayi Frazer were among those we talked to about ideas that became known as the Millennium Challenge Account (MCA), a proposal for hundreds of millions in new grants to countries that were pledged to good governance and fast-tracking their economies. It could be for a highway in Tanzania or a dam in Niger, but the numbers would need to add up, and it had to fit a fiscally conservative playbook. Leaders such as Ghana's John Kufuor and Mozambique's Joaquim Chissano embraced this because it was a new kind of relationship with America, away from patronage and toward partnership.

The danger was that the MCA began to emerge as the big idea, guided by national security deputy Gary Edson, and it felt as if the door was closing on an AIDS initiative. MCA? Hard and rigorous. AIDS initiative? Warm and fuzzy. And expensive. Very expensive. It was a worry. But in the middle of these conversations the voice of

Dr. Rice was sure-footed and precise. Condi, as we were now calling the future secretary of state, was an academic, a sophisticated thinker, a concert-level pianist, and a fluent Russian speaker. Born in Birmingham, Alabama, she was a "believer," in the sense that she seemed to possess religious faith, but she was not happy-clappy, hers was not a dancing-in-the-aisles kind of church. When she worked out in the early mornings, sometimes next to the president, she told me it might be rock 'n' roll music in her ears, and that was a picture of the classicist I couldn't get out of my mind.

"Like who?" I asked.

"Actually, Led Zeppelin is one of my favorites," she told me. Why was I not surprised? Because nothing was surprising about this woman who was tougher than the rest, this hawkish presence in the White House and later State Department, moving effortlessly from Chopin's nocturnes to "Whole Lotta Love." As a lifelong member of Amnesty International I had to push her on the torture of Islamic extremists in custody. "The United States doesn't believe in torture, as it accrues inaccurate information and invites the same practice for our own combatants."

This would have to be a conversation for another time.

Condi had an ear that could sort through the discord on different issues and locate the top-line melody for the president. She was the soprano voice in the choir that I was starting to believe would get George W. Bush across the line. But right now, for all our access, we were not making progress on a major AIDS initiative.

Our anxiety came into sharp focus in March 2002 with news that the pro-business MCA, what Bobby called "start-up money for new democracies," was going to be announced with no mention of the AIDS emergency. As we'd helped shape the initiative, it was explained that I was expected to stand at the side of President Bush as he launched it to the world at the Inter-American Development Bank. I should pause to emphasize that this was an additional $5 billion in development assistance—and from a Republican administration—to build infrastructure like roads, electrical grids, and steel smelters. It was a very big deal for the countries that would benefit. It was also a very big deal for DATA.

And awkward.

Very awkward.

Our supporters had been campaigning for universal access to AIDS drugs, and this would have no mention of that.

Awkward for me too.

Very awkward.

A photo op with a pugilistic president who, having successfully invaded Afghanistan, was now saber rattling about war in Iraq. With his cowboy rhetoric and added swagger, George W. was now even alienating conservative moderates. A war in Iraq was seen as a step too far by an overreaching president too much in the thrall of the neocons on the right flank of his party. To get wonky, the neocons believed that if the significant Iraqi Shiite majority threw off their Sunni overlords and became a democracy, then Iran and others in the region might likely follow, heralding a strategy known in the world of foreign affairs and the Atlantic Council as the Pax Americana. (Pax?)

Publicly, I had kept out of the news on Iraq. For an Irish big mouth this had been almost impossible, but I forced myself to button it. Privately, I had conversations with both Dr. Rice and Karl Rove about British troops who arrived in Northern Ireland and at first enjoyed a warm welcome from the Catholic minority they were there to protect. All too quickly those troops became the enemy. Nothing like being stopped and searched on your own street by soldiers speaking a whole other "language" to create alienation. In a moment of candor, Karl Rove exhaled and said, "Well, put it like this, Bono, if we get this wrong, you won't be dealing with us very much longer because there's an election coming up."

This put my own little conflict into context, but what sort of photo op would I be walking into? Was I going to be the liberal patsy, applauding at the launch of something that our team had played a part in but was not our raison d'être? While the AIDS emergency, the very thing we'd described as the moral fulcrum of a generation, got passed over.

I was in danger of wasting Prudence Mabele's time while providing a tacit endorsement of a warmongering president.

I could already hear the booing, and that was just from my own band. Our fans as well as our critics in the media would cry foul.

"Speak truth to power . . . where's your white flag of nonviolence now?"

Surely, I told myself, if this was the biggest U.S. aid increase in ten years, I could live with a flogging in the media. What about the band, though? They never asked for this. God bless their patience. The optics, as we learned to say later, were all wrong and we got the jitters. Bobby called Condi to explain that without some kind of accompanying initiative on HIV/AIDS the MCA announcement was not going to work for us. We saw these two elements as part of the same strategy.

Condi, who never lost her cool, lost her cool. "She's *really* pissed" was how Bobby put it.

If we reneged on her, this might be the end of DATA's work with the administration. I was in a bind. I didn't want to let Condi or the White House down—plus the MCA *was* a significant move—but nor did I want to appear the patsy. I needed to talk to her myself. On a Wednesday afternoon I was hurried through White House security at the West Gate, past the TV cameras, through the West Wing lobby, where I was no longer an oddity under the gaze of the saluting marines and receptionists sitting in the antechamber outside her office. Condi closed the door behind me for what I immediately felt was going to be one of the most critical conversations of my life. With its mahogany bookshelves and comfortable chairs it's not an unusual office, but Condi has an unusual power, businesslike but never cold. But is her smile a little more earnest than usual? Is she as nervous as I am? "Bono, I'm a relationship person, relationships are everything to me, and if you do not turn up for the president tomorrow, you embarrass us."

Straight to the punch.

"The Millennium Challenge Account is $5 billion of new money. If that's not enough for you, I sense our relationship is coming to an end. Certainly mine."

"Condi, of course we're grateful for the access, you know we really are, but please see us as representatives of every campaign organization who are working on this night and day, year after year, but our closeness to your administration has also aroused suspicion that we will sell out. Access to antiretroviral drugs is the only access this movement is interested in."

"Who's suspicious?"

"The Global AIDS Alliance for a start; even our good friend Dr. Paul Zeitz is calling us sellouts, saying we're giving you cover for inaction on the AIDS emergency."

"Bono, we will get to the AIDS problem. Just not yet. Fighting AIDS is one pillar of four or five that will make for good development policy."

Sister Anne comes back to me, her office over the drains. I'm in Condi's office, one of the most powerful in the world, but I need her to be in Sister Anne's office. I wish Prudence was here to look her in the eye. I believe Condi is making a mistake. She believes I am. But I also want to believe in her; I believe she wants to do the right thing. I feel as if I've got to know her these last couple of years, that I have a sense of who she is under her elegant armor. I think she has a sense of who I am too. I try one last time.

"Condi, this little virus is more than just a monumental health emergency; it is undoing everything your administration is working for."

(I could have gone on. I did.)

"We get it, we've got this, okay? I give you my word," she said. "We will do it. You have to believe me. Any real relationship requires trust."

No arguing with that. And there was something different in the way she said this. I wasn't sure what it was, but I knew what it wasn't. I knew I was not being played. I trusted her.

"Okay, let me get this right. You are committing to an AIDS initiative?"

Yes.

All hinged on the next question: "A historic one?"

Pause. "Yes."

I reached out and she met my hand. "Okay. I'll be there tomorrow."

Deep breath.

I walked out of Condi's office to face my own firing squad and had to pretend I hadn't made up my mind. We'd set up a conference call with DATA board members including George Soros's Open Society and the Bill and Melinda Gates Foundation. The tone of the discussion met my expectations. From Bobby—we might just get away with it—to Jamie and Lucy, borderline alarm. Have I completely lost the plot? Jamie is agitated about our reputation on the left, where most AIDS activism lives; Lucy rattled by my failure to put any parameters on "historic."

I explain that I understand that our honor as an organization—and my honor as an individual—is on the line, but I believe it's a risk we should take. The reputational risk to us is nothing compared with the risk to the lives of the people we claim to be working for if we lose our relationship with the White House.

My explanation is unconvincing, and it is pointed out that we are called DATA but I seem to have just done a deal without any.

Before the line disconnects, we hear the unmistakable Hungarian-tinged accent of George Soros.

"Bono?"

"Yes, George."

"Bono, you have sold out for a plate of lentils."

Next day, with indigestion from the plate of lentils, I'm back in the even paler splendor of the Oval Office to meet George W. Bush for the first time. I remember Bill Clinton sitting behind that desk, but that was then. When Jimmy Carter sat there, it was rumored that Willie Nelson brought some pharmaceuticals with him, smoking them on the roof. I, too, have drugs, three little pills, which I hand to the current occupant. ARVs.

"Mr. President, paint these pills red, white, and blue if you have to, but in Africa these pills will be the best advert ever for the United States of America."

As we head out to the presidential motorcade, I remember Harry Belafonte telling me about Dr. King and Bobby Kennedy's bishop. Have we found that door?

Through the window of the presidential limo green leaves are returning to trees and new shoots appearing in gardens as we hurtle by on this spring day. On the pavement people pause to take in the sight of the long dragon's tail of this motorcade, maybe twenty-five vehicles moving in unison, pulled by the dragon's head screaming its flashing lights. People stop and wave. More than I'd guessed. Bobby Shriver once told me that since the murder of his uncle Jack—

JFK—in a presidential motorcade in Dallas, an ambulance always travels in the motorcade. Just in case. An eerie thought.

It's March 14, 2002, five months since the United States brought war back to Afghanistan and six months since 9/11.

"You're pretty popular round here," I offer up as the president waves back toward the pavement.

"Yup," he says, sighing. "It wasn't always that way. When I came here first"—he pauses—"people used to wave at me with one finger."

I laugh because he's funny.

And I'm not stupid. Five billion dollars is a whole lot of hard cash to spend on the poorest countries even if it wasn't to fight HIV/AIDS. A few months later they did begin to turn in the direction activists had been discussing all over Congress. The rocket man himself, Sir Elton John, touched down at a Senate committee hearing to submit evidence while also putting in a request: that the richest nation in history end the worst pandemic in history.

We knew there were leaders in the halls of Congress who would get behind something much bigger. Nancy Pelosi said tackling AIDS in America was the reason she was in Congress. Twenty years later, the familial but forceful Democratic leader was just as committed to this fight in the rest of the world, having never forgotten what she'd witnessed in her own district of San Francisco. With her California colleagues Maxine Waters and Barbara Lee, these three women took no prisoners except the disease itself. Then there was conservative physician Bill Frist, who I bumped into in Uganda, where he was volunteering in the local hospital as a heart surgeon. On his holidays. His advice? "You can get anything done in D.C. so long as it's not your idea."

John Kerry, a Purple Heart vet as tough as any iron man. I had a cycling accident and spent six weeks in bed. Kerry had a cycling accident, and I don't think he even noticed. Then there was the Vermont mountain lion, Pat Leahy, whose roar was at its mightiest when some hyena threatened his pride in protecting the poorest.

We pushed and pushed.

There was an announcement of $500 million to halt the mother-to-child transmission of this vicious virus. Senator Jesse Helms lobbied the president on it himself. This sum was still nowhere near what was needed for a historic AIDS initiative where the scale of the response matched the scale of the problem. But speaking to reporters in the Rose Garden, President Bush planted a seed. "As we see what works, we will make more funding available."

Act 2, Scene 3: Speaking to Oprah to Speak to America . . .
and a Diagnosis from Anthony Fauci (The Queen and the Doctor)

. . . a seed that must not fall on stony ground. I'd read in *The Boston Globe* an article in which Andrew Natsios, head of USAID, was ridiculing the argument for combating HIV with antiretroviral drug therapies. Africans, he said, "don't know what Western time is . . . Many people in Africa have never seen a clock or a watch their entire lives. And if you say, one o'clock in the afternoon, they do not know what you are talking about."

While he later apologized for the remark, it was astonishing that anyone—let alone the head of USAID—might suggest that one billion people on a continent couldn't be trusted to take their medication reliably. When Bobby Shriver got a call from the White House our fears intensified. "You won't believe this," he said. "They're saying Tony Fauci is putting the brakes on something big and bold."

Dr. Anthony Fauci? The brilliant immunologist and HIV expert? Head of the National Institute of Allergy and Infectious Diseases?

"Apparently, his advice is to take it step-by-step."

Everest was getting higher, but I had to be in Chicago for a more immediately daunting ascent, America's most popular daytime TV show with Oprah Winfrey. Not to talk about music, but about AIDS. I was unable to sleep the night before, more nervous about 250 audience members in the studio than any stadium gig.

We chat about the band's performance at the Super Bowl after 9/11, naming all those who were lost, and how America—which liberated Europe in the war—had become so unpopular in some parts of the world. We talk about fatherhood and about spending the currency of fame. Then Oprah cuts to the chase: What does AIDS in Africa have to do with her ten million viewers, a lot of them, she says, women at home worried about their own children?

Okay . . . well, Oprah . . . the way I see it, this is about the value you put on the life of a child. You might have to explain this to a music fan, you might have to explain this to men in general, but there's one kind of person where no explanation is necessary.

"I don't think you have to explain to any mother that the life of a child in Africa has the same value as her child."

There's a shudder. The studio audience erupts. We're all taken aback by the response. It's an extraordinary sound, the sound of connection. Speak to Oprah, as someone had told us, and you're speaking to America. She connected our dots.

Relieved it had gone well, I was set to head back to Dublin to join up with the band I used to be in, when Bobby brought up Dr. Fauci again.

"You have to call him in D.C. Tell him you need to see him before you leave."

"But I'm leaving now."

"Stop on the way. Tell him you'll see him anywhere. Offer to read his children bedtime stories. Do whatever it takes."

As Lucy, Jamie, and I turned up at Dr. Fauci's Georgetown redbrick, I noticed, through the window, his wife, Christine, and their girls. Was she helping them with their homework? I missed my kids and wanted to be home, but we needed to understand Dr. Fauci's concerns. Which, it transpired, were not quite as the White House leaks had made out. And he was not happy at all to hear his name being used to block the scale of ambition. We fell into a conversation about Dr. Paul Farmer's fieldwork in Haiti. Another brilliant physician, Farmer had adapted a system he'd developed to curtail tuberculosis outbreaks in poor, rural communities. It was known as DOTS (directly observed treatment, short course) and showed that where local people adopted a strategy of monitoring each other's drug regimens, there were higher adherence rates than in Europe or America.

"Access to ARVs is our moral duty, and we can make it possible," said Dr. Fauci as we left. "You guys turn up the heat, as you call it, and I'll turn up the cold science."

Act 2, Scene 4: Into the Heart of America with
Agnes, Ashley, Chris, and Warren (The Players)

"I'm a Teamster. Did you say half of the truck drivers in Southern Africa are going to die because of AIDS?"

"Yes," I replied. "Unless they can get hold of the kinds of drugs that line the shelves in any pharmacy over here."

Asking for a pen and paper from the waitress behind the diner counter, this truck driver, face covered in tattoos, who'd brushed past me at a stop off I-80, passed me his phone number.

This was a moment on the Heart of America Tour, a journey into the other America, away from the coasts and the big cities, when we began to get a sense that people wanted to help. Where I started to understand that those who call the Midwest "flyover country" should really be driving through it.

Beginning on World AIDS Day in December 2002, the tour was designed to show to politicians in the administration and Congress that ordinary Americans cared about people on another continent living and dying with AIDS. We picked key strategic districts such as that of Henry Hyde, chairman of the House Foreign Affairs Committee, and went to local churches, schools, and diners, as well as dropping in on local newspapers.

It was an eclectic touring circuit and a campaigning caravan the likes of which I'd never previously traveled with: a children's choir from Ghana, the actor Ashley Judd, the comedian Chris Tucker, Lance Armstrong, and a carousel of expert AIDS physicians, including Jim Kim, who would later run the World Bank. At the last minute we remembered we'd need someone to run the sound and lights—I called Rocko Reedy, the band's longtime stage manager.

Problem solved.

The time-freezing moment? That was Agnes Nyamayarwo from Uganda, recounting the real-life story of what AIDS was doing in her country.

America is physically and demographically a much bigger and less traveled landmass than most touring rock groups experience. For twenty years in the band we'd come to love touring the Midwest and the South, feeling the common decency of people who placed a high value on conservative themes like good manners and self-reliance, even though many held political views very different from our own.

Tom Hart, a former Jubilee 2000 campaigner now leading DATA's advocacy in Washington, D.C., had some wise advice: "Just don't mention guns. One killer is enough for a trip like this." Americans, it seemed, have the same problem with firearms that we Irish have with alcohol. The problem being that we don't think we have a problem.

Warren Buffett, the venerable investor and CEO of Berkshire Hathaway, might have become the richest man in the world, but the "Sage of Omaha" was still as real an American as you could hope to meet. With his daughter, Susie, he drove himself to our opening night.

Endearingly shy, he was free from bluster, and when I sat him in a corner to get his advice, I was taken with his ability to think clearly and mint aphorisms.

Sage Advice

I've picked up a lot of wisdom from the "Sage of Omaha" down the years.

On mixing business with friendship: "I'd rather not invest in a company where I wouldn't want to have lunch with the CEO."

On disappointing people: "My favorite word is 'no.' I really do love the sound of it."

On exercise and a healthy diet: "I don't go in for it."

On stress: "I don't go in for that either."

On giving his fortune away: "I'm not giving away anything that means anything to me. A personal fortune has no utility for me."

"What are you asking people to do here tonight?" he asked.

"We're putting a postcard on every seat," I explained, "to make it easy for people to contact congressional leaders and senators."

That's too easy, he came back. "People don't trust you if you ask them to do stuff that's too easy. Ask them to do more difficult things, and you'll increase your chances."

Okay, thanks, but what do you think about our basic premise, that America should be showing more leadership on a pandemic wreaking havoc in Africa? (As a percentage of gross national income, the U.S. aid budget was half that of most other industrialized countries—0.15 percent in the United States compared with 0.4 in the U.K. or 0.9 in Norway.)

"Don't appeal to the conscience of America," he replied. "Appeal to the greatness of America. That's how you'll get the job done."

I couldn't have hoped for two more penetrating psychological insights, one into citizens and one into country. The second has framed every campaign we've mounted in the United States. Unlike Europeans, and especially Irish people, Americans are not motivated by attempts to guilt them into action. But offer them the role of the cavalry, and they're right there with you.

The star of every show was Ashley Judd, whom I'd known since she was seventeen, when we were fans of her mom Naomi and sister Wynonna's act, the Judds. She was as brilliant a campaigner as an actor, making complex thoughts accessible with her brightly constructed sentences and warm communication. Standing ovations followed her around. Wynonna joined us for a couple of evenings, adding her extraordinary voice. Chris Tucker, too, lightened the load onstage and backstage, and, as had happened on an earlier trip to Ethiopia, people would trample the rest of us to get to him. His humility was as impressive as his humor.

Night after night we found that the heart of America was beating; we felt its warmth as we traveled through the winterscape of places like Iowa City, Louisville, and Chicago. The so-called moral compass of these people was real, and while we might have had a different view of the magnetic north, even the most cynical of us felt a surge of spirit when we ended the tour at Wheaton College, in part because it was alma mater to so many influential evangelicals, including Mike Gerson, speechwriter for President Bush.

Agnes continued to steal the show, describing her life as a nurse and activist in Uganda who tested positive for HIV in 1992. Listening to her onstage, I realized that she was all about the numbers—but not just the number it would cost the U.S. Treasury to fight HIV. The numbers of her daily life: the year of her husband's death, the number of kids she'd lost and was left with, the length of a diagnosis, the age of her youngest son, and the time of day that he passed. I noticed how often we brush over the details of people's lives when such details *are* in fact our lives.

Agnes's numerate lyricism was rarely louder than a whisper, and then came the choir of Ghanaian schoolkids aged between four and eighteen, who were rarely quieter than a playground. Life had led them to the sanctuary that was the Accra home of their choirmaster, Ruth Butler Stokes. I tried to bottle their lightning in a song that Dr. Dre was mixing for us called "Treason." Rehearsing in a studio in L.A., Andrews, one of the young choristers, came up to us with what he felt was a message from on high intended for the doctor.

"I think the doctor is in danger. Can I pray with him a prayer of safety?"

I wondered which doctor he was referring to, but it turned out that Dr. Dre was open to the idea of a prayer, even if he wasn't wild about the intrusion to the recording schedule. This maestro of Beats, this brain surgeon appreciated he'd made a few enemies over the years—so much so that he was often accompanied by security fit for a president.

Another song that came out of that Dre session, a collaboration with Dave Stewart and Pharrell Williams, was "American Prayer," which Beyoncé Knowles ended up singing in front of Mandela at the 46664 Concert in 2003, with Andrews preaching by her side. Even at twenty-two, it was clear that Beyoncé could read the choreography of political change better than most.

For such a cinematic figure, she got the small-screen stuff of how often history changes more prosaically than poetically. I was twice her age before I understood that.

"Dear Madiba," she later wrote, "you made it possible for so many people like me to reject impossibilities and understand our capabilities. We have made your dreams our own . . . your work and your sacrifice were not in vain."

She brings to my mind another great torch singer, Alicia Keys, whom I see recording Marvin Gaye's "What's Going On?" in 2001 for Artists Against AIDS Worldwide. On the other side of the control room glass, I'm watching the birth of a star. She's watching the red light come on. Looking through me and the world that is staring at her through the control room window. It's a look that wants to shatter the glass that might separate her from her music. Or her activism. She's indivisible from the values that drive her music toward justice. At age twenty-two she founded Keep a Child Alive. And because of her, countless children are alive.

On our last day of the Heart of America Tour we said our goodbyes, and I quickly jumped from this band back to my other band, racing to meet them for the New York premiere of Martin Scorsese's *Gangs of New York,* for which we'd written the song "The Hands That Built America."

Act 3, Scene 1: Dublin, Nervously Watching Late-Night TV . . .
Waiting for That Call ("Of science and the human heart/There is no limit")

January 28, 2003, and I'm back on the music in Dublin, when word arrived that President Bush was going to make some kind of AIDS announcement in the State of the Union address.

The band and our partners were all out at a restaurant in St. Stephen's Green with Chris Thomas, who's worked with everyone from The Beatles and Pink Floyd to Roxy Music and INXS. I can't concentrate. I can't think about the state of the music; all I can think of is the State of the Union. Condi had called earlier to say, "You are going to be pleased tonight. I am very proud of the president. You will all have what you're looking for. We're announcing it at the State of the Union."

I had asked her, "What's the number? I need to know the number."

She said, "I can't tell you the number yet. They're still hashing some of it out. But it will be serious, and it will be significant. I'll call you just before the speech."

At the dinner, I am all over the shop. I whisper to Ali that I've got to leave; she's the only one who knows what it's about. I make my excuses and head home, which is where I'm sitting late on a winter's night with the fire flickering and our two dogs, Chanty and Helena, climbing up on me as CNN brings up an image of George W. Bush walking into the chamber to address the U.S. Congress. In the crowd applauding him I notice one of my heroes, Dr. Peter Mugyenyi, a Ugandan physician who'd been arrested earlier that year for trying to bring generic AIDS drugs into Kampala.

This is an impossible juxtaposition.

I'm nervous. Even the dogs are getting jumpy. Outside the family, have I ever been more invested in an announcement like this? And then, the phone rings. It's not Condi, it's Josh Bolten on her behalf.

"Okay, here's the number. It's $15 billion over the next five years."

For a moment I'm a little dizzy. It's new money, he says, knowing I'll worry it's been taken from some other worthy account. "It's unprecedented."

"Wow, yes, that is, indeed. Thank you, Josh, please thank Condi and the president . . . in fact thank any passing strangers you might meet this evening."

It would be called PEPFAR—the President's Emergency Plan for AIDS Relief—and I watch as the president asked Congress to commit $15 billion to fight AIDS starting with fourteen of the hardest-hit countries. Until COVID-19, it would turn out to be the largest health intervention to fight a single disease in the history of medicine.

I think of the intensity of my last two years and wonder at the staying power of the activists who've been doing this for decades, groups like ACT UP, never letting up. I think of Agnes or Prudence or Sister Anne, or any of the people responsible for my being here. Driven by the loss of their families, friends, colleagues. On their shoulders we have stood.

A fax arrives from Rupert Murdoch. My strange place in this activist ecosystem will never feel familiar. A short note: "Congratulations, let me know if there is anything I can do?"

I reply with his own words from our first meeting. "Dear Rupert, thank you for your kind note, could you please 'come on like the tide'?"

The tide arrived, warm coverage splashed across his conservative media empire, even at Fox News.

But . . . but . . . the drugs didn't.

Act 3, Scene 2: Picking Up the Lentils at the White House . . .
and Bugging the President (The President)

. . . at least not on the timeline the president had promised in his State of the Union or the day after when he'd spoken of the urgency of getting the drugs to people on bicycles and motorcycles. I went to see the president at the White House, thanking him for his speech but asking him why all these months later there were no wheels on the ground. My understatement quickly turned to overstatement, which seemed to ruffle the president to the point where he started banging his hand on the Resolute Desk.

"Pardon me for interrupting, but I don't make speeches just 'cause I like to hear the sound of my voice. I meant what I said and I mean what I say and yes there are logistical problems but we will sort them out."

The next part of this story is redacted. This involved a press line and an overzealous rock star getting in the face of the man whose initiative will save the lives of more children, women, and men than anything since the invention of vaccines. Later I will apologize for my shrill behavior . . . and be forgiven.

In the coming years, more than $100 billion of U.S. taxpayer money would be invested to ensure those children, women, and men did not lose their lives to a preventable, treatable disease. The scale of the response will almost meet the scale of the emergency.

One hundred billion dollars. That's a lot of lentils.

31

Vertigo

The night is full of holes
As bullets rip the sky of ink with gold
They sparkle as the boys play rock and roll
They know that they can't dance—at least they know.

Vertigo.

The feeling I get at the moment I shout out the broken maths and language that is "Unos. Dos. Tres. Catorce!"

Dizzy.

The countdown to "Vertigo," the moment before a song takes off. Vertigo. Let me try to describe it.

Maybe the maths is not so broken. It was Bruce Springsteen who said that this opening line is actually correct when it comes to a rock 'n' roll band. "For in art, and love, and rock and roll, the whole had better equal much more than the sum of its parts, or else you're just rubbing two sticks together in search of a fire." That's beyond true of U2, but there's another player in the mix of any real rock 'n' roll band, and that's not a person but an audience. Critics speak of the fifth member of a four-piece being a manager, like Paul McGuinness in our case, or a producer, a Brian Eno or a Danny Lanois. At times people like these and others have been all four members of our band, but they'd be the first to admit that as a band U2 only really becomes itself onstage. With our audience.

U2 live to be live.

Yet try as hard as we can to bring that live feeling to our albums it's always nearly impossible. Except for "Vertigo." A song that comes as close to the sound of a band breaking out of itself as any we've recorded. It was Steve Lillywhite, one of our earliest studio collaborators, back with us in 2004 to help finish up our album *How to Dismantle an Atomic Bomb,* who told us what to do. "You need to play this song like you're in a small club," he said, with the same boyish smile we'd known since he produced our first three studio albums. Steve's gift was a kind of naïve clarity, born out of experience. When I was stuck on a lyric, he would challenge me.

"How long is the song, Bono?"

"Three and a half minutes," I'd say.

"How hard can that be?" Steve always wanted to know: "What's the chorus, what's the hook, what's the point?"

If you can't play a song like that without a guitar in your hand, then it isn't a real song. All insights that I hold on to tighter now than then.

Until meeting us, in 1980, Steve had been the youngest man in any room he'd worked in. A quarter century later, recording "Vertigo," neither he nor we still ever had a day job, and I picture him now turning on the red light in our studio on the docks in Dublin. Although, on second thought, there was no red light, and we were recording in the warehouse attic next door. But there's no mistaking the sound we made, a three-piece at its elastic limit, as economical and effective as only a power trio can be. There's very little information being communicated from each instrument, which means the human ear can tolerate it at higher volume. Even at a lower volume, "Vertigo" sounds loud.

A FOX RAN ACROSS THE ROAD

I was sitting in Renards Nightclub in Dublin with the prodigiously talented actor Cillian Murphy. Renards, French for "foxes," after its owner, Robbie Fox—who's hosted U2 in dancing and drinking holes since the mid-eighties. A good man and generous, born and raised in Ballymun, Robbie bears an unfortunate resemblance to Saudi arms dealer Adnan Khashoggi. I have often joked with him that a mustache like his can get someone in a lot of trouble. He has often joked with me that I'm not funny. Part of the fun of being out late is getting into the right kind of trouble, and Renards is happy to host the spontaneous combustion we expect from being out late. Like the name of a horse or a boat, the name of a good nightclub is usually bad. Renards, as in fox, as in cunning, which begs a question of myself, "If you're so cunning, why are you here?" A question anyone over thirty should be asked regularly. What am I doing in a nightclub in the small hours, now that I'm well past forty years old? (A question I still ask myself, now that I'm past sixty.)

My stock answers:

1. To dance. Half-true but not enough true to fully excuse.
2. To continue drinking. More true.
3. To deny you are growing up. Even more true.
4. To be around people who haven't grown up yet. Too true.
5. To have somewhere to go with your mates when the pubs close. The whole truth and nothing but.

I'd gone through some of these answers with Cillian, who, being both much younger than me and a fine Cork man, had helped me laugh some of them off. We may have been what Irish people refer to as "mildly overserved" when the conversation took a turn toward the honesty exit off the motorway that a great night out can be. I sensed we were going to go there.

There being a heart-to-heart about our lives as artists. Mano a mano on the effect of fame on form. Are we changed by it? Yes, and why not? Saying no to change is a sad kind of stasis. To be made better is the possibility we long for, I suggested, as a waitress with gothic makeup and a large Latino crucifix served us champagne from a pewter ice bucket. A fox ran across the road; a wolf howled on a distant hill. (You get the idea . . .) We talked of the genius of Pat McCabe and the movie of his novel *Breakfast on Pluto* that Cillian was featuring in—along with Gavin Friday, sitting a few clubbers away. Honesty, we agreed, is the irreducible minimum in creativity, and it never gets easier. At which point Cillian grabbed the wheel and we made a sharp left turn into *vino veritas*.

"I used to be such a big fan," he said. "I loved your early stuff. I loved *The Joshua Tree* . . ."

Dramatic pause.

". . . but then I lost you."

He starts reciting the lyric of "One Tree Hill."

> *We turn away to face the cold, enduring chill*
> *As the day begs the night for mercy, love.*
> *A sun so bright it leaves no shadows*
> *only scars carved into stone on the face of earth.*

And here comes his question. "Where has your lyricism gone? You used to write about real love and real life, you wrote about characters like Victor Jara or the strikers in Red Hill Mining Town."

Pause.

"'Vertigo'? What *is* that song? Who are you talking to?"

In vino veritas. You have to admire it. This great actor cannot tell a lie, not even to the person pouring his champagne. "Vertigo," I explained, is about us. I'm writing to you and to me.

> *Lights go down, it's dark*
> *The jungle is your head can't rule your heart*
> *A feeling so much stronger than a thought*
> *Your eyes are wide*
> *And though your soul it can't be bought*
> *Your mind can wander . . .*
> *The night is full of holes*
> *As bullets rip the sky of ink with gold*
> *They sparkle as the boys play rock and roll*
> *They know that they can't dance*
> *At least they know*

> *I can't stand the beats*
> *I'm asking for the cheque*
> *The girl with crimson nails*
> *Has Jesus round her neck.*

At which point the girl with crimson nails, or someone very similar, was asking us if we needed another drink and, both of us laughing, I said to Cillian, "You have to write what you know, write where you are." I'm grateful to know Cillian and his partner, Yvonne, and delighted to still see them at U2 shows, but more grateful still for the exceptional performer who cannot tell a lie.

AT HOME WITH THE MAXIMAL MINIMALIST

In October 2004, a month before "Vertigo" was released, Edge, Paul McGuinness, Jimmy Iovine, and I made a visit to Steve Jobs. We had a hunch that we thought might benefit both Apple and U2.

Steve lived with his wife, Laurene, and their three kids in a low-key brick-and-slate Tudor-style house on a prosperous street in Palo Alto. Their Anglophilia also inspired a cottage garden full of wildflowers and stuff you could eat, with a gate opening yards from a front door he never locked.

Apple had a history of groundbreaking commercials, and their latest iPod spots were modern Day-Glo pop art. This new song "Vertigo," we suggested, was a perfect fit for one of those ads. If we could agree terms. There was a small complication in that our band doesn't do commercials. Never had. A decision of principle with a price tag that was rising. Over quiche and green tea Steve explained that he was flattered but didn't have the kind of budget that a band like ours would expect.

"Actually, Steve," I said. "We don't want cash. We just want to be in the iPod commercial." Steve was thrown. The spots contained only the dancing silhouettes of music fans, their heads holding those iconic white earbuds, white arteries pumping the music from tiny MP3 players now called iPods.

"Maybe it's time to shift the emphasis to artists as well as fans," Edge added. "Don't you think we'd look quite good in relief?"

Steve, intrigued, said if that was the deal, he didn't have to think twice, but he'd need to run it by the creative team.

"There's one other thing," added Paul McGuinness. "Although the band are not looking for cash, some Apple stock, even a symbolic amount, might be a courtesy."

"Sorry," said Steve. "That's a deal breaker."

Silence.

"Well," I tentatively suggested. "How about our own iPod? A customized U2 iPod in black and red?"

Steve looked nonplussed. Apple, he said, is about white hardware. "You wouldn't want a black one."

He thought for a moment.

"I can show you what it would look like, but you will not like it."

When, later, he showed the design to us, we loved it. So much that he'd ask Jony Ive, the company's design genius, to look at it again, and okay, maybe even experiment with a red component on the device too. To reflect our *Atomic Bomb* album cover. Jony was Steve's secret weapon. English. Art school type but studied industrial design. Deadpan humor and the good looks of a Buddhist monk on steroids. Two months later this man who could teach a gentleman manners came to Dublin carrying the U2 iPod as if he was carrying the ark of the covenant. As far as we were concerned, he was. The iPod was about to turn Apple from a medium-sized world-class hardware and software player into a global Godzilla. As Paul would often remind us, even if we'd received half of what the band might command for such an endorsement deal, that, say, token Apple stock we'd suggested at that lunch would be worth thirty-five times more within a decade or two. Paul would always rue losing the stock argument—not that Steve was ever going to discuss it—but in truth we were fortunate to ride the Apple wave through that period. The fantastically kinetic commercial brought the band to a younger audience and thousands of people bought the U2 iPod just because it wasn't white. Apple was on a ride to infinity and beyond; we were just lucky to hitch a lift. You couldn't buy a ticket.

When we'd first met Steve, Apple wasn't yet famous for the iPhone, but in his mind his company was already the number one nexus of art and science on the planet. Even as the Apple tree grew and grew, Steve remained Zen-like in both his business and domestic lives. It was clear he was a serious student of the East anytime you had lunch, which, with Steve, might include just one item. I have heard tell of people sitting around a table to share a cauliflower. He was trying to pursue a path of simplicity at the same time as leading what was becoming the biggest company in the world. He was a maximal minimalist, a man who lived small while thinking large.

Later Steve advised myself and Bobby Shriver on the setup of (RED), our attempt to take our HIV/AIDS activism into the world of commerce, of giant companies and big brand communications. A guru of both communication and design, Steve was all about distillation: the fewest clicks, the least interference, the shortest route from there to here.

Keep it simple, his constant instruction. (Not something he ever needed to remind Jony about.)

"You need to keep repeating that if the people don't have the pills, they die, but if they have the pills, they stay alive. Think of this as a mantra. A hook."

After a meeting with Bobby to discuss some proposed commercials, Steve was characteristically, er, blunt.

> BOBBY: "He said that you and I are in the wrong business, that we think we are in the mercy business but that's not where we need to be."
> ME: "And what business does he think we need to be in?"
> BOBBY: "In the magic business. The same business as him, putting ten thousand songs in someone's pocket, a magic trick."

It's true, the iPod was a piece of magic, carrying your entire record collection around with you wherever you went. Now, recounting the conversation with me, Bobby breaks into laughter.

> BOBBY: "He was going on about how these ARVs are like penicillin; they're like magic. Like Magic Johnson is magic."
> ME: "Magic Johnson? The basketball player?"
> BOBBY: "He's HIV positive and Steve thinks Magic Johnson looks pretty great, his point being that we need to show the effects of these drugs, we need to show before and after, in photos, in film."

———

Following that conversation, we commissioned a film, *The Lazarus Effect,* made by Spike Jonze and Lance Bangs, which did precisely that, documenting in a time lapse how, thanks to two pills a day, a person infected with this killer called HIV/AIDS, an emaciated parent or child, body scarred and at death's door, can come right back from death, can be back in the bosom of their family within a few short weeks.

Magic.

Like Magic Johnson.

Magic advice too.

Like Steve Jobs.

(RED) launched in 2006 with Freud Communications, and was made famous by some high-voltage star power, from various worlds . . . Oprah, Julia Roberts, Penélope Cruz, Damien Hirst, Theaster Gates, David Adjaye, Scarlett Johansson, Bruce Springsteen, Annie Leibovitz, Christy Turlington, Gisele Bündchen, Mary J Blige, Kanye West, Chris Martin, Alicia Keys, Lady Gaga, Olivia Wilde, Phoebe Robinson, Jimmy Kimmel, Kristen Bell, The Killers, Jony Ive, and Marc Newson.

(RED) arrived just two years after ONE, which arrived two years after DATA. Three new organizations in five years and I was starting to feel the fallout.

Meanwhile, *the* band—the other one, remember them?—had put out two albums. And done two tours. I hadn't anticipated that the business of activism might be complicated so much by the business of managing people, and my knowledge of "organizational development" was not as up to speed as my knowledge of international development. I remembered my brother, Norman, talking about "seagull management," where you fly into the office, shit over what everyone is doing, and fly off again. Some days my ability to shapeshift was leaving me out of shape. Exhausted.

I was too far in to get out, but nor did I want to get out.

I was also still in a band. I didn't want to get out of that either.

———

I was also acutely aware of our teenage girls and our toddler boys. This family and their mother who had got used to watching me head off on tour with U2 were now watching me disappear to Africa.

Mission? Yes.

Mission creep? Yes.

Still running away from home like the teenager I was when I first found myself in a band? Yes.

Thinking that keeping the wee small hours drinking and debating art and activism in noisy clubs and pubs is my job? Yes.

But it wasn't.

Where was Ali? Well, sometimes she was right beside me. But mostly she thought I needed to take the horse for a gallop on my own.

Sometimes she has a word with me. Sometimes I have a word with myself.

Enter a man with wisdom and charm who has made his name and fortune speaking the language of teenagers and young adults. Over the course of our career we'd watched MTV become a global phenomenon and, from afar, seen Tom Freston build it from scratch. Bobby used to call him the "Walt Disney of Pop Culture," overseeing breakout hits from *SpongeBob* to Jon Stewart's *Daily Show,* later leading Viacom, including Paramount Pictures. People loved Tom Freston for his good values as well as his good humor, and after a year of wooing on our part—and weighing on his—Tom decided to take us on. DATA and ONE merged, and ONE's new chairman, Tom, decided to bring (RED) under the same shared governance. It was a step change, and a step up. Not only did it give me back some of my life, but it meant these start-ups were no longer hamstrung by my personal time commitment. They were match fit and ready to sprint on their own.

They now have two hundred activists working across eleven capitals on three continents. I'm taken aback by the relentlessness of these people who've committed their lives to social justice . . . policy wonks, agitators, irritators, and history makers. And humbled by how little they need me.

Back to "Vertigo." Back to garage band rock 'n' roll. The song became a tour of the same name when night after night "Vertigo" picked up a momentum that made it feel like a hit song. We were at our punk rock best with crowds reacting as if we were a band in our twenties. When Edge first played us the guitar riff, I read it wrong, but I remember thinking "very good is the enemy of great." Neither good nor bad, is this just *very good*? Edge's guitar parts are often so subtle that only after repeated listens does the hook prick the skin in a way that you can't imagine your life without it. They are like those fine-line-drawn geometric tattoos.

I sometimes wonder about the songs that fall into obscurity not because they aren't great but because they have nothing to propel them. My favorite moment performing "Vertigo"—probably my favorite U2 45, even though it's a long way from a pop song—was in the River Plate Stadium in Buenos Aires in March 2006. Improbably large 3D cameras placed around the venue, we were shooting for a film we would imaginatively title *U2 3D*. Highly sensitive cameras, most of them were instantly rendered useless when the audience began their vertical journey at the sound of "unos, dos, tres, . . . catorce!" which, on the beat, landed so hard the entire stadium seemed to tremble.

It is a phenomenon U2 has experienced before, the hopes and dreams of a hundred thousand hearts and minds so electrically charged that the atoms of the very concrete begin to wobble. Now there might be other explanations. Sometimes these venues are vulnerable to their age; sometimes, in their youth, they have sprung floors and added bounce for basketball. But I'm in no doubt about the real explanation.

Adam Clayton.

The bass part in "Vertigo" is the match of the guitar figure. It is a mirror of it but not exactly the same. When Joe O'Herlihy has to manage the acoustics of a high-decibel roar, he oftentimes goes under rather than over the noise. He allows the bass to drop lower to stomach-churning frequencies that can affect the body in weird and wonderful ways. Once at an early show in Belgium, Adam's bass registered on the Richter scale, with news reports of a woman pointing to cracks in the walls of her house. She believed it was an earthquake. We knew it was Adam Clayton.

South American crowds remind us that the beating heart of our band at its most excited is a Latin one.

It's operatic. It's flirtatious.

It's a bit macho, but it can be reduced to tears by choral singing.

The breakdown of "Vertigo" is the temptation of Christ, but it's overpowering to hear the crowd chant in their non-native English the devil-revealing lyric

> *All of this, all of this can be yours*
> *All of this, all of this can be yours*
> *All of this, all of this can be yours*
> *Just give me what I want and no one gets hurt.*

It is the bass that answers the question and not the cry for help that is

> *Hello, hello . . .*
> *I'm at a place called Vertigo*
> *It's everything I wish I didn't know.*

To be a man of the world but not this one is, I guess, the idea behind the song. You get the sense that the singer is not sure if that's possible but he's gonna try as hard as hell. In the end it's the bass that offers the devil denial, the bass that offers the great "fuck off."

Maybe "Vertigo" would have been a big song for us anyway, but I ended up grateful to Steve Jobs for all kinds of reasons, not least because this was when culture and commerce collided for us, a relationship I'm still experimenting with.

Over the years I witnessed a tenderness in him that few beyond close friends and family talked about. In 2010, I'd been hospitalized in Germany for emergency back surgery, and no sooner was I home than a treasure chest of books and movies turned up at our door, along with a jar of homemade honey. That would have been thoughtful enough, but it came with a handwritten note.

"This honey is from our garden. Our neighborhood bees." The samurai's wife, Laurene Powell Jobs, a Jedi with an MBA from Stanford and a mind to best Steve's, could light up a room like a movie star. Laurene shared with Steve a protective instinct for people they enjoyed, and I was fortunate to catch some of that.

The last time Steve and I spoke he'd called out of the blue to say he was worried at how I'd looked when we'd last met.

"You looked ill."

We'd had a quiet but lovely evening together, and I sensed how frail he was as he struggled to walk me to the door.

Now he was calling me, worried about my health and telling me he cared for me.

Steve knew he was dying.

"Personally, you're not looking after yourself. Politically, you need to think harder about whose company you're keeping. And you've put on weight. You looked upset. What was upsetting you?"

The man who brought the world smartphones on "dumb signal" had not even a trace of the ego that might have pointed out that he was the reason I was so upset. I'd been a little overcome that night reading to him and Laurene from Oscar Wilde's "Ballad of Reading Gaol." I'd come across a signed edition which I knew they would appreciate, but when I bumped into those most famous last lines, I became all too aware of Steve's own prison sentence. The words caught me in the throat.

> *In Reading gaol by Reading town*
> *There is a pit of shame,*
> *And in it lies a wretched man*
> *Eaten by teeth of flame,*
> *In burning winding-sheet he lies,*
> *And his grave has got no name.*
>
> *And there, till Christ call forth the dead,*
> *In silence let him lie:*
> *No need to waste the foolish tear,*
> *Or heave the windy sigh:*

The man had killed the thing he loved,
And so he had to die.

And all men kill the thing they love,
By all let this be heard,
Some do it with a bitter look,
Some with a flattering word,
The coward does it with a kiss,
The brave man with a sword!

No wonder I looked so bad to Steve. I felt so bad. The scene must have come back to him a few weeks later when he realized he wasn't going to make it but was concerned that everyone around him did. Steve escaped the prison sentence of his illness on October 5, 2011, and he left with characteristic distillation, a wordless utterance to match the moment.

"Oh wow. Oh wow. Oh wow."

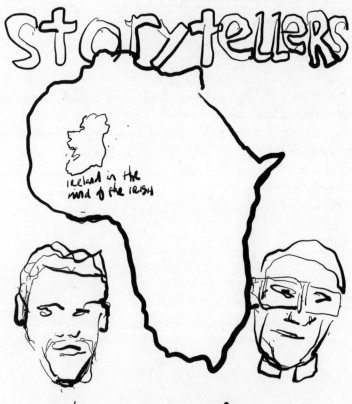

32

Ordinary Love

The sea wants to kiss the golden shore.
The sunlight wants your skin.
All the beauty that's been lost before
Wants to find us again.
I can't fight you anymore
It's you I'm fighting for.
The sea throws rocks together
But time leaves us polished stones.

My favorite version of our song "Ordinary Love" turned out to be the acoustic one we played at the 2014 Oscars ceremony. The song was nominated for its part in the movie *Mandela: Long Walk to Freedom,* a biopic starring Idris Elba and Naomie Harris that explored the stormy relationship between Nelson and Winnie Mandela. At the last minute we about-turned on a big production, the one we'd been preparing for weeks with show director Hamish Hamilton, in favor of a quieter, acoustic one.

Among the fanfare and parade of the most popular awards show on earth, perhaps we could prick the showbiz bubble and create a more meditative moment. Would a more gentle telling of this broken love song break through? One producer thought not and pulled a "You'll never work in this town again!" on us. After all this time it was quite sweet to hear one of those lines. Even though we recognize that TV is not our natural medium, we'll always do our best to serve the moment if it's waiting to be served.

The stripped-back song, simply lit with images of a young, pensive Mandela staring out to the audience caught an emotional current in the room, but it would be dishonest to suggest our band was so elevated that we didn't mind missing out on the Oscar to a children's song sung by an animated character. We did. We were also miffed for Pharrell Williams, whose "Happy" was a stone-cold classic. The song that took the gong, "Let It Go," was clever and catchy and boasted the most psychedelic line of the night: "My soul is spiraling in frozen fractals all around." Quite something. We had to let it go. I have to find my own animated character, I thought to myself.

But at least the songwriters showed up. Last time we lost out—with "The Hands That Built America" in 2002—Eminem was in bed in Detroit and had to be woken with news that his street opus "Lose Yourself" had won.

At the Oscars, you notice the strangely competitive aspect in the shared ego of being in a band. Once you put your arse in those plush cushion seats, that arse is far from comfortable. It feels as if it were right out the window, a bare bottom with a sticker saying "Kick Here." As the overture began, Larry reached over and tapped me on the shoulder.

"We're not just happy to be here, right?" he whispered. "We really, really want to win this, right?"

Right.

It's a lot of trouble to go to lose.

From that day on we would describe ourselves as having come second at the Oscars.

> Birds fly high in the summer sky
> And rest on the breeze.
> The same wind will take care of you and I,
> we'll build our house in the trees.
> Your heart is on my sleeve,
> did you put it there with a magic marker?
> For years I would believe,
> that the world, couldn't wash it away.

Nelson Mandela. This giant of the twentieth century, silver-white crown and smiling, his good humor lifting him head and shoulders above his times. If laughter is the evidence of freedom, then Madiba, the clan name that he encouraged his friends to call him, was freer than the rest of us. A wellspring of joy that defied the weight he carried.

"Why would a young man like you want to sit here and be bored by an old man like me?"

Whenever I got the chance to visit, he would turn the tables, with a lesson in grace.

He could charm the morning from the night and the cash out of wallets. He told me Margaret Thatcher, the former British prime minister, had personally donated £20,000 to his foundation.

"How did you do that?"

The Iron Lady was known to keep a tight grip on the purse strings.

"I asked," he said, with a grin. "You'll never get what you want if you don't ask."

At the time, her donation had nauseated some of his cohorts. "Didn't she try to squash our movement?" they challenged him.

His response?

"Didn't de Klerk crush our people like flies? I'm having tea with him next week. He'll be getting the bill."

I wondered what had happened to this man locked up for twenty-seven years in an eight-by-seven-foot concrete cell on Robben Island. The scholar was not afraid of hard work and saw his body as a machine that needed to be oiled and maintained. He was in great physical shape, having run on the spot for forty-five minutes every day, before doing two hundred sit-ups and one hundred fingertip push-ups. At the same time, brutalized and beaten, he'd seemed only to grow as a person and a leader.

The answer, he told me, was to be found in reading. Can it be that simple? It was books, he said, that made him a better man. He found greatness through reading and would often mention Irish authors, in particular George Bernard Shaw. He had such a thirst for reading that when it was denied him during his early incarceration, he hid Shakespeare in a Bible, knowing that his Afrikaner Protestant over-lords would never deny him access to the scriptures.

Nelson Mandela aroused so much emotion in so many, and yet few knew he was a man who could not cry. Mandela was born into royalty, his great-grandfather a tribal king, but as part of the daily grind of imprisonment he'd been forced to work in a limestone quarry. He could not have known the corrosive glare effect the limestone would have. It cost him his tear glands and Nelson Mandela could not cry. This moves me still.

I was intrigued by his natural grace and self-assurance. It was as if, after twenty-seven years, fear had lost interest in him. By the end of his time on Robben Island, Nelson Mandela's ambition was just as great, but now expressed itself as modesty. If I'd any suspicion this was just a front to put others at ease or to get things done, one sunny Spanish evening I discovered up close that it was at his back and side too.

"FROCK 'N' ROLL"

The invitation arrived with the best of intentions and from the best of names—Adam Clayton's former supermuse Naomi Campbell. Naomi has been fighting racism her whole life and saw the economic injustice facing Africa as another expression of that. Naomi, like many of us, had a giant *grá* (let's say that's Gaelic for "crush") on Nelson Mandela. A feeling that to these eyes was reciprocated. It was a special sight to notice Graça Machel, herself an icon, break into the widest smile as she observed her husband so taken with the British supermodel. "Grandad," as Naomi called him, came alive in her company, joking, laughing, and leaning in to whisper. He was a boy again through her eyes.

All this lovely static formed into an idea in the summer of 2001 in which the best of fashion and the best of music would go to work for Madiba in Barcelona, under that unforgettable portmanteau— "Frock 'n' Roll." Think fusion. Or confusion. From the outset, the Catalonian press didn't quite believe the big names would turn up, least of all the biggest, Nelson Mandela. But to be fair to the fashion people, they delivered, with a cast of superstars like Kate Moss and

Elle Macpherson, wearing collections from Versace and Alexander McQueen.

Less so on the music front, and as media coverage took a dive, everyone abandoned ship. It was left to me and reFugee man Wyclef Jean to supply the notes, and with advance sales of two thousand in a venue built for almost twenty thousand, people were right to be worried.

The President of the World, as I thought of him, was to bless the proceedings at eight. This was pushed to eight thirty when only a thousand people had taken their seats. Then nine when there were maybe three thousand in the house. But Nelson Mandela had a flight to catch, and the promoter had the idea of turning off the lights so the huge empty cavern would not look so huge and empty. Asking us to join him, he stepped out onstage, Naomi on his right, me on his left.

"Young people of Barcelona, I must tell you from the bottom of an old man's heart you have given me a welcome I have no right to deserve."

I stared at a hole in the stage.

"I came to Barcelona with high expectations, and I am happy to say that those high expectations have been fully realized."

At first I thought he was taking the piss, but it began to dawn on me that he was not. It wasn't that his glass was half full. His glass was spilling over. To have three thousand people turn up for him was his world spilling over at the brim. Nelson Mandela was the embodiment of gratitude, and as I looked out into the audience, it really seemed to look fuller.

"NOT CHARITY, JUSTICE"

In December 2013, when Ali and I walked by Nelson Mandela's coffin in Pretoria, my mind took me back to a winter's day in London's Trafalgar Square in 2005. It was a rally for the Make Poverty History campaign, and in that characteristically measured delivery Mandela made one of the most spellbinding speeches I'd ever heard.

"Like slavery and apartheid," he said, "poverty is not natural. It is man-made, and it can be overcome and eradicated by the actions of human beings. And overcoming poverty is not a gesture of charity. It is an act of justice. It is the protection of a fundamental human right, the right to dignity and a decent life."

Some things you believe and some things you know. I already believed what he was saying, but on this frozen February day I came to know it on a whole other level. His words seemed to bring the world into focus so that I could see more clearly than ever the injustice of global poverty. As Madiba spoke, I heard his words as a kind of call.

"Sometimes it falls upon a generation to be great. You can be that great generation."

Could we? Our generation?

There was something daunting about the very idea and reflecting on it I recall the words of Ellen Johnson Sirleaf, who became the first female president in Africa. "If your dreams don't scare you, they are not big enough."

In these first years of the new millennium, the antipoverty movement had some wind in its sails and in both the U.S. and Europe the left and right were finding areas of higher ground in order to reach common ground. In the U.K., for instance, the work of Richard Curtis, Emma Freud, and others in organizations like Comic Relief, with its biannual Red Nose Day, kept the injustice of life in the poorest countries in the minds of people in one of the richest. Activist organizations, aid agencies, and NGOs had rare political access, a chance to influence the political agenda of Blair and Brown. (Later, ONE would join these networks as they worked to successfully persuade David Cameron's coalition government to enshrine in law that the UK would commit 0.7 percent of its national income to overseas aid. It's less than 1 percent but still a gigantic number, and a monumental decision by a postcolonial power. Only those ignorant of the relationships of the future, as well as the past, would attempt to dismantle it. They did.)

I wanted to believe we were part of a real movement to materially change the relationship between the rich and the poor, but in my desire to be useful, there were more lessons to be learned. While the faces of the famous cannot be disqualified if they genuinely draw attention to a situation everyone is looking away from, you have to be suspicious of rock stars or supermodels or actors or billionaires lining up in a photocall with the sick and the dying.

I'm suspicious.

My suspicions are not always founded. I've never seen a campaigner work as hard on the ground as Sean Penn following the hurricane in New Orleans and the earthquake in Haiti. And I've never seen an actor get such animus for taking on a second role, *one in which he was not acting.*

Another lesson white faces like ours needed to learn was to avoid the kind of framing in which the poor of the world are symbolized by Black faces. Often emaciated. Often "African." It's not accurate, as well as not fair. It's the opposite of justice. The youthful energy, the entrepreneurial activity, the artistic creativity in Africa's dynamic capital cities is still rarely storified elsewhere in the world. Take a five-minute walk down the two-step streets of Dakar, Durban, or Lagos and you'll feel like you're sprinting. Just standing on a street corner is a double-espresso shot.

Nollywood in Nigeria makes more movies than Hollywood. More Africans—650 million—have mobile phones than Americans or Europeans. African tech leads the world in mobile money. The Democratic Republic of the Congo holds over 70 percent of the planet's cobalt used in batteries, while South Africa has 90 percent of the platinum reserves we need for fuel cells and electronics. The world's oldest continent has the world's youngest population, and before COVID-19, it was home to six of the world's ten fastest-growing economies. You don't have to ask the Chinese where they think the future is. You'll meet them in pretty much any African market or stock market they can enter.

How can it be that this sprawling super-continent, home to more countries, languages, and cultural diversity than any other, is still overwhelmingly portrayed in the global north in terms of its poverty despite its wealth. All countries who struggle to get out from under the jackboot of colonialism usually end up with a period of poor government. But the struggle to get out from under the stereotypes? Maybe that has something to do with us campaigners.

Campaigners can be a pain in the arse. I know I can. In our own heads those of us working for global development are fighting for the lives of others.

So we're right.
Right?
Wrong.
But don't we have the clincher to every argument, the punch line
to end any dispute?
Lives depend on us.
Also wrong.

WHITE MESSIAH SYNDROME

Welcome to White Messiah Syndrome. If you're fronting a rock 'n'
roll band, you need a bit of a messiah complex, but such a complex is
less helpful for the antipoverty activist.

The political and cultural winds which had been in our favor had
now begun to turn in certain countries in the global south. Some
activists had had enough of what they called "poverty porn." "Keep
Your Aid" became their theme song. I felt we needed to talk about
this. I needed to listen. Chris Anderson at TED offered to host the
TEDGlobal 2007 conference in Arusha, Tanzania, and invited me
to take part. Knowing the audience would be skeptical of the usual
donor-recipient aid dialogue, I was not anticipating a rapturous
response . . . but nor was I anticipating being booed. The Ugandan
radio host and journalist Andrew Mwenda began to tear down the
arguments of those who contend that international aid is one of the
levers the poorest countries should be able to pull as they climb
from poverty. Name one country, he asked the audience, that has
benefited from foreign aid. I put my hand up.

Oh, yes, Bono? I can't wait to hear this answer . . .

Ireland, I said.

Ireland?

Yes, Ireland, my country wouldn't exist in the state it is without
money from Europe. Aid from Europe has helped make Ireland into
a modern economy.

Okay, maybe Ireland. Let's give Bono that. Anyone here can name
even one other? I put my hand up again.

Germany, I suggested. This prosperous modern country wouldn't exist were it not for the Marshall Plan after World War II. But for all my smarty-pants answers I was listening and I could sense a genuine resentment in the room that I knew we needed to figure out. We'd always seen aid as an investment—the idea being that the business of aid is to put itself out of business. However, there were plenty of examples of this not being the case. In her book *Dead Aid* (parodying *Live Aid*) the economist Dambisa Moyo had shown how aid can be misplaced and misspent and at its worst can prop up governments that are not accountable to their own people.

The voices in this room reverberate around my head, clashing with voices from other rooms, urging more, not less, aid. I know that targeted interventions can save many lives, but I also know that unless they help a country to move away from poverty toward prosperity, they perpetuate dependency and can even undermine democracy.

I know that debt monies and international resources to fight AIDS helped strengthen health and education sectors in many countries. But then I look at the global response to COVID-19 in 2020–21 and can't see it. Because there wasn't one. The dependency of poorer nations on the beneficence of richer ones was laid bare, as vaccines were promised but not delivered. Worse than that, African countries with the resources to buy their own were blocked from doing so because the wealthy West bought up the supply chain.

Strive Masiyiwa, in charge of procuring vaccines on behalf of the African Union, described it like this: "Imagine we live in a village, and there is a drought. There is not going to be enough bread, and the richest guys grab the baker and they take control of the production of bread and we all have to go to those guys and have to ask them for a loaf of bread: That is the architecture that is in place." It's why Cyril Ramaphosa, the president of South Africa, warned of vaccine apartheid.

I still believe aid is essential, but how it is decided upon and delivered is just as important as the money itself, as is listening to the people it is designed to support. As is partnership rather than patronage. As is holding governments accountable for what is given, and what is received. People like Kenyan journalist-turned-activist John Githongo have put their lives on the line to uncover corruption and demand transparency. The Sudanese-born businessman Mo Ibrahim tells me there is a one-word answer to the challenge of development and the quest for more equal prosperity within and between countries. The word is "governance." No success can last without it, he says. "Unless we're ruled properly, we cannot move forward. Everything else is second. Everything."

But if Nelson Mandela was right, that living in poverty is a human construct which must be dismantled by humans, then *how* we dismantle it becomes the most pressing question of our shared history.

"LET US BOW OUR HEADS"

The answer will be found in many rooms and in the voices of people whose lives, like Nelson Mandela's, embody that quest to end poverty. I've heard that voice when I've been in the room with Agnes Nyamayarwo in Uganda or Florence Gasatura from the University Teaching Hospital in Kigali, Rwanda. But never as loud and clear as in the room with Archbishop Desmond Tutu.

"The Arch," like Nelson Mandela, was one of those who enlisted me in the fight against what he called economic slavery. And he gave me a priceless gift to take with me: he taught me to listen. This, it turns out, takes a serious spiritual resolve for someone like me, with a big mouth and a big foot that's often in it.

I can't forget the look on his face one day in 1998 when the band were among the guests crowded into his office of the Truth and Reconciliation Commission in Cape Town. A look that was polite but verging on dismissive.

"Let us bow our heads," he said, addressing our traveling circus, half of whom were not at all religious. "Let us ask the Holy Spirit into the room to bless the work going on in this building, and to search of our hearts for how we can do more to fulfill Your Kingdom on Earth as it is in Heaven."

He talked about the philosophy behind truth and reconciliation— his deep belief that they have to happen in that order, that we need to see ourselves before we can be redeemed. Only after the truth has its way can a clenched fist become an open hand.

Then he trundled us upstairs, where he had assembled a hundred or so volunteers, and to our surprise announced, "Ladies and Gentlemen . . . U2 are here to play for you!"

Awkward. We had no instruments and we've never been known for a cappella. We attempted "I Still Haven't Found What I'm Looking For," to which the Rev added the "amen" that meant so much more coming out of his mouth.

Despite our best intentions, some of us activists can burn out in the fire of our own do-goodery and the secret is to know when to shut up and listen. I once asked him if it was hard, with all his work, to find time for prayer and meditation. He shot me one of those looks. "How do you think we could do any of this work without prayer and meditation?"

He taught me that prayer is not an escape from real life but a passage toward it. Like him, we do have to dine with our enemies, to make ourselves known to each other, but he knew that if we are to face difficult truths, we first need a thorough outing of how we became ourselves, both as countries and as individuals. We are wounded and scarred and divided but we need to see ourselves, in all our brokenness, before we can mend. Every one of us needs truth and reconciliation.

From Poverty to Power

To end extreme poverty, to shape a sustainable equitable world, a place where everyone determines their future with dignity . . . here's eleven things I've learned from activists and activism.

1. PEOPLE POWER
   "The people have the power," sings Patti Smith. "The people have the power to dream, to rule, to wrestle the world from fools." She knows. She always knows. In the end it's dull boring things like town hall meetings, knocking on doors, marches, and petitions that change the

world. Voting. Angélique Kidjo always knows too: "You
cannot transform the society of people if the people are not
part of the change."

2. THE PEOPLE IN POWER

Ideas are more important than ideology. You can disagree
on everything but still work together on one thing . . .
if that one thing is important enough. This has been
sphincter-tightening at times. Excruciating. Look out for
the "activists on the inside," the advisers to the president or
PM. They often call the shots.

3. SPEAKING TRUTH TO POWER

You can kick arse when politicians don't do what they
promised, and you don't have to kiss arse when they do . . .
though, on occasion, I have. There should be applause if a
representative of the people changes position and does the
right thing for the people.

4. GIRL POWER

Data and facts tell us that different approaches work
in different geographies but also that there are some
universal truths . . . like how gender equality is a force
multiplier. "Poverty is sexist," says Serah Makka-Ugbabe,
ONE's campaigning director. "When people say it's a
women's issue," adds Gayle Smith, ONE's CEO, "it usually
means it's an everyone issue."

5. WHO'S GOT THE POWER

If you don't have a seat at the table you're probably on the
menu. Who's got the power really matters. Why does
Africa, a continent of fifty-four countries and the world's
second-largest population, have no representation at the
G7 or the permanent UN Security Council? And just one
seat at the G20. What century is this? What planet are
we on?

6. SOLAR POWER

Not only is there more renewable energy to unlock in the sun, there's also fusion. Climate change, like conflict, is development in reverse.

7. POWER CORRUPTS

Make daylight the detergent. Transparency is the vaccine for corruption. The rules of governance work when citizens can see who's breaking them. In countries, companies, communities.

8. POWER IN THE POCKET

Vote with your purse or wallet. The biggest corporations can be brought down by what people choose to spend their money on—or not to spend it on. Commerce has lifted more people from poverty than anyone has guessed. It can help defeat poverty or defend it. It can green the planet or heat it. It's about us. Consumers and producers. Investment and divestment.

9. THE POWER OF LETTERS

The alphabet soup of do-gooding. HIPC, PRSP, PRGT, GFATM, SDRs, MDGS, SDGS, IDA, IADB, ADB, COP, etc. . . . How about a Campaign for Responsible Acronym Production. If the acronyms make us feel less than smart, then the people who come up with them are not smart enough.

10. THE POWER OF NUMBERS

Evidence-based activism—aka factivism. Data holds solutions and stories. Statistics can sing. One is the most important number because, as John Stuart Mill put it, "One person with a belief is equal to a force of ninety-nine who have only interests." More power to you.

11. SOFT POWER

Think globally, drink locally (Sláinte).

THE SELLING OF DREAMS

It's 1998 and I'm sitting with one such servant of the people, Kader Asmal, in the garden of "the Nellie," one of the finest hotels in Cape Town. The Mount Nelson hotel is named for the English colonial pirate that was Lord Nelson. Despite this tranquil setting, as we talk, Kader becomes angry. But not about the state in which the colonialists left his country. Having returned from exile to South Africa in 1990, and now minister for water affairs and forestry in the first African National Congress (ANC) government, his fury at the colonialists is outdone by his fury at the state that he and his government have so far failed to make of South Africa. His fury, he tells me, is sparked every time he hears the sound of grass being watered by automatic sprinklers, and I remember that Joni Mitchell song, "The Hissing of Summer Lawns."

"We promised every South African they would be no farther than three hundred yards from running water, and we failed," he says. "And yet we grow begonias and pelargoniums to scent the garden for visiting elites."

He pauses. "No offense."

None taken, I assure him. I get the point.

Kader's story underscores the difficulty of political transformation. After the historic handover from white rule, change is coming so slowly to South Africa that it isn't just causing Kader acid reflux; it is seeding undemocratic instincts in a country still in the first blush of universal suffrage, one person, one vote. Everyone is equal in the eyes of the law . . . except they're not.

The crumpled minister stands up to take a call and a smoke. He holds the cigarette between his thumb and first finger, the ash protected by the palm of his hand like a corner boy from Cedarwood Road keeping his smoke lit, out of the wind. I imagine him as a younger man, the exiled ANC activist, teaching law at Trinity College Dublin for nearly three decades, cofounding the Irish Anti-Apartheid Movement where U2 played our first agitprop as teenagers. In Ireland, the ANC was not seen as a terrorist organization, and I see Kader at his kitchen table in Foxrock, notepad on his lap in

1987, writing what would later come to be seen as some of the most significant parts of the South African constitution.

Is this what revolt looks like up close and crumpled? In the end only one theme matters: Have things got better for most people?

If the music of revolt is not in tune with the maths of economic progress, it's all so much dissonance.

When Nelson Mandela was released, recalls Kader, and about to broadcast his first speech as a free man, he was determined it be a declaration of self-determination. He told us he would announce the nationalizing of the diamond industry, a handover of incandescent light to the people.

"Madiba thought the symbolism eloquent, the wealth in the ground now belonging to the people who stood over the land."

Kader Asmal looks at me, pausing that South African accent with its faint hue of India. It sounded great, he continues, but it was never going to work.

"Madiba, we do not want to be in charge of the diamonds. We want De Beers doing it; that's what they do."

"And why," retorted the president, "would we leave such wealth in the same old hands?"

"Because, comrade, only in the hands of a cartel are these diamonds valuable at all. You see, there are many more diamonds in the ground than we let on. But if this became public, the value of these wonderful concentrations of carbon would be no more than costume jewelry made of glass."

Mandela's expression changed.

"Comrade, are you suggesting there is something of the world of show business here, which is perhaps not our forte?"

"Yes, Madiba. The selling of diamonds is the selling of dreams that don't really exist."

A COUNTRY IS A STORY WE TELL OURSELVES

Kader's story stayed with me. If countries on every continent need competent governance, they also need myths . . . and mythmakers. Diamonds, like countries, are a story we want to believe in. I wonder what time has taught me in these years as an antipoverty campaigner. How Ali and I think differently than the naïve twenty-five-year-olds we were volunteering in Ethiopia in the 1980s.

I go further back to school history lessons, how it was only recently that our own country emerged from poverty. In the nineteenth century, Ireland had a population of eight million, which after famine and emigration had fallen to three million by the middle of the twentieth century. How did our country jettison that history of poverty?

We're an island people who found ourselves driven all over the globe as political and economic refugees. Poverty made us globetrotters and we brought our discoveries home. The remittances of our diaspora were not just material. They were emotional intelligence, they were a more educated view of the world that came from having been all over it. And, like the Jews, one of our biggest discoveries was that ideas are more portable than objects. It was religious thought, literature, and music that were our first forays into the weightless world of software manufacture.

From the 1970s, we were able to rewire our hardware thanks to the aid and trade of EU membership. The land of saints and scholars began its transformation into the land of sinners and software engineers, our once-light industry now entirely weightless.

This small rock in the North Atlantic, battered by gale-force winds and rain, came up with an alternative climate to attract interest and investment in our young and well-educated population. Tax competitiveness became a central plank of Ireland's industrial policy, a way to attract businesses to Ireland and enlarge its tax base to increase investment in education, health, roads, and infrastructure. In tandem with the economic transformation of the tech sector were incentives for art and artists—our band among the beneficiaries. From intellectual property and pharmaceuticals to tech and biotech, the nascent computer industry found a thousand welcomes in Ireland. Far from people leaving our country, now people were arriving, and a new story of Ireland was being told.

The success story that is Ireland was not written for us, it's a story we wrote for ourselves. And though it isn't finished, we have made a modern myth out of it. Mandela's life, the one I was singing about at the Oscars, is a story that's impossible to believe. A magnificent story. A mythic story. A true story.

The stories a country tells of itself are essential to its identity and its development. That's true in South Africa and in Ireland; in Europe and the United States. For America to take root, it has taken novelists, poets, filmmakers, and composers, artists in every medium, to depict the diversity of America on a single canvas. The country is still stretching that canvas; the easel can still be wobbly.

Europeans, in contrast, are not so involved in the storytelling of Europe. Fluent in the narrative of their own countries, less well read in the meta-narrative of our continent. But if the French philosopher Simone Weil is right, that "imagination and fiction make up more than three quarters of our real life," then Europe is often missing a sense of "grand design." European identity can feel like so much cold concept . . . until we see the people of Ukraine facing down Putin's tanks parked in the way of their freedom. These people are ultimately yearning to be part of the European story, and in the process they are beginning to rewrite it . . . for all of us.

We need our artists to tell a story we can share. The way Idris Elba and Naomie Harris tell the life of Nelson and Winnie Mandela in *Long Walk to Freedom*. The way I now find myself in exhortation on behalf of this most impossible vision, Europa, a choir made up of old enemies and ancient warring tongues attempting to sing with one voice. A romantic vision.

I remind myself that this Europe is a thought that needs to become a feeling and that artists are essential to locate that feeling.

I remind myself that it was Hollywood, a little village in County Wicklow, that is said to have given its name to Hollywood.

A story line is everything.

It's not a place, this country is to me a sound
of DRUM and bass, you close your eyes to look around
It's not a place this ___ is a dream
the pilgrims take a ___   the whole world owns
to call her home   she had your heart

CITY OF BLINDING   lights   us lies

Blessed are the bullies
For one day they'll have to stand up
to themselves
Blessed are the liars for the truth
                              can be AWKWARD
Blessed are the pregnant
For theirs is the KINGDOM OF THEIR OWN
Blessed are the FILTHY RICH Company
you can only truly own
what you give away ...
I like your pain

33

City of Blinding Lights

The more you see the less you know
The less you find out as you grow
I knew much more then than I do now.

"Let freedom ring. On this spot where we're standing, forty-six years ago Dr. King had a dream. On Tuesday, that dream comes to pass."

It's January 2009, and I'm standing in front of a frozen U2 speaking from the same stage as Martin Luther King when he delivered his "I Have a Dream" speech in August 1963.

Abraham Lincoln is imperious as he stares down at us from his granite seat. This man, so famous for his height, sitting down in a chair. Maybe if he was standing, he would cast too large a shadow. Could he have imagined a day like this? A day when the next president of the United States would be a Black man.

There look to be a million people gathered here before the Lincoln Memorial, and many of them are also finding it hard to believe.

After "Pride (In the Name of Love)," written in honor of Dr. King, we perform "City of Blinding Lights," a song Barack Obama played when he announced his campaign for the presidency in Springfield, Illinois, on another cold winter morning, nearly two years before. Today I've updated the lyric.

America, let your road rise
Under Lincoln's unblinking eyes.

The Black man with the Muslim name who is about to become president is sitting beside his wife, Michelle, and their two girls, Malia and Sasha. Through my work with ONE, I've known Barack Obama since he was a senator. At first I found him a little guarded but later understood it was just his manner. He's not a man for the casual acquaintance. He will find Washington, D.C., a capital of contradictions, a place where he will be both beloved and damned by a political culture more factionalized and fissured than at any time since the Civil War. And not just because of the inherent racism in the power structures but because the grease that makes the wheels turn and the cogs bite in the Capitol has now become an oil slick of social media.

My generation had grown up with a politics that shared facts and diverged on opinions, but Obama inherited a Washington with few shared facts and plenty of opponents determined to push back on anything that might resemble a real conversation or the possibility of compromise.

W. B. Yeats was there a hundred years ago in his poem "The Second Coming": "Things fall apart; the centre cannot hold; Mere anarchy is loosed upon the world."

Here on the National Mall, crowds stretching back as far as the eye can see, Barack Obama is spellbinding. If anyone can reach for higher ground, he can. Yes, he can. But will the polarizing politics allow him even to reach common ground? He and his family will call this city home, without ever feeling completely at home here. Good. This is a tale of two Americas. A tale of two inaugurations.

But what am I doing here? This is not my country. My answer is in the lyric of a song, "American Soul," I will write ten years later.

It's not a place
This country is to me a thought
That offers grace
For every welcome that is sought.

A song written nearly forty years after we first landed on these shores.

> *It's not a place*
> *This is a dream the whole world owns*
> *The pilgrim's face*
> *She had your heart to call her home.*

THE IDEA OF AMERICA

It goes deep.

Deeper than Wim Wenders's idea that America has colonized our unconscious through cinema and literature, through TV and music. Deeper than how American rock 'n' roll shaped a generation before me and everyone after. Only when I look deeper still into the mythology of the United States can I understand my determination to wake up in the dream that is America, the dream of a country where you really have the right to life, liberty, and the pursuit of happiness.

"You are the light of the world. A city that is set on a hill cannot be hidden."

Not for the first time, some words in the gospel dare me to imagine what this country could be in history. Outside it's America. But for me it's inside too. America lives in my imagination. The campaigning senator Obama spoke of there being no red states, no blue states, only the United States, but I've always seen two Americas. Not a Republican one and a Democratic one, or even a rich one and a poor one, rather a real one and an imagined one. An operational America whose entrepreneurial capitalism is changing and charging the world and a mythic America that is a poetic idea in which we all have a stake.

Ireland is a great country, but it's not an idea. Great Britain is a great country, but it's not an idea. America is an idea. A great idea. We can argue that it might be a French idea—*liberté, égalité, fraternité*—and that a French gift, the Statue of Liberty, reminds every new arrival of this, but we also see how the idea of America suggests a fresh start, a new beginning.

The promised land is there for those who need it most
And Lincoln's ghost
Says . . .

Get out of your own way.

—"Get Out of Your Own Way"

Before transatlantic flights, when Irish people left their homes to go to America, it was like a death. They would never be seen again. And yet they would be reborn in this land of promise. The myth of America. But does America still belong to the whole world? Does it even belong to a lot of Americans?

Black Americans, for instance, so many of whom don't feel at home, when this is their home. Even though it has been four hundred years since their ancestors were forcibly brought here to carry "the white man's burden." America is a song yet to be finished and far from recorded. For many Americans, America doesn't yet exist. And yet perhaps this is an inspiration. Perhaps America is the greatest song the world has not yet heard.

FINALLY, THE PROMISED LAND

There is nothing mythical about this weather today. The temperature is subzero, and I can see Larry's breath freeze against the January sky. Adam is dressed to climb the Matterhorn, in 1928, while Edge looks at me as if to ask how you play guitar when you can no longer feel your fingers. "City of Blinding Lights" became a song the forty-fourth president of the United States took as his signature theme for the hundreds of rallies that paved the road on his way to election. A song about the loss of innocence and naïveté, about discovering what a big city can offer you and what it could take away. It's not as strange a choice as it seems.

"And I miss you when you're not around."

A memory of youth, of the naïveté that makes you so powerful when you're young. The music resonates with the crowds who believe in this man. Maybe it's the promise in that idea of a city on a hill.

Oh, you look so beautiful tonight
In the city of blinding lights.

Thump, thump, thump. At 12:22 on the dot, the whirring blades and shifting air pressure as a helicopter lifts and arcs over the Mall, carrying, for the last time, George W. Bush as sitting president. Neither he nor the Second Family seems to look back over the great crowd as some wave and some boo.

"Off to cash in his chips with his Texas friends."

"Back to the oil business, eh, W.?"

"Still time to start another war."

Around me people are high-fiving the arrival of this new era and giving the finger to a man who will have the quietest retirement of the modern era. Meditating on the portraits he painted of the men and women he sent into harm's way. Into a war that made no sense to me, but a war I sensed he would have fought himself if he'd had to.

But now history will be rewritten in front of us, all the big problems—health care, climate crisis, financial meltdown—set to be fixed. Obama's gonna put manners on Wall Street.

Finally, the promised land. (Not exactly.) The forty-fourth president has the high ideals and storytelling skills to explain them.

During his presidency I came to know Barack Obama a little more. Became aware of a deeply ingrained integrity, saw the softness behind the seriousness. Listening with him to some early mixes of new U2 songs, I was taken by his intellectual curiosity as to how music was put together. More writer than politician, but not narcissistic like us songwriters, I noticed how profound was his commitment to his family, and theirs to him. Michelle was the definition of what the hip-hop entrepreneur Andre Harrell described as "lioness energy." Protective of her family and their ideals in the extreme, she and Ali were always going to get on—neither willing to let her life be defined by her partner. The Obamas' was a soulful White House but more than that a rigorous and reasoned one.

Careful, considered, free from hysteria and fake theater. "No Drama Obama" was the West Wing trope. "Hard things . . . are hard," he used to say to Gayle Smith, who led USAID and we later poached to lead the ONE Campaign.

CITY OF BLINDING LIES

Fast-forward another eight Januarys. Like a flashback from some psychotropic drugs but worse because this is a flash-forward. Now the first steps are being taken to dismantle the Republic. For starters it's not an inauguration but a coronation, and the crown is orange, not gold. King Trump begins his reign of compulsive lies with a cropped image of the Mall, its boundaries surging with people, when actually it is barely three-quarters full. Is the size of a crowd worth an argument? When we discover that the forty-fifth president has ordered these fantasy photos to hang in the West Wing, we know we have entered a new dimension in American life.

"IT'S NO SECRET THAT A LIAR WON'T BELIEVE ANYONE ELSE"

At ONE we decided we had to at least try to engage with the Trump administration. We tried until we couldn't try anymore. The protagonist will never admit he is wrong and will double or treble down when challenged. And he controls the narrative. How does he do this?

Because he was made for social media. Because the virality that empowers the platform rewards shock and outrage, which is his lingua franca. Because he is the storyteller for this new present tense that holds only 280 characters and every story is a Grimms' fairy tale where the monster is under your bed or at the door or on the border. And you cannot get the monster out of your head. I never understood professional wrestling until it was explained to me that everyone is in on the joke, that it's not competition, it's theater. The audience members are not dim; they're just enthralled by the drama, the name-calling and trash-talking, the huff and the puff as the big, bad orange wolf blows another house down. It's the pantomime— "Look behind you!" That she won the popular vote was all the more remarkable an achievement considering Hillary Clinton had not spent her whole life preparing for politics to become a branch of the entertainment industry.

Waking to news of his election, I felt more nausea than shock, but like so many others I was already coming to understand that Trump is not the problem. He's the symptom of the problem. He's not the virus. He's the super-spreader. The virus is populism, and it's deadly as the plague. The real host is fear. As Chuck D, the rapper/public intellectual had reminded me when we toured together in 1992,

> *I've been wonderin' why*
> *People livin' in fear*
> *Of my shade*
> *(Or my high-top fade)*
> *I'm not the one that's runnin'*
> *But they got me on the run*
> *Treat me like I have a gun*
> *All I got is genes and chromosomes*

> —Public Enemy, "Fear of a Black Planet"

BENDING THE ARC

My fear is that I/we have fallen asleep in the comfort of our freedom. The story arc of our band mirrored the arc of our times. My generation had been firsthand witnesses to a series of impossible moments. The fall of the Berlin Wall. The end of apartheid. The Good Friday Agreement. Even marriage equality in Ireland. Had we lazily come to believe we were on some unstoppable journey toward the more just world we believed in? Even us activists and do-gooders. Especially us.

I found myself returning to some words of Martin Luther King's, about how "the arc of the moral universe is long, but it bends toward justice." I did not believe them anymore. The arc of the moral universe does not bend toward justice. It has to be bent, and this requires sheer force of will. It demands our sharpest focus and most concentrated effort. History does not move in a straight line; it has to be dragged, kicking and screaming, all the way down the line.

Michelle and Barack Obama would leave office with a quiet dignity, the major controversy of their tenure the outrage they caused simply by arguing that all Americans deserved equal access to health care. Why health care? They understood that the right to "Life, Liberty and the pursuit of Happiness," promised in the Declaration of Independence, was a fatuous claim without equal access to health care. The Affordable Care Act, "Obamacare," would not be everything the forty-fourth president wanted, but it would be transformative for so many lives, unless, of course, someone tried to destroy those freshly cemented foundations.

COMATOSE ON LINCOLN'S BED

Did anyone appreciate quite what a loss the departure of the Obamas would be to the world? Our family, forgetting we were Irish, took it as a personal loss. At a last lunch at the White House with just the two of us, I got to thank him properly for following through on President Bush's breakthrough AIDS work. He would add an extra $52 billion to Bush's $18 billion. Presidents normally want ownership of such expensive items. Writing the check to continue your predecessor's legacy shouldn't be extraordinary, but it is.

This includes cash for the Global Fund to Fight AIDS, Tuberculosis and Malaria, which Obama has keenly supported alongside champions like France's Emmanuel Macron and Canada's Justin Trudeau.

He brushes off my thanks, but then the man who has a photograph of the Rumble in the Jungle hanging in his office (Ali standing over Foreman) lands one final, mortal blow.

44: "What's the maximum number of terms you can run as the singer in U2, though? Ha-ha!"

ME: "Every new record is an election, I always say. Two crap albums and you're out."

There were eight of us one night in the private quarters of the president and First Lady as their eight years were coming to an end. Because the kids were a little older, Michelle and Barack more frequently invited friends over for dinner. If I'd stuck to the cocktails, all would have been well, but I allowed myself a glass of wine with the meal. Or was it two?

Have I mentioned I like to drink wine? This comes with a warning. I am officially allergic to it. I am allergic to salicylates, allergic to salicylic acid, which is found in everything from fruit to aspirin to tomato sauce. Which is found in red wine and explains why a big night that includes pizza, red wine, and an aspirin may mean my head will swell up and my eyes disappear. Ali says that I should take a hint, but instead I take antihistamine. If I don't, if I drink without the right medication, I can go right out. Sound asleep. Wherever.

I've slept on car bonnets and in shop doorways. I once fell asleep on the lighting desk at a Sonic Youth gig. It doesn't matter where I am. I could be in the White House.

Being precise, 44 does not drink like an Irish person; 44 likes a cocktail. If only I'd stuck to the cocktails.

As I started to fall asleep, I excused myself, and what happened next is a little blurry, but, according to Ali, it took about ten minutes before the leader of the free world asked her, "Bono's been gone a while. Is he okay?"

"Oh yes," she said dismissively. "He's probably gone for a sleep."

"What do you mean? He's gone for a sleep? Where?"

"Well, he normally finds a car, but I wouldn't know where he'd be now. Don't worry, it's usually only ten minutes. He'll be back."

"Hold on a second," interrupted the president. "Hold, hold, hold on. You think he's gone somewhere for a sleep?"

"Yes." Then, sensing his concern, she said, "He didn't sleep on the flight from Dublin. I'll go and find him. Don't worry about this, Mr. President."

She gets up to go, but he follows her.

"I have to see this. Where could he be?"

Ali says, "I haven't a clue."

The president replies, "He was asking me earlier about Lincoln's speech, the Gettysburg Address."

Good instinct. They walked into the Lincoln Bedroom, and there I was, out cold, head in the bosom of Abraham Lincoln, on his very bed. "Falling asleep in the comfort of our freedoms," as I spun it afterward.

The president woke me up, and as I came around, I tried to laugh as hard as he and Ali. He doesn't for a minute believe I have this allergy. He thinks Ali made this up to cover for me. He tells people he can drink me under the table. Rubbish. But he does make a strong martini.

34

Get Out of Your Own Way

I can sing it to you all night, all night
If I could I'd make it alright, alright
Nothing's stopping you except what's inside
I can help you but it's your fight, your fight.

I'm sitting in the front seat of a red Range Rover. The driver, who has just picked me up from John Lennon Airport in Liverpool, is Paul McCartney.

He's taking me and Jimmy Iovine on a magical mystery tour through his hometown, showing us the neighborhoods where the Fab Four grew up. He's pointing here, there, and everywhere. And apologizing.

"You sure you're interested in this?"

"Oh yes," I reply. "I couldn't be more interested."

"Yeah? Okay, well, that's where George's neighborhood was. It was actually a rough neighborhood, George's. Really Ringo's was a little tougher. I'll show you where he was in a minute. John's was like a little nobby. Not too nobby, but a little nobby. And mine, my family were okay. We were over there."

As he drives, he points out the window.

"There's the 86 bus. Myself and John used to ride there, just gone by. You sure you don't mind me telling you this?"

"Oh no, I don't mind. Please go on."

Do I mind?

It's like Moses giving you a tour of the holy land.

It's like Freud giving you a tour of the brain.

It's like Neil Armstrong giving you a tour of the moon.

It's like Paul McCartney driving me through the geography of a music that has transformed my life. We pull up at a light.

"See over there? That newsagent? It's changed a bit, but that's where I had my first real conversation with John."

Now I know a bit about The Beatles lore and wonder if his memory is playing tricks.

"But I thought your first conversation with John was when he was in the Quarrymen and they played at that fete in St. Peter's Church."

Paul looks at me with, I feel, some respect.

"Yeah, that's true," he says, smiling. "But I'm talking real, insightful stuff, not just 'What sort of guitar do you use?' or 'What sort of tunes are you listening to?'"

"Insightful? How do you mean?"

"Well, John bought a bar of chocolate, Cadbury's chocolate, and when he came out of the newsagent's he broke it in half. Gave me one half. I was amazed because, you know, back then, chocolate was really something. Most boys would break off a little square, but John gave me half his bar."

I was musing on this as Paul put his foot on the accelerator and we moved off.

"I don't know why I'm telling you that."

Perhaps he did know. I knew. In an instant it was clear to me that the greatest collaboration in the history of popular culture started with a fifty-fifty deal on a bar of chocolate. Lennon and McCartney. Born over a bar of Cadbury's chocolate.

WHEN MUSICIANS SEIZED THE MEANS OF PRODUCTION

It was 2008 and I was in Liverpool to present Paul with the MTV Ultimate Legend Award. If Elvis brought rock 'n' roll into the mainstream, The Beatles kept it there by taking it to the next level. They were the blueprint. But fifty years on, the era of independence they heralded was under threat. For a few brief decades the artists had been sitting at the top table, but that period was coming to an end. Technology was disrupting culture, and the music industry was struggling to keep up.

Patronage has been the way of the art world from the beginning, nowhere more so than in music. Who could afford an orchestra? You think Tchaikovsky could afford an orchestra? You think Mozart could? That's a big band. No, they had patrons. And plugged into that system. Before the phonograph, sheet music was the nearest most people got to the sound of Tchaikovsky or Mozart. It was all patronage.

Minstrels would travel from town to town, same as now, but then they had to sing for their supper. Sorry. Then *we* had to sing for our supper. To the lord of the manor. And if we played well, we would eat fine food and drink fine wine, depending on the beneficence of our overlord.

But when John, Paul, George, and Ringo looked up and through the glass of Studio 2 Abbey Road and saw EMI engineers in white coats, they dared to think the unthinkable. Maybe we don't need the white coats, the engineering degrees, to be in charge of our music. Sorry, to be in charge of this technology that translates our music. Not only are we performers who write our own material, but we are writers who would like to be in charge of our own recordings. Of how they're recorded and how they're published.

Where they led, others followed, and in the 1960s the artists, to quote another Lenin, "seized the means of production." It was a renaissance for music. Not just a renaissance in quality and social impact, but a renaissance in remuneration. Artists started getting paid. Not all of them and in particular not all Black musicians, the people from whose music rock 'n' roll emerged. They would continue to be ripped off, an injustice only partially righted much later. But many musicians did begin to get paid properly for their work— all the more cruel an irony, then, that after the death of their manager, Brian Epstein, The Beatles themselves discovered they were bound to some bad deals. A new technology—the CD—would rescue their cash flow but not in time for John, who sold up his place in the U.K. in favor of an apartment in New York City.

In 1968 The Beatles, who would become Steve Jobs's favorite band, founded Apple Records. By April Fools' Day 1976, Steve wanted the same independence for his Apple as The Beatles had had for theirs. A symbol of desire and temptation. A symbol of the Tree of Knowledge, Steve took a bite out of the Apple. The Beatles sued.

Over our own career Paul McGuinness had made sure we struck good deals, but not everyone had a Paul McGuinness. Not even some of the most talented artists on the face of the earth.

> *Fight back, don't take it lying down you've got to bite back*
> *The face of liberty is starting to crack*
> *She had a plan until she got a smack in the mouth and it all went*
>   *south like*
> *Freedom.*

A ROYAL VISIT

In show business you need a great entrance and a great exit. The entrance of the artist who would become known as "the artist formerly known as Prince" was flamboyant. His exits, even more so. Going out for a drink with Prince, the night might end with him leaving by hopping from table to table to table. It's quite the sight to be sitting with someone and then watch as they stand up, clamber onto your table, jump to the next table, and then on to the next, arriving at the exit before people have clocked what's happened. Except that he's left. (What they haven't clocked, and neither did I at first, is that his people are standing by those tables, holding them steady, as he dances over them.)

I'm at heart, always, a fan. That's how I got into music. Among the benefits of this ultra-life I have been given is that sometimes fortune grants me the chance to spend time with someone I will always be a fan of. Like Prince.

I had this honor and this pleasure on several occasions. It was like being in the company of an untouchable, a Duke Ellington or a Hendrix. As well as being an actual genius, Prince was also a self-confessed one . . . which begs a question.

What precisely is genius?

I believe that genius is not a person but a process, a process in which someone determines to uncover their gift and, for a period, is able to step inside it. The "gift" is a self-explanatory state, and like a prize awarded in a DNA lotto—say, being born into beauty or into wealth—genius is no reason for arrogance.

But that line of thinking all goes out the window when you meet Prince. The world was just brighter for being in his glare. He still occupies my musical imagination as much as a Roxy Music or a James Brown or a Miles Davis—artists I don't just love but need.

I saw him—a showman of the highest order—do "the exit" a few times, but most memorably after a night Ali and I spent with him in the Kitchen Nightclub in Dublin in 1994. The word "slave" was written on his face. Ali, being an Irish Protestant, is bound to ask questions. For instance . . .

"Why is the word 'slave' written on your face?" (I wouldn't have asked that.)

"I'm a slave," he replies, in a kind of deadpan voice, "because I do not own my own music."

He is dead serious, but also licking a lollipop while talking.

"I think I know what you mean, but maybe I don't?"

I over-pronounce to be heard over the bass banging on the walls from the dance floor just through the door.

The great artist maintains a metallic whisper, but I hear him as if he's the only voice in the room. If not the world.

"I do not own my master tapes. I do not own my copyrights. The record label owns them. If you don't own your masters, your master owns you. Therefore, I am a slave."

We're listening; he's compelling.

"I don't like that a record label believes it can own me, that it can own my name. It's a slave name, that's why I've abandoned it."

I can't know what it was like for an unknown Black teenager from Minneapolis, a solo artist, a one-man band, to negotiate with a major American record label in the 1970s. I'm certain Prince had to face obstacles U2 never encountered, but part of the ritual of going out to a bar in Dublin is people you don't know very well getting in your face. Even if I agree with him, I'm going to press him.

"I don't feel like a slave to these people."

The Irish Protestant now has the same look for me as she did for our guest's lollipop.

"That's because you're not," he replies. "It's well known that your manager negotiated for you to keep ownership of your music, master recordings, and copyrights."

"That's true," I reply.

"So how did he do that?" he asks.

"Well, Chris Blackwell, who founded Island Records, played a key role," I reply, "but lower royalty rates played their part."

"Lower royalty rates?"

"Paul McGuinness made a trade."

"What kind of trade?"

"We, like you, discovered recording contracts often have an 'in perpetuity' clause where they have you forever . . . that's what's pissing you off, and it pissed us off too. We got rid of that with a painful trade-off. Less money up-front, lower royalties, but it meant that at the end of a period of time we'd get back our rights and regain ownership of our recordings."

"Everybody should have that right," he pressed.

We both agreed, but I think now that I should have listened more and talked less in that conversation. That I should have been more of a friend and less of a fan who wanted to impress a great idol. There was something prophetic about Prince turning his face into a neon sign, and it was dawning on me that ownership was something I was taking for granted.

We did laugh about the costs of independence. It could get expensive doing things your own way. Whatever our contracts, by anyone's standards we'd both made a fortune and spent a fortune. I mentioned we were sitting in the basement of the Clarence, a Dublin hotel the band bought, thinking we were experts in innkeeping because we had slept in so many. I asked him about the cost of Paisley Park, his famous recording complex . . . and that's when genius made its great exit.

Freedom is such an intoxicating concept, elusive on so many fronts.

We were no longer economic slaves. Paul's message had always been that if we care about our art, we have to care about the business of our art. Paul knew that in the music business, business broke up more bands than music. Paul brokered some of the best deals in a business where often managers would rather negotiate for higher advances and royalty rates because their own slice of the pie would be so much bigger. Paul was inclined to put what was right for us ahead of what was right for him.

There have always been artists indifferent to how their art is hung on the walls of the world, but our band isn't among those who don't care. We care. And when you care about your work, then you care about its presentation: who will represent you, where your song will be played. Perhaps because he came from the film business, Paul never bought that slacker stuff. He knew from personal experience that a film director didn't just get up one morning and go make a movie. It's a financial equation and an artistic equation and a logistical equation, a whole series of problems that have to be solved in order for the filmmaker to make their art. Cash. Culture. Collaboration.

Growing up on Cedarwood Road, politics and culture were always meshed, but the ol' man always encouraged me to look further than the obvious stuff. Age fifteen I was reading everything I could find by George Orwell, and transfixed by the allegory of *Animal Farm,* where the pigs rise up against the farmers and then become worse than the farmers they've overthrown.

Orwell turned me on to the power of political satire and left me, years later, well in credit but with a troubling question. Am I now pig or farmer? Can you be both? I was once asked if I'd become a "capitalist pig," and though I don't think they had George Orwell in mind, I answered with another question. "Can I be a non-pig capitalist?" I've come to accept some of the orthodoxies of the free market, but I don't accept that it comes "free."

DAS CAPITALISM

A civilized country can't suddenly sacrifice hardworking communities because the wages for that hard work are cheaper somewhere else. These transitions have to be managed. We know competition is often the driving force of innovation, but we don't want to be a part of its Darwinian unfairness. Survival of the fittest is a long way from Jesus saying that the last shall be first.

Capitalism may have taken more people out of extreme poverty than any other ism, but it has also destroyed too many lives. Capitalism is not immoral but amoral. It is a brute, a wild beast that requires our instruction to heel and serve. Capitalism needs reimagining. A reboot.

But if it is wise to be wary of money, it is also wise not to ignore it. My father said I was the least likely person to make money because I didn't seem to have any respect for it. Even when I was broke, I always felt like I had everything I wanted. From when I was a kid, Guggi and I shared everything. In my teens it was my friends who used to pay my way. Tickets to a show or the bill for a meal, a pair of jeans and boots, luxuries paid for by someone else. Usually Ali. I presumed that if things worked out with the band, I'd have more than enough to reciprocate.

When we were making our first publishing deal, Paul called a meeting to convince the four of us to credit the songs equally, no matter who wrote what. "Money," he said, "has broken up the best bands." I was already there.

Our pact accepted that as long as we continued to try and "outgenerous each other" on all fronts, then not all our talents had to be the same or in the same departments. There are so many areas that require a band to pool its talents: the artwork, the videos, the staging, the merchandising, the meeting and greeting the people who work hard for you and your music. Still more important, meeting the people who pay to hear you or see you play. These are the people paying your wages.

So many bands, formed with the most communal of intentions,

dissolve in fights over who did what and what for. But as Paul never stopped banging on, "It would be stupid to be good at the art and bad at the business of art." He found us the best lawyers and deal makers, explaining that Principle Management had to be tough-minded as well as high-minded. These were not, he insisted, contra-dictory impulses.

Maybe we went too far when we moved one of our companies to Holland to save tax. Some found it unpatriotic. We argued if Ire-land could brand itself as tax competitive so could our band. We dug our heels in. Looking back, I can see our stubborn streak at play. Maybe there are some arguments that just by being in them you have already lost.

In the '90s, Paul lost a few friends by arguing that there were sav-ings to be made going out on tour by dealing directly with a single promoter, that we might need to upend the traditional relationship between band, local promoter, and agent.

"Keep going with these big touring productions and you'll bank-rupt us," he said. "We need partners to shoulder the risk."

Live Nation entered our life, and Arthur Fogel and Michael Rap-ino still wrestle with us on costs; they only stop fighting when it's clear the fan experience will be much better for those costs. "'Cause if we put the fan first, they will come back."

Live music was becoming more and more of a lifeline for most recording artists in the 2000s, when technology was upending the economics of the music industry. The upsides were clear: for fans it was easier, and usually cheaper, to access music, and for music mak-ers this was a revolution in proliferation. But there was/is a poten-tially disastrous downside. Now that it was so easy to pass music around as free files, songwriters and musicians were getting paid less and less . . . and might even be on the road to not getting paid at all.

Paul called it "the great brain robbery."

"Your friends in big tech are about to eat your friends in the music business for lunch. Who was it who said, 'If you're not at the table you're on the menu?'"

Probably you, I thought to myself.

———

The nagging question led me to Roger McNamee, a tech adviser to the Grateful Dead and one of the founders of the investment firm Silver Lake, and we pulled together a team exploring the audacious idea—"ridiculous" might be a better word—of taking over one of the major music conglomerates. Could we storm the Bastille and mount an artist-centric revolution?

We couldn't.

But we came close, which is how Roger invited me to form another "band" with him. A band of investors in the world of media and technology. Another ridiculous idea, as I had no time. So I said yes. We cofounded Elevation Partners, named after the U2 song, which over the next ten years became my schooling in the curriculum of tech transformation.

The freethinking and wildly altruistic Roger became my tutor on this new campus. I was reminded, as I'd found in my early studies under Jeff Sachs in international development, that this teen who spent less than a week enrolled in a university is a perpetual student. And I learn by doing.

More recently, I studied at the feet of Jeff Skoll, the tech entrepreneur whose Participant Media produced Al Gore's *An Inconvenient Truth* and an array of other socially impactful movies. With his brain for business and soul for service, Jeff was out to prove that a group of "badass" investors backing innovators committed to "good stuff" could help bring into being "woolly" concepts like "a sustainable future for people and planet." I was in need of another software upgrade.

Another new band? A ridiculous idea. I had no time. So I said yes. I cofounded the Rise Fund with Jeff, Bill McGlashan, Jim Coulter, and David Bonderman at the investment firm TPG. The Rise Fund remains a work in progress, and I get why people are cynical about do-gooders in any field, especially the ones dug by commerce. But Rise, and now Rise Climate, guided by the towering figure of former U.S. Treasury secretary and environmentalist Hank Paulson, have already helped build some groundbreaking companies. These funds are making a bigger social impact than I'd have imagined possible just a few years ago.

But here's the rub.

For all the success of these endeavors, at the time of writing, the worlds of tech and music still fail to fairly reward those countless musicians who are not mega pop stars. And that feels like a personal and professional failure to me. Despite the regular reminder of "overreach" from my nearest and dearest, and for all I have learned about new media, I still feel bad that U2 failed to help shape a fairer music business. It still galls me to meet so many songwriters whose songs are sung but whose bills are not paid.

ARTIST SLASH ACTIVIST SLASH INVESTOR

I am not sticking to my lane but I am not swerving all over the road either. You might say I'm flying a hot air balloon over some very interesting terrain.

The landscape that stretches out in front of me is the canvas, the artwork. I don't see a difference between what I do as an artist and what I do with the rest of my life. I don't have a "rest of my life." I don't want one. I just have this life.

Björk—singer/composer/artist/producer/activist—told me how in Iceland an artist is just one more community service, like being a carpenter or a plumber.

"All so valuable . . . well . . . depending on how your seat sits or your toilet flushes," she added, smiling like some mythical creature.

I like this view. Is art more important than, say, designing lifesaving pharmaceuticals? No. Even though I do believe there are days when art will save your life. While I'm sitting at home trying to make a lyric for a song feel less like a crossword puzzle, I know that at that moment there are nursing home carers or social workers or garbage collectors who are doing something more essential than what I am doing. But I confess to hoping that what I *am* doing may eventually become essential to them.

Why would there be a tension between someone's life in the material world and in the immaterial world? Art is not necessarily on a higher plane than business, and an artist is not a more sacred soul because they make art. Some of the most self-absorbed people I have met are artists (I'm one of them . . .), and some of the most selfless have been business leaders, trying to treat their employees with proper dignity.

The rise of rap and hip-hop rendered such binaries useless. Here was a culture where artist, activist, and investor collided spectacularly, its fashion and philosophies permeating the whole planet in a way rock never did. Black musicians have often been less sentimental than white musicians about making an accommodation with capitalism. They've had to be. Sam Cooke set up his own label. So did Curtis Mayfield. Berry Gordy built a musical empire. James Brown owned radio stations. Prodigiously gifted musical artists like Jay-Z and Beyoncé, like Puff Daddy, Kanye, and Rihanna, developed a take on entrepreneurial capitalism that would help propel them to superstar status.

It was the eighteenth-century economist Richard Cantillon, born in County Kerry, who first introduced the modern idea of the "entrepreneur" and suggested it's someone who takes risks on what they don't know with what they do know. (Or something like that.) I don't think of myself as an entrepreneur. When I'm feeling uppity I think of myself as an "actualist," a term I made up . . . until I found it in the dictionary. An idealist who's also a pragmatist.

What works? That's what I'm always asking. When whoever said the job of the artist is to describe the problem, not to solve it, I wasn't paying attention. I want to be with the people who follow through and actually make things actually better. Actually. I like functionality.

Also I like alliteration. Artist, activist, actualist. Maybe that's why Bill Gates fascinated me.

PICKING THE POCKETS OF BILL AND MELINDA

When I'd first gone after Bill and Melinda Gates, I was trying to slip my hand into an inside jacket pocket to redistribute some of their substantial resources to what would become the ONE Campaign. But what was in that pocket turned out to be less valuable than what was in their brains. And in their friendship.

Melinda may have had a lower profile than Bill but no less energy and commitment to outcomes, for all that she was the more reflective and meditative member of their long partnership. There is always something clear-eyed about her, always searching out answers both to the material problems she has dedicated her foundation to solving and for a better understanding of the immaterial world, the one her faith seems to open her up to. In twenty years of friendship and collaboration, I notice how she is the speaker in the room who is not overly enamored with the sound of her own voice, which might explain the power when she does speak and offer a clue to its clarity. Words matter. I can use too many of them. Not Melinda.

Meanwhile, Bill was becoming a stadium act. This was partly because he was Bill Gates of Microsoft but also because he was uninhibited by the lights, camera, action; he isn't vain. So it was Bill who took to the stage at Live 8 in 2005, a global series of shows on the twentieth anniversary of Live Aid, to remind the world that the despair and anguish of extreme poverty were not inevitable. To remind the politicians at the G8 meeting in Scotland that problems are for solving.

"I have learned that success depends on knowing what works and bringing resources to the problem."

Not exactly a pop song, but a clear melody line; Bill was as comfortable addressing a crowd of music fans as I needed to be addressing a crowd of economists.

A year later, Ali and I hosted a meeting of staff and board members of the ONE Campaign down in France when there was a call from Bill.

"We're missing you," I told him.

"Missing me?"

"We're at the ONE board meeting."

"I forgot about that."

"Is that not why you're calling in?"

"No," said Bill. "Are you sitting down?"

"Just about to."

I glanced around the room, sky and sea silhouetting earnest activists and patrons carrying their board books. People who rarely get a day away like this.

"You should be here," I admonish the man who, with Melinda, over time, will back ONE and (RED) with more resources than any other supporter. "What's going on with you?"

"It's not me. It's Warren. He'd like a few words . . ."

Warren Buffett, one of history's most successful investors, has an unusual demeanor, the student rather than the professor. Always humble, inquiring.

"How's Ali? How's everybody in France?" he asked. "Susie loved that place."

"We're doing great, Warren. What are you up to?"

"Well," he said, "since Susie passed, I've been doing some thinking."

Susie, his wife of fifty years, had died of cancer two years previously. "All I Want Is You" was her favorite song, and I'd performed it at her funeral, her grandson Michael on guitar. I have great affection for this family. Their daughter, Susie, one of our board members with the same midwestern moral compass, is both good friend and good patron.

"I've got all these resources," Warren continued.

"You mean 'cash,'" I interrupted, laughing, a little nervously.

"Well, yes, and this money, it has no utility for me. I need to find a purpose for it."

The chatter and clatter seemed to be sucked out of the air. I can tell from the tremble in this normally wry voice that he's dead serious. I notice a child walk by in a bathing suit, a blow-up ring around her waist; the sea over her head doesn't even bother with a wave.

"It's about thirty-one billion dollars, and I've just given it to Bill and Melinda's foundation. They know how to spend that kind of money on the stuff that you all care about. The kind of stuff Susie cared about."

"Warren," I said, momentarily struck dumb, trying to process what I think I had heard. Maybe I'd need him to say it again, just to be sure. Maybe all these people in our meeting needed to hear it.

"Warren, would you mind if I put you on speakerphone?"

As everyone around the table leaned in, Warren's words emerged from my old Sony Ericsson, and people's faces lifted and fell as they grasped what this moment could mean in the fight against extreme poverty that had brought us all to this table.

The world's first- and second-wealthiest families combining fortunes to improve global health and fight deprivation among some of the world's poorest families. The poetry in that moment was hard to miss, but neither did it bypass anyone involved that the world should not have to depend on such charity. Justice will always hold us to a higher standard.[*]

NOISY WORDS, QUIET WORDS

When I wrote my first song as an eighteen-year-old, money was the last thing on my mind. What was on my mind was making something from nothing. What was on my mind was music. Art. I've made no secret of this paradoxical life that I've ended up living, the one where the overly rewarded rock star bangs on about the plight of the poorest people.

> Don't believe in excess
> Success is to give
> Don't believe in riches
> But you should see where I live . . .

—"God Part II"

Thanks to philanthrocapitalists like Bill and Melinda, like Warren and Susie, at ONE we never had to ask the public for money. Thanks to super-rich donors like Mike Bloomberg, George Soros, John Doerr, Mellody Hobson . . . or, come to think of it, the superficial rich like me and the band.

I've sometimes looked around the table at some high-minded do

---

* That call from Warren and Bill was to be transformative for our work at ONE. As well as strengthening our presence in London and Washington, in Brussels and Berlin, we'd be able to expand our offices on the continent of Africa. Until our movement had taken root south of the equator, until our African membership could equal our European and American membership, I used to tell people we should really be called HALF. But if ONE was to be true to its name, Africans would need to shape our organization. And as people like Ngozi Okonjo-Iweala, Aliko Dangote, Zouera Youssoufou, and Mo Ibrahim joined us, and as we were able to hire people in Abuja and Johannesburg, Dakar, Nairobi, and Addis Ababa, so our movement began to change how it looked and spoke.

with such exceptional people and wondered how this unexceptional baked-bean-boy from Cedarwood Road—the one who got through his school years on a diet of cornflakes and Cadbury's Smash, and through band rehearsals pinching sandwiches from Edge and Larry—ended up in this kind of company.

But if we all have our different origin stories, these people who bankroll NGOs like ONE share in the conviction that while individuals can change the world for better or worse, sustained change takes social movements.

Then the rate of return is to the nth.

I can't change the world. We can.

Enter the word "advocacy."

A word that is less touchy-feely than directly funding schools and medicines, but when NGOs like Amnesty or Global Citizen, Oxfam or Save the Children, are effective, they can transform policies, which in turn transform life for millions of people. At our best, organizations like ONE become a PA system for people and countries who rarely get invited on the global stage.

Because in the end, our ask is of governments.

Our ask is to remake the global architecture in favor of those being locked out of the house.

Our ask is for justice.

And it turns out the fight for justice comes down to boring words that don't look good on a T-shirt.

Competence.

Governance.

Transparency.

Accountability.

Words that bring transformation.

The non-shouty words. The quiet words that turn the world right side up.

Words matter.

Words carry the people; people carry the words.

Though, as I write now, these words are being severely tested in Russia, Yemen, Syria, Ethiopia . . . fill in the blanks.

We want to believe the Egyptian activist Wael Ghonim when he says, "The power of the people is much stronger than the people in power."

The word is that all the money in the world, all the influence, including all the rich, fancy folk like me, will get rolled over by the people in the end.

Even the tanks rolling over the people of Ukraine, they will be rolled over.

If you go your way
and I go mine
always dressed for the occasion even if it wasn't
hand made shirts from Turn Bull and Asser
tailored. suits from Edward Sexton or
Paul Smith and the faint whiff of a ridiculously
expensive Japanese scent trailing in his wake
...then his eyes sparkled a little
in anticipation of the
grudge he was going to bear
PRINCIPLE
Tropical
MELODIA
player of
the West
our office

35

Every Breaking Wave

Every sailor knows that the sea
Is a friend made enemy
And every shipwrecked soul, knows what it is
To live without intimacy
I thought I heard the captain's voice
It's hard to listen while you preach
Like every broken wave on the shore
This is as far as I could reach.

Temple Hill, Dublin. A June day staring out at the marine pines as verticals over the horizontal that is Killiney Bay.

A conversation with a friend.

"Life without you is unthinkable."

Nonplussed eyes staring back.

"You know I don't deal well with rejection . . . abandonment issues." A growl.

Part Irish wolfhound, part collie, part lurcher, Jackson, our dog, man and woman's best friend in this house, has been given months to live. Every goodbye reminds me of every other goodbye, and I'm thinking that for a man who's written more goodbye songs than most, I really don't like them.

The iron handle of the kitchen door is wrenched open and Lemmy, our other dog (named after the Motörhead singer), pads in. Both dogs have learned how to open the door with their paws, and Lemmy is always breaking and entering to scrounge supplies. Part lurcher, part rat, she's always hungry and difficult to manage. I identify with Lemmy. At least for most of my adult life I've had Paul McGuinness trying to manage me.

I hate goodbyes.

GOODBYE TO OUR FIFTH BEATLE

Paul McGuinness had grown into quite the character over the years. An extraordinary presence extraordinarily presented.

Always dressed for the occasion and making it an occasion even if it wasn't. Handmade shirts and ties from Turnbull & Asser, Jermyn Street, tailored suits from Edward Sexton or Paul Smith, and the faint whiff of an expensive Japanese scent trailing in his wake. Just enough. If he had a hangover, Paul would meet it with a steaming shower and a very clean shave. And in your meeting with him on that morning, you'd never guess he'd had such a big night out, plotting and scheming on your behalf. Although, if it was an extra-late big night out, maybe those tiny pieces of tissue sticking to his razor cuts bore witness to a more bloody carnage. There is something old world about Paul, someone hardly prepared for the life of a gentleman by his schoolteacher mum or his Liverpudlian father, who'd become a bomber in the RAF. Paul lives large, and largesse was his nature right up to the point where he felt you'd betrayed him. Then his eyes sparkled a little in anticipation of the grudge he was going to bear you.

In Principle Management's headquarters, on Sir John Rogerson's Quay on the banks of the Liffey, I'm looking out over the new smart, stylish Dublin that Paul had in some small but significant ways helped to create. A modern city driven by right-of-center politics and left-of-center economics. At the end of his wood-paneled office, a large two-meter-wide canvas of Harry Kernoff's *Melodeon Player of the West Ireland* resting on an old-school easel. On his desk, incoming paperwork stacked a little higher than the outgoing. Just behind him, images capturing big moments in a large life. Portraits of significant people. Friends. Former friends. Some portraits of people he really didn't like. As well as trophy moments and personalities, a rogues' gallery of people who'd fallen out with him. Not that he did it easily, but if it came to it, Paul had no problem falling out with you. No abandonment issues here. Nor (note to self) did he make any excuses when turning down a request.

"I write to let you know the band won't be able to make your TV show/radio program/whatever/event."

Not so much as an "Unfortunately, we're out of town" or "We're busy."

And not just Paul. He'd trained the company in his own unapologetics. No one in Principle Management was to make excuses, to exaggerate, or to fib on his behalf. Paul had principles to live by and style to go with them. If he'd been written in fiction, his character would not have been believable, but, fortunately for us, this magnificent man actually existed. And existed for our band.

Now here he is in 2013, sitting behind that desk, suited and tied to perfection, explaining to the singer from that baby band that he raised to adolescence and then to some maturity that he can no longer go along with any more of the singer's plans for world domination. The latest is my "Roadblock Theory," to create a management roster across musical genres which would be impossible to get around if you were a new format or digital platform attempting to use music as a loss leader.

> PAUL: "Bono, I just don't have the time or the inclination and as regards management, I've not much interest in the next big thing or in expanding Principle Management."
>
> ME (interrupting): "But you're the perfect person for the job. All the other managers look to you. Principle Management is the perfect convener. It should be called Principle . . ."

Paul stops me.

> PAUL: "You're not listening. I'd have to want to do this, and I don't want to."
>
> ME (about to interrupt):
>
> PAUL (interrupting my interruption): "And may I ask who would manage U2 if I'm managing all of this?"

ME: "You. Of course. You wouldn't have to do this on your own. And it would be easier if there were other managers to help. Guy Oseary is prepared to speak to Madonna about this new setup. I like him; I trust him. Younger than us, innovative, gets tech."

PAUL: "Would Guy Oseary understand that you can't manage U2 on a BlackBerry? That managing the four of you is not managing Madonna. That it's managing four Madonnas. I'm already speaking out on behalf of artists and the fate of the music business. I'm guessing I've thought about it a good deal more than you. Have you even read the speech I gave at Midem?"

ME: "Yes. You asked me last week and the week before . . . and the month before that. 'The Online Bonanza: Who Is Making All the Money and Why Aren't They Sharing It?' Of course I read it. This conversation is me following through."

PAUL (eyes to heaven): "I'm not the man for this kind of thing, Bono. Plus, you'll get mission creep and want to include every artist out there. Anyway, I like the star system because it means not everyone can shine. Look, I really don't have the energy for this. I've been playing with the idea of getting out of the music business and going back to film and TV where I started. If this is what you're thinking, then maybe this is the time for me to move on."

We both take a breath.

This was a telling moment because Paul had always had limitless ambition and energy, and now he was making it clear that it was finite. Paul was looking for a simpler life, not a more complicated one. Maybe by sixty he figured he'd rather stay friends with us than face any more battles with us. With the record business changing faster than ever, Paul had the intellectual honesty to say, "I can't go on the next part of your journey if your journey is to rearrange the music business."

I knew that was code for "This next hill that you've got to climb, you need to find a new base camp."

Paul continued with a throwdown. "Why don't you speak to Arthur Fogel and Michael Rapino at Live Nation? See if they want to buy Principle Management out?"

And with one more pawing of that shaved face, the man who produced and directed the dreams of four upstart suburban kids begins to write his own exit from our life.

His parting line?

"I can't go there, but I'll always be here for you."

Later, I'm sitting alone, wondering what just happened. What to do with goodbye?

Two memories come to me.

First memory. "You know why I want to work with you for the rest of my life?"

It's a Friday night in 1979, and Paul is shout whispering conspiracy in the snug of the Dockers, around the corner from Windmill Lane Recording Studios. His baritone easily heard over the din of a crowded pub. Glasses are landing and taking off on tables like aircraft on a runway. To me, at nineteen, his phrase "the rest of my life" sounds like twenty-six or twenty-seven.

"Because you understand the whole equation." He looks at me.

"Do you know what I mean?"

"Yes," I say. Absolutely not knowing what he means. Later I discover this is a reference to F. Scott Fitzgerald's *The Last Tycoon*.

Second memory. Twenty years on, it's 1999, and I'm walking out into Giants Stadium without the band. I'm performing at Net Aid with Wyclef Jean. Debt relief is our cause and it's huge. The audience tonight? Not so huge. I'd guess fewer than twenty thousand out of a capacity of eighty thousand. Paul at my side, shout whispering to me one more time, as if I will never learn.

"I spent my life making sure this never happened to you. Look what you've done to yourself."

Onstage, Quincy Jones conducts an orchestra. "Quincy," I say, "there's nobody here."

He looks at me and says, "Bono, I don't have to turn around."

OLD BRIDGES BREAKING

I know that Paul is going to be okay. But what about us? At the funeral of a friend I hear Seamus Heaney's poem "Scaffolding." Seamus is there when you need him:

> Masons, when they start upon a building,
> Are careful to test out the scaffolding;
> Make sure that planks won't slip at busy points,
> Secure all ladders, tighten bolted joints.
> And yet all this comes down when the job's done
> Showing off walls of sure and solid stone.
> So if, my dear, there sometimes seems to be
> Old bridges breaking between you and me
> Never fear. We may let the scaffolds fall
> Confident that we have built our wall.

I wonder if the wall will stand without Paul and Principle. Or if it's past time to knock it down anyway.

Build something else. Abandonment issues.

Is this the end of something? Or the start of something else?

Another foundation stone loosened when Jack Heaslip, our spiritual guide since Mount Temple, became ill and wouldn't have long to live. These people who have tethered us on good and bad days, these people we'd moored to in rocky waters . . . either their absence would leave us drifting or we would have to begin again. Again.

Did the world really need a new U2 album? And if so . . . why? That was the question I wanted to answer.

Was the band ready to go to the place where the music lives?

The gates to the great warehouse that contains the music are locked and few keys offer entry.

Humility verging on humiliation is one, but with the arrival of success, that's one key that most artists grow out of.

Asking for help. That's a key. Another is accepting criticism.

The male ego is made more, not less, brittle by success. ("Listen, I'm in U2 . . . Don't talk to me like that just because . . . you're in U2.")

Dishonesty keeps the door of the Warehouse of Songs firmly locked, the a-little-too-successful writer now under the false impression that all his or her thoughts are worth sharing. The key is lurking deeper, down in the depths of your spirit. More prosaically . . . what scares the shite out of you?

What's really in your heart?

I found myself diving into our early days as a band, then diving deeper, down to my earliest memories of 10 Cedarwood Road. To the box room that was my bedroom, to the struggles inside and outside our house. Ali's timely arrival so quickly after Iris's untimely departure. How did a street gang and then a band so suddenly replace a family?

I listened again to that music that formed me and especially the shot of adrenaline, the speed hit, that was punk rock. I recalled why we'd formed the band in the first place, the joy of simple melodies, the slashing, crashing guitars backing up those simple words. The innocent up-frontness of it all. Had we strayed too far from our roots in that last album, *No Line on the Horizon*? Was it time to go back to first principles? Punk principles.

"Nostalgia," said Edge, "it's a thing of the past."

Ha! . . . But, for selfish reasons, I had to go there. I had to walk back down Cedarwood Road and rediscover the corner I was still writing my way out of all these years later.

I started to write about the singers who shaped me. I began a song about Joey Ramone. I began writing about going to my first punk rock show, The Clash, on their first tour. And how, after that, a part of me never returned home to Cedarwood Road. A song called "This Is Where You Can Reach Me Now."

> *On a double decker bus*
> *Into College Square*
> *If you won't let us in your world*
> *Your world just isn't there*
>
> *Old man says that we never listen*
> *We shout about what we don't know*
> *We're taking the path of most resistance*
> *The only way for us to go.*

I began rereading the eighteenth-century English painter and poet William Blake, a fascination I'd picked up from Van Morrison, Patti Smith, and Kris Kristofferson. Blake had written two completely different points of view on his life—one as innocent in 1789 and one as experienced in 1794. Five years between them. I realized I was writing our own *Songs of Innocence,* which meant we were also signing up for *Songs of Experience.*

It was a line on our second album, *October,* that led from one record to the other. In 1981, a young man, I'd sung, "I can't change the world but I can change the world in me." Now, in my fifties, I found myself writing something different: "I *can* change the world, but I can't change the world in me."

The pivot.

Two albums and, like Blake, it didn't matter that there were only a few years between them.

WISH YOU WERE HERE

Making *Songs of Innocence* was much harder than it felt like at the time, probably because we had so much fun after work. We were recording in an old church in Crouch End, and because Adam already had a place in London, it became an excuse for the rest of us to share a house. Something we hadn't done in a while. Nearly four decades after we'd last shared a house in the city, it was as if we were reliving our innocence. With a lot more experience.

POSTCARDS FROM LONDON (24 HOURS)

#1: 4:30 a.m. in U2's Big Brother House

I cannot sleep because Edge is playing guitar in the room above me. An acoustic, Spanish catgut strings, it sounds like. He'd woken me just after two o'clock, but I'd fallen back asleep. Now it's gone four, and he's still playing the same part. I mean . . . the exact same part. For two hours now. The arpeggiation that carries "Song for Someone" appears to be carrying him into the land of nod. The Edge may not be casual about the instrument that made him famous. He's not a man to "sit in" with other guitar players, but I'm here to tell the world that . . . he plays guitar in his sleep.

#2: 4 p.m., Noel Gallagher in the Church Studios

"Me mam would love this. Is it a Catholic one?"

Our band has known Noel since the first Oasis album, *Definitely Maybe*, when after an early show, we went back to his basement flat on Albert Street. As clever as he is funny, Noel worships at the shrine of unreachable melodies and untouchable attitudes. He is the greatest tunesmith out of the U.K. since Paul McCartney. Songs are like a collection of guns or knives to him. "They can get you out of a spot of bother if you're stuck . . . what have you got?"

#3: 10 p.m., Chiltern Firehouse

Rabelaisian scenes as Brian Eno arrives late to eat with us. Noel and Sara, Damien Hirst, Stella McCartney, and Ant Genn start singing, football-crowd style, "EEEENO, EEEENO." Brian looking puzzled but flattered, an incident to be remixed for some future sonic marvel. The night will carry us forward.

#4: Midnight with the Mayor

Ethical fashion trailblazer Stella McCartney feels like the mayor of London tonight as the room appears to revolve around her. She and her husband, Alasdhair, both devoted to design, the circular economy, their kids, and . . . fun. Stella makes a point to mention how wonderful it is to see the four members of U2 hanging out, as she has no memory of her father hanging out with his bandmates (some beat group from Liverpool). "Don't just glance at this, stop and look," she tells me. "Stare at what you have."

#5: 5 a.m., "What Are You Having?"

Larry is working behind the bar with our engineer/producer Declan Gaffney serving a crowded room at five a.m. when we'd promised the hotel manager we were going to bed. (After the manager left, we all returned to serve ourselves.)

"How did we become grown-ups?" I think it was me who asked Larry, as the sun begins to come up.

"I'm sorry?" He readies the question mark to place over both of our heads. "On what grounds are you making such an accusation?"

Songs of Innocence brought us so much experience. We went back to the well and discovered we could still drop our pail if we were thirsty enough. If we still wanted to be in the band, we would need to remind ourselves why we had joined. It was an album recalling our first journeys—geographically, spiritually, sexually. It was a clear thought even if we didn't have clear heads. We mixed the record in Electric Lady Studios in New York, another studio I felt like I should take my shoes off to enter.

THE FORBIDDEN FRUIT

Our new manager, Guy O, as Guy Oseary was known, was far from anxious about digital technology. He was excited by it, suggesting that in the end more people were going to access more music, and in time it would work well for songwriters and singers and players. He also believed artists could surf this technological wave and speak directly with our audiences. That was the plan for the release of *Songs of Innocence*. Why make fewer CDs for people buying fewer CD players when you could go straight to everyone who has ever bought a U2 album and deliver the new one digitally?

"Free music?" asks Tim Cook, with a look of mild incredulity. "Are you talking about free music?"

Tim is the CEO of Apple, and we're in his office in Cupertino. Guy, me, Eddy Cue, and Phil Schiller, and we've just played the team some of our songs of innocence.

"You want to give this music away free? But the whole point of what we're trying to do at Apple is to *not* give away music free. The point is to make sure musicians get paid. We don't see music as a loss leader."

"No," I said, "I don't think we give it away free. I think you pay us for it, and then *you* give it away free, as a gift to people. Wouldn't that be wonderful?"

Tim Cook raised an eyebrow. "You mean we pay for the album and then just distribute it?"

I said, "Yeah, like when Netflix buys the movie and gives it away to subscribers."

Tim looks at me as if I'm explaining the alphabet to an English professor. "But we're not a subscription organization."

"Not yet," I said. "Let ours be the first."

Tim is not convinced.

"There's something not right about giving your art away for free," he says. "And this is just to people who like U2?"

"Well," I replied, "I think we should give it away to everybody. I mean, it's their choice whether they want to listen to it."

See what just happened?

You might call it vaunting ambition. Or vaulting. Critics might accuse me of overreach. It is.

If just getting our music to people who like our music was the idea, that was a good idea. But if the idea was getting our music to people who might not have had a remote interest in our music, maybe there might be some pushback. But what's the worst that could happen? It would be like junk mail. Wouldn't it? Like taking our bottle of milk and leaving it on the doorstep of every house in the neighborhood.

Not. Quite. True.

On September 9, 2014, we didn't just put our bottle of milk at the door but in every fridge in every house in town. In some cases we poured it onto the good people's cornflakes. And some people like to pour their own milk. And others are lactose intolerant.

I take full responsibility. Not Guy O, not Edge, not Adam, not Larry, not Tim Cook, not Eddy Cue. I'd thought if we could just put our music within reach of people, they might choose to reach out toward it. Not quite. As one social media wisecracker put it, "Woke up this morning to find Bono in my kitchen, drinking my coffee, wearing my dressing gown, reading my paper."

Or, less kind, "The free U2 album is overpriced."

Mea culpa.

At first I thought this was just an internet squall. We were Santa

Claus and we'd knocked a few bricks out as we went down the chimney with our bag of songs. But quite quickly we realized we'd bumped into a serious discussion about the concern people have about the access of Big Tech to our lives. The part of me that will always be punk rock thought this was exactly what The Clash would do. Subversive. But subversive is hard to claim when you're working with a company that's about to be the biggest on earth.

For all the custard pies it brought Apple—who swiftly provided a way to delete the album—Tim Cook never blinked.

"You talked us into an experiment," he said. "We ran with it. It may not have worked, but we have to experiment because the music business in its present form is not working for everyone."

If you need any more clues as to why Steve Jobs picked Tim Cook to take on the leadership of Apple, this is one. Probably instinctively conservative, he was ready to try something different to solve a problem. When it went wrong, he was ready to take responsibility. And while he couldn't fire the person who put the problem on his desk, it would have been all too easy to point the finger at me. On the contrary he continued to trust us, not least by spending over a quarter of a billion of Apple's dollars supporting (RED), money going directly to the Global Fund to Fight AIDS, Tuberculosis, and Malaria.

We'd stepped into a communications and civil liberties mine-field. We'd learned a lesson, but we'd have to be careful where we would tread for some time. It was not just a banana skin. It was a land mine.

There were other urgencies. A tragedy, two days before we debuted the songs in Vancouver at the opening of the Innocence + Experience Tour. Larry's father, Larry Mullen Sr., died at the grand age of ninety-two. Larry returned four and a half thousand miles home for a day to bury this most unquantifiable figure in his life. But he was back onstage for the opening night, and as the shows came and went, I felt that the band had more love for the music it made than ever.

And for each other.

Love. That's a big word to throw around.

LOVE SONGS

Harder for me to write love songs to men than to women. We'd done it with "Bad." The Beatles had "A Day in the Life." The Rolling Stones, "Waiting on a Friend." The Clash, "Stay Free." On *Songs of Innocence* we had more male protagonists than on any album before. "Raised by Wolves" and "Cedarwood Road" gained extra momentum as we played them live, but personally, the sirens "Song for Someone" and "Every Breaking Wave" rocked my house in a different way. One, a naïve portrait of two lovers committing. The other, a more cinematic depiction of lovers way further down the road running out of rhythm and momentum.

Friendship can run out of gas. Romantic love always will.

Romantic love, an epic subject, wears itself out unless it moves toward the real and away from the fantasy. I wish I could better write such songs. I wish I could better honor the women in my life. My wife, our daughters, our friends.

I sing, "Women of the future / hold the big revelations."

Ali says, "Don't look up to me or down on me; look across for me. I'm here."

ANATOMY OF A LOVE SONG

Heartbreak is a subject I return to again and again . . . even when my heart isn't broken. While that has something to do with being in a marriage I never want to risk, it's also to do with a mood I'm drawn to. The duality I require from great art in general and great music in particular. The haunted and hunted love songs of Roy Orbison, Bruce Springsteen, and Cole Porter. My idea of perfection is the near-obsessional version of "Something's Gotten Hold of My Heart" by Marc Almond and Gene Pitney. As I've mentioned, Harry Nilsson's "Without You" was in the back of my head when writing "With or Without You," and maybe an echo of Echo and the Bunnymen's "Killing Moon."

Something in me always goes looking for the despair underneath the joy or the bitter in the sweet, maybe because I know that no relationships can avoid that kind of complexity. Great relationships, like great songs, deserve better than sentimentality. As pure love songs go, I can't get past "Nothing Compares 2 U," written by Prince, recorded by Sinéad O'Connor. It's the details, time and place. In fact as great singers go, I can't get past her. Duality again.

"If you're the best thing about me then why am I walking away?" A line I threw into a song called "You're the Best Thing About Me," a line designed to give dimension to what might have been hagiography. I was writing it at a time (not long after the opening of this book) when I had serious health concerns and for the first time in my life was anxious I might not have so much time left with this woman I'd got to know as a girl. I'm always looking for the liminal space, the outer edges of emotion. If I write a song about faith, I express it through doubt because "I still haven't found what I'm looking for." If I write a song about a "beautiful day," it's also about the longing for a lost friend.

Over the years there have been times when I've been mesmerized by a figure in my imagination that I mistook for someone real. A crush that could have crushed my partner's feelings. At such a moment, while you may not be in control of who or what is beguiling or besotting you, you are in control of what you do about those feelings. The choices you make. Romantic love can enlarge a person or shrink them. Sometimes the most convincing act of love is to just let someone be who they are. Without you. As a songwriter I am attracted to any territory or subject that's just out-of-bounds, a someone or something new who might take my imagination by surprise.

As a man too. This can be problematic. I can have a crush on a person who doesn't exist.

Ali finds other obstacles in the way of her love.

Were there days when both of us might resent the obligations our marriage makes of each other? Sure, but neither of us would want to live outside each other's love as expressed through this old-fashioned but still functional construct called marriage.

We enjoy the poetics but also know we can't always live off our feelings. We've long intuited that a long-distance marathon like ours must be run on more than romance. We delight in each other enough that when we don't, we still push each other to push through the pain barrier. To try to make it to the next level. Ali calls this "the work of love," and maybe some days that's shorthand for me being hard work. But she's right: love is work. Good work. We may let the scaffolds fall, but we have built our wall.

Ali gets fidgety when I get too serious. As I am now. Struggling to express how every day that we give to each other adds both weight and . . . weightlessness. Gravity and grace.

Am I more desperate for our marriage to make it than Ali, who is never as desperate as her husband? I have the most to learn from this relationship, and one of the profoundest lessons it has taught me is in raising children. I'd had that blood-brother compact with my childhood friend Guggi to never grow up, but as Ali and I had kids, I slowly understood that you can't have a child and remain a child.

I really don't like goodbyes, but sometimes you have to say goodbye.

Even to yourself.

36

I Still Haven't Found What I'm Looking For

I have spoke with the tongue of angels
I have held the hand of a devil
It was warm in the night
I was cold as a stone.

The white dude who would do more than most white guys in the music business to help break hip-hop in America, the most important musical force since The Beatles reinvented rock 'n' roll. The man who would bring streaming to Apple. The successful producer who would partner and befriend one of the most significant producers of the century, the rapper Dr. Dre, formerly of N.W.A, and build an empire with him by positioning Beats headphones as a cultural badge. The white dude who more than any I have known in the music business has fought for the expression of Black genius and its rightful remuneration. This dude is about to reveal some of the key characteristics that will explain why one day he will accomplish all of the above. He is offering a cautionary tale about musical tourism and what these days some might call cultural appropriation.

In short, white guys dressing up in the genius of Black music without a real understanding of the music or its context. And until we remind him of the very good reasons we all decided to come here, well, he'd rather not get off the bus.

Now, to be fair to him, the bus is not at our destination, which is a church attempting to contain the fire of a gospel group called the New Voices of Freedom. On the way to this destination I have asked to stop the bus at a random street corner. A corner that looks kind of cool where some cool activities are going on. I would like the record of this trip to have some atmospherics as well as cinema verité.

"Bono, this is a part of Harlem that's not for tourists. I have too much respect for this place to just turn up as part of a film crew. And stick cameras in the face of these folks.

"You're Irish," he continues. "You want to take some photos, good for you. I'm Italian. Believe me, I grew up in Red Hook, Brooklyn, and Italians are not natural neighborhood hoppers. We didn't stray far from where we got off the boat, you know? We know where you stop and where you start."

He's not finished.

"New York in the '70s, it was territorial. You entered someone else's territory, you'd want to have a good reason. Are you sure we're not wasting these people's time? 'Cause there's a part of me, as you well know, that is still in the '70s."

"Are you suggesting," I ask, "we might not be serious enough or cool enough to be here?"

"A bit of both," he says. "Look, I understand why we're here. You wanna record this choir. By the way, it's a white guy who organizes the choir. I'm not saying it's impossible for white-ass music people to be 'cool' here, but you need a certain pass, a certain composure, a certain respect."

Edge, Larry, Adam, and I are wondering what happens next, if our producer chooses to not get off the bus.

"Just leave me here for a minute to get my attitude together. I'll get used to it."

THE IRISH ABROAD

This man is Jimmy Iovine, and he's in Harlem with us to record a gospel choir. The New Voices of Freedom are going to sing on "I Still Haven't Found What I'm Looking For" and then join us onstage at Madison Square Garden. This is a bit of a moment in our late 1980s genuflection to American music because gospel is as close to the heart of rock 'n' roll as the blues, central to the quest for a deeper understanding of where this rock 'n' roll music came from. If Jimmy Iovine is overly self-conscious about being a white guy in Harlem, we probably aren't self-conscious enough. We're innocents abroad, wandering into church, thrilled by the possibility that our own gospel song might be about to find another level.

Somewhere at the heart of "I Still Haven't Found What I'm Looking For"—an Edge song title—is John Bunyan's idea of the pilgrim's progress. Or in my case, the lack of it. If I mostly find religiosity annoying, right up at the top of the annoying is the pigheaded certainty of the devout without the doubt. Not just no room for doubt in the God they follow, but no doubt in their ability to decipher the holy tracts. No doubt their version of events is the right one.

What's the point of a conversation with someone who's already made up their mind? I was still trying to figure this out in 1987, how life was about constant refreshment, every day breaking away from the negative influences, in nature or nurture. How we might break free from the number we're given in the DNA lotto but only if we break free every day. Life as a constant dying and being reborn, dying and being reborn.

The rabbinical Bob Dylan was already there. "He not busy being born is busy dying." So here are these Irish boys in a church in Harlem singing about "the kingdom come when all the colours will bleed into one."

I'm trying to look relaxed, but I'm a little self-conscious and I'm also in some pain from a broken clavicle after running—slipping—across a rainswept stage in RFK Stadium, Washington, D.C. But now, as my voice joins with these new voices, I find their freedom more effective medicine than any painkillers. I find I am transported. I'm watching tributaries reach the mouth of a great river, real lives and real life stories gathered right there in these pine pews. Souls disappearing into each other through the mystic that is music, and I know that the reason we are here is that Black church music just feels more honest. I am reminded again that it's okay if brokenness is the place we sing from, how our emptiness is always an invitation to be filled. As the band and I and even Jimmy lose our awkwardness, I feel the many spirits present in the assembling of this song. Brian Eno, who turned us on to the Swan Silvertones, the Golden Gate Quartet, Dorothy Love Coates, and a coal miner from Kentucky called the Reverend Claude Jeter. Danny Lanois, who cracked the code on how to get the rhythm section to feel almost reggae, his flattened picking style helping out on guitars while he sang old soul classics into my ear, improvising the melodies. This, our most gospel-like song, is about the quest, not the arrival. And that's how I find faith.

The song brings you to an ecstatic end when "all the colours will bleed into one," but the race is not done. "Yes, I'm still running." The story of every pilgrim is the running toward and the running away from enlightenment. From the Holy Spirit. From Jehovah. Moses, terrified by the burning bush, the bluesman Robert Johnson with a hellhound on his trail.

LOOKED OVER JORDAN, WHAT DID I SEE?

Around that time, when the band was in Australia, I had a recurring voice problem and was advised to visit a doctor with a reputation for helping singers. The doctor had a sense that anxiety explained this constant sore throat rather than, as several of my nearest and dearest had suggested, the cheroots, the alcohol, and the talking into the small hours. It was in my interest to trust the good doctor, and because he also had such good references, I agreed to something I'd never previously agreed to. I allowed him to put me under hypnosis.

Well, almost . . .

"Imagine," said the doctor, "a room with all your best memories around you. Be in the room. Now open the drawer. Find those memories. The best things that have ever happened to you. The affirmations. Your partner, your children, your best friends. A moment that changed your life's direction. All the best things. Be in that room."

I was in that room. It might have been a rehearsal room as a new song dropped by, but soon enough it was a walk down a country lane.

"Now," said the doctor, continuing. "Pull out the feeling that makes you feel safest and strongest and describe it for me."

"I'm walking along a river with my best friend," I said. "And everything is just as it should be. I have confidence in my footsteps; I feel I am learning judgment but not being judged. I can say anything I want. Sometimes there's a reply; sometimes there's not. It's just a conversation between friends."

"And your friend," inquired the doctor. "Who is it?"

I said, "I think it's Jesus."

I heard the doctor shuffle, nervously, in his seat. Maybe I wasn't that deep in his hypnosis.

And he asked, "Where are you?"

I said, "I'm just walking down a country lane by a river. It's not the Tolka or the Liffey or even the Mississippi. Could it be the Jordan? I've always had a thing about the river Jordan."

Emerging from this "deep relaxation," I could sense that the great physician had not expected me to find Jesus in my bottom drawer. The doctor was polite but evidently disappointed. Instead of discovering the source of the vocal problems, he had uncovered the source of the messianic complex. I thanked him because I knew for sure these images were deeply comforting ones from childhood, from the Sunday singing of gospel songs like "What a Friend We Have in Jesus." In truth, he would never know how he'd opened to me an experience that helped me understand myself. Why I view friendship as a kind of sacrament and how my traveling companion in the way of faith had metamorphosed from the father figure of the Old Testament to the companion and friend of the New Testament.

Thirty years after that hypnosis, April 2016, and I am at the Jordan River in the country of Jordan with my daughter Jordan.

Actually, all the family. It's a muddy brown at this time of year, the river running low, and we're on the eastern bank at Bethabara, one of the names given to the place where Jesus is said to have been baptized by John the Baptist. It's about thirty kilometers from Mount Nebo, where they say Moses was granted his view of the promised land. A few hundred yards away a Russian Orthodox Church and a Greek Orthodox Church, in their Byzantine ornateness, are sucking gold light out of the sky. The family is overcompensating for the despair we have witnessed firsthand on the border of this mystic country. We've traveled here from Zaatari, Jordan's largest refugee camp for Syrians fleeing civil war. Fleeing to a country where 20 percent of the population are already refugees from elsewhere. Our boys had been helping out at the UNHCR, and I was visiting with the ONE Campaign to try to throw a spotlight on the work of this great humanitarian agency, which had only a fraction of the resources so desperately needed. The camps are called "permanent temporary solutions." The average length of stay in one of these camps is seventeen years.

The only soul with us is our guide, a well-dressed professor well-versed in the Hebrew scriptures as well as Islamic texts.

"Yes, this is where John baptized Jesus."

I smile at his certainty. "How can you be so sure?"

The scholar, himself an archaeologist, explains, "Actually it's easier than you think. There weren't that many people around here at the time, so major events—where Jesus was born, for example—were marked with a shrine from early on. Dig and dig and chances are you'll find someone built an altar to mark a place of reverence. That's why we're pretty sure this is where John baptized Jesus."

"As there's nobody around," I ask, changing the subject, "would you mind if we jump in? For a swim?"

"You're the guest."

And so devoid of obvious piety but still with deep respect for our environs, the Hewson family duck ourselves in the river Jordan in some kind of baptism. We're laughing out loud until we're not. Surprised by joy. Stilled by the ancient present.

Going under the water in this mythic river that means more to me than I can figure out. The symbol of baptism is about submerging into your death in order to emerge into new life, a powerful poetry, and I'm a fortunate man to have a family of foolish pilgrims who will follow me into this symbolism. I get that this moment sounds more than foolish. Preposterous.

The baptism site, Bethabara or Al-Maghtas—"immersion"—is where the river meanders through reeds into a natural pool, and my eyes follow some ancient steps down from red clay into clearer, brighter water. The bees, buzzing, give me the honeyed thought that this place is hardly changed in two thousand years as the professor becomes a time traveler, peeling off the layers of history and taking us inside the stories that so many seekers here inhabit. "In local lore," he explains, "John the Baptist was a man in the wild living off locusts and honey so that some thought of him as the ancient prophet Elijah returned once again. But all around you will find the present and the past dancing around each other."

As his musical voice rises and falls, I hear the faint tinkling of a still tinier tributary at our feet. "Elijah's stream," he says, describing how the Jordan is drip fed from many streams including one from the little hill of Hermon, or Elijah's Hill. Another source is Mount Horeb, which we can just about make out, squinting at us from a distance. Where Moses is said to have received the Ten Commandments on two tablets of stone, the people wanting clarity on how best to live.

We step back and marvel at the big picture beyond the frame, how in this place even the physical landscape seems to surrender to the storytelling. These details first written down on animal skins and then papyrus and now presented as fragments of stone and color have me standing back, looking for another perspective, trying to take in the whole picture.

At best you get to hear a rhyme in the poetry of it all. I am in awe of the poetic power of the scriptures, how you can't approach the subject of God without metaphor. All the way from Adam and Eve these fantastical stories help us make a way through our metaphysical lives. If science is how we navigate the physical universe, then religious texts offer to navigate the more than physical, the existence we can't even prove exists.

Stories that are instruments of inquiry into an invisible world we strain to see, a world we glimpse through art and family and friendship. Stories of a love that has no beginning and no end.

I am comforted by this idea of infinite love, the bigger picture beyond the frame. It throws me back to a Christmas Eve in the mid-1980s, desperately trying not to nod off during a carol service at St. Patrick's Cathedral in Dublin. Not long back from traveling, the body still in some other time zone, Ali and I slip into the crowded cathedral at the last minute and happily settle for a pew right behind one of the great limestone pillars holding up the twelfth-century vaulted nave. Unable to see the choir or players in the Christmas narrative, I focus on listening to the soprano boys.

> *Once in royal David's city*
> *Stood a lowly cattle shed,*
> *Where a mother laid her baby*
> *In a manger for His bed*

But soon enough, despite Ali's elbow in my ribs, I am drifting off. Drifting back to my brief days at the school next door, musing on the Irish writer Jonathan Swift, of *Gulliver's Travels,* once the dean here. Another elbow and I cold water myself by trying to visualize mother and child sharing a delivery room with goats and sheep. The vulnerable nature of the Nativity, the messiness of childbirth swaddled among shit and straw.

Funny how your senses work, I can smell the scene; poverty has its stench. The poetry and politics of the Christmas story hit me as if I were hearing it for the first time: the idea that some force of love and logic inside this mysterious universe might choose self-disclosure in the jeopardy of one impoverished child, born on the edge of nowhere, to teach us how we might live in service to one another is overwhelming.

Its eloquence is overwhelming. Unfathomable power expressed in powerlessness. I nearly laugh out loud.

Genius.

Inexpressible presence choosing to be present not in palace but in poverty. "And He feeleth for our sadness, And He shareth in our gladness."

The family is discussing this thought when we visit Bethlehem and the church said to be built over that lowly cattle shed. Our guide reminds us that the stable Jesus was born in was not the one on sentimental Christmas cards but more likely a cave, commonly used as shelter for livestock in the region. Our youngest, John, gets the picture of homelessness it consciously presents, and we talk about the divinity sleeping under the cardboard boxes in our own cities.

I'm still thinking about that cathedral epiphany when we visit the Church of the Holy Sepulchre, in the old city of Jerusalem, this one said to cover the site where Jesus was crucified. Where his followers believe death itself died. A wild thought if you dare entertain it, but immortality remains a stretch too far for most of us mortals. And anyway, round here the business of miracles drives the miracle of business.

I'm thinking of it as we meet the mayor of Jerusalem, Nir Barkat, who tells us that once a week two-thirds of the planet wakes up thinking about his city. And I'm still thinking of it as I ponder the rocket fire and rubber bullets that punctuate its current politics.

DREAM BENEATH THE DESERT SKY

A pilgrimage will often take you into the desert. Odysseys. Road trips. Wanderings. There was a lot of desert on that pilgrimage to the Holy Land, but it's been an enduring metaphor in the band's work. From a desert we look out on the world on our most famous album.

American deserts like the Sonoran and the Mojave offered us the Joshua tree as one of our most enduring emblems. On those photo shoots with Anton Corbijn, we discovered how cold and unforgiving the desert can be in the night. Or, in winter, in the day. On the gatefold sleeve Anton's photography captured us huddled in a cold landscape, gallantly refusing the role of actors pretending to be warm. I went to the next level and posed in a singlet in six degrees.

Such commitment. We took endless enjoyment that Anton, the Dutch master, could not quite pronounce the name Joshua. "Yoshua," he would say, *The Yoshua Tree*. In fact his pronunciation might have been closer to the original Hebrew, *Yeshua*, which, years later, we discovered was the same name but a different pronunciation of "Jesus." *Yeshua*. We called our most popular album *The Jesus Tree*. Typical . . .

That album and tour had taken the band to another level of recognition, taken us to the kind of success that wants to trick you into forgetting who you are. Sometimes you need to get away to come home, which might have been behind the idea Adam and I had for our own pilgrimage. By car. A desert road trip. A journey that might disclose some more about the music of this country we'd been falling in love with. Chet Baker's "Let's Get Lost" was our theme song, and so we did, all the way from Los Angeles to New Orleans. We filled the car with all kinds of Americana and set off through the Painted Desert. Drove through towns with names like Truth or Consequences in New Mexico and headed into Arizona, reading, talking, listening to music, and eating great Mexican breakfasts . . . and then rolling down the windows.

Al Green, one of the finest soul singers of all time and now the pastor of the Full Gospel Tabernacle Church, was not around when we arrived in Memphis, but one of his team drove us to church, an exhilarating experience that became still more spine-tingling as the preacher reached his apogee.

"I don't care where you've come from. If you've been up through the desert and down through the valley. If you've been on the highway all the way from L.A. You're in danger. You have no guard rails where you're going. You might be famous. You might be at the top of the world. But your car is about to come off on a mountain road. I don't know who you are, but I feel you're here."

Was he talking to us?

Were we the ones about to come off the mountain road?

We both had the sweats until we deduced maybe our driver had had a word with the preacher about today's visitors from rock 'n' roll Babylon. Shamanism, show business, it's a fine line.

THE HOUSE OF CASH

Adam and I didn't quite know where our pilgrimage was taking us, but we knew whom it was taking us to and he was in Nashville, an original pilgrim making a unique progress. I'd got to know Johnny Cash in the 1980s and in Ireland, where his popularity never waned. The Irish folk tradition revered his brooding country style, the truth unvarnished, and everyone knew that the first thing he did on landing at Dublin Airport was down a pint of Guinness.

People had not put that together with alcoholism, but on this Nashville day in 1987 it's a clean Johnny Cash inviting the pair of us in for lunch. And only slightly disconcerting as we walk through the door of their dining room to find a table set for forty. And here's his beloved, June Carter Cash.

"Hi, boys. I'm doing a photo shoot for my cookbook. We're eating in the kitchen today."

The four of us sit down in the kitchen and bow our heads as Johnny delivers the most poetic grace I've ever heard. But then, smiling under his breath, as if June couldn't hear or see, "Sure miss the drugs, though."

The house was filled with intricately carved nineteenth-century oak furniture from France, the U.K., and Ireland.

"I'm interested in history. June too."

"You're Irish, right?" inquires Adam.

"No, actually, the Cash name we've traced to Scotland. The House of Cash. Scottish baronial class."

I say, "Johnny, even though you are royal to me, you might want to double-check that, as you've quite the resemblance to horse people from County Wexford in Ireland. Horse people by the name of Cash.

"Did you know Cash is a name associated with the Traveller community at home. This community had a history of great expertise in tin and metal, and as a kid I remember their people going door-to-door sharpening knives or repairing pots.

"Alchemists maybe, like you, Johnny. Turning base metals into gold . . . gold records in your case. The Travellers have some great musicians, too, like Finbar Furey or less well-known like Pecker Dunne."

Johnny took this potted history a little better than June. "Would you like to visit our zoo?"

"Zoo? There's a zoo here?"

"Right here. We have a Carter Cash Zoo, and I'd sure be thrilled to show you."

"You boys really should see Johnny's zoo," June chimes in. "Make him tell you the story about the emu. He won't want to."

Johnny drove us out in his pickup and proudly showed us around. The locals were regular visitors, he told us, and it was gated to keep every living thing safe. Some of the residents could be a little unpredictable.

"June mentioned the emu. I'm not pleased to tell you, but you should know an emu is a dangerous creature and not to be trifled with."

His voice going from gravelly to grave, he described a confrontation with this "prehistoric chicken from hell."

"I'm not kiddin' when I say I nearly died on this very spot. I mean I was attacked. I was kicked. This giant bird knocked me off my feet and showed no mercy when I was on my back in the dirt, stompin' on my chest.

"Boys, if there hadn't been some wooden stakes for fencin' layin' around that I used to beat off this dinosaur, I was a dead man. Not a word of a lie."

Adam, smiling, tells me later that he'd imagined the newspaper headline: "Johnny Cash Killed by Emu." Hard to dislodge once it enters your head, but the man in black had a very white face just recalling the incident. The man who sang "I shot a man in Reno just to watch him die" had not so easily shrugged off this Australian outlaw.

Later I spent some time with Kris Kristofferson, who filled in some more details about this man who left every other man feeling that maybe they weren't one. John had been properly wild in his day.

"He would sleep at the top of trees, like a creature, the wildest thing you could meet in the wild, and that's why we love him." When Johnny first had the house in Nashville, before June put manners on it and him, it had only one piece of furniture.

"It was a wooden chest that Johnny used to sleep in. He called it his coffin; he laughed at death."

Only June Carter Cash could tame the man. But for all his deep faith and conviction, he could never be the pious type, and maybe that's why so many are drawn to him. If gospel music has a joy that in some hands comes off as sentimental, a sweetness that can turn saccharine, with Johnny Cash you always felt the angels were just around the corner from the devils. He'd made his choice to pitch his tent "at the gates of Sheol." Johnny didn't sing to the damned; he sang with the damned, and sometimes you sensed he might prefer their company.

Reasons to Love Johnny Cash

1. He wrote "I Walk the Line" and tried harder than most.

2. At six feet two he never looked down on anyone.

3. He made prison visits to San Quentin and Folsom feel like a treat to himself, and his recordings of those encounters are still freedom for so many.

4. He discovered Kris Kristofferson when Kris was down on his luck and working as a janitor in Nashville's CBS recording studio, whistling his tunes for John as he took a bathroom break. He did not call the cops when Kris, a former U.S. marine helicopter pilot, landed in Johnny's garden with a demo of "Sunday Morning Coming Down."

5. He formed the Highwaymen with Kris, Willie Nelson, and Waylon Jennings, forging a non-veneered outlaw country music that sought to straddle the chasm between left- and right-wing views in the country. And in the band.

6. Jesus Christ took his initials.

THE WANDERLUST IN THE WANDERER

A few years later, in 1993, we asked Johnny to sing on a piece of electronica we were working on for the *Zooropa* album. I was thinking about Ecclesiastes, one of the books of wisdom in the middle of the Old Testament. It's about a searcher, a pilgrim.

I impertinently wrote the lyrics of "The Wanderer" in his voice for his voice.

> I went drifting through the capitals of tin
> Where men can't walk or freely talk
> And sons turn their fathers in.
> I stopped outside a church house

Where the citizens like to sit.
They say they want the kingdom
But they don't want God in it.

"This electronic music may not be your cup of tea, but it will be some contrast with your voice."

"I ain't drinkin' tea. I don't drink anything except water these days. I'll try it."

It has to be said Johnny Cash was the heavyweight champion of every room he entered except one that contained June Carter, a country great herself. In "Ring of Fire," June wrote the finest of cautionary wedding songs, and she wrote it for her and John. She understood the gravitational pull that life exerts on a marriage because she'd endured it. In the early zeros, hearing John was gravely ill, I called the house and June picked up.

"Well, hi, Bono. How's Ireland? How's Ali? How's the band? How's the Burlington Hotel?"

We spoke for fifteen minutes, and I guessed that Johnny was too sick to come on the line.

"Well, June, please pass on our best to John."

"Oh, why, Bono, he's right beside me! We're in bed. I'll put you on right now."

That unmistakable baritone was now a bass and a grumble. "Sorry about that."

Nothing more had to be said. He was in the arms of his beloved and she with him. In the end it was Johnny who survived June. His music kept him alive. Thanks to a phone call with Rick Rubin years earlier.

"I need to record. If I don't, I'm gonna die."

A call that led to American Recordings and some of the finest musical readings in history including Johnny's stone-cold-sober version of our song "One."

"Sure miss the drugs, though."

That was Johnny, just trying to make us feel at home.

In U2 land, in the summer of 2013, we were in a meeting with our longtime creative director, Willie Williams, along with Es Devlin, the artist and designer, and Mark Fisher, the rock 'n' roll architect who was instrumental in helping us design our own touring universe. A great lover of public art, Mark had left an imprimatur on live music, from Pink Floyd's *Wall* onward, that was unrivaled. Now in the final months of his life, he couldn't be with us in person, but he joined us online. How could we stage the upcoming Innocence + Experience Tour, its songs inspired by Blake's poetry collection of the same name?

Willie was insisting, correctly, that we can't decide what we want to show until we decide what we want to tell. So what do we want to say? Es wondered if the street I grew up on, Cedarwood Road, the subject of one of our new songs, could be like a physical street, connecting two stages, a kind of spiritual thoroughfare. At which point, out of the dark digital space, comes the voice of Mark, a rebuke delivered in the stentorian style of a major general addressing a cowardly meeting of top brass.

"Why don't you build a big fucking cross at the center of the arena? That's what you really want to say. Am I right?"

"Well," I reply, "not exactly, but you're not wrong. The image of the cross is something we hold tightly to. The horizontal reaching out in community, the vertical rooting our heady dreams in the solid ground."

Maybe I sensed Mark thinking, "Fucking get on with it," but what he said was "Well, that's what William Blake would do."

And Johnny Cash, too, as I thought about it. And that's the line I want to walk. The wanderlust in the wanderer. The spirit that still hasn't found what it's looking for, a life and a gospel song about doubt as much as certainty, about the journey, more than the destination. That's how this band goes on. Just when you reach the promised land, you discover you haven't.

In the ancient-wisdom literature known as the book of Ecclesiastes, written several hundred years BC, there is a wanderer I borrowed from, a sojourner who discovers that sex, drugs, money, fame . . . are apparently not the promised land.

Instead, says the writer—maybe Solomon—these are the vanities of vanities. The best thing in life, he discovers, is to enjoy your work. To do what you love.

The promised land will always be somewhere else.

I think I can grasp this. I don't know if I can reach it.

Dearest
Elijah & John.
if you can step over the shite
love is bigger than anything in its way
papa nu guinea

37

Love Is Bigger Than Anything in Its Way

The door is open to go through
If I could I would come too
But the path is made by you
As you're walking, start singing and stop talking.

Love is bigger than anything in its way. But it has to be said, there is a lot in its way.

SCENE I: A ROCK 'N' ROLL SHOW

A hot and heaving music venue in Dublin. A young crowd is attempting to get airborne, lifting themselves out of their bodies to get closer to the band. The singer has pulled two stunts that no one was expecting. After jumping up on the drum kit, he's fallen over and is lying lifeless on the greasy stage. Boys gasp, girls scream, but he has not been electrocuted. He is involved in an act of show business.

I am not the boy. The boy is my son. But the scale of the show this young man orchestrates in the winter of 2018 holds a mirror to the shows I was playing with my own schoolmates. When I, like him, was a teenager.

His mother is here. She comes to his shows. Is that weird? It isn't. It's amazing and moving for me to see how our third child and older boy, Elijah, is capable of realizing his own musical vision. He is aware his father's face will bring him mixed blessings. He's thought about it. For all of six minutes. He is not being precious or too cool. He will sometimes ask my advice, and I have told him I envy his ease on a stage, and off it. How being so comfortable in your skin is the most attractive thing an audience can observe of a performer.

"To be yourself is the hardest thing, and it's easy for you. I've never once been myself. But you play beautifully; you don't have to be a big performer to make a big dent."

"Are you saying I'm not a big performer?"

He challenges his old man, with an Elvis-like smile. That was the week before the fainting stunt. That's who he is. Hound dog. This boy can be any man he wants to be.

SCENE 2: A RUGBY MATCH

I'm standing at a rugby match in a club called the Wanderers whose team of sixteen-year-olds are getting the confidence run out of them by a club called Coolmine. Number 3 is sixteen and six feet, and in our house that makes him a giant, but in his head what makes him a giant is his mates. His teammates are losing badly to a team that doesn't like them, and in this moment I get to witness our boy John's ability to be a great sportsman. A great boxer, they say, is made by his ability not to throw a big punch but to take one, and the same is true of a great person. John, the youngest in our family, is also kind of the eldest. He was born in a rush. I can clearly remember his arrival into this world as, on the drive to the hospital, Ali had me crash the lights.

"That boy will drive a getaway or a cop car," I told her. "He'll grow up to be either a robber or a big guard."

"There are definitely speeding tickets in his future."

Our John keeps his eye out for the lost sheep we can all sometimes become. John is the man we'd all like to be.

We begin by looking out for our children, and in time, if we are so blessed, we find they are looking out for us.

SCENE 3: A FAMILY REVELATION

To be close as a father shouldn't be so easy for me, because I wasn't that close to mine. Fatherhood is taught at home, not at school, but my da was not close to me, because he didn't like kids. My da was not close to me, because I was a bit stroppy at a time when he was vulnerable himself. I now know at least part of the reason my da was not close to me was because he was close to someone else. It's September 2000, and I'm sitting at home in Dublin when Norman calls out of the blue.

"I've some family news. You'll never guess what I'm about to tell you."

"That our cousin is our brother?" I interrupt. "Scott Rankin."

Where did that answer come from? Somewhere in my subconscious, the news that Norman was about to tell me must not have been news to me. He is incredulous.

"How did you know what I was going to tell you?"

"Middle-child syndrome," I suggest, reading his response as confirmation that I had just become a middle child.

Such intuition is, I know, eccentric. Even more unusual, I was not perplexed.

Strangely, it was as if I felt better about an ache I didn't know I'd had.

My cousin Scott was always close to us, and at times both his brothers, Adam and Michael, felt like our brothers. After Iris died, their family kind of took me in. We all knew that my father and my auntie Barbara had been close, but Iris and Jack were sister and brother so not that unusual for their spouses to be. We were a close family, and we'd never witnessed more than friendship. But maybe, just maybe, something had permeated my prepubescent brain. Norman's call is not a shock, but it is a revelation. I have to think it through, and my mind goes back to that caravan in Rush, those balmy summer nights and days. The animated conversations.

Scott was born when I was eleven, three years before Iris, my mother, died. Iris never knew the truth. Bob, her husband and my father, said nothing to anyone, nor did Barbara, Scott's mother. For three decades only the two of them knew. When Jack, Scott's father, was eventually told, he and Barbara stayed together, and he continued to be the loving father to Scott he'd always been.

Since this disclosure Scott and I have become even closer. He's smart, sincere. At peace with his past and present. He told me lately that he doesn't want to be part of any fabrication of facts for his children or by them. He wants his kids to be comfortable with their dual Rankin/Hewson identity. I now honor that. It's probably much harder for Scott and his family having a noisy name attached to their quiet one. I know his discretion had him protect my family's privacy as much as his own, which was hard at times.

Families and our secrets. Is there a family without any?

This news fills my mind for days, and I begin to wonder. Was this at the heart of my aggression with my father? Maybe it wasn't his lack of interest that had set me off. Maybe it was a sense of diminishment of my mother. Could this explain some of my rage? My mother had no choice in her departure from my life. With this revelation about Scott suddenly I understand that my da had this other life that I wasn't in. So that's where he was. To be physically present in any relationship is not everything. Emotional proximity is. I was starting to understand that this man wasn't with me growing up, even when he was.

I needed him to answer one question. I also needed some courage to ask it. I drove across the city to his apartment in Howth, overlooking the beach where Iris had swum as a child. He was weak and his eyes were a little red as he stared out to the sea.

"Did you love our mother?"

"Of course I loved your mother. Things happen."

I asked him again. "Did you love her?"

"Yes. I loved your mother."

In that moment I knew he was being truthful.

Finding out that Norman is not my only brother, that now Scott is, too, forces me to ask myself what a family is, who my other brothers have been. The ones I found after my mother died, when my own family became lost to me.

Family has always been at the center of who I am. I have attempted several surrogates since Iris passed. Families I found to join . . . or founded to join. It started in my teens on Cedarwood Road with surreal street gangs like Lypton Village, and it continued at school,

Mount Temple, when I joined U2, this family I found in Larry's kitchen in 1976.

I found another one around about the same time, when I was sixteen and Ali's father and mother let me into their family knowing I really needed one. Later, after all our success, maybe I was looking for it again in the world of activism and politics. Looking to be needed.

SCENE 4: ONSTAGE, BERLIN, NOVEMBER 2018

It's the last night of singing our songs of innocence and experience. We're in Berlin, playing a song called "Acrobat" on the circular stage, and it is an acrobatic feat that I am witnessing. Four men dressed as street performers on the high wire. Not falling off, walking across it, dancing on the pinhead of gravity. We are high on a song we haven't played in twenty years—it is so difficult to play—but tonight Edge is "shredding," as they say in guitar magazines, his cream Les Paul. The Zen Presbyterian now as High Mass as Halloween. A whirling dervish in some kind of guitar exorcism, expelling the devil from me in the stage drama where I have blacked-out voodoo eyes. Releasing the bat in all our hells.

I look at Larry, who has become the drummer that his father always wanted him to be. A true jazzman, leaving far behind anyone's expectations except his own. I watch him rolling around the top of his kit no longer a student, a master, his sticks slapping the skins and snapping the snares as if he were Buddy Rich or some Be Bop Irishman out of the 1950s. He has become Larry Mullen "Jr.," surely the name of a jazzman, a nod to another era when being junior meant there was a senior. Meant you had a father. You had lineage. The quotation marks around "Jr." were an ironic dig at jazz from us punks. I always look forward to the moment of heraldry in the show when I can hail, "On the drums, Larry Mullen Jr." The crowd roars, but tonight I don't hear them, I'm in a trance where the high-decibel scream is sucked into silence.

I can't hear anything. All is quiet. All gone. The crowd disappeared like time, just the four of us left onstage.

It's just me thanking Larry not only for excelling himself but for asking me to be in his band. I'm back in the red corridor in Mr. McKenzie's music room in Mount Temple Comprehensive watching the not-as-shy-as-anyone-thinks kid reveal a wide smile of gratitude that he's found some people to play the drums with. That's all he wanted.

In the yellow corridor I see Adam Clayton with his Afro of strawberry-blond curls, his afghan coat over his Pakistan '76 T-shirt. The greatest bluff in an era of so many was no bluff at all. A century later the boy with no plan B, the teenager with no idea in his head other than four strings are better than six, is now in complete control of his bass and his life. Adam Clayton Superstar is exactly the same as he ever was and entirely different. Yes, he is flirting with every woman he can meet eyes with from the stage, but now he has a wife and two children and so much more wisdom than the knowledge of the world he once sought. I introduce him as a luxury good, tease him for teasing our female audience, but I am in awe of how far we have traveled. Maybe Adam has traveled the greatest distance from the clichéd corpse he could have been to the no-cliché-at-all life force that he has become.

As the guitar solo crescendoes, here's *The* Edge, this singular talent and freak of nature, still ringing those bell-like harmonics that he made famous on our first single. I see him earlier still, at fifteen, sitting in the green corridor in the new breeze-block building, guitar in hand, plucking the sounds from his favorite LP, *Close to the Edge,* by the prog rockers Yes. The boy who would buy a guitar the same shape as his head, the could-be code writer and code breaker who became the programmer of hearts and minds. "Edge is from the future," I am about to tell everyone, as I often do, "and he says it's better there." But in this moment I'm having, there is no everyone. It's just the four of us in the music room in Mount Temple, and this Edge is from the past. I tell him that the three of us owe so much of our present to him, to the hours and days, the months and years of staying in his bedroom and getting it done. The cruelty of genius that so often doesn't come in a flash.

The time it takes to stop time. To squeeze the eternal out of the instant. The time it takes to stretch time. Now, time has vanished, and everyone with it. I'm standing in the middle of this great arena at the end of a circular stage, and all I'm thinking about is the start and the end of this band called U2. Us four.

There's a phrase we've used touring these songs of innocence and experience: "Wisdom is the recovery of innocence at the far end of experience."

What have I found here at the far end of experience? Gratitude.

In my case, to be alive. One year, eleven months, and five days since I was in the operating room in Mount Sinai hospital.

You're never more alive than when you nearly weren't. Now you see things with a new clarity.

For example, I now know that this band is not a collection of songs. It's more like a single song, an unfinished song. It's why we keep returning to rehearsal room, to studio, to stage, to try to finish this song, to complete U2. Perhaps ever since we started this band, we have been trying to finish it, to complete it. This song that has become our life. To be released from it. This must be it. As good as it gets.

Are we complete? Are we done? I am grateful.

I hear the words I have offered our fans most nights of our life onstage, but now I'm speaking to my brothers, these fellow travelers who had no idea when we first met what kind of road we'd be taking. Thank you for giving me a great life. Thank you for letting me be in your band. Thank you for letting me harass you and hector you, push you and pull you.

Inspire and disappoint you.

Tears are streaking down my clown face. They are not tears of joy.

I find myself apologizing for using a little too much force in the pursuit of liftoff. In the gathering of their best selves, I might not have always been at my best, but if this is the end, so be it. At the peak of our accomplishment I wonder if we have run out of road, run out of reasons to share the road together.

Why am I thinking this?

Are we still an unfinished song? What if the song is complete? It is not an unreasonable question.

Plus, there is a cost to this on everyone's nervous system. And it gets more expensive the older you become, the longer you're together.

For a lot of people, certainly a lot of performers, there is a degree of bullshit required just to get out of bed in the morning and get dressed. Facing the day is hard enough without having to face yourself. Or worse still, face those three other selves who can see right through your bullshit. If the person you are telling yourself you are doesn't ring true with the person your band knows you to be, you are most likely "on one." The snake or lizard is allowed the metamorphosis, but these beloved brothers are walking around and over the skin you've shed. They may be delighted you've shed your origin story, but they know what it is. And if you can't live with that, maybe it's time to look for the door.

Why do bands stay together?

We hear rumors of bands who barely speak any longer, whose most intimate meeting is onstage or in the accountant's office. Are the financial rewards really worth that sinking feeling? We understand a band is a family business, that it's putting food on a lot of tables, that sometimes this means certain behaviors are given a wide berth. And also that a family business may be the greatest of endeavors because a family is the place where you are free from self-consciousness, where you can be yourself in all your different colors and moods. Family is where you can be fearless. Maybe, at its best, it's a place where "perfect love drives out all fear."

So why am I looking around at my friends on this stage thinking these thoughts? It's not as if we haven't thought about it before. We break up all the time, after tours or albums where we have had to stretch a little too far. The best albums are often the hardest to complete. The best songs are often the most costly because four creative people are fighting for them. Fighting in a family can leave scar tissue, but sometimes it's when you stop fighting that you stop functioning.

The writer Jon Pareles once asked us if it was real respect for each other that had us so decorous in our relationships, or if it was prison etiquette. The fear of a knife fight with someone else in close confinement. Next question, please.

I've tried to be honest in these pages while respecting the perspective of these three people I love and work with. We've never been critical of each other in public, but it's no criticism to say we've sometimes run out of love. It happens. The well of friendship can run dry in a family, a marriage, a community, a band.

A good strategy for me is to continually go back to the source. To drop my bucket in the well in hope of a refill. Why am I always talking about the scriptures? Because they sustained me in the most difficult years in the band and they remain a plumb line to gauge how crooked the wall of my ego has become. To getting the measure of myself. This is where I find the inspiration to carry on. The exhortation that makes this struggle with the self workable. The wisdom that makes it doable.

I return to a spiritual master like the apostle Paul, way back in the first century of the modern era. I go to someone who overcame himself.

SCENE 5: THE JOURNEY INTO BEING STILL

I have so much to learn from this ancient writer. How does someone who first shows up as a monumental pain-in-the-arse fundamentalist become someone who can write the greatest ode to love in two thousand years? Somewhere on his spiritual path he discovers love is bigger than anything in its way. That "no matter what I say, what I believe, and what I do, I'm bankrupt without love."

> *Love never gives up.*
> *Love cares more for others than for self.*
> *Love doesn't want what it doesn't have.*
> *Love doesn't strut,*
> *Doesn't have a swelled head,*
> *Doesn't force itself on others,*
> *Isn't always "me first,"*
> *Doesn't fly off the handle,*
> *Doesn't keep score of the sins of others,*
> *Doesn't revel when others grovel,*
> *Takes pleasure in the flowering of truth,*
> *Puts up with anything,*
> *Trusts God always,*
> *Always looks for the best,*
> *Never looks back,*
> *But keeps going to the end.*

> —St. Paul, 1 Corinthians 13, *The Message*

This zealot scholar who ended up a traveling tent maker, paying his passage with manual labor. Who faced jail and death for his beliefs and learned that love is not sentimental but tough, that it's about speaking hard truths to power or hard truths to yourself. The man who fell off his horse on the road to Damascus to begin the most important journey of them all. The journey into being still. The vast distance from talking to listening.

The man who first appeared a contemptible human being is now transformed into the teacher who finds comfort in chaos and peace in conflict. It's while incarcerated for his beliefs that he writes some of literature's greatest explorations of love. This is a spiritual maturity that feels so far out of reach for me. If I think clearly in emergencies, in conflict I so often resort to fight or flight. So often I'm right back on Cedarwood Road, with my fists in the air.

But if my faith is a crutch, I want to throw it away. I'd rather fall over. I remain more suspicious of religion than most people who'd never darken the door of a church. I've never quite found a church I could call home, and I tell the kids to be wary of religion, that what the human spirit longs for may not be corralled by any sect or denomination, contained by a building. It's more likely a daily discipline, a daily surrender and rebirth. It's more likely that church is not a place but a practice, and the practice becomes the place. There is no promised land. Only the promised journey, the pilgrimage. We search through the noise for signal, and we learn to ask better questions of ourselves and each other.

I call the signal "God" and search my life for clues that betray the location of the eternal presence. For starters we look to who is standing beside us or down the road, the ones whose roof we share or the ones around the corner who have no roof. The mystics tell us God is present in the present, what Dr. King described as "the fierce urgency of now."

God is present in the love between us. In a crowd. In a band.

In a marriage.

In the way we meet the world.

God is present in love expressed as action.

I sang the statement "I still haven't found what I'm looking for" as a question when I was twenty-seven. But in trying to make peace with my own uncertainty, I grew to be certain in one regard. That whatever our instincts or ideas about the great mysterious He or She or They, whatever the differences of the great faith traditions, they find common ground in one place: among the poor and vulnerable is where the signal is strongest.

So where is God?

Well, while I hope God is with those of us who live such comfortable lives, I *know* God is with the poorest and most vulnerable. In the slums and cardboard boxes where the poor have to play house. In the doorways as we step over the divine on our way to work. In the silence of a mother who has unknowingly infected her child with a virus that will end both their lives. God is in the cries heard under the rubble of war, in the bare hands digging for air. God is with the terrorized. At sea with the desperate, clinging onto drowning dreams. God is with the refugee. I hear his only son was one. God is with the poor and the vulnerable, and God is with us if we are with them.

They say you choose your friends but not your family; maybe they're still doing the research on how this works with a band. Maybe the music chooses us.

But with this band I heard the signal, and now I'm hearing it onstage in Berlin. This wave of sound we all find ourselves in, and it's what I hoped for as I walked out onstage in the early pages of this story, how, even more than the music, perhaps our friendship itself is some kind of sacrament. This alchemy that turns the base metal of individual talent into the gold fever that makes a good band great.

I think of Joey Ramone and a song we wrote for his band, for their beautiful sound that sent us out on this pilgrimage that we still find ourselves on. How "I woke up at the moment when the miracle occurred / Heard a song that made some sense out of the world."

That signal.

> *If you listen you can hear the silence say*
> *"When you think you're done, you've just begun"*
> *Love is bigger than anything in its way.*

And as I sing, I am reaching out my arms into the night, stretching to grasp hold of another hand.

at the moment of
surrender
I folded to my knees
I did not notice
the passers by
and they
did not
notice me

38

Moment of Surrender

I was speeding on the subway
Through the stations of the cross
Every eye looking every other way
Counting down 'til the pentecost

At the moment of surrender
Of vision over visibility
I did not notice the passers-by
And they did not notice me.

I'm under the table, holding Ali's hand, in one of our favorite restaurants. La Petite Maison, in the old town of Nice. We often bring friends here, and some are with us now. Also under the table. Along with Ali and our eldest child, Jordan, we're with Anton Corbijn, all six feet four of him—how did he fit under here?—his partner, the clothes designer Nimi, and also Nonie and Miki, who live with us. And Emmanuelle, my assistant. We're comforting Theo, a little boy, who in turn is comforting his mother, who can't speak.

I've never really liked fireworks. The sky exploding with a riot of color, the "oohs" and "aahs" at those supernova Roman candles. Today, it's Bastille Day and France gets to celebrate and to be celebrated. The storming of the Bastille, the seizing of power. The

French are good at riots and revolutions; they sort of invented them. Bastille Day is a big night out on the Promenade des Anglais, where the French get to blow up the sky and remind the world that France's citizens are royal and allowed a little pomp. I'm told that if you've been under siege in war, the flares and phosphorous of fireworks are chillingly familiar. The instant before the death and destruction.

Less than an hour earlier on this July evening in 2016, I'd turned to Ali on the promenade and whispered, "If everyone has seen enough, maybe we should head to the restaurant?" Five minutes later we're outside La Petite Maison, en route bumping into the city's "green mayor," Christian Estrosi. We're chatting about the tramline he wants to build along the coast when a police car, at high speed, reverses toward us up a side street. Estrosi is whisked away on some emergency, without so much as an "au revoir." Wondering what that was all about, we notice the rising crescendo of screaming and shouting. A stampede is charging our way, from where we were just standing, along the route we just walked. We're in the midst of something singularly disquieting. Fight and flight. We can feel terror. I grab the family and push them inside through a half-open window.

"Everyone, get under the tables!"

I'm shouting at the clientele, ridiculous as it feels. Do Irish people know stuff like this? And now we're under the tables, because if explosions follow, the windows will shatter. Theo's mother is hyperventilating, and he pats her on the head.

"Mama, Mama, it will be okay. Don't worry."

The staff close the shutters and get out of sight, and we wait. We don't know that just up from where we'd been watching those fireworks, a thirty-one-year-old Tunisian has driven a lorry into the crowds. We don't know that eighty-six lives will be lost and that this is a terrorist attack. We don't know if terror remains on the loose. We do know not to panic. Nonie, a chef, says, "Shall I go to the kitchen and see what I can find to distract the little boy? Maybe some ice cream."

My mind takes me back to Paris, eight months earlier. Friday, November 13. A day off between four shows. We're at the arena, rehearsing a section about migrants crossing into Europe, when, without warning, everything is shut down and we're pulled offstage. Paris is under terrorist attack and music venues are being targeted. An attack is under way right now at the Bataclan theater during a show by Eagles of Death Metal, a band we know through the drummer Josh Homme. Back at our hotel, everyone gathering in my room, the shutters are down as we hear live rounds being fired, a sound I will never unhear. The news reports the butchering of music fans, of attacks taking place at other nightspots and at the Stade de France, during a football match. No one says what we're all thinking. This could have been our audience.

Next day I found a number for Jesse Hughes, the singer in Eagles of Death Metal, and called to see if we could help. Jesse was in shock, probably PTSD. He kept calling me "sir." The police had kept the band in for questioning. The venue was a live crime scene. He explained how he'd survived. While he and his girlfriend were fleeing down a backstage corridor, an assailant's rifle had locked as both were about to be gunned down. The moment the rifle froze was the time they needed to escape.

"I know how these weapons work, sir. I grew up around guns."

"Jesse. You don't have to keep calling me 'sir.'"

"Yes, sir. I understand that, sir. But I need you to know that I know the sound of firearms and I knew I could count the rounds and I knew when we'd have a break, when they were changing mags. It was a slaughterhouse, sir. I can't believe I'm alive."

He stopped talking, and I heard him weeping.

This is all going through my mind as we wait under the tables of La Petite Maison. At first I'd thought this was new, terror making a target of musicians and fans. But I'm reminded of another massacre, when I was a teenager. The Ulster Volunteer Force murdering members of the Miami Showband as they traveled back to Dublin after a show in Banbridge. I'm taken back to another day of carnage when I was fourteen, when I didn't take the bus to school, when Guggi's da and his brother Andrew Guck Pants Delaney Rowen were caught up in the terror. Under the tables the little boy has calmed his mum, and our friend Serge Pactus gets us a message that outside are a group of French soldiers who can get us all to safety if we leave La Petite Maison.

The soldiers look frightened. Not sure of who or where the enemy is. "Put your hands over your heads!"

The order is screamed at us, and we walk across the old square, our hands reaching to the sky in surrender.

INFINITY IS A GREAT PLACE TO START

"'Surrender' might be the most powerful word in the lexicon," suggests Brian Eno as we discuss heady stuff like the photography of Sugimoto and how tricky it is to cook risotto. I am persuaded by the thought that the only true way to be victorious is to surrender. To each other. To love. To the higher power.

These are the kinds of conversations you can have with Brian Eno and not feel pretentious. We are talking about calling the band's new album *No Line on the Horizon* and thinking that the Japanese artist would be perfect to contribute album artwork.

"Those seascapes of his are something you could stare at forever."

At home I love staring out across Killiney Bay when there's just enough mist to blur the separation of sky and sea, when you feel as if you catch a glimpse of infinity. Infinity in my case is often a religious pursuit, but, hey, we're trying to keep it sexy on the new album, so I try the old favorite, comparing the sea to a woman.

> *I know a girl who's like the sea*
> *I watch her changing every day for me, oh yeah*
> *One day she's still, the next she swells*
> *You can hear the universe in her sea shells, oh yeah*
>
> *No, no line on the horizon, no, no line*
>
> *I know a girl, a hole in her heart*
> *She said infinity is a great place to start.*
>
> —"No Line on the Horizon"

We're in the ancient walled city of Fez, Morocco, in 2007, where the four of us with Brian and Danny have set up a studio. Brian's talking about how in sacred songs the singer has to surrender their self, let themselves be taken over by whatever it is they worship.

Islam has sometimes been translated as "surrender." Like Christianity, like Judaism, like so many great faiths, Islam has been appropriated, recommodified, and sometimes disfigured. What kind of distortion is it that suggests a religion that purports to serve God can hate women or hate music? It was the turn to Islam that led Cat Stevens, one of my favorite singers as a teenager, to turn from music. Later, post-9/11 and now Yusuf Islam, he gave up on that stance to try to remind people that though Islam may be uncomfortable with aspects of modernity, it is not a hostile force in the world. At its heart is service to community above the individual. Islam. *Salām* or salaam.

Arabic for peace.

Peace through surrender.

Surrender is an idea at the heart of many great faiths. "Not my will but thy will," as Jesus prayed on the night the Roman soldiers came for him.

PILGRIMAGE TO FEZ

We'd set up in a small *riad,* using the open courtyard to record, writing and playing our new songs under a square of sky, framed by the roofs. Birds flecking the bright geometry above, their full-throated song more effortless than ours. At times their boisterous improvisation was a little annoying, but still they made it onto some of the final tracks. In the Moroccan nights, the square of sky over our courtyard would mesmerize me as it turned from turquoise to cobalt to sapphire and finally this most viscous black, studded with silver stars.

I'm drawn to the graphic power in the North African landscape, the geometry of architecture and design that feels both ancient and modern. It was the people of Arabia who brought the world mathematics, their algebra still fascinating to me as pure shape, quite apart from the human yearning to understand quantity, form, measure, the lunar cycle. Sitting at a chessboard, I think of the Arabs who conquered Persia and brought this game to us Europeans. Taking chance out of strategy is what all three Abrahamic religions hold in common. The Arab world fascinates me, and fascination has brought me everywhere.

We'd been invited to the Fez Festival of World Sacred Music, a place to hear the devotional singers of Jewish, Islamic, and Hindu traditions, and now we were on a pilgrimage to this city that is holy for musicians. It was inspirational to walk through the narrow streets and souks of the medina, to enjoy the religious inquiry of a city that still has a synagogue along with Christian churches of all inclinations. Not only does it feel as though tolerance has been enshrined, but I sensed a respect for religious tangents, the lens of the Sufi or the Cabalist. We recorded with local musicians, including an oud player and master percussionists from the Gnawa and Sufi traditions.

In this beautiful city that celebrates diversity in the middle of the Muslim world, I'm sitting under a great tree with Larry, Adam, Edge, Brian, and Danny. We're watching the great Sufi singer Parisa and her voice—the ululation, the heart cry—is the same as mine. But the skills, the ability, the agility are at a higher level than mine. But I know that's where I want to go now. That I want to master my own singing instrument to allow me not just to praise God, but to sing for my wife, to sing for our children, to sing for our audience, to sing my life. Music offers a language to a part of us we weren't sure was there . . . our spirit, our essence, whatever it is, it's beyond our mind and body, it's the something other.

To be a nerd for a minute, I can sense a kind of genomic connection between the musical cultures in Morocco and Ireland, the pentatonic scales, the natural gift of the singers. In the 1980s musicologists and musos had trailed Irish melodies all the way back to the Levant.

Fascination brought the Arabs to Ireland. And the Irish to North Africa.

SING YOURSELF RIGHT OFF YOUR FEET

Sing yourself on down the street
Sing yourself right off your feet

Sing yourself away from victory and from defeat
Sing yourself with fife and drum
Sing yourself to overcome
The thought that someone's lost
And someone else has won.

—"Soon"

Singing erupts from somewhere we don't understand and communicates with a part of us we can't otherwise reach. Though it unlocks emotion, it seems to break into feelings deeper than the obvious. In my notebook I jot down, "Some people sing for a living / some people sing to survive / I sing cause I don't want to be alone tonight."

Working with Danny and Brian in this ancient setting proves fertile, and among the songs that emerge, one is named "Moment of Surrender." Danny encourages us to play in a circle, and inspired by Parisa, I'm experimenting with different sides of my voice, and as I push myself into new territory, I find new characters to explore. This song is a melodrama, a modern opera, drawn from some emotional photography I'd snapped and stored. The most dramatic image is a grown man falling to his knees in a busy street. Weeping and wailing. His moment of surrender. Adam tells me that in AA meetings they call it bottoming out: you're robbing your own bank, and you haven't enough gas for the getaway car. Kaput. Rock bottom. End of the road.

I drew scenes like a movie: a wedding where the couple were high; a subway ride to score the drugs; a scene at the ATM machine.

The recording of the song came out of the blue, just when none of us were expecting it. Brian was playing with a "camel" loop, an off-center rhythmic motif that runs through the track and which he hadn't anticipated would work for us. But then Larry started drumming over the loop, Brian came up with a harmonium/church organ sound, and when I came in with the vocal, it felt as if something special was arriving. Brian told me afterward he "got the shivers" and nearly forgot he was playing. He didn't, though, and his memory is vivid: "I think that was the most intense experience I ever had in a studio. I have no idea how long it lasted. Could have been half an hour or all day. I was in the zone, in flow state, and for one of the few times in my life I knew exactly what I should be doing."

———

The moment of surrender is the moment you choose to lose control of your life, the split second of powerlessness where you trust that some kind of "higher power" better be in charge, because you certainly aren't.

Since 1998, when Adam checked himself into the Priory in London, a clinic specializing in addiction issues, I've had the honor of watching "surrender" work through this man's remarkable life and times. I've watched this most elusive word become flesh in a series of good decisions that gave Adam back his life, so much so that at fifty he was able to surrender not just to his higher power but also to the earthly power that is Mariana Teixeira De Carvalho, a brilliant and beautiful Brazilian human rights lawyer whom he met through their mutual love for art.

Adam's long obedience in the same direction now looks like a road that could only have brought him to her door; they are such a perfect destination for each other. Have I seen this man as happy as I see him on our last tour, chasing his new daughter, Alba, down the aisle of the plane, laughing uncontrollably as she chases him back up toward the cockpit? I see him strapping her in before we land, a metaphor inviting a writer on.

The moment of lift.

The moment of landing. I've had these moments. But also others.

Sinking moments, when I feel as if I were drowning, or about to be dragged under by someone who is. Rescuers so often think they are doing the saving when really *we* are the ones who need to be saved.

"Not waving but drowning," as Stevie Smith wrote.

These struggles are not related to the usual addictions, to drink or drugs, and I ask myself if I have another kind of compulsion. I am drawn to the difficult, the extreme challenge. I am drawn to the Everest. I see a summit and am compelled to figure a way to climb it. A high. What kind of addiction is this? To climb the mountain that is your own ego.

The plus side of these absurd explorations, mountaintop or diving bell, is in pushing at the limits of my potential. And then there's the downside. Living on my nerves, getting on other people's. Believing

I can breathe underwater . . . and when I surface too quickly and cannot brush off the bends, I will still want to go one step higher. Take one more gulp of salt water.

And yes, Dear Reader, I will want everyone to come with me.

"U2 can happen to anyone" was the slogan on our first button badge in 1978. I believed it, and it came true. I claimed to be a singer long before I knew how to sing. A songwriter long before I could play an instrument. A performer who so resented how the stage kept me from our audience that I told myself I could leap the divide. And when I jumped off the stage during a show, I never doubted someone would be there to catch me. Our audience, this higher power. A "busload of faith to get by," as Lou Reed put it.

The impossible happened for us, so was that what led me to become intoxicated by the impossible lift and the dangerous dive? This mission to deliver on my teenage conviction that such providence is there for everyone. But as I get older, I see the danger in this desperate desire to get out of my depth. Slowly, reluctantly, I am learning to let go. Because if you do, then that may be the very moment when you discover that your spiritual potential lies not in what you have, but in what you have not. That the trouble or torment, the weights you cannot carry, that these may carry you. Your afflictions and addictions are some kind of gift. They brought you to the empty place that you are compelled to fill. You almost want to thank them.

For example, the need to be loved at scale.

To have all these people every night screaming your name to feel normal is of course a little pathetic. But the best performers need their audience much more than their audience needs them. A crowd can feel that.

THE MELODY THAT FINDS YOU

Some people see a picture. Some hear a voice. Some repeat a prayer or mantra. Me? I have heard a melody that even now can soothe my soul if I'm disquieted. I don't know how I came across it, perhaps

I first heard it when I was nine or ten, a piece for a boy soprano. I know I learned it long before my voice broke. It's a melody put to the words of the Lord's Prayer.

"Our Father, who art in heaven, Hallowed be thy name."

On restless nights when sleep eludes me, I sing it in my head. In those moments when I feel lost, this melody finds me. It takes me beyond concept or idea, beyond the theory of a higher power. The melody brings me to a name, and for a split second I am named by this name. I discover who I am. I sense my original identity, my real self behind whatever masks I am wearing to cover up fear of abandonment or loneliness. The masks of a performer who's long believed that his insecurity has been his best security. The masks of being a star when there's no light left in you. The collapsed ego when you realize you are not the center of any universe, not even your own. The mask that falls off your face when you're over being stared at. Or admired. That now reveals the self-loathing that follows self-aggrandizement. The mask that eats your face, as John Updike wrote about fame.

The moment may not be dramatic. It may be the imperceptible snowmelt, the faintest possibility of spring. Like the author C. S. Lewis, sitting on the top deck of a bus in Oxford, England, and feeling as if he were "a man of snow at long last beginning to melt."

For me this process of discovery is a continuum of dripping. Miniature moments of revelation and realization. But when I find myself asking the deepest of questions about existence, mine and those I love, my breath elongating, the intimate sense of something "other," I know it's okay. That sometimes life needs to speak to us. A heart murmur that crescendoes, then fades.

All my life I've had these epiphanies, but the one that holds me now as I enter the third act of this life is not so comforting. It challenges me to overcome myself, to get beyond who I have been, to renew myself. I'm not sure I can make it. I doubt myself.

Carl Jung observed that the very things that made you successful in the first half of your life not only no longer work for you in the second half; they positively work against you. The Franciscan friar Richard Rohr put it to me like this: "It's our strengths rather than our weaknesses that often hold us back."

———

Service, ambition, duty, loyalty, the desire to be the best, the desire to say yes—not such bad character traits to have cherished. I always thought of them as strengths, but lately I wonder if somewhere along the line they became a cover for something more suspicious. The demand to be at the center of the action. To make God in our own image, to help her across the road as if she were a little old lady. This perpetual longing to be filled with the extraordinary so that you begin to lose appreciation for the ordinary.

If your shoulder is black and blue from trying to enter every locked room, maybe there are rooms you do not need to enter. Or maybe some doors have a key in the lock that will gently turn. This long struggle for art, for justice, for self-aggrandizement. All this ambition, all this ego. Are these goals fired by the engine of a sense of duty or of a swollen sense of self?

So often the fight is not with the world but with yourself.

I was always fascinated by the story of Elijah, who is told to wait on the voice of God in a cave on a hillside. There he was, waiting for the earth to shake, and shake it did, but it did not offer up a word. Neither did the melodrama of the celestial fires or cyclone offer any clues. When it arrived, the divine communication was such a whisper that Elijah almost didn't recognize it. In one translation it is described as "the still small voice"; in another it is translated as "the sound of silence."

Maybe Paul Simon heard it too:

> And the sign said "The words of the prophets
> Are written on the subway walls
> And tenement halls
> And whispered in the sounds of silence"

—"The Sound of Silence"

A call to shut up and listen is not what I want to hear. "Be still" is hardly an epiphany. But "Be still" is all I hear from the silence. I was hoping for something a little more rock 'n' roll.

"Surrender" might be the most powerful word in the world, but now I'm caught between the life I know and the one I don't. Can I just take a walk on Killiney Hill with my best friend, who happens to be my wife, and sit on that wooden seat that overlooks the bay and not check the phone to see what's going on somewhere else in the world?

Can I take in the view without having to be in it? Can I not take that call, in favor of this other call, to stillness? Is this what vision over visibility looks like now? I bow to no one in my love and respect for Leonard Cohen, but I can't see myself following him up that mountain on his Zen retreat. I'm not sure I'm made to climb that hill. But then the drip, drip, drip. I hear the words of another Sufi, the poet Rumi.

> Out beyond ideas of wrongdoing and rightdoing,
> there is a field. I'll meet you there.
>
> When the soul lies down in that grass,
> the world is too full to talk about.

Maybe I'm discovering surrender doesn't always have to follow defeat and may be all the fuller after victory. When you've won the argument you now understand you never needed to have. The argument with your life that's no longer necessary.

THE POWER TO DREAM

We went back to Paris, to play the shows canceled by the terrorist attacks, and Eagles of Death Metal returned with us, facing down their fears. At the end of our set, we handed over our stage and instruments to them so that rock 'n' roll, in their voice, not ours, would have its say.

"Is everyone here having a good time? Can I hear you? I said, Is everyone here having a good time?"

Overwhelming. That's what it feels like on the side of the stage, watching Jesse Hughes in his white calico suit back in front of his band and getting all rock 'n' roll on twenty thousand Parisians. These utterances now transformed into touching sentiment.

"You're beautiful," he says to the crowd. "You really are beautiful."

He's right, they are beautiful. And so is he. As we all perform Patti Smith's "People Have the Power," Paris is lifting us, and the healing power of the song is clear. It reminds us all why we're here, of the vision a great song can hold.

> *I was dreaming in my dreaming*
> *Of an aspect bright and fair*
> *And my sleeping it was broken*
> *But my dream it lingered near*
> *In the form of shining valleys*
> *Where the pure air recognized*
> *And my senses newly opened*
> *I awakened to the cry*
> *That the people have the power*
> *To redeem the work of fools*
> *Upon the meek the graces shower*
> *It's decreed the people rule*
> *The people have the power*
> *The people have the power*

The previous night Patti herself had closed out the show with us, another surprise, like a dove released, walking onstage to an ovation in a country where she has never lived but has always been beloved. Singing with Patti, I'm conscious that she is one of those spirit guides I cherish. Her first album, *Horses*, gave us a chance to express our faith as doubt. "Jesus died for somebody's sins but not mine." This voice coming to me in my early twenties, showing me that you could have visions, that you could sing about them. *Radio Ethiopia* and that voice pointed me to that place. On *Wave*, she speaks to the pope in a vision, while the fiery prayers of *Easter* in 1978, this reverent irreverence, were everything I wanted. The way she allowed her religiosity to flow through would shape the way I see music.

She is sixty-eight now, elegant and feral in the same moment, jumping out of her skin. I'm watching the singer not just serve the song but become the song. It's transformational to witness, and even more so to have experienced it as a singer myself.

Why would I want to do anything else with my life?

What would Edge, Adam, and Larry do with their lives? More to the point, what would I do without them?

It's healthy to question why anyone should still be listening to us as a band. Asking if our song is complete. In this moment I am questioning this question.

Now I find myself wishing away the freedom to be anything other than the singer and the song. This image of the singer becoming the song is not one I am growing away from. It is one I am growing toward. I want to be free to do only this. Patti Smith has served words and melody, and I notice that I am jealous of her singularity and purpose.

> I believe everything we dream
> Can come to pass through our union
> We can turn the world around
> We can turn the earth's revolution
> We have the power
> People have the power

So many of the characters I wish to inhabit come together in Patti Smith: the poet, the seer, the spitting-venom punk rocker, the revelry and reverie, the animal-like physicality, the howling voice, the prayerful hush, the reverence for the sacrament of music.

Above all the pilgrim. Leaving home to find home. How far am I from home?

Every wave that broke me
Every song that wrote me
Every dawn that woke me
was to get me home to you, see
every soul that left me
Every heart that kept me
the strangers that protected me
to bring me home to you
Every magic potion
Every false emotion
How unswerving our devotion
to the lies we know are almost true
Every sweet confusion
Every grand illusion
I will win and call it losing
if the prize is not for you

39

Landlady

Roam, the phone is where I live till I get home
And when the doorbell rings
You tell me that I have a key
I ask you, how you know it's me?

The road, no road without a turn
And if there was, the road would be too long
What keeps us standing in this view
Is the view that we can be brand new.

It's two days after the Paris show. I took a dive into sleep five hours earlier, round about one a.m., and now it's six and I'm swimming in the clean sheets of my own bed in Temple Hill in the town I grew up in.

Our bed is a large bed at the top of a house on the side of a hill over a beach where we have lived for over thirty years. It's a bed big enough to fit a whole family, and there have been many times when all six of us have been in the bed to watch a movie or talk something through but not now. The only conversation now is with myself and my Maker.

There is a cold breeze waiting if I was mad enough to stick my head out of the duvet, but I'm not.

I'm in a conversation that's actually long overdue.

It's not in silence.

I can hear Ali breathing, and even with my ears dulled by the roar of the crowd and the noise that comes with putting up and pulling down a rock 'n' roll show, this is better than silence.

This is a meditation on tiny things.

The noise of the tour and its kinetic energy now replaced with the soft crashing of waves on Killiney beach and the murmurings of the woman I have loved since we were teenagers.

Normally, if I can, I get up before anyone else, especially if I'm just back from tour. Johnny Cash used to say that the best feeling in the world was walking in your backyard in your bare feet! For me it's walking through my own house in the dark in my bare feet, stopping in each room, whether they're empty or full, just to feel the room and, I guess, my own absence.

Often, if not always, it is a prayerful moment when I give thanks for shelter. Many's the time over the years that I've walked into the kids' bedrooms and just stared at them sleeping, watching them for ages, whispered prayers over their sleeping heads, prayers for their potential, their future, prayers for their future partners, but not this morning.

This morning I don't move from the bed. I let my mind stretch out, not to where I've been, but to where I am. The bashing and bruising a front man takes in throwing himself at twenty thousand people can have me awake in the night with an "Agh, no! Fuuuuuck! Why did I do that to myself!"

And there are other self-inflicted wounds that will wake me, but they all subside in this twilight moment before morning. I am not in a rush to proper consciousness, but I am awake on another level, more awake than I have ever been in my life.

I stretch out my body and feel every inch of myself alive. My fingers, my toes, my neck, my torso. At this moment my aching frame is aching with aliveness.

I reach out for you, the reason I have stepped back from so many precipices . . . you, the woman I met as a girl in Mount Temple, wearing a tartan skirt, saffron woolly jumper, and Wellingtons.

I feel your outline, but I want to see it.

———

I reach for my phone, which is always on but always on silent, and I use the light to stare at your face, and when you unconsciously turn away from that light, soft as it is, my eyes hover over you, blinking at all your different selves, the finite to the infinite. You are lying sideways. I can see the cowlick of your hairline and brow. I can see into those closed eyes that suggest so much, and I sense, too, that there is so much more for us and I thank you and I thank our Maker and I thank the whole universe . . .

that the reason I set out on this adventure

the reason I have sojourned with such extraordinary company for over forty years

the reason for all this wandering in what has mostly been a wild and extravagant desert, drawing circles in the sand

the reason I have filled the hole in my heart with music and making love to the unknown

that reason has now disappeared

the wound of my teenage years that had become an opening is now closed

the search for home is now over

it is you

I am home

no longer in exile

even here

and

I need to learn

how

to be home

to be still

and surrender

in the end a new beginning . . .

IRIS

the star that
gives us light
has been gone awhile
but its not an illusion

why at 55 years old I'm still waiting for my mother
and why the apple doesn't fall far from the tree
but it can roll

Breathe

To walk out into the street
Sing your heart out
The people we meet will not be drowned out
There's nothing you have that I need
I can breathe.

Those arc lights.
Those arc lights pour a cold fluorescence over the whole scene.
This scene is not for me.
That room is the temperature of a fridge. A fridge I don't want to be in. A fridge that is no place for a warm-blooded creature like me. I like to be under the waves or floating on top of them.
I love this oceanic feeling.
Amniotic.
Hypnotic.
I hear a heart beat.
I'm not drowning where I am.
I am breathing underwater.
I am comforted by the sound of a heart beating louder and louder in my ear. Or next to it.
Some kind of underwater drum.
A tom-tom.
Ba bum ba bum ba bum ba bum ba bum

Iambic pentameter.
Shakespeare found the rhythm of the heart to propel his words.
"But, soft! what light through yonder window breaks?"
I love Willie Shakespeare
I love a raver. I love a rave. I love dance music.
Electronic dance music found the heart of a marathon runner.
120 BPM. EDM. Techno.

I am about to sprint in the marathon.

There's a pounding at the door of a heart. It's not my heartbeat.
The heart belongs to Iris, my mother, who I'm excited to meet.
In one way I couldn't be closer to her. Already know her. Inside but
not out.
But I have to leave her shelter if I want to see her face in the outside
world.
And I do.
And I don't.

It's cold out there. Unfriendly. And a big move from the universe of
Iris's swollen belly to the circular world of the North Circular Road
and Dublin's Rotunda Hospital.
My bloody head is spinning. Like the world outside. Turning as I
turn, but this childish world won't take its thumb out of its mouth.
This week the adult world is turning on itself.
My da says, "You can't get a copy of Edna O'Brien's *Country Girls*
here in Ireland, 'cause it's too racy."
Da says Europe is going to become a country and be bigger than
America.
Da says the Americans and the Russians are getting closer and closer
to what my uncle Leslie is calling an extinction event.
He says they have a bomb that can blow up the whole world. It's
May 10.
Just last week the Russians shot down one of America's most secret
spy planes.
The U-2.
Time magazine is putting the pilot on the cover of their next issue.
There's a rumor an Irish American presidential candidate thinks

peace is possible—if you can explain it to people—and that space is the new frontier.

JFK says astronauts are the new cowboys. I guess the countdown has begun.

TEN
from the life of water to the life of air
NINE
from the womb life to the wild life
EIGHT
from the dream life to the dream wife
SEVEN
from my home in Iris to "I'll never be at home in this world!"
SIX
is it a boy? Is it a girl?
FIVE
minutes for God's sake
from damburst as waters break
to make an entrance—it's one take!
FOUR
screens in the Savoy
from scarlet sleep to crimson joy
from behind the velvet curtain comes the boy
THREE
inches wide in dilation
from murmur to murmuration
sky too stretched for an island nation
TWO
eyes scrunched in the spotlight
I enter from stage right
from the dribble and drivel of a
good night
I know how to find my light
stage fright. I don't think so
I don't even blink no
I'm comfortable
on the big screen
it's now a crime scene
blood and the mud of imagination

from projector to projection
I will long for your protection
I already hear your voice
I'm already exercising choice I sort through the papers
to find THE WORD
children will be seen, they will be heard
TWO
Iris shouts at the second stage
of the rocket as it leaves in love and rage
to take us out of earth's atmosphere
"sure it's only gravity that keeps us here"
orbiting the sun. I am a wife but I am some . . .
ONE
Iris screams into the abyss
ONE
from the comfort of agony and the terror of bliss
ONE
all those mouths to feed and kiss and fill with this
this . . . this . . .
ONE
story of surrender . . .

My heart is beating so loudly I can no longer hear Iris's.
This is my heart.
This heart has to last me my whole life.
This is my start.
I am getting ready to take my first breath.

> *To walk out into the street*
> *Sing my heart out*
> *The people we meet will not be drowned out*
> *There's nothing you have that I need*
> *I can breathe . . .*

40

I waited patiently for the Lord.
He inclined and heard my cry.
He brought me up out of the pit
Out of the miry clay.

I will sing, sing a new song.
I will sing, sing a new song.

How long to sing this song?
How long to sing this song?
How long, how long, how long
How long to sing this song?

You set my feet upon a rock
And made my footsteps firm.
Many will see, many will see and hear.

I will sing, sing a new song.
I will sing, sing a new song.
I will sing, sing a new song.
I will sing, sing a new song.

How long to sing this song?
How long to sing this song?
How long, how long, how long
How long to sing this song?

AFTER WORDS

On how these thoughts of mine met your thoughts, on how I came to put my life into words, on how a writer meets a reader. The answer is mostly found in the previous five hundred pages. But writing is mainly editing, and once I'd understood that it was the songs that would lead me through this more episodic telling of my life, many significant figures and transformational moments have had to remain in the books I *didn't* write. One of the toughest things in setting all this down is not being able to include so many people I've learned from and leaned on . . . comrades, colleagues, crew.

Not for the first time, all the errors here are mine. I have a pretty good memory, except for the things I've forgotten. The conversations I've written about all took place but in the writing I've sometimes embellished the dialogue. I've learned from Ali that I benefit from a good edit. If we are each of us the stories that we tell ourselves, I hope in the telling of these I have done justice to other people's.

I wouldn't have written this book without some pivotal people talking me into it. First, Ed Victor, for many years persuading me across the table that our conversations should be text. When I took his advice and began writing, his introduction to Sonny Mehta was crucial. I nervously sent Sonny some early chapters and took courage from his message back to Knopf: "He can write." If Sonny Mehta thinks I could do this, maybe I could. It was Patti Smith who'd pointed to Sonny's provenance, and for her encouragement to follow through, I will always be grateful.

When Ed and then Sonny passed away within a couple of years, it crossed my mind that the project might have passed with them, but then Jonny Geller and Gail Rebuck in London, and my new editor, Reagan Arthur, in NYC, kept it alive in the publishing world, their skilled teams taking oversight with insight.

In my world, I had an editorial sounding board that kept putting the pencil back in my hand, that were sharpener, rubber, and parchment: Martin Wroe and

AFTER WORDS

Lucy Matthew, I thank you. For your compassion and your compression, for a candid view of my life from beyond it. To get the book done and dusted would not have happened without Emma, Leah, Catriona, Jenn, Kelly, Nadine, Guy O, Gavin, Anton, Shaughn, Saoirse, Candida, Kathy, Douglas, Didi, Callan, Regine and Bri, Hackin' Mackin, and the Freuds, Matthew and Jonah. This wealth of encouragement and wisdom was complemented by the scissors and paste of those who took time to read different chapters: Edna O'Brien, Norman, Scott, Sian, Orlagh, Kathy, Paul, Bill, Bobby, Jeff, Jann, Josh, Jamie, Tom, Serah, Kate, the Sheridans, and the Carmody. My thanks to Mannix Flynn, who inspired that I end by counting down to my beginning.

Jordan, Eve, Eli, and John gave me permission to write about their lives. I believe there's a good chance that Ali will at some point.

Life gave me a song to sing and Edge, Adam, and Larry gave me a story to write.

U2 fans give me a reason to keep writing, song and story.

No one teacher taught me to love language, but there were two who taught me the much more impossible lingua franca of communication with myself and with my maker. Thank you, Donald Moxham and Jack Heaslip, teachers at Mount Temple Comprehensive School, I remain your student.

AFTER THE AFTER WORDS

PAGE 276: "Love and Fear," courtesy of Michael Leunig.

PAGE 543: "The Sound of Silence," written by Paul Simon. Copyright © 1964 by Sony Music Publishing US (LLC). All rights administered by Sony Music Publishing US (LLC). All rights reserved.

PAGE 546: "People Have the Power," words and music by Fred Smith and Patti Smith. Stratium Music Inc. (ASCAP) and Druse Music Inc. (ASCAP). "In Excelsis Deo," words and music by Patti Smith. Linda S Music Corp (ASCAP). All rights administered by Warner Chappell Music Publishing Ltd.

* Reprinted by permission of Hal Leonard Europe Ltd.

Thanks to:

PAGE 527: *The Experience of God: Being, Consciousness, Bliss* by David Bentley Hart (Yale University Press, 2013).

PAGE 544: *The Essential Rumi* by Jalal ad-Din Rumi, translation by Coleman Barks (HarperOne, 2011).

Thanks to my band mates and our publishing house, Universal Music Publishing Group, for permission to quote from our songs and, in case some of you had noticed, yes, I have sometimes been rewriting some of the lyrics. During lockdown we were able to reimagine forty U2 tracks for the *Songs of Surrender* collection, which gave me a chance to live inside those songs again as I wrote this memoir. It also meant I could deal with something that's been nagging me for some time. The lyrics on a few songs that I've always felt were never quite written. They are now. (I think.)

Thanks to the immortal invisible for permission to quote from many different versions of your holy book and in particular to the late and much missed Eugene Peterson for permission to quote from his very special modern translation *The Message*.

Thanks to all my mentors, teachers, and inspirational friends in the world of activism, to everyone who reminds me that there is no them . . . there's only us. Thanks especially to Amnesty International (amnesty.org), Chernobyl Children International (chernobyl-international.com), Greenpeace (greenpeace.org), The Irish Hospice Foundation (hospicefoundation.ie), The ONE Campaign (one.org), (RED) (red.org), Special Olympics (specialolympics.org), The UN Refugee Agency (unhcr.org).

PHOTOGRAPHS

A NOTE ON THE TYPE

This book was set in Monotype Dante, a typeface designed by Giovanni Mardersteig (1892–1977). Modeled on the Aldine type used for Pietro Cardinal Bembo's treatise *De Aetna* in 1495, Dante is a modern interpretation of the venerable face.

Composed by North Market Street Graphics, Lancaster, Pennsylvania
Printed and bound by Friesens, Altona, Manitoba
Designed by Anna B. Knighton

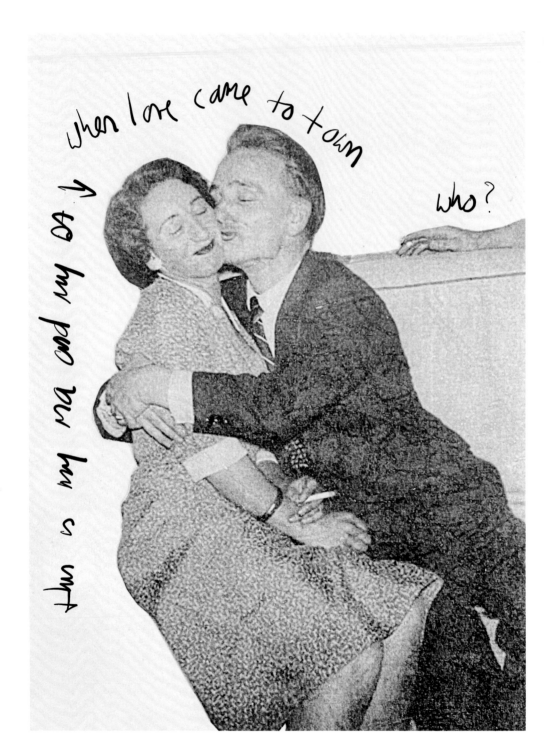

"lion king" and his castles
in the sand
                    godfather
                    &
                    godchild
                         embrace.
          this tide is never coming in

the comfort of being held
and
the joy of holding....

me & Eve

Bob &
Iris

Fathers & daughters cannot be apart especially when we are together.

the star that gives us light
has been gone awhile
but it's not an illusion
the ache in my heart is so   such a poet
                                    of who I am
                    standing in the hall
IRIS   she tells me   I can do it all

IRIS   wakes   to my nightmares
                                    don't fear the world
                                    it isn't there

IRIS   playing on the strand
                    she buries the boy
                    beneath the sand
                    says that I will be
                    the death of her
IRIS   it was not me

Hold me close
    like I'm someone
        that you might know

teans into twenties

FERNS WEXFORD JORDAN teaching me to write + EVE of EVE the artist Parc Monceau Paris

the youngest as the eldest...
lil John

stage coach

me, Bob + Elijah 3 generations of Henson

terry & Joy took me in as a
stray dog and fed me in
every which way.

Grandad 'Gramps' Rankin

Mrs RANKIN.
& all the RANKINS

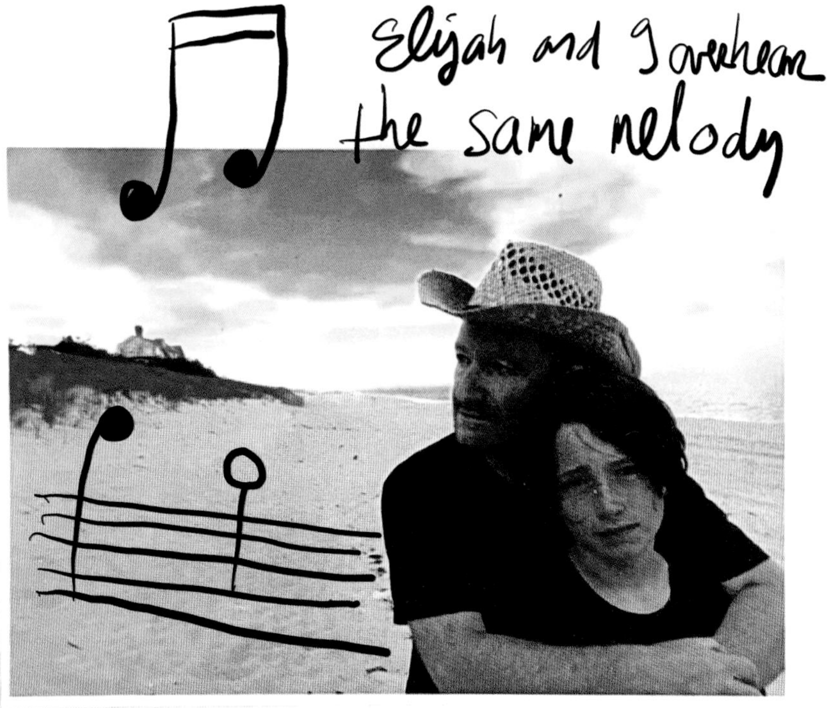
Elijah and I overhear
the same melody

summers of love & cousins

Paul DAVID
eh Hensen, Dae Evans Larry Muller
ADAM CCLAYtay
won our 1st
Recording
Session

U2 from Malahide, Dublin, winners of the Pop '78
contest at Limerick (left to right) Paul Hensen, Dave
Evans, Larry Mullin and Adam Clayton (leader).

U2 & the
virgen prunes
Glasnevin

Bill Graham

the Hype becomes U2

guggi   me not singing HARMONY   GAVIN

posing came easily to some of us

ADAM the best man for a couple of
reasons 1. best at being M.C and
critical for Irish wedding, give the best
2... maybe my teenage front   best man's
didn't always appreciate   speech
ADAM getting more out Front!
but he was just better at lots of
" vision are visibility?" things   "gig" "Circuit"
                                        "demo tape"

the blonn leading the blind......

U2 + the Virgin Prunes

"IF U2 IS GOD then the prunes are the devil"

CAVLN FRIDA
HOT PRESS 1980

STRONGMAN, GUGGI, DIK

CAVLN, DAVE (D), MARY

U2 COULD

U2 HAPPEN

U2 TO

U2 ANYONE

the man who would let me in
to his life, home wide daughter
~ son Ian 40 years
later
TERRY
STEWART

Jot
Stewart

JoJo
brings the
family
closer

70 St Assams Ave Raheny Dublin.

either Paul McGuinness getting
U2 to sign mgn+ contract
or we getting him to buy us
a drink or a van .....

First meeting with our soon to be manager Paul Mc Gui

Project Arts aftershow 18/9/78

piggy and gavin looking on as we play at being in a band

Edge the marksman, Larry the fly moustache,
me perfecting "the stockled look"
adam perfecting "potty mouth"

two hans ʒ and two boiled eggs

the Bono
the Ali
'enlightened', with class of 78 at the most
Mount Temple Comprehensive

the edge

Class of 1978, Mount Temple Comprehensive School

Windmill lane recording studios
recording "BOY"

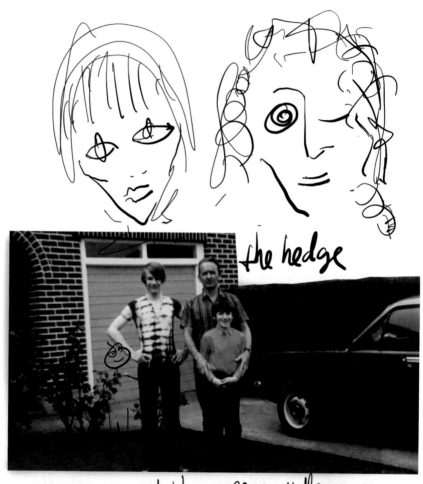

the hedge

10 CEDARWOOD RD and the avenger Hillman

mullet in Madhattan seeks
and finds a girl who will know better
about such things

dont know if this photo is taken by Ali or Edge but I know it was 1981 in Nassau where we were miting 'Fire'

the swing is in Goran but I greu up in Ireland AUG, 1980 that's Ali's head on my BODY I think......

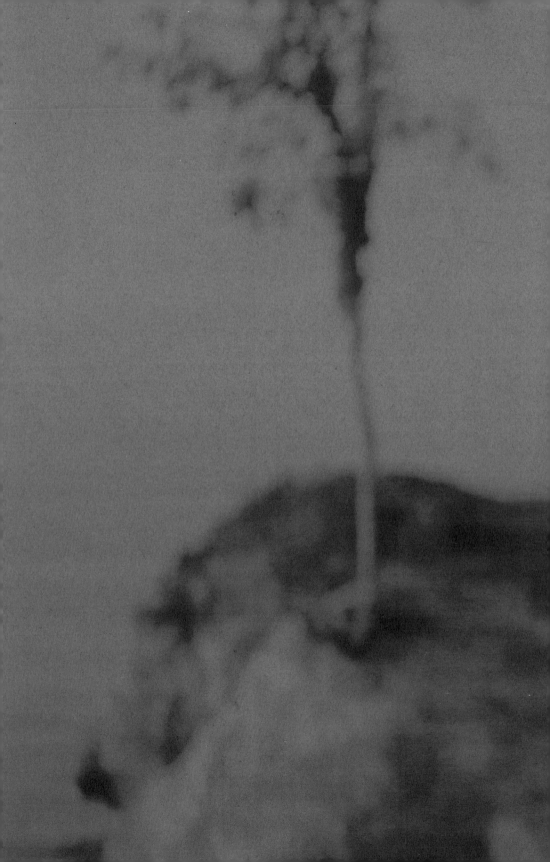